THE QUEST FOR

SECURITY

1715-1740

THE RISE OF MODERN EUROPE

Edited by WILLIAM L. LANGER
Harvard University

* *In preparation*

THE QUEST FOR

SECURITY

1715-1740

BY PENFIELD ROBERTS

HARPER TORCHBOOKS ❧ THE UNIVERSITY LIBRARY

HARPER & ROW, PUBLISHERS · NEW YORK, EVANSTON, AND LONDON

TABLE OF CONTENTS

LIST OF ILLUSTRATIONS

*The illustrations, grouped in a separate section, will be
found following page 82 of text.*

PREFACE

Due to the exigencies of the recent war, this volume is being published posthumously. My lamented friend, the late Professor Roberts, submitted the draft of the book to me in the autumn of 1941, after I had already entered government service. I was able at that time to do some work on it and at first had real hopes that the manuscript could be put into final shape with little more than the usual delays. But Pearl Harbor brought all my expectations to an abrupt end. During the ensuing years I had no opportunity whatever to devote myself to private activities. The manuscript was, therefore, still resting on my shelves when Professor Roberts unexpectedly died in the autumn of 1944.

Under the circumstances I have had to complete work on the manuscript without the author's aid or advice. In this difficult assignment Professor Crane Brinton of Harvard, a close friend of the author, has been of inestimable help. He has gone over the entire manuscript with great care, has made a number of changes and emendations which seemed desirable, and has rounded out certain sections which were deficient. The final product is of necessity a trifle patchy and uneven, but the author had so nearly completed the job that it would have been unfair to his memory as well as professionally unjustifiable not to finish off his work as best might be. Professor Roberts, had he lived to write his preface, would have wished to thank for their aid his friends Professor H. L. Seaver of the Massachusetts Institute of Technology and Dr. O. H. Taylor of Harvard.

WILLIAM L. LANGER

INTRODUCTION

Our age of specialization produces an almost incredible amount of monographic research in all fields of human knowledge. So great is the mass of this material that even the professional scholar cannot keep abreast of the contributions in anything but a restricted part of his general subject. In all branches of learning the need for intelligent synthesis is now more urgent than ever before, and this need is felt by the layman even more acutely than by the scholar. He cannot hope to read the products of microscopic research or to keep up with the changing interpretations of experts, unless new knowledge and new viewpoints are made accessible to him by those who make it their business to be informed and who are competent to speak with authority.

These volumes, published under the general title of *The Rise of Modern Europe,* are designed primarily to give the general reader and student a reliable survey of European history written by experts in various branches of that vast subject. In consonance with the current broad conception of the scope of history, they attempt to go beyond a merely political-military narrative, and to lay stress upon social, economic, religious, scientific and artistic developments. The minutely detailed, chronological approach is to some extent sacrificed in the effort to emphasize the dominant factors and to set forth their inter-relationships. At the same time the division of European history into national histories has been abandoned and wherever possible attention has been focused upon larger forces common to the whole of European civilization. These are the broad lines on which this history as a whole has been laid out. The individual volumes are integral parts of the larger scheme, but they are intended also to stand as independent units, each the work of a scholar well qualified to treat the period covered by his book. Each volume contains about fifty illustrations selected from the mass of contemporary pictorial material. All noncontemporary illustrations have been excluded on principle. The bibliographical note appended to each volume is designed to facilitate further study of special aspects touched upon in the text. In general every effort has been made to give the reader a clear idea of the main movements in European history, to embody the monographic contributions of research workers, and to present the material in a forceful and vivid manner.

Probably no phase of modern European history has been so long and so generally neglected as the period covered by this volume. The explanation for this lack of interest is not hard to find. The early eighteenth century spanned a generation that was anything but spectacular. There were few if any imposing personalities, there were no widespread or desperate military struggles, and there were no world-shaking social upheavals. The period was one of exhaustion and recovery after the long wars of Louis XIV; once this difficult phase was over, Europe passed on to the generation that prefaced the French Revolution. An undramatic period, then, but not necessarily for that reason unimportant. On the contrary, much can be learned from transitional periods of history. In this case the author has analyzed in an interesting way the general war weariness of Europe, the difficulties of political and territorial adjustment, the financial and general economic problems of recovery. Quite rightly he has titled this volume *The Quest for Security*, for throughout these years men were not only striving to return to well-established forms and procedures, but also struggling for some measure of stability in a world already stirred by new forces and new requirements. So the main theme of the book is the effort to reconcile attachment to the old with demands for the new. Ultimately failure to effect such a reconciliation led to the cataclysm of revolution. But the late Professor Roberts has wisely abstained from unbridled use of hindsight. He has examined this period in terms that would have meant something to people of that day and thereby has made a real contribution to our understanding of a neglected and but little appreciated phase of Europe's growth.

WILLIAM L. LANGER

Chapter One

STABILIZATION IN THE WEST

I. THE END OF THE AGE OF LOUIS XIV

ON AUGUST 26, 1715, Louis XIV of France, dying, spent much of the day in a series of solemn farewells to his court, his relatives, and to Madame de Maintenon. Toward evening he ordered Madame de Ventadour, the great lady who was in charge of his orphaned heir, to bring the child to his bedside. What he said to his little great-grandson was both a confession and a warning: "Try to keep the peace with your neighbors. I have loved war too well; do not copy me in this, nor in the lavish expenditures I have made."

Louis XV, according to his historiographer royal, Voltaire, kept by his bedside all his life a copy of his predecessor's farewell address to him, in one of the several somewhat varying texts noted down by the courtiers who listened to it. The French government, through much of the period to be covered in this volume, acted on the advice contained in it.[1]

Louis XIV had not merely outlived all his legitimate male descendants save the frail child of five, who was his heir, and the Spanish Bourbons; he had survived into a new era which was impatiently awaiting his end. His death made it possible to hope for a stabilization of external and internal affairs, so long troubled by his wars.

From 1688 to 1697, and again from 1701 to 1712, the great conflict had been world-wide. These wars, and not that of 1914-1918, were the first world wars. Even in 1713 the Emperor Charles VI, unwilling to accept the settlement arranged between England and France, had tried, without success, to fight France alone. Europe was bankrupt and exhausted, yet Louis XIV in the last year of his life was meditating an alliance with Charles VI, and giving aid to the Stuart Pretender to the English throne, who hoped to overthrow George I and upset the Protestant succession which France had guaranteed in the Treaty of Utrecht. Louis

[1] Voltaire, *Siècle de Louis XIV*, in *Oeuvres*, ed. Beuchot (Paris, 1829-1840), XX, 213.

I

XIV's renunciation of war, if sincere, was literally a deathbed repentance. But almost everyone else in 1715 wanted peace in western Europe.

II. THE PROBLEM OF STABILIZATION

The treaties of Utrecht, Rastadt, and Baden, negotiated before the death of Louis XIV, had ended the fighting without really ensuring a durable peace. That no major war followed until the conflict over the Austrian succession in 1740 was owing to the events and the negotiations subsequent to the death of Louis XIV. These events and negotiations are extremely involved. To anyone not a specialist in eighteenth-century political and diplomatic history their importance lies in certain general principles and broad outlines, not in the intricate detail. They do, however, illustrate the difficulties inherent in the problem of avoiding world war, a problem as real under the Old Regime in Europe as it has become in the present-day world.

There would seem to be three devices by which to keep peace in Europe: an empire, a federation, and a balance of power. Only a state strong enough to conquer and tolerant enough to control peaceably all of Europe could establish an empire on the Roman model. No such state existed in the eighteenth century. If Louis XIV had not revoked the Edict of Nantes, and if the dream he once cherished of being chosen emperor had come true, it is barely possible that his era of French preponderance might have led in the seventeenth century to a French empire more durably founded than the subsequent one of Napoleon. But the coalitions formed against her had by 1715 so weakened France, absolutely and relatively, that no such dream was realizable. No other European power seemed capable of succeeding where France had failed.

Though the Abbé de St. Pierre prepared at this time plans for a European society of nations, as Henri IV and Sully had prepared their *Grand Dessein* during a time of troubles a century earlier, there was in 1715 no real, no popular demand for a federation, a United States of Europe. There was not even sufficient administrative and political organization or experience to make such a philosopher's dream function.

There remained, then, only the third possibility, the establishment of a balance of power, of a European equilibrium. It has been said of this equilibrium that it was established after great wars, when everyone was ruined and exhausted, and that it could never be permanent because of the mutability of all human affairs. If any state impoverishes or reforms itself, the balance is inevitably upset. The truth of these observations is illustrated by what happened between 1715 and 1740.[2]

Furthermore, the nobility and gentry as well as the monarchs of the Old Regime could not in the nature of things desire to abolish war. Their position, still quasi-feudal, as well as their outlook required their wearing and using the sword. World wars had proved ruinous, but little wars, gentlemanly wars, waged at the expense of neighbors too weak and too friendless to make conquests overcostly, were still thought of as necessary to provide young gentlemen with their chance to win glory and honor. Pacifism is essentially a bourgeois ideal. Even the most enlightened of the ruling classes of the Old Regime were brought up to regard war as a natural, normal thing. The problem of stabilization did not in 1715, then, involve any widespread desire for perpetual peace. It was not war as such, but world wars that the exhausted powers wished for the time being to avoid.

To make the balance of power, the European equilibrium, function successfully, it had to be supplemented by some form of periodic consultation and negotiation among the great powers, and by some degree of willingness to allow every strong power at least a little scope for its ambition to add to its territories and its influence. The perplexing series of minor wars, negotiations, conferences, congresses, and treaties between 1715 and 1740 merely reflected an unorganized and chaotic effort to achieve a Concert of Europe which might avert another *general* conflict by a more or less tacitly agreed-upon division of the available spoils among the strong powers.

Sorel, like most nineteenth-century historians, stressed the immorality of eighteenth-century international politics. *The Prince* of Machiavelli, he says, gives an accurate description of the situation then existing. But, to use the terminology of Machiavelli's famous eighteenth chapter, the cunning of the fox was in the age of absolutism employed to give the king and the dynasty the power and the glory of the lion. The means employed might be cynical, but the end, summed up in the word Louis XIV had used to characterize his aims, was *gloire,* something more refulgent than our English for it, "glory." This noble and often quite unprofitable end justified any means necessary to attain it. Such an ideal may be feudal, may be barbaric, but it is not sordid nor materialistic. The question of international stabilization in western Europe in 1715 may, then, be summed up as the problem of how to work out in detail arrangements which would give to each strong power its quota of the

[2] Albert Sorel, *L'Europe et la révolution française* (Paris, 1930), I, 33-35.

spoils, and its portion of *gloire* without letting any one power become too strong.

One caution is necessary. The units involved in the balance of power in the early eighteenth century were dynastic states, not nation-states. National patriotism certainly existed, especially in those states already unified like Spain, France, and Great Britain. There were, however, provincial and local differences, even within these states, and therefore local rather than national patriotisms. The Germanies and Italy were divided into hundreds of small states, and at most "German" and "Italian" suggested somewhat disputed cultural inheritances. To the east and southeast, in the Balkans, Poland, and Russia there was in 1715 hardly even a nascent nationalism of the kind that emerged a century later from the French Revolution.

Dynasties, then, rather than nations fought these wars and made these treaties of balance of power. They could, however, especially in western Europe, count on an embryonic national patriotism fairly widespread among their subjects. And they must not be thought of, especially in the three decades after Utrecht, in terms of great and forceful individual monarchs. These years were rather short of such monarchs until Frederick the Great appeared. The competing dynasties were actually rather large groups—sovereign, royal family, court, government, high business and financial circles. The kind of competition they indulged in was not worlds apart from the kind that has been the tradition in American big business. Most monarchs were literally cousins. The nobilities and the very important men of affairs in all countries spoke French and knew one another. There were all sorts of interlocking directorates, agreements, and concessions—and cutthroat competition. The rights of nationality, all that was later summarized as "self-determination of peoples," had no more place in the minds of those who conducted the affairs of these dynasties than had concern for social security, the closed shop or industrial democracy in the minds of American capitalists of the Gilded Age. The problem of self-determination of peoples did not exist in 1715, or at any rate had not come to the surface of politics.

III. THE FRENCH SUCCESSION

Dispute over the legitimacy of any major ruler was fatal to European peace. In two of the greatest powers, France and Great Britain, there was in 1715 at least uncertainty about the succession and this uncertainty had to be overcome before European stability could be attained.

In France, the uncertainty, which seemed real in 1715, did not last very long. When Louis XIV died the life of a sickly boy of five, Louis XV, was the only guarantee against a conflict over the succession which would probably have led to another world war. This prospective war, which after all did not occur, furnishes the clue to much in the internal history and the international relations of France during the minority of the young king. The threat was not felt to be finally removed until the birth of a dauphin, on September 4, 1729. A Europe which had been plunged into the War of the Spanish Succession by the death of one royal boy, the electoral prince of Bavaria, may be pardoned for what might seem undue anxiety for the continued health of another such child.

If Louis XV had died, the only remaining legitimate male descendants of Louis XIV would have been Louis XV's uncle, Philip V, King of Spain, and that king's sons. But the Spanish Bourbons were barred from the French throne by the terms of the Treaty of Utrecht. Philip V did not hold the renunciation extorted from him to be valid, and in fact the French had warned the English negotiators that in French law no such renunciation would hold good. Kings inherited by the grace of God, and if heredity imposed upon them by the mystery of "divine right" the duty of reigning, they could not evade the will of God. These theories may seem nonsense, but Philip V, whose faith was far stronger than his critical faculties, unquestionably believed them. He therefore meditated giving up the Spanish throne to a son, and becoming King of France if his royal nephew should die. In that event, then, Philip V would have claimed the French throne and would probably have found a good deal of backing from influential persons in France.

The legal heir of Louis XV, according to the peace treaties, was the Duke of Orleans, son of Louis XIV's only brother, "Monsieur." He and Philip V had long been bitter personal enemies. Philip V apparently believed not only that the Duke of Orleans had poisoned the father, mother, and elder brother of Louis XV, but that he had meant to have the Spanish Bourbons murdered too.

The Duke of Orleans had renounced his claims, as a Bourbon, to the Spanish throne in favor of the House of Savoy, which by the Utrecht settlement was given the right of succession after Philip V and his male descendants. In 1715 the duke seems to have taken his position as heir to the French throne even more seriously than he had once taken his claim to succeed to the crown of Spain. That he did not eliminate the sickly boy who alone stood between him and the French crown proves, if proof were needed, the baselessness of the gossip about his poisonings.

These malicious rumors seem to have had no foundation beyond the fact that the Duke of Orleans, whom Louis XIV had called a *fanfaron de crimes*, paraded not merely his immorality and atheism but his very amateurish experiments in chemistry. To the pious and conventional majority at court, so scandalous a man seemed capable of any crime, no matter how horrible. A known homosexual and atheist, strongly suspected of incest, drunk nearly every night, boasting that his friends and companions were most of them deserving of being broken on the wheel, "roués," he was not likely to be credited by respectable people for his very real intellectual abilities, genuine kindliness, and generosity. His most durable contribution to France and the world was this mocking word "roué," which has become part of the English as well as of the French language. His position as heir presumptive to the French throne was the key to his internal and foreign policy during his regency.[3]

Louis XIV had made a will putting the Regency in commission, with the Duke of Orleans as chairman of a council. The Duke of Maine, one of the legitimatized bastard sons of Louis XIV, was to have charge of the person of Louis XV and command of the guards. Philip V had hoped to be made regent, but the old king had not dared to violate the provisions of the Treaty of Utrecht. He probably did not expect his will to be carried out. When on the day after Louis XIV's death the *Parlement* of Paris overrode the will and made the Duke of Orleans sole regent, the Duke of Maine refused to serve in a subordinate capacity.[4]

The Duke of Orleans had been obliged to concede to the *Parlement*, in return for the regency, the right of remonstrance to royal decrees, of which Louis XIV had deprived it in 1672. Lord Stair, the British ambassador, had written to Lord Stanhope, March 8, 1715, that it was extraordinary how the French detested the regime of Louis XIV and envied the conditions existing in England. Some members of the *Parlement* dreamt that their institution might come to resemble the English Parliament in more than name. They were able to decide who should be regent. The new regent recognized that no royal decree was valid until entered on their register and restored to them their right to protest before registering obnoxious edicts. If a dispute over the succession were to follow the death

---

[3] On the renunciations and the dynastic situation in France and Spain, see A. Baudrillart, *Philippe V et la Cour de France* (Paris, 1890-1901), II, and Emile Bourgeois, *Le secret du Régent et la politique de l'abbé Dubois* (Paris, 1909). Dom H. Leclercq, *Histoire de la Régence* (Paris, 1921-1922), is by far the most complete and authoritative treatment of the facts about the period it covers.

[4] Leclercq, *Histoire de la Régence*, I, 1-32, 97-126, is a full and thoroughly documented treatment of the will and the action of the *Parlement*.

of the boy king, might they not be able to play the part the English Parliament had been playing since 1688?

The Duke of Orleans made concessions to each major group opposed to the royal absolutism of Louis XIV and his ministers. He curried favor with the nobles of the gown in the *Parlement*, and made the Cardinal de Noailles, leader of the church party which opposed the ultramontanism of the Jesuits, head of a new council on church affairs, one of six (later seven) new councils through which the administration was to be carried on. On these councils the great nobles of the sword, excluded by Louis XIV from all real power, were well represented, though members of the bureaucracy of the former reign were also included. The Spanish envoy, Cellamare, said of these councils that the French had now decked out their government in Spanish style.

The new regent's internal policy, according to his friend Saint-Simon, was to "divide and rule." He reconciled the diverse opposition groups, baffled and powerless under Louis XIV, not with one another, but with himself. He was free from conventional prejudices, eager to break with tradition, and genuinely if superficially interested in new ideas. His real reliance was on what may be dubbed a "brain trust," with a shifting membership. John Law, a Scottish financier called by his enemies an adventurer, and Abbé Dubois, a French priest of humble origin, were to become his most influential advisers. As the "Old Court" or old guard of hangovers from Louis XIV's reign were sure to favor Philip V and close friendship between France and Spain, the regent was intent on a foreign policy which would frustrate the interests of the rival claimant to the French succession. Hence the alliance he presently made with England on the advice of Dubois.

IV. THE JACOBITE FAILURE

The Elector of Hanover had succeeded Queen Anne as King George I of England, August 1, 1714, in accordance with the Act of Settlement passed in 1701 by a Tory majority in Parliament to ensure the Protestant succession. The Jacobite followers of the exiled Stuarts were able to list in their propaganda pamphlets more than fifty Catholic princes with a clearer hereditary right than George I, whose mother, the Electress Sophia, was a granddaughter of James I.[5]

The new king owed his throne to the determination of a majority of

---

[5] A. and H. Tayler, *The Old Chevalier* (London, 1934), reproduces in an appendix a table of 57 persons besides James Stuart who in 1714 had a better hereditary claim.

Englishmen, both Whig and Tory, that no Catholic should again reign in Great Britain. The heir by divine right was James Stuart, James III to his adherents, the Old Pretender to Whig historians. The Whig propaganda in 1688 and later spread a baseless story that he was not really the son of James II and Mary of Modena, but a changeling brought to the queen's bed in a warming pan at the hour of his alleged birth. There is little doubt, however, that if the exiled Stuart prince had been willing to follow Henri.IV's example and change his religion to win a throne, he might well have succeeded his half sister Anne without much opposition. But his Catholic faith was genuine. He declared plainly in 1714 that he would in no event become a member of the Church of England. This statement ended all prospect of Jacobite success, though at the time the hopelessness of the Stuart cause was not always realized. A recent writer has suggested that it was unfortunate that the issue was not clearly joined in 1714 by a determined Jacobite attempt, so that the adherents both of the Stuarts and of George I might have seen the utter hopelessness of James's cause.[6]

But if James had changed his religion after 1715, or if his son and heir Charles Edward, the Young Pretender of the 1745 uprising and of Sir Walter Scott's romances, had done so, the British people, with whom the Hanoverian dynasty was never really popular, might have rallied to the Stuarts. George I and George II after him maintained the British throne because their Stuart cousins were steadfast in their faith. *Cujus regio, ejus religio* really meant in England that the monarch must be of the faith of the people, not, as in Germany, that the people must follow their ruler's creed.

George I was fifty-four when he became King of England. He had been Elector of Hanover since 1698 but until the death of his mother, June 8, 1714, she and not he had been next in succession to the British throne, according to the Act of Settlement. George did not know the English language and even as king made no effort to learn it. He was obliged to converse with the ablest of his ministers, Robert Walpole, in Latin, and with others in French. The British throne he had accepted only with reluctance, and his chief aim as King of England was to further the foreign policy of the electorate of Hanover. As a Lutheran he conformed only nominally to the Anglican church. The services he attended on Sundays were conducted in a tongue unintelligible to him and they obviously bored him. He was both unwilling and unable to perform the ceremonial functions of the crown in the customary manner.

⁶ Basil Williams, *The Whig Supremacy* (Oxford, 1939), 145.

His wife, whom he had married and divorced to keep the possessions of the House of Brunswick-Lüneburg united in his hands, was a prisoner at Ahlden. His mistresses, nicknamed "the Elephant" and "the Maypole" in the political satire of the period, were middle-aged German women quite incapable of filling the gap left by the absence of a queen, even though George raised them to the English peerage as Duchess of Kendal and Countess of Darlington. The king was economical with his civil list, and refused to go through the ceremony of the levée, which Louis XIV had made almost obligatory for all royalty. He got up and dressed, not with the aid of members of the nobility and gentry, but attended only by two Turkish men servants. It is easy to see why he was never personally popular in a country which he neither loved nor understood.[7]

George I's right to name a ministry preponderantly Whig was not questioned by a Parliament which had still a Tory majority. Most of his Tory supporters, when offered ministerial posts, declined the honor. The election of 1715 gave the Whigs a large majority in both houses, and enabled the victors to proceed against Bolingbroke, Ormonde, Oxford, and other Tories whom they had declared guilty of plotting to restore the Stuart Pretender. The flight of Bolingbroke and, somewhat later, of Ormonde to France, and the fact that they both presently entered the service of "King James III," made their guilt seem apparent. Yet it could not be proved. Oxford was eventually released from the Tower and acquitted by the House of Lords in 1717 because the Commons did not press the impeachment. It does not appear that most of the accused had, prior to 1715, ever actively favored putting a Catholic king on the British throne. They had hoped that James would change his religion; they had kept in touch with him and had made him promises. But we know that the Duke of Marlborough, the Duke of Shrewsbury, and other lesser men with Whig sympathies had tried to reinsure themselves against a Stuart restoration by letters and gifts of money sent to James.[8] Oxford certainly did not want James restored, and Bolingbroke probably believed what he said when he remarked that "England would as soon have a Turk as a Roman Catholic for King."

[7] Wolfgang Michael, *England under George I* (London, 1936-1939), I, 178 ff. On the divorced wife, Sophia Dorothea, see Adolf Köcher, "Die Prinzessin von Ahlden," *Historische Zeitschrift*, XLVIII (1882), 1-44, 193-236, also C. G. Robertson, *England under the Hanoverians* (London, 1922), appendix I. The surviving evidence does not prove the princess guilty of misconduct, but the Hanoverian rulers did their best to suppress discussion of her fate and that of her alleged paramour, Königsmarck.

[8] The evidence of Marlborough's correspondence with James after the accession of George I is to be found in the Historical Manuscripts Commission, *Stuart Papers* (London, 1902-1923), I, 349, 357, 364, 365, 372, 383, 385, 387, 407.

The Whig effort to discredit their Tory rivals provoked the Jacobite rising of 1715, an armed rebellion which was suppressed without much difficulty with the aid of Dutch mercenary troops. Louis XIV, whose support had been enlisted by the Jacobites, died just as the revolt began in Scotland. His successor, the regent, refused to furnish either men or money, though he was willing to connive at the embarkation of troops and finally of James himself. By September the Pretender realized that all his effort was "but rowing against the tide," and doubted the loyalty of his professed adherents in Great Britain. "If indeed they are resolved to submit tamely," he wrote to Bolingbroke, "the evil is without remedy."[9]

The collapse of the revolt early in 1716, with the departure of James from Scotland, not to save himself so much as to enable his defeated followers to make better terms with the government of George I, did not end Jacobite hopes. Plots and attempts continued until the final failure in 1745. Only the disgruntled Highland clans and the few thousand Roman Catholics really wanted James III as a Catholic king in 1715. The size of the Whig vote in the election merely emphasizes what all other evidence shows, that tranquillity was universally desired in a Britain weary of war and disillusioned with the conflict of ideologies which had troubled the preceding century. For the Whigs were really still a minority, a coalition of about seventy great landed families with the London merchants, who were the state's principal creditors. An England primarily agricultural was still Tory at heart. But George I and later his successor "had no choice but to take Whig servants and had therefore to accept their terms." The king still tried to follow the advice of his Hanoverian ministers, Bernstorff and Bothmer, who were with him in London, but his English ministers presently thwarted him and finally, in 1721, he did what he had tried to avoid, resigning himself to the guidance of an English prime minister, Robert Walpole.[10]

George I, then, reigned in England with the active support of an oligarchic minority, but constantly under threat of attempts to restore the Stuarts, with or without foreign aid. At any moment his rival might strengthen his position among the English by what to skeptics and rationalists seemed the simple expedient of becoming an Anglican. Like the regent in France, George felt insecure, a circumstance which largely determined his internal and his foreign policy. In both England and

[9] *Stuart Papers*, I, 424-427.
[10] See epilogue to G. M. Trevelyan, *England under Queen Anne* (London, 1930-1934), III, 310 ff.

France the dynastic situation contributed to the desire for European stabilization.

V. THE BARRIER PROBLEM

The peace settlement embodied in the treaties of Utrecht, Rastadt, and Baden had sought a means of restricting France and also the Empire by setting up neutral buffer states in Germany, Italy, and the Low Countries. A most important item in this policy was the establishment of Dutch garrisons in the barrier forts on the border between France and the former Spanish Netherlands, after 1715 to become the Austrian Netherlands, and by the nineteenth century, Belgium. In the south, Savoy was similarly to guard the old battlefields. But the buffer states were, of course, powerless against either France or Austria without the aid of one or the other of the great powers, or better, of a concert of powers. England was to seem in these years the especial guardian of the small powers and of the European balance; indeed, England now appeared for the first time as a universally acknowledged leader among the great powers.[11]

George I and his ministers in the first year of the new reign wished to revert to the old system of alliance with the Dutch and the emperor against France, since Louis XIV was showing renewed hostility by constructing a port at Mardyke in place of the one he had been obligated to destroy at Dunkirk, and by his secret encouragement of the Stuart Pretender, in violation of his public recognition of the Hanoverian succession. It therefore became necessary for the London government to mediate between their former Dutch and imperial allies in the question of the barrier, if possible in such a fashion as to obliterate the ill feeling created when the Tory ministry negotiated separately with the French in arranging the Treaty of Utrecht.

The Emperor Charles VI in 1715 still spoke of Philip V of Spain as "The Duke of Anjou." He had not yet accepted the Treaty of Utrecht. His separate peace with Louis XIV in the treaties of Rastadt and Baden left the Dutch barrier question unsettled. After protracted negotiations he eventually agreed to a treaty with the Dutch States-General and the British (signed in November, 1715, and ratified in January, 1716), by which Dutch garrisons, paid from the revenues of Charles VI's Belgian territories, were to occupy certain frontier fortresses, among them Namur, Tournai, Menin, and Ypres. The Dutch were ceded outright some terri-

[11] Pierre Muret, *La prépondérance anglaise, 1714-1763* (Paris, 1937), 10-13. The view expressed in the title of this book is that of Emile Bourgeois. See, for example, Bourgeois, *Manuel historique de politique étrangère* (Paris, 1925-1927), I, 243.

tory necessary to enable them to close the Scheldt River, a measure which they claimed was indispensable to the flooding of the country for defense. Pending the negotiation of a new commercial treaty, which neither the British nor the Dutch wished to see consummated, the tariff schedules were to remain substantially as they had been fixed during the joint Anglo-Dutch occupation begun in 1705, at rates favorable to the trade rivals of Antwerp both in Amsterdam and London.[12]

Actually this Dutch barrier was no longer needed in 1715 for defense, nor was it destined to be defended by the Dutch in the War of the Austrian Succession in the 1740's. Charles VI was very reluctant to consent to it, as it involved an infringement of his sovereignty. He and his successors wanted either to gain complete control of their Netherland possessions, or else to exchange them for Bavaria. Why, then, was an obsolete barrier thus set up by international agreement? One answer, already indicated by the terms of the economic and commercial clauses of the treaty, was that in this instance, as throughout the whole War of the Spanish Succession, trade interests played a decisive role; the Barrier Treaty reflects an attempt of London and Amsterdam to crush their trade rival, Antwerp.[13]

It may well be that, as Pirenne has suggested, there entered into the creation of the Austrian Netherlands some anticipation of a Belgium the neutrality of which would be guaranteed by international treaty. For such a treaty the arrangement actually made was an imperfect substitute. This is shown by the agreement between the Dutch and French governments signed on November 24, 1733, which excluded Belgium from all military operations during the War of the Polish Succession. Louis XV's *chargé d'affaires* remained at Brussels, which was nominally Austrian, though France and Austria were at war. Charles VI thought it unbecoming his dignity as a sovereign to take an open part in an arrangement between foreign powers involving a portion of his dominions. He was, however, as Pirenne says, "only too happy to profit by it," and carefully refrained from carrying out a threatened invasion of France through Luxembourg, which would have involved violation of Belgian neutrality.[14]

[12] Roderick Geikie and Isabel A. Montgomery, *The Dutch Barrier, 1705-1719* (Cambridge, Eng., 1930), is the fullest treatment. There is a good summary in Michael, *England under George I*, I, 225-247.

[13] Max Immich, *Geschichte des europäischen Staatensystems von 1660 bis 1789* (Munich and Berlin, 1905), 234. See also J. R. Seeley, *The Growth of British Policy* (Cambridge, Eng., 1930), and the books of Bourgeois and Muret, cited above.

[14] H. Pirenne, *Histoire de Belgique* (Brussels, 1902-1932), V, 207, 220; R. Dollot, *Les origines de la neutralité de Belgique* (Paris, 1902), 413.

The settlement of the barrier problem left the Italian question the chief obstacle to stabilization in western Europe. It was clearly to the interest of the Dutch and the British that Belgium be, in effect, neutralized by restricting Hapsburg sovereignty there. The Spanish Netherlands, now under the nominal rule of a great power, would not again become a bone of contention except in the event of another world war. But over Italian possessions and dynastic claims, if Spain and Charles VI remained unreconciled, such a war might easily arise. The empire of Charles V had been maintained in partition by the Utrecht settlement, though Charles VI had hoped to succeed to all of it. Philip V, given Spain and the colonies, coveted Italian territory. He and his rival were still in 1715 nominally at war.

Italy, of course, was merely "a geographical expression." By the Treaty of Rastadt (March 7, 1714) Charles VI received Milan, Naples, Sardinia, Mantua, and the Spanish ports in Tuscany. Savoy gained Sicily, a little more territory in north Italy, and recognition as a kingdom. Philip V resented more than anything else the complete exclusion of Spain from the peninsula, where his rival obtained most of the disputed Hapsburg heritage. On the other hand, Charles VI objected most strongly to the arrangement about Sicily, which he felt should have come to him along with Naples. The English had preferred to see Sicily in weak hands, because their new strongholds at Gibraltar and Minorca now gave their navy control of the western Mediterranean.

Mantua had fallen to Charles VI because its ducal line had become extinct in 1708. In Parma and Tuscany the Farnese and Medici rulers had no male heirs, and the Hapsburgs hoped to succeed to these territories also. But the niece and sole heiress of the Duke of Parma, Elizabeth Farnese, was in 1715 the second wife of Philip V. When their first son, Don Carlos, was born in 1716 the Spanish queen began to insist to her husband, and through him to the world, that her boy, whose half brother, later the king, Ferdinand VI, was heir to the Spanish throne, be recognized as heir to Parma and also to Tuscany, since the Farnese and Medici families had intermarried. "An appanage for Baby Carlos" was needed, as Carlyle put it, by the "Termagant of Spain." Eventually Don Carlos was to wear, successively, three crowns. He became Duke of Parma in 1731, King of Naples from 1734 to 1759, and King of Spain from 1759 till his death in 1788, thus fulfilling his mother's ambition. But this could not be foreseen in his boyhood. Elizabeth's ambition for her son and Philip V's own resentment at the loss of his Italian possessions combined with his claims to the prospective French succession to make Spain's foreign policy after 1715 strongly aggressive.

Venice at the time was at war with the Turks, who had taken from the republic the Morea (the Peloponnesus of the Ancients) which the Venetians had regained in 1686. The pope was preaching a crusade against the infidel and using the old weapon of excommunication against the Piedmontese, because the new king refused to acknowledge any form of papal suzerainty over his Sicilian domain. Among all the Italian states only Genoa was at peace.

The pope, as a temporal sovereign, had a foreign policy of his own which included, besides the crusade against the infidel, a scheme of alliance among Austria, Savoy, and Spain to pacify Italy and, incidentally, to restore the Stuarts in Great Britain. This projected alliance was to counteract the triple alliance between Great Britain, Holland, and France which was taking shape in 1716. The failure of these grandiose schemes was necessary to convince the papacy of its impotence in temporal affairs. Stabilization in Europe after the Treaty of Utrecht depended on a balance of power which could only be maintained by a concert of the great powers. Italy was the only region in western Europe where scope for the ambition of the stronger states might still be found if the arrangements of Utrecht had to be altered.

In May, 1715, Philip of Spain had sent an expedition which seized Majorca, where there was still an Austrian garrison. As Philip was still at war with Charles VI, this operation was legal, but as he had previously accepted mediation in the dispute and now acted in disregard of the mediators, the Spanish king had really defied the other powers. "The Archduke and the King of England," wrote Philip to his grandfather, Louis XIV, "are much mistaken if they think that I cannot procure myself satisfaction." This success, coming after Philip's dealing with the conquered Catalans according to his own ideas and not those of the powers responsible for the Utrecht settlement, may have encouraged the Spanish rulers to think that they could successfully force a revision of what they felt to be the unsatisfactory settlement in Italy.[15]

In the summer of 1717 Spain surprised Europe by suddenly resuming her war with Austria, alone and unaided. The Italian prelate Alberoni, whom Elizabeth Farnese had promoted from envoy of Parma at Madrid to chief minister of Philip, had made great exertions to restore the military and naval forces of Spain. England and France were about to

---

[15] Michael, *England under George I*, I, 273 ff.

intervene and impose a settlement of the outstanding disputes over Italian territories. Spain therefore took the initiative and seized Sardinia, which Charles VI, to whom it had been awarded at Rastadt, was about to exchange with Savoy for Sicily. As there was no Hapsburg navy, and as Charles VI's armies were busy in the Turkish War, this act of aggression involved little immediate risk. It drove Savoy away from any hope of alliance with Spain against Austria, and made mediation by England and France between Philip V and Charles VI indispensable if a general war was to be averted.

In 1718 a Spanish expedition conquered Sicily. George I and his principal minister, Stanhope, had tried to avert this by first promising Philip the return of Gibraltar and, when that proved insufficient, by communicating to the Spanish court the instructions given to Admiral Byng, commander of the British fleet which was sent to the Mediterranean to "hinder and obstruct" any Spanish attack on Naples or Sicily. Alberoni's reply to Byng was curt: "His Catholic Majesty has done me the honor to state that the Chevalier Byng may carry out the orders which he has from the king his master." To Lord Stanhope, who had taken the unusual step of himself coming to Madrid in August, 1718, Alberoni explained that this Sicilian enterprise represented not his personal views but those of his sovereigns.[16]

The conclusion by Charles VI of the Treaty of Passarowitz with the Turks (July 21, 1718), which the British had mediated, no doubt hastened British aid to Austria against Spain. The fleet under Byng dispersed the Spanish armada at Cape Passaro, August 11, and the British transported Austrian troops to Sicily, which had been overrun by a Spanish army. But the Austrian forces took some time to conquer the island from the Spaniards, who had twenty-three thousand infantry and six thousand cavalry. Victor Amadeus of Savoy, though he had agreed to exchange Sicily for Sardinia by adhering to the Quadruple Alliance, had not withdrawn his troops, and the co-operation between the Savoyard and the Austrian armies was imperfect. The Spanish had not been completely subdued either in Sicily or in Sardinia when peace was finally concluded. Since the English were afraid that there might be an agreement between Savoy and Austria and Spain by which this Spanish army would be allowed to return home, Byng had

[16] For Spanish policy in these years, see E. Bourgeois, *Le secret des Farnèse* (Paris, 1909), the second volume of his trilogy *La diplomatie secrète au XVIIIlième siècle*; and for Alberoni's share in it, Pietro Castagnoli, *Il Cardinale Giulio Alberoni* (Piacenza, 1929). For Lord Stanhope's Madrid visit, see Basil Williams, *Stanhope* (Oxford, 1932), 304, 309 ff.

orders to prevent this. Even if the Austrians were to transport them in their own vessels the British admiral had orders "to sink everyone of them to the bottom of the sea" if possible, lest these Spanish troops be used in Spain or France against the forces of Britain and France, so lately at war, and now allies.[17]

This now almost forgotten war of 1719 was undertaken solely to coerce Spain into accepting a negotiated settlement of the Italian question. Stanhope said it was to be a war only in name; Dubois too wished to limit it. Charles VI, who alone desired to crush his Bourbon rival, was told that the English nation had only been brought to accept the war by the prospect of an early peace. His request that British troops be sent to Italy was flatly refused. While the British navy kept Spain's best troops immured in Sardinia and Sicily, a French army under Berwick invaded Spain and destroyed the naval base and dockyards at Pasages. But a British fleet, sent to attack Corunna, was obliged to content itself with an attack on Vigo and with co-operation in an expedition against another naval base at Santona. Berwick's troops avoided engaging the Spanish army sent to meet them. The allies insisted that not Spain but Alberoni was the enemy, in order to give Philip and Elizabeth Farnese a means of saving their faces by dismissing their energetic minister.

Alberoni's view of the situation in 1718 was that the British and French scheme for Italian pacification was intended by George I to preserve his throne, and by the French regent to procure one for himself. Charles VI's aid was needed by both rulers, hence the Italian interests of Spain and of the Farnese would be sacrificed by the pacificators as a bribe to Austria.[18]

Until the destruction of the Spanish fleet by the British, Alberoni hoped to drive the Hapsburgs not merely from Sicily but from the whole of central and south Italy, where the Farnese would then become dominant with Spanish support. But when he learned in October, 1718, the extent of the naval disaster, Alberoni tried in vain to persuade Philip V and the queen to compromise. He enlisted the support of the confessor of the king, Father Daubenton. Together they persuaded Philip, but Elizabeth was unyielding and her influence over Philip undid their work in a night. If the cardinal had really been merely selfish he would

---

[17] For the details about the confused situation in Sicily, see H. Benedikt, *Das Königreich Neapel unter Kaiser Karl VI* (Vienna, 1927).

[18] Letter of Alberoni to the Duke of Parma, May 24, 1718, quoted in Castagnoli, *Alberoni*, I, 321, from the Naples archives.

then have resigned and would thus have escaped the blame for the catastrophes he saw in prospect. Instead, the phrase he used to his friend Rocca in a letter of June, 1719, about the necessity of serving "the King, my master and benefactor," represents his real attitude.[19]

Alberoni's foreign policy since his assumption of control in Spain had been directed toward finding allies, and toward encouraging what in today's political slang are called "fifth columns" within the states opposed to Spain's Italian ambitions. He had sought in 1715, for instance, to assure British support of Spain by negotiating a commercial treaty with the ministers of George I and at the same time had given money to the Stuart Pretender to aid the Jacobite rebels. In 1717 he had proposed an alliance to Tsar Peter the Great of Russia, which was politely declined, and had sent emissaries to the Turks and to Rákóczi, leader of the Hungarian opposition to the Hapsburg regime. His ambassador at Paris, Cellamare, was in 1718 drawn into a court intrigue led by the Duchesse du Maine, wife of the legitimatized son of Louis XIV, and Madame de Montespan, whose share in the Regency had been curtailed by the Duke of Orleans and the *Parlement* of Paris in 1715. Madame du Maine was particularly aggrieved at the moment because the regent and the *Parlement* had just annulled the decree of Louis XIV which assured the eventual right of succession to the throne of the "bastards," as their enemy Saint-Simon always called them. But there was no serious threat to the regime of the Duke of Orleans in the overpublicized "Conspiracy of Cellamare."

Early in 1719 Alberoni without much faith in the success of his attempts, as his letters to his friend Rocca prove, fitted out an armada for a new Jacobite descent on Britain, and tried to get the co-operation of Goertz, the ambitious adviser of Charles XII of Sweden. The armada, like the famous one of Elizabeth's day, was dispersed and ruined by a storm, and the death of Charles XII at Fredrikshald in December, 1718, had caused the downfall of Goertz. By autumn the surrender of the Spanish garrison at Messina and the threat of Berwick to revive the Catalan movement for autonomy convinced the Duke of Parma that Alberoni must be made the scapegoat. He was dismissed from all his offices and ordered to leave Spain (December 5, 1719).

Alberoni went to Rome, thwarted the efforts of the powers to get him deprived of his cardinalate, and lived to write projects for peace, to serve as papal legate, and even to receive at one conclave ten votes

[19] Castagnoli, *Alberoni*, I, 341. See also *Lettres intimes de J. M. Alberoni*, ed. Emile Bourgeois (Paris, 1892), 608, 613, 631, 632.

for the papacy. His comment on Philip V and Elizabeth Farnese after his expulsion has been often quoted. Philip needed nothing but a wife and a *prie-dieu*; Elizabeth's diabolical energy would, should she find a clever military man, cause her to make a great disturbance in France and in all Europe.[20]

Spain, by agreements of January 26 and February 17, 1720, accepted the scheme of pacification and adhered to the Quadruple Alliance, but the agreement was one in principle only. The details were left to be settled at a forthcoming congress, eventually held at Cambrai. The sequel to the Italian question became a part of the War of the Polish Succession in the 1730's. But for the time being western Europe was at peace and the international situation stabilized.

VII. STANHOPE AND DUBOIS AS PEACEMAKERS

The negotiations between England and France which led to the Treaty of Utrecht had left both powers isolated. England, under Anne's Tory ministers, had deserted her allies, and had treated France more leniently than she would have been treated by the terms Louis XIV had been willing to accept in 1709. Spain, France's natural ally, was alienated by the partition of her empire and by the rivalry between Philip V and the Duke of Orleans for the French succession. The English Whigs, who came into power at the accession of George I, were forced to accept the Utrecht settlement, to which they had so strenuously objected, because, next to the Act of Settlement, it offered the surest guarantee of the Hanoverian dynasty on which their control in Great Britain now depended. By negotiating the Barrier Treaty of 1715 the British placated the Dutch and conciliated Charles VI. The ensuing Treaty of Westminster in 1716, between Great Britain and Austria, pointed toward a revival of the old system of the grand alliance, as it had existed during the war. But the rivalry between Charles VI and Philip V over their respective claims to the entire inheritance of Charles II of Spain, and especially their conflicting ambitions in Italy, was a threat to the peace of Europe, as was the threat of a war over the French succession. Stanhope in London and the Abbé Dubois in Paris, once tutor and now unofficial adviser to the regent, meditated, therefore, a diplomatic revolution in the form of an alliance between

---

[20] Mil. R. Vesnitch, "Le Cardinal Alberoni pacifiste," *Revue d'histoire diplomatique*, XXVI (1912), 352-388; P. E. Lémontey, *Histoire de la Régence et de la minorité de Louis XV* (Paris, 1832), I, 281.

Great Britain and France to preserve the peace by maintaining a balance of power, and to further thereby the dynastic interests of their respective rulers.

This scheme was worked out by the two diplomats at the Hague and at Hanover, whither Stanhope had gone with George I. When the alliance was signed in October, 1716, Stanhope wrote Dubois, "Your trip to the Hague, Abbé, has saved a great deal of human blood, and there are many peoples who will be under obligation to you for their tranquillity."

The alliance, which became triple by the adhesion of the Dutch, January 4, 1717, lasted nominally until 1744 and was a real factor in the European situation until 1731. It has lately been described by a distinguished historian, Sir Richard Lodge, as "quite as deserving to be called a diplomatic revolution as the Austro-French alliance of 1756, to which the term is usually applied."[21]

That there was a conscious and concerted plan of peacemaking is proved by the secret memorandum accompanying official instructions of May 7, 1717, to Lord Stair, British ambassador to France:

Mylord Stair may say to the Regent and to the Abbé Dubois privately that they are not unaware of the great pains which have been taken to bring repose to all Europe, and to re-establish a lasting peace (*une tranquillité solide*) by means of the plan which is under consideration, and which has been so well started that they themselves have agreed that for its success the Emperor's participation is necessary.[22]

This plan of pacification contained four main points concerning western Europe which were later embodied in the Quadruple Alliance of 1718. It also envisaged British mediation to settle the war between Charles VI and the Turks, and a hope of excluding Russia from the division of the German possessions of Charles XII of Sweden resulting

[21] Williams, *Stanhope*, 227, 229; Sir Richard Lodge, "The Anglo-French Alliance, 1716-1731," *Studies in Anglo-French History*, ed. Coville and Temperley (Cambridge, Eng., 1935), 3 ff. Lodge gives a brief and clear account. Williams is more detailed, and over-stresses Stanhope's share in the negotiations, as do those French historians of the school of Bourgeois, who emphasize English predominance in Europe after 1713 resulting from the colonial acquisitions and naval bases Great Britain then obtained.

[22] *British Diplomatic Instructions, 1689-1789* (London, 1922-1934), II (*France, 1689-1721*), ed. L. G. W. Legg, 112-113. The document is in inaccurate French, but French versions exist of British documents on foreign policy of the reign of George I, who knew no English and took a considerable part in foreign affairs. The editor, L. G. Wickham Legg, does not make any statement about the authorship, but it is probably the work either of Stanhope, or of the king himself.

from Peter the Great's victory in the Northern War, matters dealt with in detail in the next chapter.

The Quadruple Alliance provided for the recognition by Charles VI and Philip V of the partition of the domains of the Spanish Hapsburgs, for the exchange by Savoy of Sicily for Sardinia (the price of Charles VI's consent), for the granting to Don Carlos, son of Philip V and Elizabeth Farnese, of the right to succeed the Farnese in Parma and Piacenza and the Medici in Florence (the price of Philip V's consent), and a guarantee by Charles VI of George I's right to the British throne and of the Duke of Orleans' right to the French succession (the selfish motive of Stanhope and Dubois as negotiators). The European world, weary of war and bankrupt, genuinely desired to avoid another major conflict, and the way to establish a balance of power had been taken not too unwillingly by everyone concerned except the Spaniards, who gained least in the settlement. Western Europe, in principle, was stabilized. Details were left for the Congress of Cambrai to cope with.[23]

[23] The failure of the Dutch government to make fully legal the entrance of the United Provinces into the Quadruple Alliance gave Spain an excuse for failing to comply within the three months from the signature by Austria, France and England, August 2, 1718, as provided for in an article of the treaty. See Michael, *England under George I*, II, 126 ff., and H. v. Srbik, *Oesterreichische Staatsverträge, Niederlande* (Vienna, 1912), I, 574 ff.

Chapter Two

STABILIZATION IN THE NORTH AND EAST

THE SWEDISH SUCCESSION

IN NOVEMBER, 1714, Charles XII of Sweden rode nine hundred miles in a fortnight to appear unexpectedly among the defenders of his Pomeranian city of Stralsund. His sojourn among the Turks after his defeat at Pultava in 1709 by Peter the Great had not aided his country, as he had hoped it would. His Ottoman allies had used their victories over Russia for their own ends, not his. When he returned, his neighbors were engaged in partitioning his empire, through a complicated and ever-shifting series of alliances, treaties, quarrels, bargains, and conflicts, the last stages of the vast imbroglio known as the Northern War. In spite of desperate efforts, Charles failed to hold any of Sweden's remaining German possessions. Wismar, the last of them, was taken in 1716. The Baltic provinces had been lost to the tsar after Pultava. Charles's final exploit, an attempt to wrest Norway from the Danes, ended with his death in December, 1718, at the siege of Fredrikshald. The north of Europe could not be stabilized until Sweden's lost empire was finally divided among her neighbors.

This problem of the Swedish succession was aggravated by doubt as to who should inherit the crown of Charles XII. The king, still in his thirties, had never married. His heir might be either the young Duke of Holstein-Gottorp, son of his deceased elder sister, or his surviving younger sister, Ulrica, whom he had married off shortly after his return to the Landgraf of Hesse.

Count Goertz, a skillful diplomat who had been chief minister of Holstein-Gottorp, entered Charles's service in 1714. Goertz, who soon gained the confidence of his new master, tried to revive the old friendship with France, to weaken the hostile power of Hanover by aiding the Jacobites, and to make peace with Russia by conceding to her the lost Baltic provinces. He was thwarted in France and Great Britain by the alliance negotiated by Dubois and Stanhope, and by the arrest in 1717 of the Swedish envoy in London, Gyllenborg, whose seized papers were published to prove his plottings. The Dutch, at the request of their British ally, arrested Goertz himself. His collaboration with Alberoni in 1717 and 1718, and his negotiations with Russia in the latter year, might still have come to something, had it not been for the death of Charles XII and the subsequent seizure of power in Sweden by a group of nobles hostile to absolute monarchy. As it was, Goertz was executed at Stockholm, March 13, 1719, a scapegoat for the ruin Charles's failures had brought about. The Swedish crown was given not to the Duke of Holstein-Gottorp, who would have kept Goertz in power and inevitably have depended on Russian support, but to Ulrica, and then, in accordance with her wish, to her husband.

Charles XII, on his return from Turkey in 1714, had found Hanover, Denmark, Prussia, Russia, and Saxony-Poland all arrayed against him. The accession of George I, Elector of Hanover, to the British throne made England also an enemy of Sweden, at least from the German point of view. The one thing on which the coalition was agreed was a strong desire for Swedish territory. Russia was likely to keep the Baltic provinces, since nobody would make the military effort to deprive her of them. But the several German states were anxious to keep Russia out of Germany, though unable to agree among themselves on how to do this, or, for that matter, on anything else. At the Treaty of Utrecht, the kingdom of Prussia was recognized as an independent power. This gave King Frederick William I, whose reign began February 25, 1713, the oppor-tunity to conduct a foreign policy independent of that of the Emperor Charles VI. The Elector of Saxony, Augustus the Strong, could do likewise as King of Poland; and so, when the Elector of Hanover became King of England in 1714, there were three German princes really no longer subject to Hapsburg control, or at any rate, with important lands and resources wholly outside the Holy Roman Empire of the German People. By a separate peace with Louis XIV of France, April 11, 1713, the King of Prussia gave up to the French the principality of Orange and claims to territories of the House of Orange in Franche-Comté, and in return was given recognition of his sovereignty over Neuchatel and Valengin, and a portion of the upper quarter of Guelders, as well as of his right to the title of "Majesty." Not until 1732 did he abandon his long effort to gain the rest of the heritage of the House of Orange, to which the Hohenzollerns laid claim on grounds of kinship, after the death of William III. The Emperor Charles VI, who did not make peace with France until the next year, took umbrage at this desertion by his vassal. But Prussia, in contrast to Brandenburg, was not a part of the Holy Roman Empire. The king's aim was to secure for himself as much of Sweden's German possessions as possible.[1]

In 1713, after many complicated negotiations, Frederick William I by an agreement known as the Recess of Schwedt obtained Russia's recognition of his joint occupation with Holstein of Stettin and Pomerania for the duration of the war, to keep these territories neutral. In 1714 Russia promised him, in return for his guarantee of Russian conquests on the Baltic and the Gulf of Finland, aid in securing for Prussia Stettin and Pomerania as far as the Peene, or in other words, control of the outlet of the Oder River and of a first-rate Baltic port.

By military and fiscal reforms, by participation in the expulsion of Charles XII and his forces from Stralsund and Rügen, by devious and shifting negotiations with all the great powers in turn throughout the final stages of the Northern War, Frederick William sought to assure Prussian annexation of at least this much of Sweden's empire. The means varied, the end was always the same. Finally, in 1720 Prussia, deserting her Russian ally, made peace with the Swedes and paid them two million thalers for the cession of Stettin and of Pomerania as far as the Peene.

The Elector of Hanover wanted for his share of the booty the secularized bishoprics of Bremen and Verden, entrusted to Protestant Sweden by the Treaties of Westphalia. By intricate maneuvering he bought out the Danes and paid them to withdraw their troops, placated Prussia and Saxony, and finally, in 1734, obtained the consent of Charles VI, necessary to give legal title to imperial fiefs. His accession to the British throne in 1714 enabled George I to use British prestige and the British navy to further his ends as elector, although this practice was directly contrary to the intention of the Act of Settlement. These electoral interests, quite as much as Stanhope's ambitions to pacify Europe, explain the Anglo-French alliance of 1716. It was necessary to break the old tie between France and Sweden, lest the regent aid Charles XII to get back his German possessions. The Danes, besides seizing lands belonging to the Duke of Holstein-Gottorp, desired to annex Stralsund, Greifswald, and Rügen. But in the settlement of the Northern War Sweden finally retained this fragment of Pomerania, which she kept until the Napoleonic era.

[1] The best treatment of Prussian history for this period is Albert Waddington, *Histoire de Prusse* (Paris, 1911-1922), II. J. G. Droysen, *Geschichte der preussischen Politik* (Leipzig, 1868-1886), if used with caution, will supply much added detail. An admirable introductory account is S. B. Fay, *The Rise of Brandenburg-Prussia to 1786* (New York, 1937).

The policy of Augustus the Strong of Saxony was to remain King of Poland, and all his shifting alliances may be thus explained. Although he owed his throne to Russian aid, he made an alliance with England-Hanover in 1719 and with the Emperor Charles VI (Treaty of Vienna, January 5, 1719). The idea of a partition of Poland, by which he could secure hereditary and absolute monarchy over a portion of that country, colored Augustus' policies then and later.[2]

The Duke of Holstein-Gottorp was not merely deprived of his right to the Swedish throne, to which he had a claim supported by Russia and Prussia; he had also to give up to Denmark his possessions in Schleswig to compensate the Danes for not receiving Stralsund and Rügen. His marriage in 1725 to Anna, daughter of Peter the Great, was to prove less inauspicious for his house than that of his father Charles XII's sister had been. Characteristically, this weakest of the contenders for the Swedish domains fared the worst. The fact that Russia, the strongest, obtained no more was chiefly due to British opposition.

II. THE BALTIC QUESTION

Otto Hintze has pointed out that perhaps the most important effect of the Northern War on the European state system was the rivalry between Great Britain and Russia which developed in its final stages.[3] This rivalry, which was a new thing in European diplomacy, turned on the Baltic question. England's Baltic trade was important, and the naval stores from the Baltic countries were indispensable to her unless substitute sources of supply could be developed in her distant American colonies. Russian aggression in the Baltic, now first conspicuous, began to worry British diplomats.

Lord Townshend, then Secretary of State for the Northern Department, wrote in September, 1716, that "if the fleet of merchant men, now lading in the Baltick, should by any accident miscarry, it will be impossible for His Majesty to fitt out any ships of war for the next year, by which means the whole navy of England will be rendered perfectly useless."[4]

The building of St. Petersburg, the possession by the Russians of Riga and Reval, the excellence of the Russian fleet (to which Admiral

---

[2] See Waddington, *Histoire de Prusse*, II, 429; and R. H. Lord, *Second Partition of Poland* (Cambridge, Mass., 1915), 34-35.

[3] O. Hintze, *Die Hohenzollern und ihr Werk* (Berlin, 1915), 278.

[4] Quoted by J. F. Chance, *George I and the Northern War* (London, 1909), 9. See also R. G. Albion, *Forests and Sea Power* (Cambridge, Mass., 1929), chap. iv.

Sir John Norris testified), and the efforts of Peter the Great to develop Russian maritime commerce made the English and the Dutch feel that a complete Russian victory over Sweden would injure their interests in the Baltic. Yet George I, as Elector of Hanover, was an ally of the tsar by the Greifswald Treaty of October, 1715, and had guaranteed Russia's Baltic conquests in return for a Russian guarantee of Hanover's right to Bremen and Verden. George had given the tsar to understand that he would advance the interests of Russia to the best of his ability. He told the Prussians, who were also in the coalition against Sweden, that he could not let them see the written instructions with which he had sent Admiral Norris to the Baltic with an English fleet, because such a commitment would demand the assent of his English ministers and of Parliament; but he assured them that "We promise the King of Prussia on our royal faith and troth that the said squadron shall in every way second operations in Pomerania against Sweden."[5]

George I was forbidden by the Act of Settlement and by a solemn coronation oath to engage as King of England "in any war for the defence of any dominions or territories, which do not belong to the Crown of England, without the consent of Parliament." The remark of Frederick the Great about George II, that it was hard to tell whether he was one person or two, might have been made of George I also. A serious difficulty between the king and his cabinet was perhaps averted by the action of Charles XII in authorizing Swedish privateers to prey on English and Dutch commerce, and by the conduct of Peter the Great in quartering troops in Mecklenburg, next door to Hanover, and siding with the Duke of Mecklenburg in a quarrel with his nobles. George's principal Hanoverian minister, Bernstorff, had estates in Mecklenburg and, according to contemporary gossip, his interests there caused him to change to an anti-Russian policy by 1717. The Emperor Charles VI was persuaded by Hanover in 1719 to permit a Hanoverian occupation of Mecklenburg in the interest of the nobles, even while the tsar still backed the duke, who had married his niece. Charles XII had furnished a pretext for the annual naval expedition to the Baltic, and the tsar's actions had made Hanoverian policy swing back in line with English. In April, 1717, a split among the Whig leaders sent Walpole, Townshend, and others into opposition; this made Stanhope virtually the chief minister, and henceforth his policy was to prevent a complete victory over Sweden which would leave Russia dominant in the Baltic.

[5] Quoted in Williams, *Stanhope*, 231-232; see also Chance, *Northern War*, chaps. vii-ix. On the Greifswald Treaty, see F. Stoerk, "Das Greifswalder Bündiss," *Pommersche Jahr-bücher*, II (1901).

III. RUSSIA AND EUROPE

The military victory of Peter the Great over Charles XII at Pultava in 1709 and his naval victory over the Swedes at Hango in 1714 had marked the rise of Russia to the position of a great power. But the tsar's efforts to win allies among the European powers resulted for some years merely in securing treaties with small German states, whose status was that of clients pursuing their own selfish interests rather than that of equals. From the Russian point of view, Augustus the Strong of Saxony, as King of Poland, was a dependent of the tsar, and Poland was a kind of protectorate annexed to the Russian empire. Prussia and Denmark were too obviously afraid of being reduced to a similar position of dependence on the tsar to be his reliable supporters. So in 1717 Peter made another visit to western Europe in the hope of securing some great power as an ally.

Since his quarrel with George I over Mecklenburg and his rivalry with England and the Dutch in the Baltic blocked hopes of alliance with the maritime powers, Peter sought earnestly to negotiate with France. His views, as summarized by Tessé, appointed by the regent to attend him, were that he wished to take the place which Sweden had formerly held in France's system of foreign relations, that he would guarantee France's treaties, and that Prussia and Poland as well as Russia would become allies of France. Peter disclaimed any hope of a French guarantee of his own conquests and appealed to the traditional French distrust of Austria. "Put me in the place of Sweden, and I will give you by this treaty all that you could have expected from Sweden in view of the well founded disquiet the power of the emperor must cause you."[6]

But in the spring and early summer of 1717, when Peter's visit to Paris was causing the interest and amazement Saint-Simon has so entertainingly described, the English government was urging on the French a plan for a general pacification in which the participation of the Emperor Charles VI would be essential. Peter's effort to secure a French alliance resulted merely in the colorless Treaty of Amsterdam (August 15, 1717), between France, Prussia, and Russia. The only

---

[6] Quoted by Chance, *Northern War*, 219. This is the fullest account of Russian diplomacy available. The standard histories of Russia pass over her foreign relations during the period 1715 to 1721 rather hastily. Karl Staehlin, *Geschichte Russlands* (Berlin, 1923-1939), II, 110-126, gives the best account of them. See also Milioukov, Seignobos et Eisenmann, *Histoire de Russie* (Paris, 1935), I, 335-350, and the brief general statement in Dietrich Gerhard, *England und der Aufstieg Russlands* (Munich and Berlin, 1933), 1-9. There does not seem to be any monograph in the western languages on the subject.

important clause gave France Russian recognition of her right to mediate in settling the Northern War. France preferred the Quadruple Alliance to a Russian one. French persuasion, incidentally, probably hastened the departure of Russian troops from Mecklenburg, where, as the regent remarked to the British ambassador, they had remained in order to be fed and housed at someone else's expense.

Unsuccessful in obtaining the alliance of a great power and disgusted with the squabbles and obstructive tactics of his greedy German client states, Peter decided to make peace with Sweden on his own terms. He needed peace because of what Miliukov calls the "chaos" of Russian internal affairs after his first reforms, so that the administration of his dominions could be reorganized on a permanent peacetime basis after the ruinous wartime expedients.[7]

Negotiations between Russia and Sweden in 1718 at a conference in the Aaland Islands failed to bring an agreement. Goertz could not persuade Charles XII to accept the Russian terms, and Peter awaited the complete financial collapse apparently impending in Sweden. The death of Charles XII in December which ended the war and the Treaty of Passarowitz, between Austria and Turkey, altered the situation. The new Swedish regime sought only to save what it could from the wreck of Sweden's empire, and Charles VI, released from the Turkish War and strengthened by the conquests made by Prince Eugene, was no longer dependent on the Quadruple Alliance with France and Britain to guide his attitude toward the disputes in the north and east.

IV. THE HAPSBURG "DRANG NACH OSTEN"

In 1683 the Turks had been driven back with difficulty from the gates of Vienna. In 1717 Prince Eugene drove them from Belgrade. As a French historian has put it,

Thus while Louis XIV had struggled for decades merely to win Franche-Comté . . . and a disputed control over a few Flemish towns, the Hapsburgs, in a shorter time, had taken the vast regions, plains, mountains, and plateaus which brought them to Belgrade, and to the summits of the Carpathians.[8]

This Hapsburg *Drang nach Osten,* which had scored a notable success in the Treaty of Carlowitz in 1699, had again been challenged by the

[7] See Milioukov, Seignobos et Eisenmann, *Histoire de Russie,* I, 362 ff.
[8] A. de St. Leger and Phillippe Sagnac, *La prépondérance française, 1661-1716* (Paris, 1935), 409.

Turks in 1716. The Turks were once more gaining the upper hand in a war with their old enemies, the Venetians, whom they had just driven from the Morea. Turkish seizure of Corfu and Dalmatia, Venice's remaining possessions, was in prospect. That this was believed in Vienna to be a serious threat to Italy is shown by the provisions of the alliance between the republic of Venice and the Emperor Charles VI (April 13, 1716). If, for example, both Naples and Milan were attacked, the army of the allies would all be employed in Lombardy, and only the fleet at Naples. The danger to the Hapsburg possessions in Italy came, of course, not merely from the Turks, but also from Spain and Savoy. At Constantinople, however, prayers were publicly offered for the forthcoming triumph of the Moslem faith not merely in the Morea but over "Vienna and Rome," if Theyl's memoirs are to be believed. The author, chancellor of the Dutch embassy at Constantinople, added that "This prayer had a great effect on all Christendom," which to the modern reader smacks of a propaganda line.[9]

The several advisers of Charles VI were not agreed on the necessity of war with Turkey in 1716 until the imprisonment in May of the imperial resident at Constantinople, von Fleischmann. The emperor's Spanish ministers and some of his German advisers felt that his claim to the Spanish throne and his interests in Italy were more important than any conquests to be made in Hungary. Prince Eugene wanted war, they grumbled, because it would make him indispensable.

Eugene's opinion was that prolonged negotiations with the Porte would merely afford time for the complete annihilation of the Venetians. There was little to fear from the other powers, since France needed time to recover from the late war and the regent thought of nothing but how to keep himself in power. Spain was occupied in subduing the rebellious Catalans, and Philip V was far from secure on his new throne. Religion and honor would combine to make it the duty of Europe not to hinder this holy war.[10]

Pope Clement XI had already proclaimed a crusade on behalf of the Venetians, and aid was forthcoming from Genoa, Spain, and Portugal. Johann Mathias von der Schulenberg, a friend of Prince Eugene and a well-known soldier, had been employed by Venice to command her

---

[9] The standard authority on this Turkish War is still J. W. Zinkeisen, *Geschichte des osmanischen Reiches in Europa* (Hamburg and Gotha, 1840-1863), V, 461 ff. The treaty provisions are summarized on pages 510-511. On the alleged prayer, see B. Erdmannsdörffer, *Deutsche Geschichte vom Westfälischen Frieden bis zum Regierungsantritt Friedrich's des Grossen* (Berlin, 1892-1893), II, 357.

[10] A. Arneth, *Prinz Eugen von Savoyen* (Vienna, 1858), II, 381 ff.

armies, composed chiefly of mercenary troops, and Charles VI had conferred upon him the title of *Reichsgraf* (Count of the Empire). The new count was a North German Protestant, formerly in the service of Augustus the Strong. The pope now received him into the Catholic church at a private audience in the Vatican garden. Gentlemen from all over Catholic Europe volunteered to serve under Prince Eugene against the Turks, "more, perhaps, for the pleasure of being able to boast of it in days to come than for the interests of the Empire and of religion," as a skeptical contemporary wrote.[11]

Eugene's victories over the Turks at Peterwardein, Temesvar, and especially at the siege of Belgrade, which ended with its capture on August 18, 1717, were admired all over Europe. Germans still sing about "Prinz Eugen, der edle Ritter," apropos of the taking of Belgrade, although, as Erdmannsdörffer has pointed out, it had been taken before and was soon to be lost again. The prince, however, was a genuinely heroic figure, nearly always victorious in half a century of almost constant warfare, yet sensible and prudent in diplomacy, despite his impetuous energy. His reputation, unlike that of his friend Marlborough, was not tarnished by ugly rumors of treachery and bribery. Son of a prince of Savoy-Carignan and of a niece of Cardinal Mazarin, Eugene was a cosmopolitan, in whom France as well as Italy and Germany could take pride. He left the service of Louis XIV and entered that of the Hapsburgs in an age when fealty was to the sovereign, not to the nation. Even nationalist nineteenth-century historians have not held it against him. Von Sybel, for example, at the end of his published lectures on Eugene, dubs him good as well as great.

Count von der Schulenburg won great renown by his successful defense of Corfu against a formidable Turkish expedition. He spent the rest of his life in the Venetian service, and devoted much thought to preparing fortifications at Corfu which were long regarded as impregnable. The Venetian navy, however, proved unable to defeat the Turkish fleet even with the aid of ships of the "crusading" powers.

England and Holland had tried, by offers of mediation, to avert the outbreak of war between the Turks and the emperor, since such a war would hamper their profitable commerce in the Levant. After Belgrade was taken, Charles VI wrote to Eugene to "lose no opportunity of concluding peace with the enemy, as you well know that a mediation is undesirable and that it is best to treat *sub armis*." But the Turks had

---

[11] [E. Mauvillon], *Histoire du Prince François Eugene* (Vienna, 1745), quoted by Zinkeisen, *Geschichte des osmanischen Reiches*, V, 547n.

already received Britain's offer to mediate, and would not surrender; and, in view of the Spanish attack on Sardinia ten days after the fall of Belgrade, the emperor was not in a position to offend the maritime powers. He would need the British fleet to cope with a Spanish descent on Sicily.

After extended preliminary negotiations, the Treaty of Passarowitz was finally concluded at a conference which began June 5, 1718. Treaties between Charles VI and the Porte, and between Venice and the Porte, were signed July 21. A separate Austro-Turkish treaty of commerce, in which the English and Dutch mediators had no part, followed within a week. The Hapsburgs gained not merely the remainder of Hungary, but a large part of Serbia and of Wallachia as well. These gains were comparable in extent to those made in the War of the Spanish Succession. Had those territories been retained, Austria would have become dominant in the Balkans, but most of them were lost in the next Turkish war. Venice lost all but one or two of her Levantine territories, but retained Corfu and the Ionian Islands near by. She also made slight gains in Dalmatia. The Turks had threatened to continue the war rather than include her in the Treaty of Passarowitz. The grand vizier used unprintable language about the Venetians to Stanyan, envoy of George I, who reported that "They should kiss the hands and feet of the Emperor for having been admitted to the peace negotiations. Otherwise, they would have been destroyed by the Turks."

Venice had ceased to count in international relations. Charles VI, thanks to this victory over the Turks and to the Quadruple Alliance, became potentially the most powerful of European sovereigns, if his hold on the Empire and his administration of the now enormous Hapsburg family domain could be strengthened. George I of Hanover and Great Britain had scored three signal triumphs within a few weeks: his successful mediation at Passarowitz, the formation of the Quadruple Alliance, and Byng's naval victory over Spain. As Michael says, he was at "the zenith of his power," in the role of pacificator of Europe.

V. THE TREATY OF NYSTADT

When Dubois heard of the death of Charles XII he wrote to Stanhope, "We must seize this chance that Providence has sent us to complete our task of giving peace to Europe." Dubois and Stanhope planned to force Russia, by means of a naval demonstration in the Baltic with English and Swedish ships, to accept mediation in a form which would restore the lost Baltic provinces to Sweden, or at least give her back such seaports as Riga and Reval. Dubois wished her to retain a portion of Pomerania, so that she would still belong to the Holy Roman Empire and serve French interests against the Hapsburgs as before. Hanover was to receive Bremen and Verden, Prussia Stettin and the mouths of the Oder, and Denmark a guarantee of Schleswig. Sweden was to be paid cash for these cessions, and brought to consent to them by the promise of aid against Russia. When Russia had perforce submitted to all these arrangements, by which she would not control the Baltic and would remain excluded from Germany, she was to be admitted to a northern quadruple alliance to balance the one just concluded in the west.

But Charles VI, now an ally of England and France, had intended all along to have peace made in the north at a Congress of Brunswick; hitherto this Congress had been abortive, because Charles XII would not consent to negotiate, though Peter had actually sent an envoy. The proposed northern league was to be chiefly one of Protestant powers, and Charles VI was a devout Catholic still anxious to bring all his empire back to the faith. The conversion of the principal official protector of the North German Protestants, the Elector of Saxony, who had changed his faith to win the Polish crown, had led to difficulties and encouraged what were regarded as Catholic encroachments. The religious issue was by no means dead in 1719.[12]

The emperor, both as a sovereign and as a Catholic, disliked the attempts of Great Britain and of France to usurp what he felt to be his prerogative of settling disputes between states belonging to the Empire. He no longer needed help against the Turks, and as soon as Spain had been brought to accept the plan of pacification in the west he began to veer toward an alliance with Russia. He did not, however, thwart the first part of the plan for a northern peace. Prussia, deserting Russia, received her promised reward. The new Swedish regime also made peace with Hanover, and finally with Denmark, on substantially the terms George I, Stanhope, and Dubois wished.

But, despite Russia's previous acceptance of French mediation, and despite the English fleet in the Baltic, Peter the Great was not brought to accept the terms England wished to impose. The diplomacy of Carteret, and a judicious bribing of members of the Swedish senate, made Stockholm amenable to English suggestions and prolonged the nominal state of war with Russia until London became convinced that only a real war, not a sham like that against Spain in 1719, would dislodge

[12] K. Borgmann, *Der deutsche Religionsstreit der Jahre 1719-20* (Berlin, 1937).

Peter from his Baltic conquests. England herself was not prepared to wage such a war in 1719 or 1720 against Russia. She tried, however, to get Charles VI or the Turks to do it for her. Efforts to embroil Vienna with the tsar came to little. Peter was endeavoring to win the right to keep an embassy at Constantinople, with the privileges granted to the western great powers, and to free himself from the obligation to pay a tribute to the Khan of Krim Tartary. Though his prestige in the Near East had suffered from his inglorious campaign on the Pruth in 1711, and from the terms of the ensuing peace, he did win Turkish recognition of Russia as a great power and gained a mutual promise of perpetual amity by a treaty negotiated in 1720. English efforts to stir up hostilities had failed.[13]

Against the British and Swedish fleet in the Baltic, Peter had not merely a number of excellent ships of the line, but also a second flotilla of light craft, galleys, and small sailing vessels, well suited to the shallow waters, dotted with islands, in which large ships were often useless. These galleys, which could also be used to transport troops to ravage the Swedish coast, proved decisive. The British navy was unable to cope with them, and when that fact was finally realized, it became impossible to stir up various powers to furnish troops to be paid out of British and French funds. The Treaty of Nystadt, nominally under French mediation, was actually dictated by the Russians. George I resented the rejection of his mediation, and the English disliked the terms. Sweden lost all of her Baltic provinces save the greater part of Finland. The effect on British trade was less adverse, however, than had been feared, and in 1734 a commercial treaty was negotiated between England and Russia. With the signature of the Treaty of Nystadt in September, 1721, Europe was at peace. For twenty years there was not another great war, for the War of the Polish Succession in the 1730's was not much more than a series of maneuvers; this was the longest interval of tranquillity the Continent enjoyed between 1660 and 1815.[14]

VI. THE EUROPEAN BALANCE IN 1721

By 1721 a balance of power had been established in Europe, completing a peace without victory. Even the worst defeated and the weakest of the principal powers, Venice and Sweden, had been more leniently treated

---

[13] Zinkeisen, *Geschichte des osmanischen Reiches*, V, 583 ff.

[14] On the end of the Northern War, see Chance, *Northern War*, 473 ff., and Michael, *England under George I*, II, 207-268.

than they had expected amid their calamities. Each retained its sovereignty and a fragment of its empire, though neither was henceforth important in the European state system. Furthermore, it was finally settled that neither of the great dynasties, previously paramount, could hope to conquer the Continent; for the Hapsburgs were now finally excluded from Spain, and the Bourbons, beaten in the war just ended, suffered from being divided into a French and a Spanish branch. British sea power had become well established, guarding the far-flung outposts which were to develop into an empire, and British money power was gaining on Dutch. Ships and subsidies had enabled England to defeat Louis XIV, who owed an honorable peace not to British magnanimity nor to Bolingbroke's Jacobite leanings, but to British unwillingness to revive the empire of Charles V for Charles VI. But Walpole's withdrawal into an isolation more comfortable than splendid was to end any real threat of British predominance over Europe, a threat which could not have been enforced in time of peace prior to 1815. The total population and the total wealth of the entire British dominions of George I, including Ireland and the colonies, were markedly less than those of France, even excluding the important French colonial possessions; one has only to consider this fact to see that the much-discussed *prédominance anglaise* of the French historians was unreal.

The balance of power was established, but there was no mechanism for maintaining it. There was a kind of league of nations, limited in fact to the Germanies and masquerading under the false name of "Holy Roman Empire," but its emperor was more interested in his Hapsburg family domain than in an empire which, in all essentials, such as the power to levy taxes, was really ruled not by him but by his numerous and various vassals. As we have seen, the rulers of Prussia, Saxony, and Hanover were able, after 1713, to pursue in practice that independent policy in foreign relations which the Treaties of Westphalia theoretically granted to every state in the Empire. Charles VI's empire was in some ways analogous to the present British Commonwealth of Nations under the Statute of Westminster, save that it contained not only one, but several unreconciled Irelands. The Holy Roman Empire, however, effectively blocked any other attempt at an institution through which the concert of powers might be established and maintained.

Disputes between states were frequently settled by the mediation of supposedly impartial powers, such as the British mediation between Charles VI and the Turks, and the nominal French mediation between Peter the Great and Sweden. Congresses at which many powers were represented, as at Cambrai and at Soissons in the decade following 1720, played perhaps a more prominent role than such gatherings of diplomats had yet played; but the absence of guiding principles and of masterful personalities prevented their decisions from having any lasting effect. The general postwar exhaustion suppressed all desire for dangerous or far-reaching undertakings. In the settlement of disputes and the ever-shifting, often surprising complex of treaties and alliances, temporary expediency and the needs of the moment were usually decisive, rather than permanent groupings or durable institutions.[15]

Even the balance of power does not appear to have been an ideal consciously present in many minds. At least, contemporary references to it are few. The practical necessity of preventing any one power from growing predominant was obviously clearly felt, but it resulted in action, not in theorizing. The general ideas current among men of affairs were still of medieval and of Roman origin. We are told of the folly of trying to run our twentieth-century world on eighteenth-century ideas, but the 1720's were still talking in terms of the thirteenth century, of feudal investitures like that of George I for Bremen and Verden or the House of Savoy for Sicily, of a crusade against the Turks, of the divine right of kings, and so on. Meanwhile, practical men must have known that the facts were quite otherwise. In the case of Bremen and Verden George I, as Voltaire said, "had bought them from the Danes, to whom they did not belong," and when he had compensated the Swedes, the rightful owners, what the emperor said or did mattered little unless it came to a war with Austria on one side and England-Hanover on the other. The old ideas were fast losing their hold on men's minds, but no new ideas had become established.

Nationality existed, of course, but, as Hayes has shown, nationalism did not yet affect the course of events.[16] Like imperialism, liberalism, and democracy, nationalism as we understand it today had little bearing on the state of Europe before 1789. In 1720, the *theories* which were present in men's minds about relations among states were far nearer those of the Middle Ages than those of the coming two centuries. But only old-fashioned people still took these theories seriously. This accounts at least in part for the absence of guiding principles and of continuity in foreign policy which makes the detail of the international relations of the period following 1715 so complex.

One definite accomplishment of the pacifiers had been to avert the

---

[15] Immich, *Geschichte des europäischen Staatensystems*, 254-255.
[16] C. J. H. Hayes, *Essays on Nationalism* (New York, 1926), 30 ff.

grouping of the powers into long-lasting and fixed opposing systems of alliances like those which existed between 1890 and 1914. Goertz and Alberoni had striven to organize a coalition of Spain, Sweden, Turkey, and Russia against England, France, and Austria. Various other tentative groupings had appeared in the kaleidoscope of international relations, but for some years following 1720 there were no well-knit rival alliances and no major wars.

To whom should the credit for this pacification of Europe be given? Stanhope and Dubois were most prominent among the negotiators who brought it about, but the plan seems to have been largely the work of George I. Even Basil Williams, somewhat prejudiced in Stanhope's favor, admits that the prompt conclusion of the crucial Anglo-French alliance of 1716 was "owing to the king even more than to Stanhope."[17]

It is curious that these three men have been so much underrated by most historians. Stanhope was a general who had lost his greatest battle (at Brihuega), and was a diplomat more or less by accident. Dubois had an enemy, the Duke of Saint-Simon, whose portrait of him is a masterpiece of invective familiar to students of French literature. Even modern French historians, who have learned to distrust Saint-Simon's accuracy, have not forgiven Dubois for the English alliance, because it diminished French prestige and acquiesced in France's colonial losses. That George I was an unpopular King of England we have already seen. But nobody has yet denied that he was a highly successful Elector of Hanover, worthy of the praise which his grandson, Frederick the Great, accorded to him for his probity and his excellent judgment of men and of affairs. And George cared far more for his native land than he did for his British crown. Even the Englishmen who disliked him admitted that George I was a just man. His peace, all things considered, was a just peace.

[17] Williams, *Whig Supremacy*, 19.

Chapter Three

THE STRUCTURE OF POLITICS

I. THE CONSERVATIVE REACTION

THE historian writing in the mid-twentieth century seems impelled by the spirit of his age to attempt to formulate generalizations and comparisons. He cannot confine himself to the narration of events as if they were unique in space and time. Emerging from two world wars in close succession—wars which historians will in the future probably group together, as they group the wars of Louis XIV and the Napoleonic wars —we can hardly help asking ourselves how men felt and acted when they emerged from such crises in the past. But the professional training of the historian is still a powerful influence warning him against facile analogies and against rigid uniformities. The years 1715, 1763, 1815, 1919, 1945 have this in common, that they mark the end of great wars and the beginning of great peace settlements. The student of the behavior of men in society has every right to seek in the history of these periods for any valid uniformities that will help in the building of the sciences of human relations. The historian, however, can best serve the common cause, not indeed by neglecting the search for uniformities, but by insisting that this search never neglect the facts, even though some of these facts invalidate cherished ideas.

Much in the situation of 1715 was, quite literally and in common-sense terms, different from anything in 1945. Much in 1715 was unique, and much else bears to the state of the world in 1945 a relation which may be, obviously or subtly, *genetic;* but nothing in the two periods can be compared in the simple sense in which we may compare facts, data, things in the present.

As we have seen, there were in 1715 embryonic ideas for a federation of Europe, and the beginnings of a method of regular diplomatic consultation to keep the peace among the powers. It seems clear that after the Napoleonic and the recent world wars such efforts, if not more successful, have been progressively more articulate, more specific, more wide-

36

spread. Again, after each of these world wars there has been a desire, among victors as well as among vanquished, to get back to the good old days of before the war. There has been a reaction against the men who seemed responsible for the war, a feeling, pathetic against the background of recurrent modern warfare, that somehow peace is normal, natural. Yet this uniformity does not really go very deep, and it does not tell us everything about what men considered at any specific time to be "normal." Men are never unanimous in such matters.

Nevertheless, in most of the states of Europe there was discernible in the years after Utrecht a conservative reaction against royal absolutism or, to speak more generally, against the sovereignty of the state over the various groups, more or less corporate in character, which composed the ruling classes. There was no coherent or elaborate political philosophy of conservatism, only a widespread feeling that peace and what Harding two centuries later dubbed "normalcy" were both necessary and desirable. There was no program of action; but in most of the countries of Europe different groups were taking unplanned and ill-defended measures, all groping toward the same end of restoring the "liberties," the traditional privileges, which the strengthening of state sovereignty in wartime had restricted and imperiled. There was no mass movement, since politics were, even in England, still the business of the gentry, and the common man, except in purely local affairs, showed almost no interest in political questions except when they could be given a religious aspect. To rouse the mob, even in England, the best cry was still that of Sacheverell in 1709: "The Church is in danger."

After such attempts at revolt as the *Fronde*, the authority of dynastic states like France under Louis XIV had been accepted by the nobles, because the monarchy meant glory as well as pensions and honors. The rest of the people had supported it because royal authority alone seemed able to ensure internal peace and order. But the absolutism of Louis XIV had led to a series of world wars perhaps even more disruptive and disastrous—and certainly more damaging to the finances of the French crown—than the religious strife of the sixteenth century. There was no desire to abolish monarchy, but a strong feeling that it must be curbed. The best way to curb it was to recognize that the crown was only one among numerous authorities to which men owed allegiance, such as the family, the church, the landlord, the judges, and above them all, the law, both of God and of the land. According to conservative opinion in the early eighteenth century, the problem of government was not how to establish a beneficent despotism, but how to bring about a compromise between the interests of the various groups composing the governing class which would respect all traditional privileges and not permit the king, or the church, or the nobles, or the *bourgeoisie* to dominate. This compromise was, in the minds of most of its adherents, based on a reversion to medieval corporate practices, to the *Ständestaat*, already seen in a kind of historical half-light.

Though this light was not in 1715 the romantic glow it was to be for men like Burke, Walter Scott, Maistre, the Schlegels—indeed the conservatives of the early eighteenth century were mostly conventional men of the "Age of Prose and Reason"—it is quite possible to distinguish in their daily political lives a devotion to what became with Burke philosophical conservatism. Even Locke, apologist for the radical break with the past which the British Whigs had taken in their Revolution of 1688, spent page after page in an effort to show that this revolution had been a defense of British tradition, of the British constitution, from the radical innovations of James II.

The authority of anything which could claim to have "existed time out of mind" was still almost universally accepted in 1715. Therefore, those who sought to curb royal absolutism in France, for instance, asserted the right to power of the nobles, or the church, or the *parlements*, as organs of the realm, and went back to Charlemagne or to the Franks in search of proof. They did not yet appeal to an abstraction like the "Rights of Man" of 1789. If privileges or rights could be shown to have existed before the monarchy existed, that alone would suffice to demonstrate their validity. The appeal was always to tradition and only incidentally to reason. Even Locke's well-known theory about the origin of government in a social contract in a hypothetical stage of historic development was merely an attempt to supply a respectably ancient basis for the right of Parliament to dethrone the Stuarts. Filmer, whom Locke answers in the first of the *Two Treatises of Government*, had sought to defend royal absolutism on the ground that kings have an hereditary right derived ultimately from the fatherly authority of Adam over the first human family. This notion seems to us today hardly deserving of elaborate disproof, but Locke refutes it laboriously and in detail.

This reversion to the traditional would seem a commonplace, the inevitable search of a tired and tortured generation for rest and assurance after the strain of a time of troubles. Such a reversion in modern Western society is never complete, never without contrary eddies and currents, never quite as simple in political life as in political theory. There seems clearly to have been in most of Europe, and especially in Great Britain,

France, Holland, Sweden, and Russia, an effort to escape from the growing authority of *central governments*, from the already foreshadowed "leviathan" state. It was a movement which, compared with the roughly analogous movement after the great French Revolution, was almost inarticulate, at least in formal political theory and literature. Its members, leaders and led, were never united on any sweeping program, were, indeed, often quite willing to increase the power of the state to further their particular ends. In Prussia, the rise of which is one of the important facts of these years, there can hardly be said to have been a "corporative reaction" at all. The king, Frederick William I, went on calmly strengthening his army and his bureaucracy. In the Hapsburg realms, unitary central government had scarcely progressed far enough to make even the most jealous Magyar nobles feel that a reaction was necessary.

Nevertheless, there is in Europe of the early eighteenth century a tendency, if not a movement, for certain groups, nobles, gentry, burghers, and the like, to hold on to their privileges, charters, exemptions, to their status, to the little local worlds their ancestors had built, worlds now threatened by a new enemy, as yet unnamed Progress or Efficiency, and only beginning to be known as Reason.

II. REVOLTS OF THE NOBLES

The great nobles, followed more or less faithfully by the gentry, the men of affairs, and by all sorts of dependents, led the attack on the leviathan state, which in 1715 was embodied in the institution of monarchy in the grand manner—and method—of Louis XIV. They were aided by the fact that the dynastic situation in much of Europe after the Treaty of Utrecht became unfavorable for the perpetuation of strong monarchies.

In England the first two Hanoverian monarchs, George I and George II, had greater ability and industry than they have always been credited with. But until 1745 they were continually menaced by attempts to restore the exiled Stuarts. Their right to the British throne was not hereditary but parliamentary. In France, as we have seen, only the doubtful survival of a sickly boy king averted a dispute over the succession which would probably have meant another world war. The regent's authority was necessarily far weaker than that of Louis XIV had been. Cardinal Fleury, the first of Louis XV's ministers to command popular respect, had no wish to be a Mazarin or a Richelieu, and Louis himself, though highly intelligent, was not an industrious ruler. In Russia, Peter the

Great ruled with a strong hand until 1725; but after his death the succession to the throne was settled in Byzantine fashion by palace revolutions, from which no strong ruler emerged until the time of Catherine II.
In Poland Augustus the Strong of Saxony failed in his effort to make the
Polish throne hereditary in his family. In Sweden the death of Charles
XII, unmarried and childless, gave the Estates-General an opportunity
to declare that there was no heir with a legal title to the throne, and then
to choose Ulrica, Charles XII's younger sister, and soon afterward to
transfer the crown to her husband. In Spain Philip V, grandson of Louis
XIV, had won possession of the throne only after a world war. He had
neither the unquestioned hereditary right nor the personal qualities of a
strong king. In Austria Charles VI was the last of the male line of the
Hapsburgs, and after 1720 he was so intent on integrating and thus
securing the succession to the Hapsburg family domain to his daughter,
Maria Theresa, that he sacrificed all other aims to this one.

In many parts of Europe, then, the nobles, whom strong kings and able
ministers had repressed in the seventeenth century, saw a chance in the
early eighteenth to regain their traditional position as an institution of
the realm, not subject to the monarchy, but co-ordinate with it. Hence
the Peerage Bill in England, the *Polysynodie* in France, the so-called era
of liberty, or *Frihetstiden*, in Sweden, and the escape of the Russian nobility after Peter's death from the obligation to serve the state which he
had imposed.

The clearest case was that of Sweden, where the heroic ventures of
Charles XII had ended in national disaster. So many men had died in his
wars that even thirty years after his death there was still an abnormal
excess of women in the population. Travelers around 1720 speak of
Sweden as a land with only boys and graybeards. The economic loss had
been great. The impoverished survivors were anxious for peace and fearful that a strong monarchy would necessarily mean a war of revenge.
By the constitutional reforms following the death of Charles XII the
administration was put into the hands of a council, on which the king,
as chairman, had only two votes. The powers of the Estates-General were
entrusted to a secret committee, with fifty members for the nobility,
twenty-five for the clergy, and twenty-five for the *bourgeoisie*. There
were four houses in the Estates, nobles, clergy, bourgeois, and peasants,
but the peasants were not represented on the secret committee until after
1740. They were, however, supposed to be consulted about taxation. The
council was composed of bureaucrats holding office for life. This system
of government was dominated by the nobles, but it soon led to the

assumption of control by Arvid Horn, who was backed by majorities in the secret committee, the council, and the Estates.

In the 1730's two factions, or parties, arose—the "Hats," who favored a war of revenge against Russia, and the "Caps," who wished to continue the existing peace. Horn, who sided with the Caps, was finally overthrown in 1738; but the subsequent war with Russia (1741-1743) proved disastrous. Throughout the *Frihetstiden*, which lasted until 1772, when the *coup d'état* of Gustavus III restored the monarchy in the by then fashionably absolute form of beneficent despotism, foreign powers constantly bribed Swedish officials and factions. The oligarchic regime of the nobles in Sweden seemed to be leading to a partition of the country between her neighbors, just as it did in Poland. Internally, it proved not inconsistent with a fairly steady level of prosperity.

The liberties secured by the Swedish Estates in this period are medieval rather than modern in character. The nobles demanded that not merely officerships in the army but also positions in the government civil service be reserved for them. There was a dispute as to whether persons of noble blood not possessing landed property should be considered as noblemen. The clergy of the established Lutheran church demanded and received a decree against conventicles, directed against Pietist dissenters from the state church. The guild regulations were relaxed and trades opened to all comers, but this was a temporary emergency measure resulting from the aftermath of war, not part of a theoretical policy of *laissez faire*. By conscious borrowing from seventeenth-century England and France, navigation acts were passed to encourage a Swedish merchant marine, and the establishment of manufacturing industries was promoted by tariffs and subsidies. Such liberties as these were quasi-medieval. Each order of society in the revived *Ständestaat* demanded privileges fitting its position in the social hierarchy. The reaction against royal absolutism, in Sweden as elsewhere, was rather corporate than individualistic. Its basis was not contract, but status. Liberty in the *Frihetstiden* had no relationship to equality. On the contrary, the division into ranks and classes by which no two men were ever exactly equal was a bulwark of what the Swedes considered their civil liberties.[1]

---

[1] The standard work in Swedish on this period is C. G. Malmström, *Sveriges politiska historia från konung Karl XII's död till statshvälfningen 1772*, rev. ed. (Stockholm, 1893-1901). The best treatment accessible to historians unable to read Swedish is L. Stavenow, *Geschichte Schwedens, 1718-1772* (Gotha, 1908). This is not a mere translation of his volume in the Swedish work *Sveriges historia intill tjugonde seklet*, but an independent treatment addressed to foreign readers. In English a convenient summary is Carl Hallendorff and Adolf Scheuck, *History of Sweden* (London, 1939), 318-337.

What happened in France after the death of Louis XIV looks at first sight like something more than a conservative reaction against a regime that had just waged a long, bitter, and unsuccessful war. Indeed, the best modern historian of the Regency calls it "a try at revolution" (*l'essai d'une révolution*).[2] Louis XIV's will was promptly broken. The chief law court of the realm, the *Parlement* of Paris, was expressly granted its right of remonstrance at the registration of royal edicts, a right that pamphleteers for the *Parlement* were to turn into a curious anticipation of John Marshall's doctrine of judicial review. For the close-knit ministry through which Louis XIV had exercised his will, the regent introduced a series of councils recruited from among the old nobility, put aside by Louis XIV, as well as from among the professional lawyers, judges, and civil servants who, *as a class,* had done the chief work of administering and governing France since Richelieu. A Council of Regency of eleven, of whom all but three were princes of the blood or great nobles, was presided over by the regent, but made decisions by a simple majority vote. It was a kind of supreme council, beneath which were six sub-councils, for ecclesiastical matters (it was called, rather touchingly, the *Conseil de Conscience*), for foreign affairs, for war, for finances, for the navy, and for the interior, to which was shortly added a seventh for commerce. This cumbersome system of *polysynodie* went back to the ideas of the gentle intellectual Fénelon, preceptor of that Duke of Burgundy who, but for his early death in 1712, would have succeeded his grandfather on the throne. It did not work. The French, who have never lacked for able political diagnosticians, soon saw why. As a contemporary poet put it,

> Français, ne craignez plus d'évènements sinistres.
> Notre sage Régent a su tout prévenir,
> Il a soixante et dix ministres . . . .[3]

Nearly everything went wrong. The separate subcouncils quarreled within and among themselves, and with the Council of Regency. The great nobles showed themselves awkward at what was after all committee work, a task which takes special skills in which they were wholly untrained. They did not get on with their professional colleagues of the bench and bureau. It is true that posterity has probably been disproportionately impressed with the political incapacity of these nobles by

[2] Leclercq, *Histoire de la Régence*, I, lxvii.

[3] Quoted in F. Funck-Brentano, *La Régence* (Paris, 1931), 51. (Frenchmen, fear no more sinister events. Our wise regent has shown he can take care of everything—he has seventy ministers.)

the accident that one of the least sensible of them happened to be a literary genius. The Duke of Saint-Simon, whose memoirs are among the greatest of autobiographical writings, was a member of the Council of Regency. He has left a detailed record of the bickerings over etiquette which plagued the councils, and of which he was chief fomenter. Saint-Simon, as one of the *ducs et pairs*, insisted that the *premier président* of the *Parlement* should take off his hat when asking the opinion of a duke, just as he did when asking the opinion of a prince of the blood. The presidents claimed to be the equals of dukes, and refused to make the deferential gesture. Saint-Simon storms at them in eloquent pages, and with a fury reserved in other ages for theological or patriotic disputes. For Saint-Simon, rank was a part of the order of nature, a divine order, and the *parlementaires* were agents of corruption.

Serious though these questions of etiquette were, inept though the nobles proved to be, cumbersome though the machinery of *polysynodie* was, the attempt of the regent to govern with the aid of representatives of all interested groups must have failed sooner or later because these groups were already too far apart to form effective coalitions; and in the France of the Regency there was no central representative body in which there might grow up, as there was slowly growing up in the England of that time, a "loyal opposition." The council on ecclesiastical affairs failed to solve the Jansenist question. The Jansenists, sometimes called the "Puritans of the Catholic Church," who had, like so much that stood in the way of the unified and unanimous France he desired, been driven to cover by Louis XIV, sprang up in new strength at his death. They began again in public their war against their old foes, the Jesuits. The skeptical regent, like most skeptics, had an especial aversion to earnest and noisy religions. He was greatly disturbed by the resignation of the head of the council on ecclesiastical affairs, the ambitious Cardinal de Noailles, who had quite failed to settle these religious quarrels. The regent, who was in some senses a monarch, was even more disturbed by the failure of the council on finance to provide him with the first need of any monarch—money. France was in the virtual bankruptcy that faces any beaten state in a world war. The council on finance wrangled over the details of taxation and accounting, debated reforms that were to be argued on numerous occasions until 1789, but did nothing.

After three years of trial the new system was abandoned. In September, 1718, the regent dissolved the councils and went back to the form, at least, of the central government under Louis XIV: six ministers with professional administrative experts under them. More and more the regent came to rely on two men, John Law, a Scotsman with ideas on finance, whom we shall encounter in the next chapter, and the Abbé Dubois, of lower middle-class origins, who had risen in the church by his undoubted political abilities. Saint-Simon loathed Dubois and expressed that loathing so skillfully that historians for years painted him in very black colors. The balance has long since been restored, and we see the abbé, who was to die a cardinal, as an able handler of his fellows, a man of expedients and compromises, a peer of Walpole and Fleury. His private life was fashionably immoral, and he was, of course, a very bad priest.

The failure of the councils was taken by contemporaries as the failure of a class—the *gens de qualité*—and has been so taken by historians. The classic quotation here is from the memoirs of the Duc d'Antin, one of these noblemen:

Kings who will reign in the future will recall that Louis XIV, one of the greatest kings on earth, would never employ *gens de qualité* in any kind of government business; and that M. the Regent, a very enlightened prince, had begun by putting them at the head of all such business, and had been obliged to take them altogether out of the government after three years. What will they, what should they, conclude? *That men of this class are not suited to government affairs, that they are good only to be killed off in war.*[4]

There has been a tendency among the most recent historians to question the very existence of any self-conscious attempt of the nobility to regain political power in Regency France. The regent, they claim, was moved above all by his own ambition to succeed to the throne, and he therefore called all sorts of people around him in order to ingratiate himself with them. The initiative was his, not the nobles'.[5] This is to swing the pendulum of historical interpretation too far. If the Regency no longer seems, as it seemed to Michelet, "a century in eight years," it is still important as evidence that the French ruling classes, nobles, near nobles, and bourgeois alike, were already unwilling to accept the famous formula of Louis XIV, *L'état, c'est moi*. After 1715 royal absolutism of an incomplete and inefficient kind existed in France on sufferance and for lack of a feasible alternative. Its opponents could not put up a united front until the end of the century.[6]

[4] Duc d'Antin, *Mémoires,* quoted in Lémontey, *Histoire de la Régence,* I, 194-195. The italics are mine. Note the reverent tone d'Antin uses toward Louis XIV, whose policies he believed had been harmful to the interests of the nobility.

[5] This view is summarized in Muret, *Prépondérance anglaise,* 64.

[6] The quotation from Michelet is in his *Histoire de France,* new ed. (Paris, 1881-1884), XVII, *préface*.

Historical writing, both in Britain and in the United States, has so accustomed us to the view of British history as "freedom slowly broadening down from precedent to precedent" that phrases like "oligarchy" and "revolt of the nobles," which seem to us natural enough when applied to Continental history, seem inapplicable to British history. It is true that in the nineteenth century Disraeli made great use of his term "Venetian oligarchy" for precisely the ruling groups in early eighteenth-century England. But the term never caught on; the comfortable Victorians, serene with faith in the Whig interpretation of history, were sure that Disraeli was inventing, as politicians must.

Actually, the course of monarchical absolutism—or, if you prefer, that of the leviathan state—had been arrested in England by the Civil War of the mid-seventeenth century. From the last phase of this struggle, that against James II, a minority not undeserving of the title of oligarchy had come out as victors in 1688. The British nobility and its allies in the ruling classes did not need to revolt, as their likes did in Sweden and France at this time, because the British upper classes had won the Glorious Revolution, they had enjoyed the reign of a weak ruler, Queen Anne, and they now had in George I a ruler they themselves had brought to the throne, and who had to rely on them against the supporters of the Stuarts.

Even so, the British nobility felt it necessary to attempt to reinsure themselves. They passed in 1716 the Septennial Act, making the duration of Parliament seven years. This measure was taken immediately to preserve the existing Whig Parliament in a time when the Jacobite rebellion of 1715, easily suppressed though it had been, made the Whigs fearful about possible results of any kind of election. But the Septennial Act was also meant to give Parliament even greater continuity and strength against the crown. Stanhope, the Whig leader, made an attempt in 1719 to put through a Peerage Bill, which would have restricted drastically the right of the crown to create new peers. By his power of creating peers a king might, theoretically, have his way against a hostile House of Lords, might even swamp the nobility with new creations. The Peerage Bill was beaten, but not by any weakness in the oligarchy or strength in the crown; it was beaten as part of the complex and by no means principle-bound play of politics in the Commons, when the Whig Robert Walpole threw his strength to the Tory opposition to show Stanhope that the Whigs could not carry on the government without Walpole's aid. Walpole succeeded in his aim, and in 1720 entered a government he was to dominate through the rest of this period. Events proved the oligarchy did not need the reinsurance of the Peerage Bill. In 1759, at the end of the reign of George II, there were only one hundred and seventy English peers, a decrease of eight, instead of the increase of six which the Peerage Bill would have allowed.[7]

The limitations on British royal authority produced by the Whigs' success in holding George I substantially within the Act of Settlement are of more importance than the Peerage Bill. George I had brought over with him from Hanover several of his German ministers. Previous experience with a foreign king, William III, had recently taught the English that such a ruler would wish to give his foreign favorites English peerages and English offices. The Act of Settlement, passed by a House of Commons with a Tory majority in 1701, had imposed limitations to come into effect when the House of Hanover should succeed. The fifth article of this act was as follows:

That after the limitation shall take effect, no person born out of the Kingdom of England, Scotland, or Ireland, or the dominions thereunto belonging, although he be naturalized or made a denizen (except such as are born of English parents) shall be capable to be of the Privy Council, or a Member of either House of Parliament, or to enjoy any office or place of trust, either civil or military, or to have any grants of lands, tenements, or hereditaments from the crown to himself or to any others in trust for him.

George I in the early years of his reign was trying to see how much of this clause would really be enforced against him.

We have already seen that he had succeeded in getting around another clause, the second, providing "That . . . this nation shall be not obliged to engage in any war for the defence of any dominions or territories, which do not belong to the Crown of England, without the consent of Parliament." By a subterfuge he had sent a British fleet to the Baltic to take part in the Northern War against Sweden to help Hanover win Bremen and Verden (p. 25). He had given pensions and peerages to his German mistresses, the Duchess of Kendal and the Countess of Darlington. In foreign affairs he had followed the advice of his Hanoverian ministers. He had insisted on parliamentary consent (required by Article III) to his going to Hanover, and while he was there he had managed foreign affairs without referring some of the more important details to London, except for ratification after the event. He had, indeed, secured the consent of the English ministers attending him at Hanover, but he had chosen the ministers. He had paid his Hanoverian ministers in

[7] Williams, *Stanhope*, 402-418; A. S. Turberville, *The House of Lords in the Eighteenth Century* (Oxford, 1927), 165-185.

attendance at London out of his Hanoverian revenue, but he had taken their advice about English affairs as well as Hanoverian. He had conformed, outwardly, to Article I, obliging him to "join in communion with the Church of England," and had complied with Article VII, which provided for a salaried judiciary serving for life, but he wished to retain as much of his royal authority as possible.[8]

His English ministers were paid, not by Parliament, but out of the civil list, an annual sum voted to the king, for life, at his accession. They were chosen, not by a prime minister, but by the king. Although most of them were members of Parliament, that was partly because most of them, as peers, had seats in the House of Lords. Even under Walpole only one other minister was, like him, a member of the House of Commons. Walpole retained his seat in the Commons because it was necessary that he, as Chancellor of the Exchequer, be there to supervise money bills. A cabinet, that is to say, an informal committee of the principal ministers, met at regular intervals. One may seriously question the usual statement, that George I's inability to preside successfully at cabinet meetings, because he knew no English, was responsible for the development of cabinet government. Both George I and George II did sometimes preside at cabinet meetings, and there is reason to believe that under George I the discussion was carried on in French when the king was present. And the existence of the cabinet did not mean that cabinet government also existed. Under cabinet government the ministry is a committee of Parliament, whose members are chosen in the king's name by a chairman, the prime minister, who is necessarily also leader of a party able to command a majority in the House of Commons. But both George I and George II chose their own ministers, a fact obvious at their accessions. Each minister was still responsible not to Parliament but to the king.[9] George III still thought it feasible to choose ministers unable to command a majority in the Commons, until experience finally taught him (in the 1780's) that this would not work.

In the Act of Settlement as passed in 1701 there were clauses intended to restore the actual authority of the Privy Council and stating that "No person who has an office or place of profit under the King, or receives a pension from the Crown shall be capable of serving as a member of the House of Commons." If these clauses had not been repealed, with

[8] On the Act of Settlement, see Trevelyan, *England under Queen Anne*, I, 116 ff. On George I's prerogative, see Williams, *Whig Supremacy*, 15 ff.

[9] See W. Michael, *Englische Geschichte* (Berlin, 1920-1937), III, 536-592, and Williams, *Whig Supremacy*, 31-39.

some difficulty, by the Regency Act of 1705-1706, the whole constitutional development in England would have been different. It seems to have been the common sense of Godolphin rather than any general desire for repeal that brought this about.[10]

The House of Commons was still regarded as the organ of opposition to royal absolutism, and the ministers, most of them peers, were suspected of being either would-be oligarchs or tools of the king. The eighteenth century was to end with the Commons the actual seat of government power. But these first years were years of transition, and even within the Commons, men still thought of themselves as barriers to the abuse of power rather than as a source of power.

The House of Commons at this period represented not so much persons or regions as economic and social groups in the propertied governing classes. By an act passed in 1711 every county member was required to possess an income of at least six hundred pounds a year from landed property, and every borough member one of three hundred pounds. There were exceptions for university and Scottish members and for eldest sons of English peers, and it was possible to evade the act by various legal devices. The intent was, clearly, that the lower as well as the upper house of Parliament should be dominated by the landed gentry. A statement in the papers of Lord Chancellor Hardwicke, giving the composition of the Commons in 1754, is probably typical of eighteenth-century conditions. There were then among its members 63 army or navy officers, 36 merchants, 10 planters, 36 practicing lawyers, and 314 country gentlemen. As most of the officers belonged to families of the country gentry, the overwhelming predominance of the landed interest in the Commons is evident. The majority of the seats were held year after year, sometimes for centuries, by members of the same families. Sometimes this was because a decayed town had become a "pocket borough." But a more typical case was that of Bridgnorth, one of the twenty places with the broadest franchise and the least corrupt electorate in England. In the 209 years, 1661-1870, one member for Bridgnorth at least, and sometimes the other as well, was a Whitmore. These Whitmores were baronets with estates in Shropshire, where the borough is located.

A study of the genealogy of the peerage and landed gentry is necessary for any real understanding of English eighteenth-century politics. The gentry was not a single class, but made up of different economic and social groups often highly suspicious of each other. Nor did George I or George II lose all of the royal prerogative. To a considerable extent

[10] Trevelyan, *England under Queen Anne*, II, 94-97.

they governed as well as reigned. The constitutional problem in English history following 1715 was the establishment of a balance of power between the crown, Parliament, and the judiciary. Montesquieu's opinion is not as erroneous as it is often said to be. But the solution worked out in the era of Walpole, the development of cabinet government, was not achieved through institutional "checks and balances," but by a common-sense compromise. Parliament, by what Burke called "virtual representation," actually represented the wishes and desires of the governing classes, and it gradually reduced the Hanoverian dynasty to its present ceremonial and ornamental function. Only the earlier steps in this long evolutionary process had been taken prior to 1740.

George I, except in choosing army officers, showed in internal affairs a lasting disposition to keep within the limits of the Act of Settlement. When he found by experience that his English ministers resented his accepting advice from his Hanoverian ministers, he stopped bringing over Bernstorff and the others from Hanover to London. His reconciliation with his heir, afterward George II, was arranged without the knowledge of Bernstorff, and against Bernstorff's counsel. It had been demanded by Stanhope as necessary for the reconciliation of Walpole and Townshend with the ministry. Even in the final stages of the Northern War the king followed Stanhope's advice, not Bernstorff's. When in 1721 George I was especially unpopular with his British subjects because he was Governor of the South Sea Company and his mistresses and favorites were believed to have made illicit profits from the burst "Bubble," his Hanoverian advisers urged him to defy Parliament and rely on the support of the army, many of whose officers, they claimed, were in favor of a strong monarchic government. But George I disregarded this advice and put himself in the hands of Walpole as prime minister.[11]

George I, like his immediate successors, retained and exercised very considerable power over foreign affairs. He kept control of the army in his own hands, including army patronage, and took a personal interest in the details of military organization. His civil list covered many purposes, such as the payment of civil-service officials, ministerial salaries, and pensions, besides the personal and household expenditures of the monarch. This gave him a larger share of financial power than is commonly realized. Carteret (later Lord Granville) was able to say as late as his ministry in the 1740's, "Give a man the crown on his side and he can

[11] William Coxe, *Memoirs of the Life and Administration of Sir Robert Walpole* (London, 1798), I, 137.

defy everything." This proved untrue in his own case, but his more successful rival, Henry Pelham, expressed an opinion which, as Basil Williams says, "is a very fair statement of the relative strength of king and parliament during the period 1714-1760." Pelham said that when Parliament was against him he might still get his way by royal support; when the king disapproved he sometimes got his way by relying on Parliament; but against both king and Parliament he was powerless. If either George I or George II had tried to defy Parliament, he could have caused serious difficulties. But the only recurrent breaches of the Act of Settlement were the repeated gifts to royal mistresses of German nationality. Even under Walpole, for example, three thousand pounds from the British treasury were given to the Countess Platen toward the dowry of her daughter. But the lady's desire for an English peerage, and her wish to come to England like her rivals, the Duchess of Kendal and the Countess of Darlington, were not granted, apparently because she was a Roman Catholic. But the greater part of the Duchess of Kendal's wealth seems to have been gotten from bribes offered and taken for her influence with the king. As Walpole said of her, "She would sell the King's honor, if she could get a shilling for it." George I's gifts were measured in tens and hundreds, not as a rule in thousands, of pounds.[12]

In England, then, the real curbing of royal authority was not the result of any single measure or event, nor of any concerted movement of nobles, as in Sweden. It was not the Peerage Bill, nor its failure in the commons, nor the advent of Walpole as prime minister and the beginning of cabinet government that gave the stamp to these years, but a common-sense compromise between king, ministers, and the various groups in the ruling classes acting through Parliament. England remained strong and grew stronger not because she was richer or more populous or inherently more powerful than other countries, but because there were no deep-seated divisions among the ruling classes, except the long-continued split between the majority which accepted the Hanoverian dynasty and the Jacobite minority. The Jacobite threat, ever present until 1745, was no doubt the explanation of at least some of the moderation and the willingness to co-operate shown by the Hanoverian majority. Unquestionably, too, the much-publicized political genius of the British nation was at work; but there was also something in line with Franklin's well-known advice to

---

[12] Michael, *Englische Geschichte*, III, 340-343. On the constitutional position of George I, see Williams, *Whig Supremacy*, 15 ff., and M. A. Thomson, *A Constitutional History of England*, ed. Treharne (London, 1938), IV.

the Continental Congress: "Gentlemen, we had best hang together lest we be hanged separately."

Dutch historians are not at all hesitant about calling the government of their country in the early eighteenth century an oligarchy. After the death in 1702 of William III of England who, as head of the House of Orange, was stadholder of the United Provinces, no new stadholder was chosen, and the country was ruled by a merchant, financial, and shipping aristocracy. The office of stadholder, though it gave even a strong man but a precarious hold over the States-General and other organs of the federal government and even less over those of the provinces, fiercely jealous of their local rights and privileges, nonetheless smacked of monarchy to these aristocrats. They were determined republicans.

Their notion of a republic was, however, quite devoid of the democratic and equalitarian connotations the word was gradually, in the course of the second half of the century, to acquire in most of the Western world. To these Dutchmen, the republic meant the rule of custom, of established enterprises, of the banks and shipping firms they owned, of the elaborate checks and balances of the Netherlands government. Their reaction against monarchical centralization was, then, conspicuous in these years. "The ruling class grew smaller and smaller. Dominant cliques within the caste tended to form a superaristocracy and some offices, for instance that of Secretary to the States-General, became virtually hereditary."[13]

The eighteenth century in Dutch history, though perhaps it has suffered unduly from the chagrin of patriotic Dutch historians at the obvious fall from the heroic achievements of the Dutch seventeenth century, was nevertheless clearly a period of decline in the power and prestige of the United Provinces. Some part of that decline may be explained by the power of the oligarchs. They were conventional, propertied, business aristocrats. They were confronted in 1715 with the financial aftermath of a great war—in fact, with the necessity of defaulting on interest payments on the national debt. With Dutch thoroughness, they restored the financial respectability of Holland by a process of retrenchment at home and abroad which in the end reduced Holland to the position of a minor power. Had they been willing to undertake the reform of their state in the direction of *efficiency*, had they been willing to eliminate the unnecessary offices, the pensions, the nepotism, the conflicting jurisdictions, the piled-up irrationalities of several centuries, they could perhaps have continued to pay for a large navy and a substantial army, and have remained a great power. But wherever the oligarchs, the nobles, came into power

[13] B. H. M. Vlekke, *Evolution of the Dutch Nation* (New York, 1945), 258.

in Europe in these years, it was not as agents of change, of reform, but as guardians of a very old and very elaborate social system.[14]

Integration of Russian internal political history with that of western and central Europe as early as the beginning of the eighteenth century is bound to seem somewhat artificial. It is true that after the death of Peter the Great in 1725 there was an "oligarchic reaction" quite as pronounced as those we have noted in Sweden, France, Britain, and the Netherlands. In abstract analysis, the Russians like the others were revolting from a recently strengthened central authority in the name of old ways and old traditions. Even psychologically, there was no doubt a parallelism between the Russian experience of these years and the experience of many other Europeans: a desire for an end to experimentation and expansion, for a return to normalcy. But in concrete terms it is almost impossible to establish any living, active movement of ideas and programs between Russia and the rest of Europe, any "influence" of the sort that became a commonplace after 1789. Moreover, the Russian nobles thought of the normal in terms obviously very different from those of a Saint-Simon or a Stanhope.

The opposition to Peter brought in not only the nobles, but the clergy. During Peter's lifetime this opposition rallied around Alexis, the heir to the throne. Alexis had been brought up by female relatives, and had come under the influence of prominent personages hostile to Peter. The tsar had abolished the Russian patriarchate, for which the Holy Synod, controlled actually though not officially by a procurator subordinate to the tsar, was substituted in 1721. Peter had scandalized the devout and the orthodox, not merely by neglecting his religious duties, but by commanding his courtiers to take part in grotesque and obscene parodies on church services. His reform of the calendar, which had made the year 1700 date from the birth of Christ as in western Europe, and not from the creation as had been the Russian method; his insistence that men be clean-shaven and dressed in "German fashion"; his smoking of tobacco, all were unwelcome and unpopular departures. His conquests, his building of St. Petersburg which had followed these reforms, had not seemed to the conservatives to be desirable innovations. The heavy taxation and forced service, both of nobles and peasants, were bitterly and more reasonably resented.

Alexis, when prosecuted at his father's orders for being involved in an

---

[14] P. J. Blok, *History of the People of the Netherlands* (New York, 1898-1912), V, 42-96, is a good summary of conventional views of the early eighteenth century in the Netherlands. For a balanced modern corrective, see Vlekke, *Dutch Nation*, chap. x.

alleged plot to take over the throne, confessed that if the insurgents had summoned him he would have heeded their call. His mistress testified that Alexis, had he become tsar, would have lived at Moscow and let St. Petersburg be an ordinary provincial town. He would have paid no attention to the navy or its upkeep, and would have retained only those troops actually needed to defend the country. He would never have declared war on anyone, and would have been content with the traditional boundaries of Russia. The plot never matured. Alexis, under sentence of death, died in prison after torture (July 8, 1718).[15]

The language of the decree creating the Holy Synod shows Peter's fear lest the authority of the patriarch should be a rival to that of the tsar. In the words of the edict, drawn up by Theophane Prokopovich, "the common people do not distinguish spiritual from autocratic power"; the patriarch is regarded as "a second sovereign, equal in power to the autocrat and perhaps greater than he." In case of dispute between tsar and patriarch there would be danger that the masses would follow the latter and believe themselves to be fighting on God's side.[16]

Even on such apparently trivial points as objection to clean-shaven men and to smoking tobacco, the opposition to Peter the Great professed religious motives. The religion of so backward and primitive a country as Russia in the early eighteenth century was more a matter of taboos and rituals than of a reasoned theology, as the persistent opposition to the seventeenth-century religious reforms of the pious Tsar Alexis and the Patriarch Nikon shows. Peter's religious reforms, like much else that he did, merely continued the work of his predecessors and met the same reactionary opposition that they had encountered. His attempt to subordinate the church to the state was perhaps the result of what he had observed in western Europe, where even the papacy had little political power in Catholic France or Catholic Austria.

At Peter's death, then, there was an almost universal reaction against the work of this first Russian westernizer. Politically the reaction is summed up by the failure of any ruler until Catherine the Great in 1762 to dominate the various groups struggling for power. Rulers were made by revolt of the palace guards. These guards, largely recruited from the nobles, were a constant threat to the royal power they had created. The nobles on their estates escaped more and more from the status of servants

---

[15] Milioukov, Seignobos et Eisenmann, *Histoire de Russie*, I, 418. Most of the detail above is taken from the very clear and readable account by Miliukov in this collective work. See also V. O. Kluchevsky, *A History of Russia* (London, 1911-1931), IV, chap. x.

[16] Quoted by Milioukov, *Histoire de Russie*, I, 410.

of the state which Peter had held them to. Yet Russia was now inescapably a great power and needed at the top in both army and civilian services the kind of skill and technical training these Russian nobles did not have and now refused, for the most part, to acquire. Hence the introduction, especially under the Empress Anne (1730-1740), of many foreigners, of whom the most conspicuous were Germans. Able men like Biron (his real name was Bühren), Ostermann, and Münnich helped keep Russia as a power in European politics, in spite of the indifference, contempt, or hatred felt by most of the Russian ruling class for the west and its ways.

There is no sense in trying to write of an "oligarchic reaction" in early eighteenth-century Poland. There was nothing for the nobles to react against; the authority of the central government, never strong by Western standards, had by 1715 fallen so low that it can hardly be said to have existed. There was a king in Poland, a king elected by the nobles in their Diet. As king, he played a part in international politics, but hardly, save as a figurehead or party leader, in internal politics.

Poland in 1715 was, in fact, not so much a *Ständestaat* surviving into modern times as a degenerate *Ständestaat*. All political power was in the hands of the nobles, indeed in the hands of the great nobles, each with a dependent train of petty nobles. These met in local county diets, and sent delegates to a national Diet. Within this body there prevailed the notorious *liberum veto*, a requirement of unanimity which permitted minorities to stop normal political action and throw things into the hands of "confederations," of county delegates. In a confederation majority vote supposedly prevailed. The trouble was to know which confederation, which of the groups now in a kind of private war, was actually legal. In theory, the king's joining a confederation made that confederation legal, or constitutional.

Poland was in a state of disintegration and was ripe for partition. It is true that her boundaries were—and remain today—among the least defensible in Europe, and that she stood between two strong and aggressive powers. Yet economically and socially Poland as a society seems not worlds apart from Hungary as a society, and the Polish nobles not worlds apart from the Magyar nobles. Hungary survived as part of the great Hapsburg complex; perhaps Poland could have survived as part of a great Saxon complex, had there been such. But with due allowance for geographical, military, and dynastic factors, it does seem that the extinction of Poland as a state was due in part to the incredible, caricatural badness of its political structure.

III. CHURCH AND STATE

Any conservative reaction in modern European history seems bound to show a strong clerical tinge. The Catholic church, which has never admitted that the state can be supreme over it, and the Protestant churches, established and dissenting, with their insistence on the right of the individual or congregation to judge freely on matters of doctrine and policy, have never supported royal absolutism or any other form of state sovereignty without reservations. Either the church, as a universal and divinely ordained institution, claims powers co-ordinate with the state, or the individual Christian asserts the right of private judgment, and obeys God rather than the king. These generalizations can be illustrated by the conflict between churches and states in Europe following 1715, with the Jesuit ultramontane effort at one extreme, and the Quaker and Moravian Brethren's individualism at the other.

In England, after the Revolution of 1688, a considerable portion of the clergy of the established church had refused to swear allegiance to the new sovereigns, William and Mary; these Nonjurors, who had been deprived of their benefices, were still active in the reign of George I, often in sympathy with the Jacobites. It has been claimed that their protest "against the omnicompetence of the Hobbesian state" was helping to win freedom of conscience for the individual. The continuance of the Nonjuror movement long after the political hopes of its founders had become impossible of realization may certainly be ascribed to their objection to Walpole's apparent policy of reducing the church to a department of the civil service of the state. The surviving fragment of the Nonjurors, which lasted until the beginning of the nineteenth century, called itself "The True British Catholic Church." Its liturgy, revised in 1718, resembled rather strongly the revised prayer book proposed by the English bishops in 1927. But such high churchmen were hardly advocates of liberty of conscience for individuals not in agreement with their peculiar doctrines.[17]

The Jacobites like Atterbury, Bishop of Rochester, who had remained within the Church of England, insisted strongly on the constitutional rights of the historic assembly of that church, the Convocation. As many of the parish clergy were Tory, and some of them Jacobite, Atterbury's insistence on the powers of the lower house of Convocation as against

[17] L. M. Hawkins, *Allegiance in Church and State: the Problem of the Non-Jurors in the English Revolution* (London, 1928), 167-168. See also H. Broxap, "Jacobites and Nonjurors," F. J. C. Hearnshaw, ed., *The Social and Political Ideas of Some English Thinkers of the Augustan Age* (London, 1928); and N. Sykes, *Church and State in England in the XVIIIth Century* (Cambridge, Eng., 1935), 284 ff.

those of the Whig bishops appointed since 1688 was a part of Jacobite strategy. But the equality of authority of Convocation as a whole with that of Parliament was asserted in 1713 by Bishop Gibson, the stanch Whig who afterward worked with Walpole to keep order and tranquillity in the church.

England is governed by two distinct Administrations: one Spiritual, for matters of a Spiritual nature; and the other Temporal, for matters of a Temporal nature. And for the same ends, hath it two Legislatures, the one consisting of persons Spiritual and the other of persons Temporal; whose business it is, to frame the Laws for the government of Church and State.

He goes on to state that these laws, when confirmed by the sovereign, become obligatory on the people and rulers for the administration of justice in spiritual and temporal matters.[18]

Convocation had, however, been deprived under Charles II (by a private agreement between Archbishop Sheldon and Clarendon, the Lord Chancellor) of its most important power, the privilege of taxing the clergy. It had not actually sat between 1664 and 1688, and William III did not allow it to do so until 1700. Under Anne it had assembled whenever Parliament was summoned, but a bitter dispute had arisen as to whether the Archbishop of Canterbury could prorogue it if the upper and lower houses disagreed. There was, of course, a separate Convocation for the Archdiocese of York, so that the one for the province of Canterbury did not represent all of England.

The attempt by Bishop Headly, then of Bangor, to answer the arguments advanced by the Nonjuror Hickes, provoked another dispute in 1717 between the two houses of the Canterbury Convocation which caused a hasty prorogation in order to avoid attempts to censure Headly. Headly's position was objectionable not because of his demonstration that the nonjuring bishops had been rightfully deposed, but because of his insistence on unfettered private judgment as the essence of Christianity, which denied all authority to the church as such and favored complete toleration of all sincere believers in Christ. This was certainly unorthodox. It was not supported by many among the clergy. But this "Bangorian controversy" gave the government an excuse to prevent Convocation from sitting. Except for a brief trial in 1741, it did not sit again to transact business until 1855. Gibson and Walpole worked out details of church affairs together during most of the latter's ministry.

[18] E. Gibson, "Introductory Discourse," *Codex Juris Ecclesiastici Anglicani* (London, 1713), xxix, quoted in Sykes, *Church and State*, 298-299.

In France the great controversy over the Bull Unigenitus continued in an acute stage until Fleury, during the latter years of his administration, succeeded in imposing a rule of silence on the subject. Jesuit and other advisers had persuaded Louis XIV in the last years of his reign that if the pope would issue a bull condemning Jansenism as heretical, the result would be peace and unity within the church in France, instead of the controversy which had continued through many decades. Accordingly, in 1713 Pope Clement XI promulgated the Constitution Unigenitus, condemning as heretical one hundred and one propositions taken from a work of Father Quesnel entitled *Moral Reflections on the New Testament*. Aside from involved and often rather barren theological issues, this bull was an assertion that the pope was supreme on all points of faith and morals. Its acceptance was equivalent to accepting papal infallibility, which did not become the received doctrine of the Catholic church until the Vatican Council of 1870. Hence many French Catholics without interest in or detailed knowledge of the theological points at issue were inclined, as Saint-Simon was, to feel that this assertion of papal authority restricted the liberties of the church. A number of prominent churchmen wished to appeal from the pope to a council, either of the entire Catholic church or of the church in France. The *Parlement* claimed that the bull would not have the force of law until it was registered. The universities, especially that at Paris, were inclined also to object that it was not to be received in France unless accepted by their faculties.

Louis XIV before he died had forced the *Parlement* to register letters patent for the publication of the bull, and had brought pressure on the faculty of theology of the Sorbonne, through the syndic Le Rouge, to sign a formula of acceptance. Forty bishops had approved a pastoral letter which was to introduce the bull, but eight others, including the Cardinal de Noailles, Archbishop of Paris, had refused to approve it. The king, in the last months of his life, was preparing to depose the cardinal. Had he lived a couple of years longer, he would probably have succeeded in compelling France to accept the Constitution Unigenitus. The regent, by making Cardinal de Noailles head of the new *Conseil de Conscience* in 1715, showed that he hoped the dispute would be settled by a compromise. The cardinal did try to procure from the pope an "explanation" of the Bull Unigenitus which might satisfy its more moderate opponents; in this attempt he was not merely rebuffed by the Vatican, but was unable, even with the backing of the regent, to quell the violence of the various partisan groups involved in the dispute. The regent, having discovered by experience that no compromise would be acceptable, finally, after the resignation of Noailles, endeavored to impose silence on all parties. The bull was to be accepted, then more or less ignored. But even strong measures failed to silence the disputants. The appeal to the "Liberties of the Gallican Church," an appeal directed against both the papacy and the monarchy which had asked for the new Constitution Unigenitus, was never completely suppressed until the Revolution of 1789 changed the situation entirely.

The object which Louis XIV had in view in procuring the papal bull was not to support the infallibility of the pope, but to establish religious uniformity in France. The revocation of the Edict of Nantes in 1685, by which Protestantism was outlawed in France, has been explained as an effort to establish the principle *Cujus regio, ejus religio* imposed on northern Europe after the Reformation. After the Edict of Fontainebleau, repealing that of Nantes, Protestants in France were in the same situation as Catholics in Protestant states.[19] But to secure religious unity the Jansenist opposition within the Catholic church must also be suppressed.

Louis XIV, the regent, and Cardinal Fleury, judged by their conduct of relations with the Vatican, were consistent in opposing any effort of the papacy to diminish the authority of the French crown over the church. The spiritual authority of the pope was always recognized in principle, but he was denied all temporal sovereignty in France. In practice his spiritual authority was also limited, since his bulls and apostolic letters could not be published or enforced in France without having passed the scrutiny of the royal authorities. He could not without the king's consent send legates into France to interfere with the authority of French bishops. The bishops could write to the pope only with the king's knowledge and consent. Appointments to the bishoprics and other important offices in the church in France were made by the crown. The king could make regulations having the force of law on church matters, and he could tax the clergy, though he did this by asking the assembly of the clergy for a *don gratuit* which they apportioned among themselves. The assembly of the clergy, akin to the English Convocation, was dependent on royal authority, and only by that authority did it take part in administration or in declarations of doctrine like that of 1682. Thus the papacy could act in France only through the king. It had no direct authority over the clergy or laity. Pope Clement XI and his successors blamed on the "Gal-

---

[19] Joseph Déclareuil, *Histoire générale du droit français* (Paris, 1925), 1019.

licanism" of the French crown the failure of the measures taken to suppress Jansenism.[20]

The opposition to the Bull Unigenitus in France came both from people who objected to its theology and from people who objected to the extension of royal authority over the church in France. After 1715 the merely political opposition was more important than that based on faith in the doctrines condemned by the bull as heretical. Many of the political opponents were already deists and rationalists. Some of them were skeptics.

On the religious side, as Sainte-Beuve long ago pointed out, there was a decline, not in fervor, but in dignity and intelligence. There is a startling contrast between Port Royal in the time of Pascal, and the grotesque scenes at the grave of the Deacon Pâris in the St. Médard Cemetery in the 1730's, when the so-called *convulsionnaires* behaved like Holy Rollers or a camp meeting of Negro Methodists.[21]

Throughout the discussion the opponents of the bull claimed to be defenders of "the Liberties of the Gallican Church" against attacks said to be of Jesuit inspiration. But this claim can only be admitted with many reservations. These so-called "Liberties" were in practice chiefly the independence of the church in France from papal control. From the point of view of the Vatican, Louis XIV was himself the chief Gallican, not merely at the time of the declaration of 1682, but as late as January and February in 1715, when he sent Amelot to Rome with instructions to secure papal consent to the summoning of a French national council of the church to bring about acceptance of the Constitution Unigenitus. The Vatican objected that no such council had been held for seven or eight hundred years, and finally refused consent. Cardinal Fabroni, on the pope's behalf, made the remarkable counterproposal that Cardinal de Noailles be deprived of his French citizenship and then turned over to the pope to be dealt with. The implication that Louis XIV's insistence on maintaining the liberties of Gallicanism had caused the difficulties is clear.[22] On his deathbed Louis XIV was still insisting, against practical difficulties pointed out by the Archbishop of Bordeaux and others, that such a national council, from which the objecting bishops were now to be excluded, should be held. This does not look like the result of Jesuit advice from Le Tellier.

Louis XIV objected to papal control of the church in France, but wished

[20] See, for example, the comment of L. von Pastor, *Geschichte der Päpste* (Freiburg im Breisgau, 1899-1933), XV, 137.

[21] C. A. Sainte-Beuve, *Port-Royal* (Paris, 1926-1932), IX, 210-211.

[22] On these negotiations of Amelot at the Vatican, see Pastor, *Geschichte der Päpste*, XV, 178-185.

complete unanimity in that church under royal authority. His entire policy in church matters, both Protestant and Catholic, was directed not toward the triumph of the doctrines of the Jesuits over the allegedly Augustinian beliefs of the Jansenists, but toward the complete establishment of royal absolutism with supremacy of the state over any and all churches. The insistence on uniformity was necessary not so much to guarantee orthodoxy as to ensure tranquillity and order. After the unlucky experiment of making Cardinal de Noailles head of the *Conseil de Conscience* had led to dissension and bitterness, the regent undertook to restore tranquillity by making Fleury the chief member of the *Conseil de Conscience*, which was not abolished when Noailles resigned. Silence was imposed on the Jansenists, as the heterogeneous opposition was named in current discussion. But the regent had forced Pope Clement XI to abandon his effort to dictate French policy, for when the pope refused his consent to appointments which required it (such as, for instance, ordination of bishops), the regent had simply threatened to have the new clerics consecrated without the papal bulls.

Fleury was a Thomist in theology, and he therefore wished the state and the church to be co-ordinate powers. He had favored the Constitution Unigenitus from the first, because he felt that the majority of Catholics in France were opposed to Jansenism. He opposed both the papal efforts to regain *de facto* control of the church in France, and the efforts of the opposition to the Constitution Unigenitus to eliminate royal authority. The opposing bishops were trying to become in fact supreme in their dioceses, independent of both the king and the pope. The *parlements*, in supporting the opposition, were asserting their independent authority. Again it is the arguments of Filmer about the anarchy of a mixed or limited monarchy which give the clue to the conservative position of defenders of royal absolutism. What Fleury wanted was peace and order. His position on doctrine was neither that of Quesnel nor that of the Jesuits.[23]

The libertarian, and in the philosophical sense anarchic, character of the Jansenist opposition in its extreme form appears from a study of the influence which the ideas of Edmond Richer, an early seventeenth-century theologian, exercised on Jansenism in the eighteenth century. Richer's arguments against both royal and papal authority were used to defend the right of the parish priests and the lower clergy to defy orders transmitted to them by their bishops, when the bishops were mouthpieces for

---

[23] G. Hardy, *Le Cardinal de Fleury et le mouvement Janséniste* (Paris, 1925); A. Gazier, *Histoire générale du mouvement Janséniste* (Paris, 1922).

the king and the pope. This defiance is analogous to the equally barren defiance which the lower house of Convocation in England showed to the upper house, the bishops appointed by the crown. Under early eighteenth-century conditions, such defiance could only tend to perpetuate what Heckscher in another connection has called "feudal disintegration."[24]

The Jesuits were blamed in contemporary discussion for having persuaded Louis XIV and Pope Clement XI to issue the Constitution Unigenitus. But actual documentary proof of Jesuit responsibility for this act is lacking. Clement XI, a zealous and conscientious pope, himself made a careful study of Quesnel's book. The preparation of the Constitution Unigenitus was entrusted to a commission of thirteen members, chosen to represent all schools of thought and all of the monastic orders of importance, with the "utmost possible omission of Jesuits," as von Pastor says. Only one of the thirteen was a Jesuit.[25]

Nor can Jesuit responsibility for the religious difficulties in Germany, which came to a head in 1719, be proved, though in this case also the Protestant and other opponents blamed the Jesuits for making trouble. These difficulties arose in the Palatinate, and for a time seemed to threaten another religious war. The Protestant line of electors had failed, and the reigning Elector Palatine, Karl Philipp von Neuberg (1716-1742), the last of his line, was a Catholic. By the Treaties of Westphalia the Protestants were to retain their rights as of the "normal year" 1624, but Louis XIV, who had conquered the Palatinate, insisted upon a clause in the Treaty of Ryswick in 1697 whereby the Catholics, who had extended their privileges under French rule, were to retain what they held as of 1697. This "Ryswick Clause" had met with objections from the Protestants, but despite their protests it was not revoked in the peace settlement after the War of the Spanish Succession, the Treaty of Baden.

The Protestants complained to the Emperor Charles VI that a dissertation by a Jesuit professor in the Heidelberg University contained remarks about Calvin which they regarded as insulting, in violation of an imperial decree of 1715 forbidding all invectives against opposing beliefs. The Catholics then pointed out to the Elector Palatine that in copies of the *Heidelberg Catechism*, bearing the electoral imprimatur, the Mass was described in glosses on the eightieth question as "accursed idolatry." Charles tried to suppress the *Catechism*.

There was also a bitter dispute over the right to use a church in Heidel-

[24] E. Préclin, *Les Jansénistes du XVIII° siècle* (Paris, 1929).
[25] Pastor, *Geschichte der Päpste*, XV, 156. See also A. Le Roy, *Le Gallicanisme au XVIII° siècle* (Paris, 1892), 380 ff.

berg, formerly divided between Catholics and Calvinists, now to be
allotted to the Catholics alone. These apparently local questions roused
a storm all over Germany. The two Protestant electors, George I of
Hanover and Frederick William I of Prussia, authorized "reprisals"
in their dominions against Catholics, who were deprived of privileges
formerly granted. They also intervened at Vienna. The Prussian protest
was tactless and gave great offense. But a remonstrance made on behalf
of George I by his agent at Vienna, the Swiss Protestant Saint-Saphorin,
was more successful. Saint-Saphorin pointed out that the emperor, by a
prompt and judicious use of his authority, could easily restore peace and
order in the Reich, and avert the threat of a war which would upset the
whole European system. Charles VI answered at once that he saw how
necessary it was to quench this dispute which might destroy all
Germany. [25a]

It had already attracted attention all over Europe. The Archbishop of
Canterbury had written a letter (January 13, 1720) to the Palatinate
Church Council offering them encouragement in their struggle against
"false and deceitful Jesuits, and against the person known as the Pope
of Rome." This demonstration of solidarity between the Anglicans and
the Reformed (Calvinist) churches indicates how seriously the counter-
reformation tendencies in Germany were viewed by Protestants everywhere. From Sweden, too, came assurances of sympathy. That the
devoutly Catholic Charles VI should have interfered, carried on long-
drawn-out negotiations to stop these extensions of Catholic influence, is
another proof of the universal desire for peace and order, the cult of
stability. Like Louis XIV, Charles VI wished to control the church in
his domains and in the Reich, and hence resented ultramontane attempts.
Saint-Saphorin's appeal to him to use his authority struck the right note.
As the danger of another war of religion was averted, historians have
tended to ignore its reality.

IV. THE GROWTH OF CENTRAL AUTHORITY

It would be a grave error to consider the oligarchic reaction against
royal power as the most important element in European politics in the
years immediately following the Utrecht settlement. In the long run,
even in the countries where this reaction was most apparent, the future
lay with those who were working toward the modern, centralized state.

[25a] Saint-Saphorin to Stanhope, Feb. 10, 1720, quoted in Borgmann, *Der deutsche Religionsstreit*, 90. This monograph, by a pupil of W. Michael, gives a careful and judicious account
of the whole situation. On the impossibility of complete proof of Jesuit responsibility, see
pp. 33-38.

The debts with which all the great states were saddled by the long war proved, as we shall see, a handle by which businessmen increased their power over the country gentlemen everywhere in the maritime states of the west. In Austria, in Spain, in many German states, there were able, or at least adequate, kings, a growing bureaucratic tradition, and other elements making for a fairly steady growth of central power. The recent wars themselves, though they provided no such innovation as did the universal democratic conscription of 1793 in France, had been so long-drawn-out, and on such a scale, that they had helped destroy many of the habits and practices of local, corporative independence. The wars, in short, helped make the reaction against the war-built centralized states ineffective and indeed impossible. Even in England, where the forms of local independence, of picturesque variations, of corporate "liberties" seemed guaranteed by the final defeat of the Stuart attempt to rule by Continental absolutism—even in England the new financial power in coalition with the great Whig families was slowly molding the English government into the centralized cabinet system. This system in its actual working, and especially in its capacity for future development, was by no means as subject to checks and balances as contemporary theorists thought it.

Yet the *locus classicus* for the growth of centralized power in the early eighteenth century was Prussia. It is possible to trace the genesis of the Prussian state back to the beginnings of the Hohenzollern house; and it is possible to argue that by 1715 the future of Prussia had been "determined." Yet in the normal frames of reference of historical determinism —geography, economic factors, race, culture—there seems to be little that marks out the Hohenzollern state at the beginning of the eighteenth century as destined to win out over all the other German states. It is at any rate obvious that the reign of Frederick William I (1713-1740) is a decisive reign; it may even have been a crossroads, a turning point.

For under Frederick William's father, the Elector Frederick III of Brandenburg who became in 1701 King Frederick I of Prussia, there was little to distinguish Prussia from other fair-sized German states with rulers imitating Louis XIV—court etiquette, architecture, extravagance, impending bankruptcy, and all. The famous son of Frederick William, Frederick the Great, wrote that "Under Frederick I, Berlin was the Athens of the North; under Frederick William, she became the Sparta."[26]

---

[26] J. D. E. Preuss, ed., *Oeuvres de Frédéric le Grand* (Berlin, 1846-1857), I, 266. Frederick the Great was most objective in his estimate of the political achievements of the father with whom he quarreled so violently. See the estimate of Frederick William's work in Frederick's "Mémoires de Brandebourg," *Oeuvres*, I, 201-202.

If this judgment savors a little too much of eighteenth-century love of epigram and broad generalization, it has a nucleus of truth. No king could have turned the Brandenburgers and Prussians into lazy, cheerful Neapolitans. The Prussia we know was formed by the labors, the sacrifices, the voluntary restraints of a typical North German population. But political mishandling from above might perhaps at this period have allowed some other German state to take the lead, might perhaps have altered the whole course of the national unification of Germany.

Frederick William conducted the affairs of his scattered lands as if they were a proprietary enterprise. He "ran" Prussia in just the sense that the old-fashioned American businessman expected to run his business. And he ran it extremely well. He inherited an almost empty treasury, for his father's attempts to imitate Louis XIV had been expensive. By cutting to the bone expenses for everything but his army, by efficient tax collections, and by skillful management of the royal domains, he diminished expenditures and increased income. He even made money out of the Prussian post office. The nineteenth-century Prussian historian Droysen estimated that the total income of the crown rose from 3,655,000 taler in 1714 to 5,483,000 in 1730 and to almost 7,000,000 in 1740. A large part of these financial gains Frederick William used to increase his army from 38,000 in 1713 to over 80,000 in 1740. In these figures may be found one of the reasons why Frederick II could become Frederick the Great.[27]

The army is the astounding fact. It made Prussia a by no means distant fourth among European military powers, in a class with France, Russia, and Austria. And these nations had from ten to twenty times the population of Prussia (which was at most 2,500,000 at the end of Frederick William's peaceful reign) and corresponding advantages in almost everything measurable by statistics—wealth, natural resources, trade areas, and the like. The Prussian army was an excellent one, especially in the infantry, well trained and well equipped, officered for the most part by Prussian Junkers devoted to their king, and recruited, save for a third to a fourth of its ranks, from the king's own subjects. It was a *professional* army, but with some of the traits of a national army.[28]

---

[27] These figures, and many other convenient details, may be found in Robert Ergang, *The Potsdam Führer* (New York, 1941), chaps. iv-v. In spite of its misleading bookseller's title, this book is a convenient scholarly summary of both recent and older work on the reign of Frederick William I.

[28] Frederick William was obliged to have recourse to conscription to fill out the army; but it was a very incomplete conscription, with numerous exemptions, and its existence does not invalidate the usual generalization that the French *levée en masse* of 1793 began modern universal service. See Waddington, *Histoire de Prusse*, II, 517-534.

Frederick William had, of course, to work in a political structure not without corporative, medieval survivals. There were *Landtage* (assemblies, somewhat like the French provincial Estates, and representing classes, not the "people") in Brandenburg, in Prussia, and in other provinces. There were all sorts of survivals of the *Ständestaat* in the scattered patches of the Hohenzollern state in west and south Germany. In constitutional theory the Estates still had some control over taxes, and still had a hand in recruiting the soldiers on which most of the taxes were spent. In practice, Frederick William had little trouble with his privileged classes; they were neatly integrated into the Prussian service, military or civil. During this reign the standing committees and similar groups of corporative bodies, which had formed nonbureaucratic administrative groups with some real powers, fell completely into desuetude.[29] It is not that Frederick William's whole administration ran smoothly, perfectly. But the troubles that cropped up were troubles of detail, the kind that get adjudicated by due process of administrative law. They were not troubles that reflected, indeed sprang from, a class struggle, such for instance as the troubles that at this time confronted the regent in France.

Frederick William achieved his success partly by carrying through administrative reforms which made Prussia a model absolutism, with a well-trained bureaucracy and with something like a minimum of obstructive routine, jurisdictional disputes, and other classic weaknesses of bureaucracy.[30] But it is important to note that the system worked without the usual bureaucratic difficulties largely because the king himself really had absolute power, and really used it, not in grandiose pronouncements and in mere ritual, but in the thousand little details of daily life. Frederick William's ministers were his secretaries and servants. He never had what in western countries was called a ministry. Even the *Ober-Finanz, Kriegs und Domänen Direktorium* (fortunately known for short as the General Directory), which he formed in 1722, was merely a very good administrative board, any decision of which could be altered or vetoed by the king. All this exercise of royal authority, though it was unquestioned and almost automatic, meant long hours of labor for the king, and an appetite for detail. This Frederick William certainly had.

He was not an attractive personality, but his achievements for Prussia and for Germany were so great that the commonplace about his reputation

[29] O. Hintze, "Der oesterreichische und der preussische Beamtenstaat," *Historische Zeitschrift*, LXXXVI (1901), 408.

[30] The functioning of the Prussian state, which remained the same under the succeeding reign, has been clearly described in the subsequent volume of this series, Walter L. Dorn, *Competition for Empire, 1740-1763* (New York, 1940), 52-62.

being overshadowed by that of his famous son really does not hold. Historians—and not merely Prussian historians—have always pointed out that Frederick William built up the capital, human as well as material, which his son invested so riskily and so successfully in national greatness. Frederick William's work was especially lauded by the Nazis. For them the king was great, not merely as part of the Prussian tradition, not merely as the builder of the Prussian army, but more particularly as an exemplar of the *Führerprinzip* in a simple outright form that smelled of blood and the soil, and as a practical exponent of the kind of good-housekeeping socialism they insisted they meant by their full party title, *Nazional-Sozialistische-Deutsche-Arbeiter-Partei*. The claim is perhaps no more incongruous than most such soundings into the past for justification of the present.[31]

In this light, the tales of Frederick William's manias, such as that for tall soldiers, his boorishness, his bad temper, are only on the margin of history. His regiment of giants, recruited from all over Europe at a cost of seven hundred thousand talers, was his one real extravagance. It was certainly not worth the money in military value, and was, indeed, dissolved by Frederick the Great on his accession. But the Sergeant King loved his "blue boys," and got his greatest pleasure from drilling them himself. He liked his *Tabaks Kollegium*, an informal gathering of his closest advisers, held under barracks austerity, and devoted to shop, smoking, drink, bawdy talk, practical jokes, and such deliberately masculine activities. He liked to display his contempt for art and letters, for intellectuals and their theories, for anything French. He would, on occasion, beat almost any of his subjects with his stick, from an estate bailiff to a high dignitary of his court. He was, in short, an autocrat for the book; but he was an efficient autocrat, and by no means unintelligent. Working in his own way, and with very different materials, he showed the same mastery over the art of handling men that his contemporaries Fleury and Walpole showed.

In the Hapsburg dominions the reign of Charles VI (1711-1740) was part of the conflict between the proponents of the leviathan state and those of the *Ständestaat* which runs through all early eighteenth-century Europe. But the problems of the Austrian state—or better, the Austrian complex of states—were more complicated than in virtually unitary states like France, or even in a state like Prussia which, though geographically

---

[31] For an example of this devotion to Frederick William, see F. von Oppeln-Bronikowski, *Der Baumeister des preussischen Staates: Leben und Wirken des Soldatenkönigs Friederich Wilhelms I* (Jena, 1934).

and economically a patchwork, had already in 1715 many elements of unity—ethnic, religious, even "national." And the quarter century after Utrecht saw no great *administrative* or *political* changes in the structure of the Hapsburg state. The great outstanding fact, the Pragmatic Sanction, by which Charles assured the succession of the whole Hapsburg dynastic inheritance to his daughter, Maria Theresa, was a *constitutional* achievement of great importance.

For the last two centuries, Hapsburg practice had varied between an attempt on the one hand to keep intact the lands that fell to the head of the dynasty, and on the other a natural feudal family desire to share the spoils as much as possible, at least among the sons. So there had come the division of the immense holdings of Charles V between the western (Spanish) and the eastern (Austrian) branches. Now, after the War of the Spanish Succession, the western part seemed lost for good, though Charles VI, who had loved Spain, could never quite give up hope. In 1713 Charles had therefore arranged for a new protocol on the succession in order to adapt the family pact of 1703, the *pactum mutuae successionis*, to the apparent loss of Spain. The old pact had put the daughters of Charles's older brother Joseph above those of Leopold (their aunts) and Charles (their cousins). This provision is perhaps explicable in view of the good prospect in 1703 that Charles's issue would be taken care of in Spain. At any rate, in 1713 Charles modified this pact so as to ensure the succession of the whole Hapsburg dominions to his *own* issue, eldest son, or lacking sons, eldest daughter. This was at first a secret *family* compact, not public law; but by 1719 the consent of the Leopoldine and Josephine archduchesses had been obtained. The one son born to Charles had died in infancy. His daughter, Maria Theresa, seemed almost certain to be his successor. Accordingly what is known as the Pragmatic Sanction was finally published to the world in 1719.[32]

The real problem was to make the Pragmatic Sanction *public* law and, if possible, *international* law. Charles spent the last twenty years of his reign trying to ensure acceptance of the Pragmatic Sanction by all the powers of Europe, and by whatever corporate bodies within the Hapsburg lands still possessed political powers. The international aspects of Charles's

---

[32] There are many very fine points of dispute about this whole sequence of family agreements. It is clear that, though they mark a real attempt to keep the Hapsburg inheritance together and avoid feudal disintegration, they are not a kind of "constitution" marking the formation of a modern state of Austria-Hungary. For an admirable and judicious summary of the dispute between Professors Turba and Michael over the finer problems of the Pragmatic Sanction, see a review of this dispute by Basil Williams, *English Historical Review*, LV (1940), 471-473.

efforts will be considered in a later chapter. Domestically, he achieved his purpose, and at his death Maria Theresa succeeded him with no serious internal opposition.

History has generally been rather harsh toward Charles. It is true that a very able contemporary gave historians the lead, for Prince Eugene expressed the opinion that the best defense of the Hapsburg inheritance would be a good army and a well-filled treasury. At the death of Charles, the army was disorganized and inefficient, and the treasury was nearly empty. Yet the verdict that Charles gave up a possible real strengthening of the Hapsburg monarchy to chase a useless set of paper guarantees is unfair. Four centuries of Austrian history suggest that the limits to "real strengthening" imposed by the disparate character of the Hapsburg holdings fell well short of anything like Prussian efficiency. It is pretty clear that Charles conceded nothing important to his Estates in return for their acceptance of the Pragmatic Sanction. The best case one can make for his having yielded something is in Hungary, where the acceptance actually took the form of a treaty between Charles and the Hungarian Diet in 1723. But the Hapsburg bureaucracy had never got a foothold in Hungary, and that country can hardly be said to have been under less effective central control after than before the Pragmatic Sanction.

The case against Charles really comes down to an unalloyed conditional: *if* he had spent his energies doing the kind of efficient job in his land Frederick William was doing in his, *then* his daughter might have had the men and money to beat Frederick William's son. No one can ever tell. But it should be pointed out that in all three of the main subdivisions of the Hapsburg lands—the Austrian lands, the Bohemian lands, and the Hungarian lands—there were grave obstacles to any further rapid campaign for centralized efficiency. In all of them there were active *Landtage* or diets, and there were complicated structures of corporate rights. In all of them save Hungary there had been introduced at least the beginnings of royal absolutism in the form of paid bureaucrats in the service of the crown. In most of them there was a class of noble administrators, not quite in the independent position of the English justice of the peace, nor yet in the dependent position of the French intendant, but with links both to the Estates and to the crown. There was not yet a real central administration in Vienna, except at the level of top advisers to the crown. The good Catholic Hapsburgs had won their counter-reformation against the Protestants, especially in Bohemia, in part by "settling" noblemen with special privileges. The Hungarian Diet, a bicameral legislature with a House of Magnates, the great nobles, and a lower house of country gentlemen with some representation from the urban upper classes, was no mere *Landtag*, but a sort of cross between the Polish Diet and the British Parliament. Milan and the Austrian Netherlands (Belgium) had only just fallen to the Hapsburgs, and their integration into the realm was to prove an almost impossible task.

The Hapsburgs, almost inevitably in view of their background, had slowly been building on the absolutist pattern. They were slowly creating a bureaucracy, slowly encroaching on the particularism of the *Länder*. They could hardly have chosen the British method of compromise with corporate privilege. It is true that Schierl von Schierendorff, who served both Joseph I and Charles VI in the Vienna *Hofkammer*, has left writings in which he advocated much that sounds very liberal, in the nineteenth-century sense, such as a "Convocation" of all the *Länder* in a national parliament, and the adoption of the union between England and Scotland as a pattern for the solution of national problems within the Hapsburg lands. But Schierendorff was an isolated intellectual; the set of the tide was all against him.[33]

In this delicate and very typical early eighteenth-century equilibrium between royal absolutism and corporate privilege, between efficiency and custom, between the new and the old, the task of the reformer was exceedingly difficult, and the results of reform hard to calculate. It is true that, despite her wars, Maria Theresa did rather better at the task than her father had. But the daughter had lost Silesia in a foreign war. Charles and his advisers never enjoyed that kind of stimulus. Their work was essentially a work of peace, and one which may have altered the whole history of Europe. For had Maria Theresa's subjects repudiated her, had the Austrian succession been a *domestic* as well as an *international* problem, no one can even guess sensibly what kind of state or states would have grown up in south-central Europe.[34]

For the Empire, the settlement at Utrecht did but continue the work of the settlement at Westphalia in 1648. Politically, there is nothing new in the Empire in the first part of the eighteenth century. What counted for the Germans was the government of the state in which they lived; and that varied from the patrician merchant city-state like Hamburg through

[33] Schierendorff called the writings in which he discussed these weighty matters *Parerga sive otia*, which seems a good Viennese touch. See J. Redlich, *Das oesterreichische Staats-und-Reichsproblem* (Leipzig, 1920), volume of notes, 4. (The notes in this work are printed in a separate volume, separately paged.)

[34] For a brief modern account, less critical of Charles than usual, see H. Hantsch, *Die Entwicklung Oesterreich-Ungarns zur Grossmacht* (Freiburg im Breisgau, 1933), 90-94.

the tiny splinter principalities of Thuringia to states like Saxony, Bavaria, and Hanover which were to form the basis for the Napoleonic settlement of Germany. In general, most of the Germanies were in the early eighteenth century ruled as their princes wanted them ruled. Some of them, like Augustus the Strong of Saxony, who was also King of Poland, and Karl Philipp of the Palatinate, were able rulers, forerunners of the enlightened despots. But in most of the *Kleinstaaten*, and in particular the imperial cities and the states under spiritual rule, there were strong elements of rule by custom, by privilege, by corporate bodies. Germany in the early eighteenth century was far from being cut on the plan of Prussian absolutism. Especially if one looks at Germany as a whole, with its loose federation in the Holy Roman Empire, its cultural and religious variations, its subdivisions into three-hundred-odd entities with some claim to political sovereignty, and above all its confusion of internal tariffs, unstandardized weights and measures and finances, the picture is rather medieval than modern.

In Spain there can be no doubt: the Bourbon rule marks a definite strengthening of the royal power, known to Spanish historians as *el regalismo*. Though its culmination was to come only in the second half of the century under Charles III, the gentle and tactful process by which the Bourbons were to transform Spain from an inefficient oligarchy to an efficient absolutism (efficient by comparison with the last years of the Hapsburg regime in Spain and in the Indies) was begun by Philip V, and had gone far by 1740. This achievement, carried out without any great changes in the Spanish constitution, is an interesting example of the elasticity of formal institutional arrangements. This elasticity is not, of course, an absolute. We have already noted that probably no amount of administrative skill could have saved the Polish constitution.

The greatest of the Spanish Hapsburgs had not been able to overcome wholly the centrifugal tendencies of the provinces (especially Catalonia and Aragon), the nobility, the church, the Council of the Indies—in short, the corporative inheritance of medieval Spain. Under the weak rulers of the last of the Hapsburg line, the centralization already achieved by Charles V and Philip II was very considerably lessened. Affairs of state were settled in fact by a series of great councils, in which the nobles were well represented—indeed, which they dominated in 1700—and which really were deliberative bodies with wills of their own. They were much tied up with ceremonies and the dignified Spanish equivalent of what we know as red tape. But they did govern.

Philip V was fortunate in that the circumstances of the War of the Spanish Succession and the settlements at its end enabled him to clear away entirely the councils of Flanders and of Italy, no longer needed now that Spain had lost the Netherlands and Italy; and, since the Aragonese had revolted against him and sided with his Hapsburg rival, he was able to do away with the obstreperous Council of Aragon. Toward the Inquisition, the most notorious of the councils, the Bourbons had only to let the eighteenth century take its course. Not even in Spain could the fires of the Inquisition be effectively lighted in a period whose great heresy was neither Lutheranism nor Calvinism, but freethinking, indifference, deism.

Neither Philip nor his successors abolished the other councils, nor did they need to employ even the kind of *douce violence* Maria Theresa found so effective in Hungary. The councils were maintained, and became in spirit and in actual working essentially bureaucratic, even though they were recruited in part from the Spanish equivalent of the Duke of Saint-Simon. Upon them there was gradually imposed a series of ministries on the French model. Manned at first by foreigners with technical skills, the Frenchman Orry in finances, the Italian Alberoni in foreign affairs, the Dutchman Ripperdá in economic matters, they were eventually staffed by Spaniards trained in this French school of administration.

As in the case of almost all such essentially peaceful and unhurried reforms, the Bourbon reform of Spain perhaps owes a good deal to the fact that the groups it gradually wore down into compliance and conformity were not precisely in lusty youth, were not really in a fighting mood. Philip V and his successors deserve the credit a French historian has given them when he writes that after the superfluous councils were abolished "there were only innovations in detail, but innovations so numerous, so clever (*savantes*), so patient, that they ended by filling the monarchy with an entirely new spirit without having modified in any obvious way either its structure or its appearance."[35] That is all very well, but can anyone imagine this technique being applied to the crude and hearty Russians with whom Peter the Great had to deal? The problems in the two countries are really almost incommensurable.

The contrast between these two opposite ends of Europe should remind us that, no matter how earnestly the modern historian seeks to rise above the limits of national history, Europe was not and is not in fact one. Certainly the Europe of 1715 was not one. And the end term of the

[35] G. Desdevises du Dézert, *L'Espagne de l'ancien régime* (Paris, 1897-1904), II, vi.

struggle between modern centralized efficiency and medieval particularism, which we have seen may be found everywhere in Europe, was not in this period to be a definitive one. On the whole, the leviathan state was destined to win, but never in quite the same way and to quite the same extent.

Chapter Four

ECONOMIC EXPERIMENTS

I. THE IMPOVERISHMENT OF WAR

In 1715 every government in Europe was insolvent. The unprecedented costs of the world war had greatly exceeded the receipts from taxation. There was a mass of short-term obligations, of unpaid and overdue bills of many kinds, of salaries and pensions in arrears, and no apparent means to pay them, either by refunding or from any possible revenue. The situation in France, which has been studied in greater detail than that elsewhere, was typical rather than exceptional. It may serve therefore as an example.

The regent complained, in a declaration of December 7, 1715, that on taking over the administration he had found neither cash nor current revenues in the treasury to meet the most urgent expenses, that all sorts of arrears had accumulated over a long period, and that all sources of income had been mortgaged for years in advance. The receiver-general, de Bonneval, had in fact written to Desmaretz, the controller general, on August 18, 1715, that he had no money with which to pay the interest on the government bonds due the next day; that he hoped by gentle persuasion to postpone payment to some of the large bondholders, but he was greatly troubled about the following week.[1]

In England the Jacobite danger impaired the credit of a government which had been hardly less prodigal and reckless than that of Louis XIV. Adam Smith's view of eighteenth-century English government finance is more to be trusted than that of some nineteenth-century historians. He says, apropos of a proposal to make the Bank of England an institution under government ownership and control, the

orderly, vigilant, and parsimonious administration of such aristocracies as those of Venice and Amsterdam, is extremely proper, it appears from experience,

[1] Marcel Marion, *Histoire financière de la France depuis 1715* (Paris, 1914-1931), I, 41, 42, 63 ff.

for the management of a mercantile project of this kind. But whether such a Government as that of England, which, whatever may be its virtues, has never been famous for good economy—which, in time of peace, has generally conducted itself with the slothful and negligent profusion that is perhaps natural to monarchies, and in time of war has constantly acted with all the thoughtless extravagance that democracies are apt to fall into—could be safely trusted with the management of such a project, must at least be a good deal more doubtful.[2]

The drastic economies and governmental reorganization of the new King of Prussia, Frederick William, the reforms of Alberoni in Spain, the difficulties of the Bank of Sweden, which had suspended specie payments after the defeat of Pultava in 1709, the troubles of the *Banco del Giro* at Venice, all indicate that the financial distress of governments and of government institutions was everywhere acute. The Swedish case is peculiar, since the currency was on a copper standard, so that a depositor who withdrew four hundred rix-dollars had to take away a wagonload of cumbersome copper coins. Yet the public, accustomed in normal times to use paper currency akin to our dollar bills, now preferred the inconveniences of even the ten-dollar copper coins, which weighed 19.7 kilograms (more than forty pounds), to the distrusted paper currency, which had been inflated to meet war costs. The bank, unable to pay in copper, made the paper inconvertible. As it was a government institution, controlled by the Estates-General (not by the king), this decision could not be opposed successfully. It was a factor in the oligarchic reaction after the death of Charles XII.[3]

Adam Smith's alarmist view of the dangers of national debts may perhaps be as obsolete as some modern economic theorists argue, but his description of the way in which they arose is accurate and succinct.

The progress of the enormous debts which at present oppress and will in the long run probably ruin all the great nations of Europe has been pretty uniform. Nations, like private men, have generally begun to borrow upon what may be called personal credit, without assigning or mortgaging any

[2] Adam Smith, *Wealth of Nations* (first published in London, 1776), Bk. V, chap. ii. The importance of Smith's incidental remarks to historians is pointed out by J. C. Clapham, "Economic History," R. A. Seligman and Alvin Johnson, eds., *Encyclopaedia of the Social Sciences* (New York, 1930-1935), V, 316.

[3] There is no good treatment of Alberoni's fiscal reforms. On the Bank of Sweden, see E. F. Heckscher, "The Bank of Sweden in Its Connection with the Bank of Amsterdam," J. G. Van Dillen, ed., *History of the Principal Public Banks* (The Hague, 1934). On the Bank of Venice, see G. Luzzati, "Les Banques publiques de Venise," in the same very useful co-operative work, for which an International Committee for the Study of the History of Banking and Credit is responsible.

particular fund for the payment of the debt; and when this resource has failed them, they have gone on to borrow upon assignments or mortgages of particular funds.[4]

The personal credit of Charles II and the Stuart monarchy ended with the closing of the Exchequer in 1672. William III found that no reform of the revenue could raise the sums needed for the War of the Grand Alliance. Interest as high as 14 per cent was exacted on loans, and even at that rate the subscribers demanded lottery tickets in addition, all the profits of which went to them and none to the state. Only when specified revenues were mortgaged could further money be raised.

Louis XIV encountered similar difficulties in the 1690's, and resorted to expedients often paralleled in England, where they were equally ruinous, such as the sale of annuities at rates very unfavorable to the government, and the sale of new and superfluous offices, the holders of which were not merely exempt from many taxes but able to exact fees from the overburdened public. At the Treaty of Ryswick in 1697 the burden of debt in both France and England was regarded as crushing. Yet the renewal of the war from 1701 to 1713 entailed even greater expenditures.[5]

II. THE BANK OF ENGLAND AND THE "BANQUE ROYALE"

A new era in British public finance began during "King William's War," as the American colonists called it. The government, forced to borrow and unable to do so by the issue of its own bonds, called on the aid of associations of businessmen. This practice developed into what Clark calls "the eighteenth century system . . . under which the state was financed by privileged companies": the Bank of England, the East India Company, and the South Sea Company.

The most important of these was the Bank of England, established in 1694. Charles Montagu, soon to be appointed Chancellor of the Exchequer, pondered on more than seventy financial schemes for the flotation of a loan at 8 per cent; he finally selected the third of those submitted by William Paterson, a Scotsman living in London and later concerned in the unfortunate Darien Company. Recent research based on the records of the Bank of England has proved that Paterson's claim to be its sole founder is unwarranted, though it has been accepted by

---

[4] Smith, *Wealth of Nations*, Bk. V, chap. iii.
[5] On English finances prior to 1713, see G. N. Clark, *The Later Stuarts* (Oxford, 1934), 168 ff.

many historians. From his scheme Montagu, the ablest financial expert of the day, and Michael Godfrey, the first Deputy Governor of the Bank, evolved plans which were successfully carried through.[6]

The title of the act of Parliament (5 and 6 Wm. and M. c. 20), under which the Bank of England was established, is revealing:

An act for granting to their Majesties several Rates and Duties upon Tunnage of Ships and Vessels, and upon Beer, Ale, and other Liquors; for securing certain Recompences and Advantages in the said Act mentioned, to such persons as shall voluntarily advance the Sum of Fifteen hundred thousand Pounds towards carrying on the War Against France.

Of the million and a half to be advanced on the security of the new rates and duties levied, one million two hundred thousand pounds was to be raised by the subscribers incorporated by a royal charter as "The Governor and Company of the Bank of England," who were guaranteed 8 per cent interest. They were also empowered to carry on a banking business, to accept deposits, to purchase bullion, to discount bills, to grant secured loans, and to issue notes against negotiable securities to the amount of their capital. They combined the functions of a transfer bank, like the Bank of Amsterdam, with those of a modern commercial bank. The Bank of England was also the first modern bank of issue. The importance of this institution in maintaining the credit of the British government, and in stimulating commerce and enterprise in Great Britain, can hardly be overestimated. Without the Bank of England it is improbable that London could in the course of the next hundred years have replaced Amsterdam as the financial center of the European world. Without the Bank of England the British government could hardly have succeeded in raising the subsidies to Continental states which furnished the sinews of eighteenth-century wars. Without the encouragement which the success of the Bank of England gave to the accumulation of capital and to the recirculation of hoarded wealth, the so-called "industrial revolution" could hardly have been financed in eighteenth-century England.[7]

The tie between the Bank and the government grew steadily stronger. Although the former was forced, at the various renewals of its charter, to

[6] See W. M. Acres, *The Bank of England from Within* (London, 1931), especially I, 16-18 and chap. viii; also R. D. Richards, "The First Fifty Years of the Bank of England," Van Dillen, ed., *Principal Public Banks*. Both Acres and Richards were given access to the archives of the Bank. Their work supersedes that of Andreades and others. The authoritative work is now the 250th anniversary history, Sir John Harold Clapham, *The Bank of England, a History* (Cambridge, Eng., 1944).

[7] See E. Lipson, *The Economic History of England* (London, 1931), III, 240 ff.

increase its loan to the state and to accept reduction of the rate of interest to 6 per cent in 1710 and to 3 per cent in 1742, it was compensated by the profit and the influence it gained through acting as financial agent for the treasury. In 1715 the Bank began to manage and to transfer the stock of a public loan, the 5 per cent annuities of 1715. Its management of government securities has continued from 1715 to the present day. The relationship between the financiers and capitalists of London and the British government has remained intimate and highly important. A "funded interest," as conservatives like Swift complained, had become a rival of the landed gentry, another privileged class. The basis for the characteristic British collaboration between "landlords" and "fundlords"— a collaboration not without its internal quarrels—had been laid.

The success of the Bank of England in maintaining public credit and stimulating private enterprise made a deep impression on financiers and businessmen in other countries. During the War of the Spanish Succession the British and the Dutch were not merely able to pay for the armies of the German princes, who could not have maintained their troops from their own revenues or by their own credit; they were also in a position to increase the prosperity of their own trading classes. The maritime powers had fewer people and smaller total resources than France, the Austrian Hapsburgs, or Spain, yet they found it possible and profitable to mobilize a larger proportion of these resources for war purposes than their Continental allies and rivals could control. The Bank of England and its rival, the Bank of Amsterdam, were vaguely seen to be essential in this achievement, which seemed almost miraculous in its day.

Proposals for the establishment of banks were consequently made in other countries and seriously considered by the governments. In France, for example, the controller general, Desmaretz, received and studied a number of such schemes between 1708 and 1710. A decree to establish a bank was tentatively drawn up, but was dropped again upon the advice of Samuel Bernard, a private banker who had then a considerable share in financing the war. Bernard, whose profits seem to have been enormous in the long run, despite his bankruptcy (from which the government rescued him in 1716), may not have been altogether disinterested as a critic of public banks.[8]

Most of the French proposals were for an institution on the model of the Bank of Amsterdam, which would remedy the confused and fluctuat-

---

[8] See *Correspondence des contrôleurs généraux des finances*, ed. Boislisle (Paris, 1874-1897), III, 636-651, for the texts of some of these proposals, and of the projected decree.

ing monetary situation that hampered foreign and domestic business and finance. The Bank of Amsterdam's most obviously useful function was to receive deposits of coins of varying weights and fineness, against which it issued certificates of deposit, expressed in units of relatively stable value, the so-called "bank money." These were not a paper currency, but they did provide a unit on which contracts for future delivery of goods could be based with assurance that the payment would not change in value before the goods were delivered. As the French government was in the habit of debasing the coinage and of altering arbitrarily the value of particular coins (e.g. the number of livres in a *louis d'or*) as one of its desperate expedients of war finance, French businessmen in 1710 would obviously have found an institution of the type of the Bank of Amsterdam very useful at home as well as abroad.

One of the most ingenious and persistent "projectors," as Defoe termed them, who proposed schemes for a bank to the French government, was John Law. He was a Scotsman, son of a goldsmith at Edinburgh. Saint-Simon, who doubts whether Law was a gentleman born, praises his good manners and says that his extraordinary success did not spoil him, and that nobody could take exception to the style in which he lived. Coming from a nobleman with a violent prejudice against parvenus this commendation is extraordinary. Voltaire tells us that Law, who had been forced to leave England because he killed a man in a fight over a woman, lived by his skill at cards and his gift for mathematical calculation. It was his remarkable system in gambling which first attracted the attention of the regent. But, inspired by the ideas of such men as Locke, Petty, Mun, Davenant, and Barbon, and by the success of the Bank of England and the East India Company, Law had conceived a grandiose system for paying off national debts and at the same time greatly increasing commerce; since 1705 he had been endeavoring to get his scheme established in some country. He had presented projects to the governments of Scotland, England, Austria, Savoy and other Italian states, and to the French government under Louis XIV, securing usually an interested and respectful hearing but nothing more, until the Duke of Orleans came into power.

Then, by the regent's wish, he was granted in 1716 a charter for a *Banque Générale*, which resembled the Bank of Amsterdam in serving as a transfer bank furnishing an invariable monetary unit, the *écu de banque*, and facilitating exchange and discount. The notes issued were certificates of deposit, which were accepted by the government in payment of taxes. By common consent, then and subsequently, this *Banque*

Générale was a useful and highly successful institution. The regent could not but contrast its success with the drastic and dubious financial measures taken by his official advisers in the Council of Finances in dealing with the burden of debt.[9]

In 1717, accordingly, Law was allowed to found a trading company, the *Compagnie d'Occident.* That year his bank became a government institution under the name *Banque Royale,* empowered to issue notes guaranteed by the king and secured nominally by the value of land, a detail suggested, no doubt, by the various unsuccessful land-bank schemes in England in the 1690's. Law's idea was essentially that upon which Dr. Schacht established the *Rentenmark* after the German financial collapse under the Weimar republic. The real security was not the theoretical mortgage on land and revenues, but the intention to limit the note issue in accordance with the demand for currency. As Voltaire says, Law's whole system depended on credit for its success. It could succeed only if there was no credit inflation bringing a boom and a collapse.

III. SINKING FUND AND VISA

The comparison of the measures proposed and adopted in England with those suggested and those carried through in France shows not merely the very considerable influence of each country on the other, but also the differences then existing between their respective social and economic organizations. In England the merchant class was not only numerous and prosperous but also politically influential in Parliament; in France, the merchants were also numerous and prosperous, but politically they had to work indirectly through their influence on the royal bureaucracy.

The creation of a national debt based on loans raised by chartered companies forced the directors of those companies—the East India Company, the South Sea Company, and the Bank of England—to support the regime which had contracted the debt. None of them could be Jacobites without disregard for their investment in government funds, since it was obvious to everyone that the Stuarts, if restored, would repudiate the debt contracted since 1688, which was nearly the entire sum.

---

[9] For the very extensive bibliography on Law and his system, see Van Dillen, ed., *Principal Public Banks,* 296-300. See also Saint-Simon's character sketch in *Mémoires,* ed. Cheruel et Regnier (Paris, 1908-1924), XVII, 161-162; and Voltaire's account, as usual accurate on essentials but weak on some details, in *Précis du siècle de Louis XV,* in *Oeuvres,* ed. Beuchot, XXI, 17 ff. Harsin, who has edited Law's works, contemplates a definitive treatise on the man and his career which has not yet appeared.

It is misleading to speak of these fundholders as necessarily Whig, since the South Sea Company had been established by the Tory administration in 1711. They were Hanoverian, not Jacobite. One reason why Bolingbroke and Atterbury could not venture to proclaim James III when Queen Anne died lay in the attitude of the government's creditors. Shares in the three companies were widely held, often by titled and landed gentry like the Percivals, Earls of Egmont. What Swift called the funded interest overlapped with the landed interest, with which he contrasts it. In 1715 and thereafter, the funded interest was disturbed by the unprecedented and alarming total of the national debt, but anxious that the security of their investment be maintained.

In the extensive discussion of the government's financial problems in the early years of George I's reign, almost every conceivable theory was advanced. Archibald Hutcheson, for example, repeatedly proposed a capital levy of 10 per cent. As he thought that England was bankrupt, since her wartime expenses exceeded her income and the existing debt was staggering in amount, he felt that drastic remedies were needed. His ingenious plan would have set aside as a perpetual rent charge 10 per cent of the rent of real property, and levied 10 per cent of personal property. Like the capital-levy schemes in Germany and Italy following the war of 1914-1918, it practically amounted to a disguised addition to the income tax (then named the "land tax"). The justification is the familiar mercantilist notion that defense is more vital than opulence, that above all the state must be strong.[10]

Robert Walpole's proposal for the establishment of a sinking fund was the expedient first adopted under George I for refunding the debt at a lower rate of interest, and for gradually paying it off. The Bank of England, receiving 6 per cent on its holdings of government debt, which amounted to £3,375,027, consented to a reduction of the rate of interest to 5 per cent, and took over an additional two million pounds of the floating debt. It continued, however, to receive "three per cent for the circulation" of £2,561,025 of Exchequer bills left outstanding as floating debt.[11]

---

[10] The best treatment of English finances for this period by a historian is Michael, *Englische Geschichte*, III, 13-119. Only the first two volumes of the English translation of Michael's very important work have yet appeared. On Hutcheson, see Michael, III, 30-32; also John Sinclair, *The History of the Public Revenue of the British Empire* (London, 1803-1804), I, 478 ff., and article on "Capital Levy" in *Encyclopaedia of the Social Sciences*, III, 190-192.

[11] On the Bank of England's share in Walpole's sinking-fund scheme, see Richards, "First Fifty Years of the Bank of England," 241 ff.

The principal group of national debt holders in 1717 was not the Bank, but the South Sea Company, as a result of Lord Oxford's scheme for funding the floating debt in 1711. The company, too, was willing to consent to a reduction of interest to 5 per cent on its share of over nine million pounds, now increased to the round sum of ten million pounds by funding of the floating debt. The East India Company was already receiving only 5 per cent on its three million two hundred thousand pounds, a circumstance which may have contributed to the willingness of the rival establishments to accept a reduction to the same rate.[12]

Walpole's plan was that the savings made by the government through the reduction of the rate of interest on the funded debt should be used solely to redeem the principal of it, an intention which he did not always carry out in later years, as Sir John Sinclair reproachfully pointed out. But there was a great difficulty to be met. A very large portion of the debt was technically unredeemable, in so-called annuities akin to the French *rentes*. There were a number of different issues of these annuities, with complicated and sometimes picturesque provisions such as those of the so-called "tontines," where the last survivors of a group were to receive an enormous income. All of them had been sold originally on terms disadvantageous to the government. From 1695 onward, the English government had included in its annuities a provision by which they were in many cases to run for long terms and become transferable to any person on payment of a fee of four years' purchase or more. Walpole's difficulty in 1717 was that so large a proportion of the annual expense for interest on the debt went to annuity holders.

The statement of the Prussian envoy, Bonet, that a sinking-fund plan was expected to save six hundred thousand pounds a year, which could be applied to debt reduction, seems to have forecast more or less accurately the eventual result. Next to the maintenance of the government's credit, it was the annual interest charge which was of practical importance to the ministry. The act establishing the sinking fund, in 1717, states that the savings effected by the various measures for refunding debt "shall be appropriated to the discharging the principal and interest of such national debts as were incurred before December 25, 1716." The words "national debts" seem to us a matter of course, surprising only in that the plural "debts" is used where we should use the singular. But in

---

[12] I have used Sir John Sinclair's figures, e.g. *History of the Public Revenue*, I, 439, as do most modern historians. But his admission that they are only approximate, despite the delusive appearance of complete authenticity he gives them by figuring everything down to the shillings and pence, should be noticed (I, 440). The Bank of England figures are probably wholly accurate.

them lies the secret of the difference between the English government
and most other governments then existing. Here the nation's representatives solemnly pledged the nation's honor to redeem a debt not felt to be
capable of repudiation. This was not a party question as between the
Whig and the Tory supporters of the Hanoverian dynasty. Only Jacobites
like Shippen protested.

Yet in all other monarchies, including France, the notion persisted
that the debts of the crown were the personal debts of the sovereign, not
binding upon the nation. The Sinking Fund Act, and the whole plan of
which it was the essential connecting link, is a greater achievement than
it appears to modern historians, to whom the concept of national debt
is familiar. Walpole was merely the most prominent political leader of
what was a national movement. As he had resigned owing to a squabble
among the Whig leaders, he was no longer a minister, but, as he said
in moving the bill, "a country gentleman," when the various acts were
finally passed.

Before the sinking fund was established, there had always been a
scramble among the government creditors for the chance to be paid first.
Not many years after 1717 the competition was, as Sir John Sinclair said,
over who should be paid last. The government had been a poor credit risk
under William III. Under George III its securities were the most gilt
edged to be had, while those of Louis XVI's France were still no more
trustworthy than the paper of Louis XIV had been.

These generalizations may be abundantly confirmed by contrasting
the financial and fiscal measures which the French government took
immediately after the death of Louis XIV with those of Walpole and
other ministers of George I. In France, as in England, the end of the
war had left the government in financial difficulties. But the French
debt had been incurred on the credit of Louis XIV. France had not
merely a greater population and greater national wealth than England,
but also a government which was far more highly organized and efficient.
The English government had been repeatedly overturned by revolution
in the seventeenth century, and the Hanoverian dynasty in 1715 was still
obliged to suppress rebellion by armed force. But the French monarch
had defeated the seventeenth-century attempts at revolution so thoroughly
and so finally that in 1715 nobody doubted that the Bourbons would
remain as rulers of France.

What Adam Smith would have called the "personal credit" of the
French crown was, however, almost exhausted in 1715, as that of Charles
II and of William III had been long before in England. The means

Fifty-four Illustrations
Drawn from Unusual Sources
and Specially Chosen by
the Author

for

THE QUEST
FOR SECURITY

1715–1740

by

PENFIELD ROBERTS

❧

1. Four generations of French Bourbons
A painting by Largillière

2. The first British Hanoverians
From a print by J. Simon

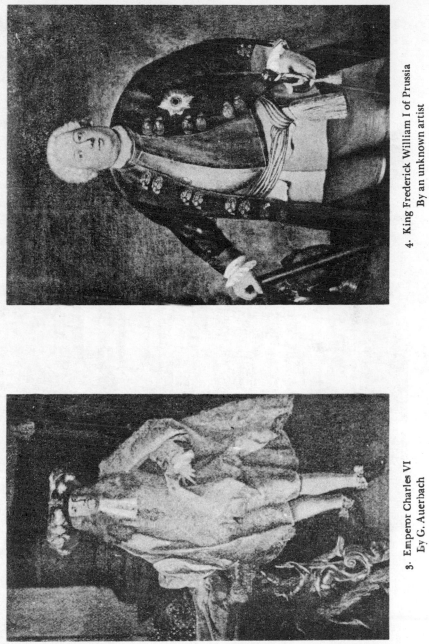

4. King Frederick William I of Prussia
By an unknown artist

3. Emperor Charles VI
By G. Auerbach

5. The corn market in Amsterdam
A contemporary print

Die Rue Quincampoix in Paris   Von Humblot. 1720

6. Crowds in front of Law's bank at the height of
the Mississippi Bubble

7. Prince Eugene of Savoy
An apotheosis by Permoser

8. The House of Commons
By Hogarth

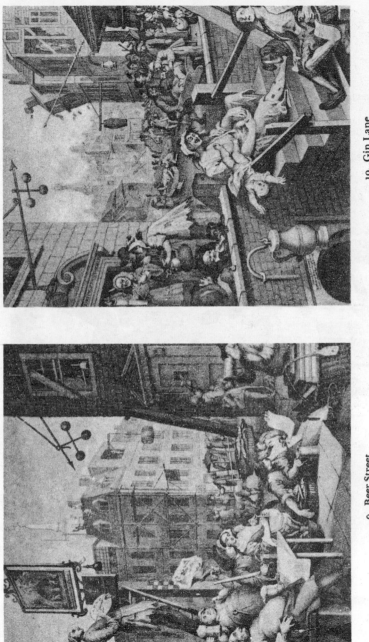

9. Beer Street
Engraved after Hogarth

10. Gin Lane
Engraved after Hogarth

11. France
Engraved after Hogarth

12. English caricature of Dutch neutrality

13. The Rear Guard
By Watteau

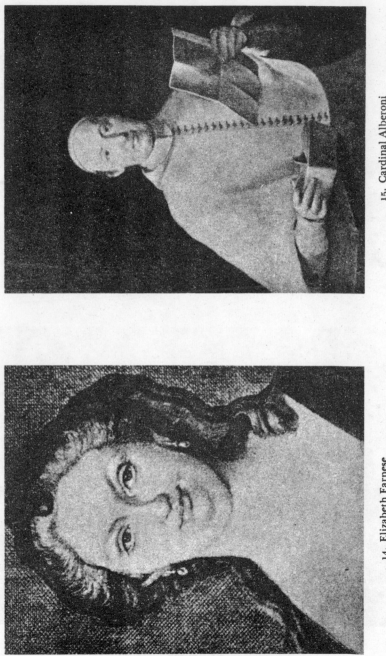

14. Elizabeth Farnese
By an unknown artist

15. Cardinal Alberoni
By Trevisani

17. Don José Patiño
By an unknown artist

16. James, First Earl Stanhope
By Sir G. Kneller

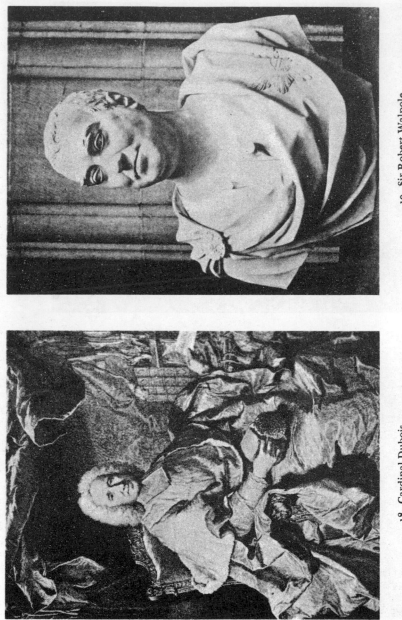

19. Sir Robert Walpole
From a bust by John Rysbrack

18. Cardinal Dubois
Engraved after Rigaud

20. The "Tabakskollegium" of Frederick William I

21. "Excise and Servitude," a caricature of Walpole

22. One of Frederick William I's famous giant soldiers

23. Gibraltar, 1718
From a contemporary print

24. Old London Bridge
By Scott

25. Peter the Great, about 1716
By an unknown painter

26. A ward in Guy's Hospital, 1725

27. Scarborough Sands, 1735

28. The Zwinger at Dresden
By Pöppelmann

29. San Giovanni di Laterano
By Galilei, 1734

**30. Hotel de Mantignon
By Courtonne, 1721**

**31. Belvedere Castle, Vienna
By Hildebrandt, 1724**

32. Frauenkirche, Dresden
By Pöppelmann

34. Interior of the Frauenkirche, Dresden

33. A lavish Spanish baroque doorway

**35. Vauxhall Gardens, London
An engraving after Canaletto**

**36. The great gardens at Herrenhausen
Drawn by J. von Sasse, 1740**

37. Berlin: the new quarter named Friedrichstadt

**38. Dresden, the old city with Pöppelmann's bridge
By Canaletto**

**39. Dresden, the courtyard of the Zwinger
By Canaletto**

40. Warsaw
By Canaletto

41. St. Petersburg
Engraved after Zubor

Prospect des Serallien.
pag. 129.

42. Seraglio Point, Constantinople
A German print of 1728

44. Fortress Church, St. Petersburg

43. The wooden church at Kizhi

45. Betrothal of Frederick Barbarossa and Beatrice of Burgundy
A painting by Tiepolo

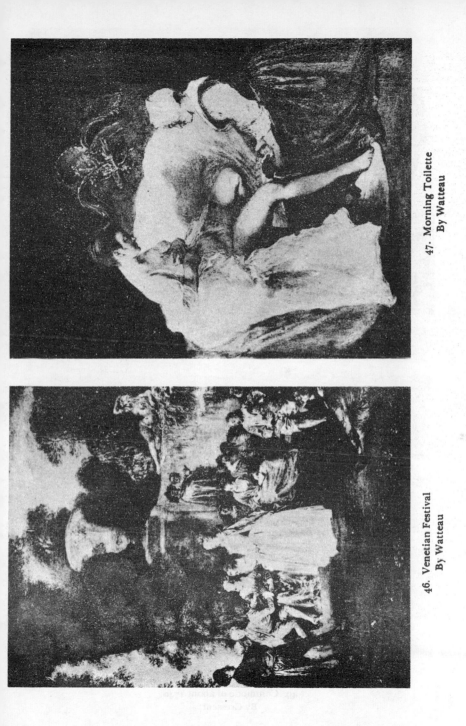

47. Morning Toilette
By Watteau

46. Venetian Festival
By Watteau

**48. Desk of the Regency period
By Cressent**

**49. Commode of about 1740
By Cressent**

50. Alexander Pope
By William Hoare

51. John Locke

52. Handel
An engraving after Hudson

53. Johann Sebastian Bach
By an unknown painter

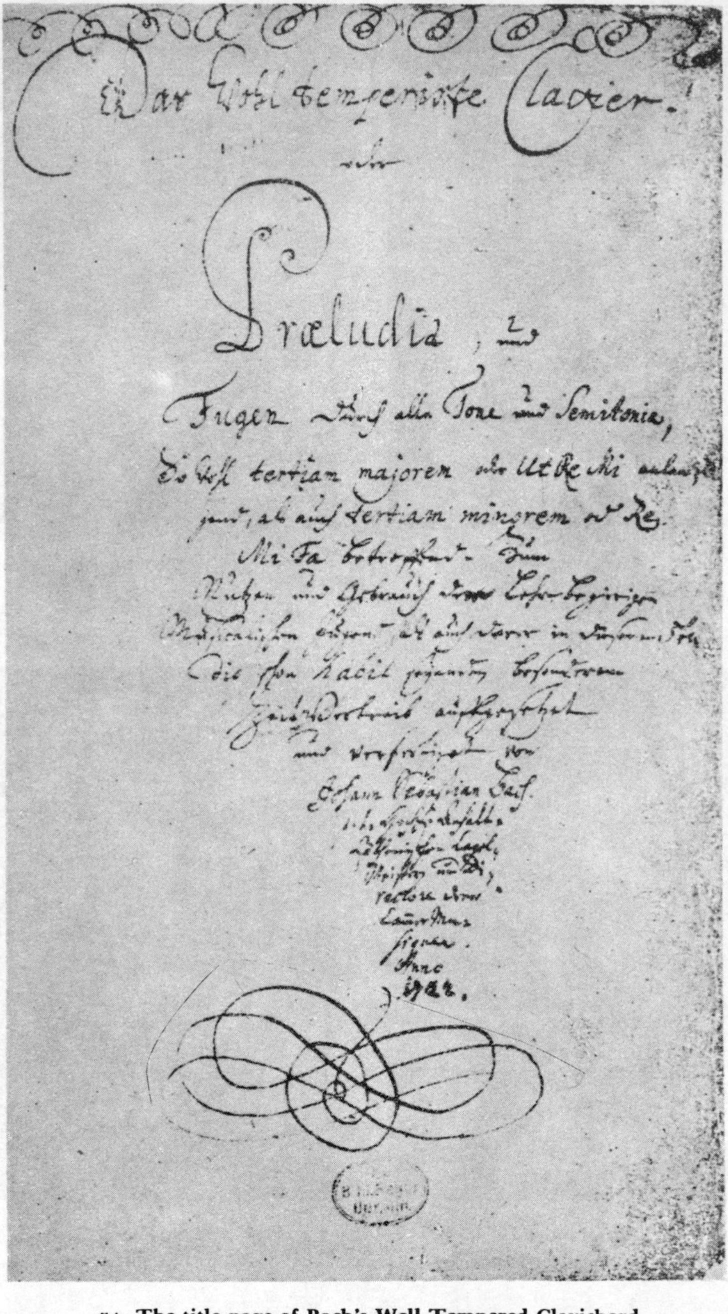
Das Wohltemperirte Clavier.
oder
Praeludia, und
Fugen durch alle Tone und Semitonia,
So wohl tertiam majorem oder Ut Re Mi anlangend,
als auch tertiam minorem oder Re
Mi Fa betreffend. Zum
Nutzen und Gebrauch der Lehr-begierigen
Musicalischen Jugend, als auch derer in diesem studio
schon habil seyenden besonderem
ZeitVertreib auffgesetzet
und verfertiget von
Johann Sebastian Bach.
p.t: HochFürstlich Anhalt-
Cöthenischen Capel-
Meistern und Di-
rectore derer
Camer Musiquen.
Anno
1722.

54. The title page of Bach's Well-Tempered Clavichord

taken to cope with the almost impossible financial situation which confronted the Council of Finances, established in place of the controller general at the beginning of the Regency, all involved a repudiation of a large portion of the debt; a step, as John Law told the regent, sure to make matters worse, not better. The real trouble, Law claimed, was not the debt, but the general sluggishness of trade and the widespread lack of confidence. But practical men of affairs and conservatives of all types naturally distrusted this Protestant foreigner of dubious antecedents, this architect of amazing blueprints for a "new deal" to bring permanent prosperity. The regent, himself inclined to favor new and bold schemes, found it expedient to wait until the usual methods of dealing with the familiar problem of the deficit had been tried and proved inadequate to cope with the exceptionally critical condition of the finances.

Not only Saint-Simon, but also Montesquieu, argued at the time for outright repudiation of the major portion of the existing debt. War profiteers had taken advantage of Louis XIV's need for means of carrying on the last great struggle against his enemies. The outstanding *rentes*, perpetual annuities issued since 1689, to be paid from specified sources of income, represented an exorbitant return on the original investment, since they had been sold below par. The outstanding notes, issued by a bewildering variety of government agencies, had also been badly depreciated. The new offices sold since 1689, often on the installment plan, carried official salaries out of proportion to the capital invested. The unpaid bills for war supplies often were swollen by waste and graft. The concept "national debt" did not really exist in the France of 1715. The rights of capitalists to a return on their investment in funds were not recognized.

It may be said in defense of the attitude of those who favored declaring the king free of debt that the nominal capital represented by outstanding government obligations was far in excess of the value in specie of the goods and services for which it was to pay. The government had no budget in the modern sense. Many different agencies could contract debt in the name of the king, long-term debt as well as short-term. The check on them was supposed to be the controller general, and the practice by which the king personally signed every order to spend. But if any one of the several royal *chambres des comptes* certified the accounts, they became incontestable. Expenses were authorized by general orders as well as by particular appropriations. There were long delays in the submission of accounts to the courts. Often, it would seem, no accurate accounts were kept at all. Government paper had depreciated by as much as 70 to 90 per cent of its face value, and speculators had bought it up, hoping for payment in full. A debt contracted by devious means represented fictitious rather than actual value. A great part of it, therefore, could be honorably and prudently repudiated, according to the notions of aristocrats under the Old Regime.[13]

The actual repudiation, however, was disguised rather than overt. The interest on the *rentes* was arbitrarily reduced to 4 per cent. The interest on the forced loan, or capital levy inflicted since 1689 on holders of venal offices (the so-called *augmentations de gâges*), was also reduced, in most cases to 4 per cent. The state lightened its burden of superfluous new offices by abolishing those which had not been paid for in full, and allowing the purchasers merely the interest on the money they had paid. They should have been reimbursed, but there were no funds in hand. As holders of offices were exempt from the *taille*, the reduction in their number was expected to increase the yield of that and of similar taxes borne by the nonprivileged.

The regent appointed the brothers Pâris as his financiers, to conduct a so-called *Visa*, to which all outstanding government notes had to be submitted. They canceled nearly six hundred million livres in various notes and issued two hundred fifty million new notes of which 195,817,103 livres were issued to holders of the old notes submitted, and the rest used to pay pressing debts. These notes, like the long-term debt, bore interest at 4 per cent. It was alleged, possibly correctly, that the old notes, canceled and supposedly destroyed, were also reissued.

Finally, the government ordered a *Chambre de Justice*, an extraordinary court of a kind often previously used, as in 1625, to prosecute the *traitants*, or contractors and financiers accused of fraud and of speculation in government notes, of buying them up in the hope of payment in full. This measure, though popular and justified morally by the existence of actual gross frauds and of speculation in government paper, was highly unwise. The same frauds and the same speculation on the part of war contractors and financiers existed in England in 1715, and in the United States at the end of the American Revolution. But they were condoned by Robert Walpole and by Alexander Hamilton. All modern wars have been and must be waged on credit. This obvious reflection, which makes the wisdom of Walpole and of Hamilton in financial matters proverbial, was not present in the minds of the Council of Finances under the Regency.

[13] For these details on French finances, see Marion, *Histoire financière*, esp. I, 447 ff., and I, 63-89; also Leclercq, *Histoire de la Régence*, I, chaps. vii and xi.

The government of France under the Old Regime was not dictatorial but essentially oligarchic in character. The regent had restored to the *Parlement* of Paris its right to remonstrate prior to registering royal decrees, and the *Parlement* had exercised the right on several occasions. In September, 1717, apropos of various financial measures, it asked for a statement of the receipts and expenditures of the government since the beginning of the Regency. The regent, irritated at first by this attempt of the *Parlement* to assert jurisdiction over the finances, eventually sent the Duc de Noailles to give a detailed account of the financial situation to a committee of the *Parlement*. This nobleman was the principal member of the Council of Finances, to which the functions of the controller general had been entrusted. Although in theory the right to levy taxes and to control the finances remained with the crown, it appeared as though in fact that control would be shared. But neither the Council of Finances nor the *Parlement* of Paris included any representative of the commercial classes, nor understood their views. The Council was composed of nobles and bureaucrats. The *Parlement*, because of the long-standing practice of venality of offices, was composed of an hereditary caste of "nobles of the gown" differentiated in theory more than in actuality from the court nobles.

The summoning of the Estates-General, which had not met since 1614, was repeatedly proposed in these years, largely to deal with the financial difficulties. But had the Estates been summoned, the deputies of the third estate, the commons, would in all probability not have represented the commercial classes as adequately as those classes were represented in the English House of Commons. The French monarchy did not feel any dependence on the nascent capitalist class. The Hanoverian regime in England was conscious of the necessity of retaining their support. In France ambitious men purchased a government office in order to rise in the world. In England, the most ambitious men were the merchants, whom the Tory Dr. Johnson was soon to recognize as "a new species of English gentlemen."[14]

The commercial classes were, accordingly, the chief sufferers from the attempts of the regent's official advisers to deal with the perplexing financial situation by other means than usual. The result of their drastic

---

[14] For the *Parlement's* attempt to control finances, see H. Carré in E. Lavisse, *Histoire de France depuis les origines jusqu'à la révolution* (Paris, 1911), VIII, Pt. II, 15 ff. On the effects of venality of offices, to be discussed *infra* in detail, see Martin Goehring, *Die Ämterkäuflichkeit im Ancien Régime* (Berlin, 1938), esp. 289 ff. This monograph in the series *Historische Studien* deserves to be read by all students of the Old Regime.

and varied expedients was a small saving at a great cost to credit, public and private. John Law, whose *Banque Générale* was meanwhile flourishing and winning universal acclaim, could therefore say to the regent, in effect, "I told you so. Now, let me show you what I can accomplish by my system."

IV. THE MISSISSIPPI AND SOUTH SEA BUBBLES

In recent years historians have come to perceive that the so-called Mississippi and South Sea "bubbles" were closely connected. They have long known that in the years after 1715 the history of France was influenced by English institutions and English thinkers; but Professor Michael was apparently the first to point out the extent of French influence on England's South Sea bubble, and the historical importance of the interaction between the two countries, which became political allies, as we have seen, in 1716.[15]

Indeed, as Hauser has suggested, both bubbles are probably parts of a general European phenomenon which only further research can clearly reveal to us. But, lacking detailed studies on what happened in the Italian cities, at Vienna, in Sweden, and so on, we can only attempt to correlate the French and the English aspects of this phenomenon, this postwar crisis, and to indicate their antecedents and results.[16]

Paul Harsin, who has devoted much effort to research on Law and his system, and to the editing of a very useful edition of Law's works, has said: "The more I study the period known in French history as the Regency, the more I am persuaded of its economic and financial importance. Law's system is to me a crucial point in the economic development of France." He goes on to enumerate its effect as "monetary, financial, agricultural, fiscal, and commercial." The much-talked-of bubble was more than a temporary outburst of speculative mania. Whatever one may think of John Law's theory and his conduct, its effects were more far-reaching and more important than people who look at it solely from the point of view of the classical economists will realize.[17]

The system of John Law has most frequently been examined either from the standpoint of economic theory, or as an example of speculative activity. To the historian it is perhaps more important to consider it as

[15] See Michael, *Englische Geschichte*, III, chap. iii, "Mississippi und Sudsee"; also Muret, *Prépondérance anglaise*, 102-129.

[16] H. Hauser, "Crises de crédit et de spéculation en France et en Angleterre au lendemain de la paix d'Utrecht," *Revue d'histoire moderne*, IX (1934), 435 ff.

[17] Paul Harsin, *Crédit public et banque d'état en France du XVIᵉ au XVIIIᵉ siècle* (Paris, 1933), 4.

an instance of economic policy with far-reaching effects. After all, it was a condition, not a theory, which Law undertook to remedy. The world wars after 1689 had greatly stimulated economic activity in all the belligerent countries. France, without banking facilities and with its currency in confusion, had found credit and cash hard to procure. Capital was needed, in short, for the expansion of industry and trade resulting from the war. The system, with an issue of bank notes to an amount regulated not by a reserve of gold or silver but by the demand for currency, could provide cash to any amount that might be necessary. Credit also would be made available to entrepreneurs large and small. The burden of government debt would be lifted, as it had been in England through the Bank of England and the South Sea Company, by conversion of outstanding securities into shares in a great government company, which would dominate French foreign and colonial trade and take a large share in domestic business. No casual brief summary can do justice to the subtlety and plausibility of Law's arguments. But the elements enumerated above were perhaps the most essential portion of his plan. Each of them had some justification in the experience of other countries, particularly of England, since the general war which began in 1689.[18]

The banks of England and of Amsterdam had set precedents for the proposed *Banque Royale*. The British and Dutch East India companies had been so successful in the more than a century they had already existed that it was easy to overlook the numerous unsuccessful trading companies, several of them French. The refinancing of government debt through exchange of government securities for those of chartered companies had been successful in the case of the Bank of England, the reorganized combined East India Company, and the South Sea Company of 1711. Law's system proposed to include the successful features of all these going concerns in one grand design, which existing theory as well as existing practice abundantly justified. It was not a wildcat scheme and involved no conscious attempt at fraud or graft on the part of its promoter. Law seems to have believed that he could actually increase the population of France to thirty million, as he promised the regent, the national income to thirty billion livres, and the income of the crown to three hundred million livres, all before the boy king came of age.[19]

[18] On the stimulus to English trade caused by the War of the Spanish Succession, see Lipson, *Economic History of England*, III, 297, and G. N. Clark, "War Trade and Trade War, 1701-1713," *Economic History Review*, I (1928), 279. The total economic effect was, of course, not gain but loss. The war prosperity was unevenly distributed and fictitious.

[19] John Law, *Oeuvres*, ed. Paul Harsin (Paris, 1934), II, 266.

What is more, even after the collapse of 1720 and the dismissal of Law, the regent appears still to have believed that the system had failed merely because its opponents interfered with its operation. There is reason to believe that only the premature death of the Duc d'Orléans in 1723 prevented the recall of Law to France and a renewal of the great experiment. After all, in Germany and Italy in our own day state capitalism financed by paper currency unsecured by any substantial reserves of specie functioned in ways often similar to the mercantilist ideas of the system. "Bubble" is too harsh a word. The losers by the French system were not the genuine investors, but those speculators who waited too long after buying shares at grossly inflated prices, with the intention not of keeping them, but of selling them at a profit. The shares of the *Compagnie des Indes*, like those of the South Sea Company, remained gilt-edged investments for those content with "safety and four per cent." They were the equivalent of government bonds, but bonds of a preferred type.

It is impossible to recount the oft-told story of the development and the collapse of the system briefly yet adequately. In outline the course of events was substantially the following: The failure of the *Visa* and the *Chambre de Justice* caused the regent to turn the responsibility for the finances over to Law. The Council of Finances was abolished, *polysynodie* abandoned, and the conduct of affairs entrusted in fact chiefly to Dubois and to Law. Most of the nobility, the *Parlement*, the bureaucrats, and the financiers and businessmen were opposed to this change. What Law wished to bring about was contrary to all French tradition. The opponents of the system tried to block it at every step, or to circumvent it. Louis XIV, once decided on such a revolution in economic policy, would no doubt have been able to suppress opposition, but the regent had neither the full royal authority, the obstinacy, nor the personal prestige of the *grand monarque*. Law could never be sure when the regent would yield to pressure from his foes.

The opposing financiers included the *fermiers-généraux*, who collected various duties and taxes. They tried to break the *Banque Royale* by presenting unexpectedly a mass of its notes for payment in specie, a measure like one adopted by the foes of the Bank of England in its early days. This attempt failed, as the one had in England. Then they got up a company, as it was nicknamed, and promised big dividends, because the security for them was the profits of the tax farm, which were known to be large. They could really pay 12 per cent, and Law's company had nothing but the 4 per cent on the government debt it had taken over (a dubious security), and the possible future profit of its colony in Louisiana and similar trading ventures. Law was forced to outbid the antisystem group, and to take over the tax farm, to which he added the tobacco monopoly and the mint. Then his *Compagnie d'Occident* absorbed the existing, but not profitable *Compagnie des Indes Orientales*, a *Compagnie de Chine*, in short, all rival trading companies, and became the *Compagnie des Indes* in May, 1719.

Up to this point Law had been successful in his undertaking, but he had made enemies of most Frenchmen with money to invest. The rival financiers detested him. So did the bureaucrats and nobles whose dismissal from office he had procured. The *Parlement* of Paris was angry with him since he had encouraged the regent to take away their power of refusing to register decrees.

Law must float a large issue of shares in his new grandiose company. Under these circumstances, he was forced to make that issue seem so attractive that even people who hated and distrusted him would subscribe. He used most of the tricks of the modern company promoter, and succeeded in starting the notorious boom by which shares of a par value of five hundred livres were sold on the installment plan for as much as fifteen thousand livres. As his new company had undertaken to assume the entire national debt, it was necessary to persuade holders of uncallable securities like the *rentes* to convert them voluntarily on terms actually not favorable to them. His first fatal mistake seems to have been the overissue of notes of the *Banque Royale* to an amount not needed by legitimate business, in order to finance the speculative boom in shares of the "Mississippi." The issue of notes, according to Law's theories, was to be regulated by the demand for currency, but this particular demand was a fictitious thing of his own creation. The inflation, of course, led to an increase in prices and a temporary feeling of prosperity on the part of most upperclass Frenchmen, as they counted their paper profits. When they tried to "realize" these, the collapse occurred.

If the public had really believed the system was anything more than a gambling device, the measures taken by Law to meet the situation might have succeeded. By varying the value of the coins, and finally by prohibiting the possession of specie, he tried to persuade people that paper money was not only more convenient to use than gold, but really better. Gold was demonetized, and silver devalued with a demonetization in prospect. In a country used to paper currency, like the United States today, the public is not unduly perturbed by being forbidden to possess gold for monetary uses. Law wanted to get bank checks as well as bank notes used as money, as we use them today. He hoped then to be able to reduce the amount of paper and of bank credit. But these steps produced indignation and panic, since the Old Regime had no real faith in any currency but gold and silver coin. His monetary theories may have been sound, though in flat contradiction to classical economics. But they were hopelessly impracticable in the France of 1720. The regent was forced to dismiss Law and to aid him to escape from France. He took with him only a little cash and died in poverty in 1729.

Another *Visa* followed, conducted like the earlier one by the brothers Pâris. Many speculators were ruined, but the genuine investors, who owned their shares outright, found the market price of a five hundred livre share one thousand livres in 1726, and over two thousand livres in 1737. The profits of the tobacco monopoly and the other ventures explain this high value. The national debt seems to have been somewhat reduced by the disappearance of some of the floating debt. The *rentes*, after the *Visa*, were about what they had been before the system began.[20]

The most important immediate effect of Law's system was the South Sea bubble in England. Walpole's sinking-fund scheme, adopted in 1717, had left a large portion of the national debt in annuities, analogous to the French *rentes* or to modern noncallable registered bonds. The South Sea directors presented to the Stanhope ministry a scheme for taking over the management of the entire debt, if the government would pay 5 per cent (after 1727 4 per cent). The Bank of England, whose share in the debt was essential to its position, outbid the South Sea Company's first offer of three million and a half pounds for the management of the entire debt, and forced the South Sea directors to raise their bid to 7,567,000. This was accepted by an act of Parliament of April 7, 1720.

The essential unsoundness of this scheme was pointed out at the time by such critics as Walpole and Defoe. The profits of the asiento agreement, which had been forced on Spain and which gave the British a monopoly of the slave trade between Africa and Spanish America and a limited permission for other trade, were greatly overestimated. The ten thousand pounds a year which the government would pay for management, and the profit on the difference between the market rate of interest, then 4 per cent, and the 5 per cent the government was to pay, could hardly suffice to meet the dividend necessary to support a high price

[20] For the liquidation of the system, see Marion, *Histoire financière*, I, 107 ff. The general reader will find a clear and witty but unsympathetic account of Law and the system in C. J. Gignoux and F. F. Legueu, *Le bureau de rêveries, 1715-1925* (Paris, 1926). Marion is clear, but not witty.

for the shares. It was essential to the plan that the shares should seem so attractive an investment to holders of annuities that they would willingly convert their holdings into South Sea stock when that stock was above par. Probably the directors expected that their bank, the Sword Blade Company, would eventually displace the Bank of England, and that their control of the national credit would enable them to embark on all sorts of profitable ventures, domestic and foreign.

The condemnation so often made of the South Sea directors as a mere group of stockjobbers, and speculative gamblers, appears unwarranted. The Bank of England, it is worth repeating, tried hard to secure the same privilege, and its directors can hardly all have become mere irresponsible gamblers and swindlers overnight. It appears to have been the influence of George I which decided that the privilege of managing the debt should be concentrated in the hands of the South Sea Company. They had made him their governor, a position he retained until his death. They had also arranged a preferred list of subscribers to the stock. Not merely the king's mistresses and his German favorites were "let in on the ground floor," but also members of the ministry, especially the Chancellor of the Exchequer, Aislaibie, to whose department the essential arrangements belonged.

The details of these transactions were probably recorded in the books of the company, which were destroyed or removed in part by its cashier, Knight; he fled to the Continent after the crash and, like Law, eventually went to Venice. But, though the books are lost, the parliamentary investigation and the comments of well-informed observers like the Harley family indicate that the assertions repeated above were not unfounded. As the stock was to be paid for on the installment plan, a delay in collecting installments from favored investors may have served as a disguised and polite method of bribery.[21]

The arguments used by proponents of the South Sea scheme may be gathered from the title of a pamphlet, with French and English texts on

[21] Historians have begun to restudy the South Sea bubble, but there is still a great deal that remains obscure about it. Detailed knowledge of the careers of the principal London merchants of the period would shed much light, since their directorships in important companies were the basis for the credit of those companies. Besides Michael, *Englische Geschichte*, III, chap. iii; Lipson, *Economic History of England*, II, 367 ff.; and Richards, "First Fifty Years of Bank of England," cited above, W. R. Scott, *The Constitution and Finance of English, Scottish and Irish Joint-Stock Companies to 1720* (Cambridge, Eng., 1910-1912), III, 295 ff., and *Portland Mss.*, published by the Historical Manuscripts Commission (London, 1891-1931), V, should be consulted. See also R. D. Richards, "The Bank of England and the South Sea Company," *Economic History*, II (1932), 348-374.

opposite pages, issued through the Whitehall *Evening Post*, by a publisher also concerned in another government propaganda venture. It ran

A Full and Impartial Account of the Company of Mississippi . . . wherein the Nature of that Establishment and the almost incredible Advantages thereby accruing to the French King and a great Number of his Subjects are clearly explained. With an account of the Establishment of the Bank of Paris by the said Mr. Law. To which are added a Description of the Country of Mississippi. . . .

The text stresses, as one might expect, the high prices to which shares of the company in Paris had risen. It does not explain the ideas of Law systematically.

Although the South Sea Company had finally been obliged to leave its holdings of the public debt in the hands of the East India Company and the Bank of England so that it did not become a monopoly, the speculation in its shares, as everyone knows, was frenzied. The attempts to "realize" were brought about in part by the measures taken against numerous rival enterprises, not all of them fraudulent. These measures were embodied in the so-called "bubble act" forbidding issues of stock except by chartered companies, a measure which determined the course of corporate enterprise in Great Britain for the next century.[22]

The collapse of the South Sea scheme in September, 1720, resulted in the rise of Robert Walpole to the position of prime minister. He alone among the chief Whig leaders had actively opposed the scheme. Although he had been made paymaster of the Forces in June, 1720, in a reshuffling of the Stanhope ministry, he was not regarded as responsible for the debacle. His management of the difficult situation won him the nickname "The Screen," because he protected most of the court personages and cabinet ministers involved. Aislaibie, Chancellor of the Exchequer, whose fortune had risen to almost a million pounds, was expelled from Parliament, but allowed to keep his estates as of 1718. Lord Stanhope, occupied with pacifying Europe, had played no part in the South Sea and was not responsible. He died from a stroke said to have been caused by the intense emotion with which he answered an

---

[22] On the pamphlet literature there are details in W. T. Laprade, *Public Opinion and Politics in Eighteenth Century England* (New York, 1936), 218. The quoted title, not mentioned by Laprade, is that of a pamphlet printed by J. Roberts (London, 1720). There is a facsimile reprint in the series *Photostat Americana* (Boston, 1936), 2nd series, No. 107. The French text may possibly mean that it was hoped George I, who knew no English, would read it, or that it would reach Dutch investors, who were large holders of English securities. On the importance of the bubble act from the legal point of view, see A. B. Dubois, *The English Business Company after the Bubble Act* (New York, 1938).

attack by the Duke of Wharton in the House of Lords; his death left the way clear for Walpole, who subsequently used all his influence in saving the late prime minister's cousin, Charles Stanhope. When the case of Lord Sunderland, the chief Whig leader involved, came before Parliament in the investigation, Walpole intimated that a conviction would certainly result in a Tory ministry, and Sunderland's acquittal was voted by a majority of sixty-one. On April 3, 1721, Robert Walpole was appointed Chancellor of the Exchequer and First Lord of the Treasury. That date marks the real beginning of the ministerial system of government in England, as well as of Walpole's long tenure of power.

His wisdom had re-established not merely the credit of the Whig party and of the Hanoverian dynasty, but that of England. The bursting of the bubble ruined some private individuals and a few political careers, but there were no lasting ill effects on the country as a whole. Without Walpole, financial chaos and the overthrow of the unpopular new dynasty would have been a strong possibility. As Lecky said of him, Walpole must be judged not merely by his positive accomplishments but by the misfortunes he averted.[23]

That England was not ruined by the bursting of the South Sea bubble is a fact familiar to historians. Was France ruined before and, more particularly, after the collapse of the system? This question cannot be conclusively answered until further research has been carried out, but it merits examination. The best history of the Regency, that by Dom Leclercq, states in its introduction that the "despotism of Louis XIV" left France exhausted, and that the ruin of the monarchy, the French Revolution, found its prologue in the many and various excesses of the Regency. He sums up this view, which would be accepted without question by most nineteenth-century historians, in an epigram, apropos of Regency finances under Noailles: "After the *taille* on the peasant came the discouraging of the merchant, the hobbling of the artisan, the ruin of the rentier. *Voilà l'ancien régime.*"[24] France, ruined before John Law, was doubly ruined afterward. Leclercq, with his customary great pains and complete accuracy, assembles in a chapter entitled "Ruins of the System" the gist of what had been published on the subject to the time of writing. It is a series of plaints and lamentations about poverty and distress, summed up in a passage which he quoted from Marion's *His-*

---

[23] W. E. H. Lecky, *A History of England in the Eighteenth Century* (New York, 1878-1890), I, 354.

[24] Leclercq, *Histoire de la Régence* I, 188.

toire financière. "The few gains were dearly bought, and the evil resulting infinitely greater than the good."[25]

Yet one cannot help noticing that under the Old Regime these complaints about ruin come from speculators who had lost in the bubble, or from cranks like Boisguillebert, who may be judged by his remarkable theory that money had done more harm than good, that it is nothing but a pledge for future transfers, "a criminal thing," the "moloch of the world." After 1789 the most notable complaints emanated from those who believed that the Revolution had meant, if not "liberty, equality, fraternity," at least prosperity and privilege for the *bourgeoisie* to which they belonged. Was the state of France really so bad under the Regency? Did Law's schemes actually result in more harm than good? One hesitates to accept obviously biased testimony on the point, and most testimony is biased. Turn to the modern royalists like Gaxotte, and they emphasize the universal well-being under the beneficent regime so mistakenly overthrown in 1789. But they, too, are biased.[26]

There is no doubt that the condition of the government finances was ruinous *both before and after the system*, though under Cardinal Fleury's regime, which began in 1726, there was a marked improvement. There is also no doubt that the personal finances of many members of the nobility were disordered. Excluded both by law and by custom from going into business, they were dependent on income from land, from investments in securities like the *rentes*, and on royal pensions or government salaries. Land tenure in France under the Old Regime did not afford the gentry fat rent rolls like those of the corresponding class in Great Britain. The failure of the system made government securities less gilt edged than they became in England. The discrediting of the idea of banking by the collapse of the *Banque Royale*, dragged down by the *Compagnie des Indes* with which Law, in desperation, had finally combined it, meant that fewer business undertakings existed in France than in England. There were numerous private bankers, most of them also merchants, but it was difficult for a gentleman to find any safe investment save land, or a mortgage on real estate, or a venal office. The pensions and government salaries were often irregularly paid and subject to arbitrary reduction; moreover, although a few of them were notoriously of excessive amount, the bulk of them were actually inadequate for the style of living expected of courtiers.

---

[25] Leclercq, *Histoire de la Régence*, II, 459-481; Marion, *Histoire financière*, I, 100-101.
[26] On Boisguillebert's monetary theories I have paraphrased the article by E. R. A. Seligman in *Encyclopaedia of the Social Sciences*, II, 619-620.

The French nobility, itself hard pressed for money, was likely to feel that France was ruined. And many of our accounts of the Old Regime were written by nobles of the gown and of the sword. The clergy seem to have been better off, save for the ill-paid parish priests. It is difficult to generalize about the condition of the third estate, the great bulk of the people. Prices and wages both rose during the system, and remained much higher after it than they had been before. Commercial activities of many kinds increased steadily after 1720. Henri Sée has pointed out that the sum total of foreign commerce in 1715, imports and exports combined, was about 215 million livres, that by the middle of the century it exceeded 600 million, and for the years 1784-1788 it reached an annual average of 1061 million.[27]

It is easy to cite details showing what looks like prosperity for particular regions or groups. The trading ports like Nantes and Bordeaux flourished, and Lorient, created by Louis XIV and revived by John Law, shared with the older coast towns. The rebuilding of Rennes, devastated by fire in 1720, was on a scale which does not suggest ruin. The peasants were no doubt not well off, but it was their relative prosperity as compared with other peasant classes in other countries, and not their relative hardship, which caused the Revolution of 1789 in France, as Tocqueville long since remarked.[28]

There were, however, bad years. If the harvest failed, as it did in 1709, 1725, 1739, 1740, and later at intervals, the common people went hungry and times were bad for everyone. Three quarters of the French nation still depended directly on agriculture for subsistence, and in the primitive state of land transportation all cheap and bulky articles were necessarily of local production. Most of the worst descriptions of the "misery and ruin" of the Old Regime are of conditions in years of crop failure, e.g. 1709. It is still not clear how much of the obvious suffering of that dreadful winter was caused by the war and how much by the weather.

On the "ruin" of France one must render the Scotch verdict "not proven." The considerable amount of recent research into the history of prices and wages sheds less light than might be supposed on the economic condition of the bulk of the European population after 1715. There were great variations between different occupations and different regions in the same country. The preserved data are not really sufficient to permit accurate generalization about levels of real wages. It is hard for anyone

[27] H. Sée, *La France économique et sociale au XVIII° siècle* (Paris, 1933), 124.
[28] Gaston Martin, *Nantes au XVIII° siècle* (Paris, 1928-1931); A. de Tocqueville, *L'ancien régime et révolution* (Paris, 1856).

in the modern Western world to realize that all people, even bourgeois and noble landlords, got a large portion of their food direct from the soil, without the articles entering any market or being priced at all. The masses got not merely food, but most articles in daily use. Adam Smith, for example, remarks casually and as a matter of course that "In every large country both the clothing and the household furniture of the far greater part of the people are the product of their own industry." Even in England in the first half of the eighteenth century the worker's money wage was only a part, often a small part, of his living. Not the state of the market, but such homely rustic items as the condition of the crop of wheat, flax, the clip of wool, the forage to be found for the family cow on the common pasture, determined the well-being of the common man. For the majority the system of land tenure was the most important economic fact, not the state of commerce or of the money market.[29]

V. THE OSTEND COMPANY

Nothing better illustrates the close relations between politics and economics in the early eighteenth century than the brief history of the Ostend Company. The politics were those of the dynastic state; the economics those of mercantilism. The result was a form of economic warfare, which in turn was one of the great factors in the embroilment of Europe and the failure of the Utrecht settlement.

We have noted that England and the United Provinces managed in the series of treaties ending the wars of Louis XIV to hamstring their Belgian trade rivals, virtually close the port of Antwerp, garrison the barrier towns with Dutch troops, and place the Belgian provinces under the distant and presumably distracted control of the Austrian emperor (p. 11). Yet the Belgian merchants were not to be downed. They began to charter foreign boats and to trade with distant China, as yet subject to no trading-company monopoly, and to encroach on British trade with India. Now the French and British bubbles, though they produced fantastic and brief stock-exchange speculations, worked in the longer run to promote the less catastrophic rise in prices which entrepreneurs welcome as "good for business." The early 1720's were a period in which,

[29] Examples of the research on price and wage history are: E. W. Gilboy, *Wages in Eighteenth Century England* (Cambridge, Mass., 1934); C. E. Labrousse, *Esquisse du mouvement des prix et des revenus en France au XVIIIᵉ siècle* (Paris, 1932); E. J. Hamilton, "Prices and Wages in Southern France under John Law's System," *Economic History*, III (1937), 441 ff. On the persistence of usufructure, see H. Heaton, *Economic History of Europe* (New York, 1937), 335 ff., and Trevelyan, *England under Queen Anne*.

in spite of medieval survivals and mercantilist restraints of trade, prices were rising, Europe was at peace, and the demand for luxury goods was increasing. Under these conditions, an Austrian trading company on the classic mercantilist model was proposed by Belgian men of affairs in 1721. After a long course through the *bureaux* of the absentee government in Vienna, these proposals emerged in 1723 as a charter for the *Société impériale et royale des Indes,* better known as the Ostend Company.

The charter set up a company well controlled politically by the imperial government, but enjoying a very generous degree of economic liberty. The company was well administered. Its six successful expeditions to China formed the nucleus for a total dividend of 6,180,000 florins in seven years, on a paid-up capital of 4,500,000 florins. Under the impulse of the company's activities, the old port of Ostend began to revive, and the stimulus spread to most kinds of economic activity in the Austrian Netherlands. The company had "primed the pump."[30]

This was too much for the mercantilist—or perhaps merely human—notions of the British, Dutch, and French competitors of the Belgians. They believed firmly that the trade that went to the Ostend Company was so much trade lost to theirs. The Ostend Company had been chartered only after complicated international negotiations. Austria was being wooed by the maritime powers, who feared an Austrian-Spanish reconciliation and the restoration of the combination that had threatened Europe under the Emperor Charles V. But by the Treaty of Vienna in 1725 Spain and Austria *had* come together; Spain had accepted the Pragmatic Sanction. The British—quite justifiably—suspected there were secret provisions making possible a closer union of the kind both they and the French dreaded. The Spaniards began lending aid to the ships of the Ostend Company.

Meanwhile the Dutch were simply seizing the ships of the Ostend Company whenever they could lay their hands on them, and in other ways putting economic pressure on the Belgians wherever possible. Belgian national feelings against the Dutch, which were to make the union of 1815 impossible, received in these years a further strengthening and intensification. The British, under Townshend, continued their attack on the Austro-Spanish combination, and when a war broke out between Spain and Britain in 1727, the Austrian emperor backed down and refused to go to war against Britain. He did not, however, succeed

[30] Michel Huisman, *La Belgique commerciale sous l'empereur Charles VI; la Compagnie d'Ostende* (Brussels and Paris, 1902), 530.

in saving the Ostend Company. In another Treaty of Vienna in 1731 the emperor ratified provisions of an earlier Anglo-Spanish Treaty of Seville, in which, among other provisions, was one for the suspension of the Ostend Company. Suspension meant extinction, for the company was excluded from the Asiatic trade for which it was founded. It continued a modest domestic trade and wound up its affairs by mid-century after a profitable career. Its promising life was cut short, not by economic failure, but by high politics.

VI. ASIENTO AND INTERLOPERS

In the early eighteenth century the progress of commerce, which finally resulted in an agricultural and an industrial revolution, depended to a surprising extent on the slave trade between Africa and America. This trade was of basic importance to colonial production and to European commerce. Ships and merchants of many nations, Portugal, France, Great Britain, the Netherlands, Denmark, and even Prussia, engaged in it. It was essential to have trading posts in Africa, to which the traders of the interior, mostly native, could bring their human wares. Spain, on the whole, had remained true to the famous division of the world between her and Portugal, to whose share Africa belonged, but in 1709 there were not only Portuguese outposts in West Africa, but also Danish, Dutch, English, French, and Prussian forts, most of them on the Gold Coast and often near to one another.[31]

Spain provided for the slave trade to her American colonies by awarding a contract of monopoly, called an asiento, sometimes to Spaniards, more often to foreigners. It had been held by a Portuguese company from 1696 to 1701, then by the French Guinea Company. The Treaty of Utrecht included a transfer of this asiento to the British. In 1711 the South Sea Company had refinanced over nine million pounds of the British floating debt, in the expectation of receiving the asiento, which would result in immense profits. In view of the fact that a share in the asiento had been promised to the Dutch in 1709, and that the Tory administration broke the promise, this contract with the Spanish government had a far-reaching effect on the international situation.[32]

The asiento was an agreement to deliver to the Spanish colonies in

---

[31] See the lists of settlements and forts in Elizabeth Donnan, ed., *Documents Illustrative of the History of the Slave Trade to America* (Washington, D. C., 1930-1935), II, 70-72, and the account of them in the introduction to the work, pp. xiii ff. This massive volume is indispensable to historians interested in the eighteenth-century slave trade and its ramifications.

[32] See Trevelyan, *England under Queen Anne*, III, 147 ff., 189.

America forty-eight hundred *Piezas de India* yearly for thirty years, beginning May 1, 1713. Because the Asientists had given a loan to Philip V, eight hundred of these *Piezas* would be admitted duty free. On the rest, a duty of thirty-three and a third pieces of eight (roughly equivalent to 4s. 6d., or a dollar) was to be paid. The term *Pieza de India* meant, in general, a young adult Negro in good condition. Sometimes several inferior slaves were counted as only a single *Pieza de India*. The Spanish government absolutely refused to consent to the cession of trading posts in Spanish America, though it did allot a concession at Buenos Aires on which only wooden buildings and no fortifications of any sort were to be erected. They consented to allow one ship a year of five hundred tons burden to bring goods to be traded at the annual fair at the Isthmus of Panama.

This asiento seems to have been useful to English commerce chiefly as a recognition by Spain that English ships had a limited right to trade in the Caribbean. Interlopers and smugglers could take advantage of the right, and if they met with any interference, could pretend to be authorized slave ships. Perhaps the most important clause in the asiento was its grant of the right to maintain commercial agents in Spanish America. The colonists, not satisfactorily supplied from Spain, were anxious to buy smuggled goods, and the restrictions imposed by the Madrid government were not rigidly enforced. The four thousand eight hundred *Piezas de India* were only a small portion of the slaves annually brought from Africa to the New World. In a report to Parliament in 1709 the Board of Trade in London estimated the needs of the English colonies alone at twenty-five thousand slaves annually, of which only five thousand were for the North American colonies, as compared with four thousand for the small island of Barbados and twelve thousand for Jamaica. The Jamaica figure included a large number to be resold in Spanish America.

Although the South Sea Company had made considerable expenditures in the expectation that the asiento monopoly on the slave trade would be granted to it, the directors hesitated to accept the terms of the contract, once they learned them in detail. One fourth of the profits were reserved for the King of Spain, another fourth for Queen Anne, and 7 per cent for Don Manuel Manasses Gilligan, who had aided in the negotiations. It was alleged that the queen's share was to be diverted into the pockets of her Tory ministers; according to some rumors, Oxford was to receive the chief share, others made Bolingbroke the probable beneficiary. Perhaps this gossip was responsible for the queen's allotting her share to the South Sea Company. Gilligan's share was an option, which, it seems, he did not exercise. The South Sea Company bought the slaves from the African Company or from private traders. It sent out only eight of the permitted annual ships, and on the whole found both the ships and the slave business unprofitable.

The time for chartered companies with monopoly privileges was really past in the Occident, where it was already possible to make individual private ventures with relative safety and greater profit. The private slave traders could always undersell the African Company and the South Sea Company. It was the so-called interlopers who really profited by the asiento. Neither the chartered English companies nor the Spanish royal authorities were able to suppress them.[33]

Arguments like those later advanced by Adam Smith against such monopolies were already current. In 1709, for example, the African Company was agitating, as it did at intervals, for a revival of its former monopoly, which had been taken away by Parliament in 1698. Against the proposal to charter a joint-stock company with a monopoly, the Board of Trade reported that

It may reasonably be apprehended should this Trade be confined to a Company by a joynt Stock exclusive of all others that such Company will contract the Trade within . . . such narrow Limits in Africa, as may best turn to their owne Profitt without Regard to the good of the Plantations or of the Publick which may be presumed from the ways of their having carryed it on for the time Past.

It will Of consequence very much to lessen the Number of Ships now Employed in the Trade, to the great Disincouragement of our Navigation, for since there has been an open Trade, the separate Traders have sent three Ships for one imployed by the Company.

The report goes on to argue that

the Plantations may suffer for want of sufficient number of able Negroes at reasonable Rates, those Marketts being best supplyed where there are most Sellers. . . . we cannot but be sencible how prejudicial it must be to Trade in generall to have but one Buyer of all such Woollen and other Goods as are annually Exported for this Trade But one Freighter of so many Ships at home and but one buyer of the Plantation Commoditys abroad.[34]

[33] See Elizabeth Donnan, "The Early Days of the South Sea Company," *Journal of Economic and Business History*, II (1930), 419-450; V. Brown, "The South Sea Company and Contraband Trade," *American Historical Review*, XXXI (1926), 662-678; J. H. Rose and others, eds., *Cambridge History of the British Empire* (Cambridge, Eng., 1929-1940), I, 330-345.

[34] Donnan, ed., *Documents Illustrative of the Slave Trade*, II, 67. See also Smith, *Wealth of Nations*, Bk. V, chap. i.

That the freedom of trade advocated by such arguments as these was a freedom within the British dominions (Ireland not included) is clear from the rejection of the commercial treaty with France which was negotiated as a part of the Utrecht settlement. The House of Commons refused to sanction freer trade with France as contrary to the economic interests of Britain. The objection to the chartered monopolies was that in the past they had tended to favor cliques of London merchants as against rivals in London, and more especially in such other trading ports as Bristol. In the growth of trade the eighteenth-century mercantile interests saw the greatest security for the strength of the state. The restriction of the asiento trade to the South Sea Company was therefore against the spirit of the age. The attempt of that company to secure a monopoly not of trade but of banking and credit was far more nearly in accordance with that spirit. It is still not clear how genuine this attempt was, and how far the opportunities for stockjobbing profits motivated the directors of the South Sea Company.[35]

Though the South Sea scheme may have been nothing but a swindle all along, Law's system was certainly a far-reaching plan meant to increase the power of France by increasing her trade and her wealth. Here the opposition between the advocates of a laissez-faire policy and those of a planned economy was obvious. Long afterward, Montesquieu wrote in his *Esprit des lois* that John Law had been "one of the greatest promoters of despotism in Europe," because he strove, contrary to the constitution of both monarchies and republics, "to level intermediate ranks and entirely destroy political bodies." Archdeacon Coxe tells us that the opponents of the South Sea scheme felt that it tended to concentrate power in the hands of the directors to a dangerous extent, since these directors could influence *both* the king *and* his ministers, as well as a parliamentary majority. If either the French or the English company had succeeded in its aims, the result would certainly have been to strengthen the state enormously and to make company and state for practical purposes one. Law's system was mercantilism brought up to date with the addition of the great power which control of bank credit gives. It was rather an anticipation—in many ways a very close one—of some of the economic practices of the National Socialist regime in Germany after 1933 than what the French call Colbertism, or the classic mercantilism of the textbooks. Law would have swept away the medieval and traditional

---

[35] E. F. Heckscher, "A Note on South Sea Finance," *Journal of Economic and Business History*, III (1931), 321-328, sheds new light on the way in which the original shareholders could profit by the issue of shares at ever-increasing prices.

ideas and institutions that made any reform of the French *ancien régime*
almost impossible. He would have made it possible for Louis XV to be
in fact as well as in theory an absolute monarch, a despot.

The failure of the system discredited the reforms the regent had attempted. By way of a return to the old system of Richelieu, Mazarin,
and Louis XIV, Dubois was made cardinal and chief minister. When he
died, the regent took his place as chief minister, the king being legally of
age. The death of the regent was followed by a ministry of the Duc de
Bourbon, who was governed by his mistress, who in turn was managed
by the banker Pâris-Duverney, one of the old guard financiers who had
done their utmost to ruin Law and then in the *Visa* liquidated the
system in order to restore private initiative to its former place in state
finance. Only with the advent of Cardinal Fleury's regime in 1726 did
France find a leader who remained long in power.

VII. POLITICAL IMPLICATIONS OF ECONOMIC PROGRESS

The first half of the eighteenth century was in most of Europe a
period of economic progress. The progress, measured in terms of increased international trade, increased incomes, indeed by any of the
norms of economic statistics, was real. It was not evenly distributed
throughout Europe by countries, nor within countries by classes. On the
whole it was greatest in northwestern Europe and least in eastern Europe.
It was probably nonexistent in the Ottoman Empire, which was not by
contemporaries considered a part of Europe. Its chief beneficiaries were
no doubt the middle classes, but it was to a certain extent spread through
all classes. It was not a progress marked by any such striking series of
technological improvements as marked the first industrial revolution
(that of steam) or the second (that of oil, electricity, automatic machinery). It was produced rather by the slight but real improvement of old
industrial and agricultural methods, by the beginnings of modern commercial methods—credit, banking, the joint-stock company—by careful
stewardship, as in Prussia or in Tuscany, by the comparative peace
Europe as a whole enjoyed.

All this was not of course new in 1715. It was part of a slow rise in
European standards of living which began well back in the Middle
Ages, and was greatly hastened in the sixteenth and seventeenth centuries. The early eighteenth century was simply its high point. It is sometimes called, especially as it speeds up in this period, the commercial

revolution. From it there arose, with the introduction of power machinery and the factory system, the so-called industrial revolution.

Now the extremely important economic and political doctrine that grew out of the eighteenth century, and dominated much of the thinking and feeling of the nineteenth century, is that called economic liberalism, or sometimes just plain liberalism. A few stock phrases will call up readily some of the political implications of this liberalism: "that government governs best which governs least, and most cheaply," "*laissez faire*," "individualism," "free trade." In its culmination, Herbert Spencer could write a book called *Man versus the State*—that is, the good man against the wicked state.

However congruous this later development may be with the *practices* of the European middle classes in the early eighteenth century, it remains true that such *ideas* were almost unheard-of in the first part of the eighteenth century. Businessmen were not hostile to the state. Most of them fully expected to use the machinery of the state for their own purposes. Many of the producers, and many of the merchants, were quite willing to do business within the surviving corporative organizations, guilds, trades associations and the like, in which they had grown up.

But in fact the most enterprising of them found these corporative organizations hampering. They found the elaborate specification of standards, the bewildering variations of weights and measures, the even more complicated tax structures, the irregularities of local government—they found that all this cramped them, hindered their expansion into large-scale production and marketing. For them the enemy was not the state, unless the state threw its authority behind local autonomy, internal tariffs, the privileges of a landed aristocracy—in short, behind feudal survivals that got in the way of the expansion of the market. They were delighted to have the state protect their markets in colonial areas by the devices of economic nationalism. They welcomed the state as patron and protector of central banks. They supported the central authority of the growing leviathan state, which was doing their work and which they helped to staff. They wanted efficiency, though they did not call it that; and the centralized state still seemed, in the years after Utrecht, the most efficient instrument available. Only later, having failed to capture the state entirely even in northwestern Europe, did they turn to "nature's freedom" and the "harmony of interests" as a better way to efficiency.

Chapter Five

RESISTANCE TO CHANGE

I. THE FORCE OF TRADITION

THE problem confronting conservatives everywhere in Europe after 1715 was the establishment of a stable regime capable of maintaining order and promoting prosperity. How was "the harmony between liberty and authority, so desirable, yet so difficult," to be established in the internal affairs of each state?[1] How was the balance of power between states, the only feasible method of ensuring peace, to be maintained? In a world bankrupted by wars, internal order and prosperity plainly depended on the prevention of another major conflict between the great powers, or at least its postponement for a generation.

Since the royal absolutism of Louis XIV had been used to wage great wars, royal absolutism must be curbed, and the authority of the sovereign state over its component bodies or groups lessened. The attempt to check the swollen power of the dynastic state at least succeeded in preventing the creditors of that state from taking control of it through John Law's system, and through similar ventures by corporate finance such as the South Sea scheme in England and the more abortive and even less understood schemes for refinancing war debts in Charles VI's dominions. The alliance between the *bourgeoisie* and the kings against nobles and church was definitely at an end after these bubbles burst.

The efforts to revive the *Ständestaat* in Sweden and the Netherlands show the impossibility of making medieval institutions function in the eighteenth-century world. Sweden and the Netherlands had been great powers in the seventeenth century. That they ceased to carry much weight in international relations in the eighteenth was due not merely to the obvious fact that they were less populous than England or France or Charles VI's domains, but also to the inability of their governments to

---

[1] Daguesseau, "Mercuriale XIX," *Oeuvres* (Paris, 1787), 213. The whole speech, a *mercuriale* delivered before the *Parlement* of Paris, is an excellent example of the curious mixture of conservatism and liberalism that went into the cult of stability.

command the lives and fortunes of their people. Prussia, less wealthy than the Netherlands and hardly more populous than Sweden, rose to become a great power while they were declining into insignificance, for it became a *Beamtenstaat,* in which the obligation to serve the state in peace and in war was imposed on nobles, *bourgeoisie,* and peasants alike, through the development of an elaborate military and bureaucratic organization under the personal control of the king.

In France the venality of offices and the unwillingness of Louis XV to devote most of his waking hours to the business of governing prevented an analogous implementing of royal absolutism. The jealousies of the many cliques and the coteries within each of the traditional groups composing the nobility were quite as instrumental as royal opposition in preventing the traditional institutions, the Estates-General and the *Parlement,* from developing into representative assemblies. In the eighteenth century the bureaucracy probably had an authority greater than it had exercised in the seventeenth, and the intendants and ministers were frequently able and well-intentioned men. Their authority, however, was never permanently reconciled with the traditional liberties or privileges (the terms were in practice almost synonymous) of the rest of the governing classes. The problem of establishing an internal balance of power, so that no one group or interest could dominate, was never solved by the French *ancien régime* save through personal rule, like that of Fleury. Had he been immortal, the French Revolution might never have occurred.

In England the existence of Parliament and its success in limiting monarchy obviously made it much easier to reconcile liberty and authority. It is evident that so long as access to the governing classes remained open to new men from the *bourgeoisie* the English constitution could gradually adapt itself to the new conditions which the industrial revolution was beginning to create, and no violent revolution would be necessary to effect the transition from the Old Regime to the nineteenth century. But it is sometimes forgotten how large a part accident played in the divergent development of English institutions, originally not very different from those of France. Suppose that Bolingbroke had been prime minister after 1721 instead of Walpole, for instance, and it is unlikely that cabinet government and the party system necessary to make it work would have been evolved. George I, or even George II, would probably have been less unsuccessful as a "patriot king" than George III, who was more or less guided by Bolingbroke's theories, eventually proved to be.

In the development of the governmental and social institutions of modern Europe the years following 1715 marked a turning point. Since the attempts to return to the medieval *Ständestaat* were impracticable, if only because they tended to render the state incapable, like Poland, of defending itself from "fifth columnists" and aggressors, the choice lay between continuing the trend toward highly centralized bureaucratic autocracy begun in France by Richelieu, Mazarin, and Colbert, or furthering the development of parliamentary institutions. The bureaucratic autocracies in the Germanies and Russia developed and were transformed by national unity and the revolt of the masses into the totalitarian states of Hitler and Stalin. The parliamentary system on the other hand evolved into the present representative democracies in Great Britain and the United States. France, as the two Napoleons indicate, wavered between the two tendencies. Furthermore, the increasing economic interdependence within the nations compelled the democracies to an immense extension of state activity and of bureaucracy so that actual interference by government in the daily lives of the citizens is far greater today in the United States and Great Britain, even in peacetime, than it was even in the Prussia of Frederick the Great. The revolution in methods of production and distribution has necessitated a revolution in government and society everywhere in the Western world. But the changes have been gradual, and there is no single magic clue by which to explain them.

In the years after 1720 the task of the governments was to effect a working compromise which would stabilize and pacify the internal affairs of the great powers. Walpole, Fleury, Charles VI, Philip V, and Frederick William of Prussia were in their several ways equally devoted to the cult of stability.

II. THE UNCHANGING COUNTRYSIDE

The conservative cult of stability after 1715 had its roots in the unchanging European countryside. The major changes in Europe since the Middle Ages had been caused by the growth of towns and cities, by the extension of trade and commerce, and by the expansion of Europe overseas. The Protestant Reformation has been attributed in the main to the rise of the *bourgeoisie* and the eighteenth-century revolutions in industry and in politics were likewise of urban origin. After 1750 even the countryside began to change its traditional methods of cultivation and its traditional social order. But in 1715 and in 1740 the countryside was still for the most part living and working in the established way, a way in some respects of immemorial antiquity, older than the Roman Empire, rooted in pre-history. It is curious that so little attention has been paid by historians to the great part played in the whole social and political framework of the Old Regime by its agricultural basis. Attention has been concentrated on what happened at the apex of the social pyramid, at the court of the monarch, and in wars waged by professional soldiers officered by gentlemen amateurs. But more is known of the rural organization of the twelfth and thirteenth centuries than of that in the early eighteenth, which, as an economic historian has lately said, "is rather more difficult to understand."[2]

The difficulty is to determine to what extent the growth of the dynastic states and the money economy of the commercial revolution really affected the lives of the rural masses. The survivals of medieval feudalism were obviously still highly influential everywhere. The techniques of agricultural production remained for the most part those of the Middle Ages. The church, in Protestant as well as Catholic Europe, still functioned in rural parishes much as it had for centuries. Parish and manor had both been forms of organization suited to the methods of agricultural production and distribution of the natural or subsistence economy. Even in England parson and squire remained the natural and respected leaders in each neighborhood as late as the nineteenth century. In the eighteenth, it is clear that in countries like France, where absentee landlords were numerous, the clergy and gentry still exercised a quasi-medieval and feudal authority which had its good as well as its bad sides.

In 1715 there were three different types of rural organization, each widely distributed in Europe. In central England, parts of northern France, most of the Germanies, and central Russia the plowland was in large unfenced "open fields" subdivided into small strips of perhaps an acre each, normally ten times as long as they were wide. In Spain, southern France, Italy, portions of the British Isles, and a large part of Russia, there were open fields divided into fairly small parcels of irregular shape and varying size. In other regions, such as southwestern England, the Netherlands, and Brittany, the fields were completely enclosed under individual occupation and control.

The origin of these variations in the arable or plowland is not known. It is possible that the enclosure had always existed in certain places, e.g. in parts of England, and that many such areas have been wrongly assumed

[2] W. Bowden, M. Karpovich, and A. P. Usher, *An Economic History of Europe since 1750* (New York, 1937), 45. Despite the title, the first three chapters are devoted to "Economic conditions and organization in the early eighteenth century," of which the book gives an excellent short account.

to have been first enclosed in the eighteenth or sixteenth centuries. The nature of the soil and the type of plow traditionally used may explain the existence and varying shape of strips in the open fields.[3] On heavy soils a wheeled plow was used. As this was hard to turn at the end of a furrow, long narrow strips were the most convenient holdings.

In the open fields or, for that matter, in the enclosed fields it was necessary to allow the fertility of the soil to be restored by bare fallowing at least one year out of every three. The land was plowed and cultivated, but not planted to any crop. Weeds were destroyed, the mechanical condition of the soil improved, and nitrates allowed to accumulate. Modern research has shown that the accumulation of nitrates was the most important result of bare fallowing, but the practice in earlier centuries was empirical and traditional. By it, a farming community could use the same plowland for centuries without exhausting its fertility. As artificial or chemical fertilizers were not known, and as animal manure was scarce, this technique was essential. Traditional systems of crop rotation were used, in which grains were alternated, and every field regularly lay fallow "to rest the soil."

The main object of the farmer in the early eighteenth century was subsistence. Cash crops were needed to pay for the few articles not homemade or home-grown, and to pay such taxes and rents as were exacted in money. For a subsistence farm it was necessary to have land in each of the open or common fields used in the local traditional crop rotation. This land, whether in strips or in irregularly shaped parcels, was individually held. The theory that the common fields had originated in a primitive and supposedly idyllic communism is not supported by historical evidence. The farmer needed also to get hay from a meadow, wood from a wood lot, and to have pasture for his cattle, sheep, and other livestock. He must, finally, have sufficient land near his house for a garden, pigs, and chickens.

The house and the adjacent garden plot were, like the strips in the common fields and in the hay meadow, individually held, but the pasture and the wood lot were common land of which the use was shared by the citizens of the parish or manor, not necessarily equally. In Yorkshire, for example, the pasture was divided into "cattle gates" and each farmer could have as many beasts on the common pasture as he held gates. These gates or rights of pasturage had become attached to certain houses by the

[3] See H. L. Gray, *English Field Systems* (Cambridge, Mass., 1915); Marc Bloch, *Les caractères originaux de l'histoire rurale française* (Paris, 1931); C. S. Orwin, *The Open Fields* (Oxford, 1938); Max Weber, *General Economic History* (New York, 1927), chaps. i-vi.

eighteenth century, and the lord of the manor owned a large number which he might allow tenants in other houses to use.[4]

This traditional organization of agricultural production, which had existed from time immemorial in the three types indicated by the three ways of dividing plowland, had distinct advantages from the point of view of the peasant farmer of the early eighteenth century. It gave even the man with a small holding, say a single strip in each field of plowland, the pasturage, wood, and hay he must have to subsist. As the plowland fields were the best land in the parish, it permitted even the poorest land-holder to share in the best land, instead of being relegated to marginal land as he was likely to be after enclosure[4] acts. The pasturage on the common, usually a scrubby, partly wooded waste resembling a New England pasture today, was supplemented after the harvest by the turning of all the village beasts to pasture on the stubble in the common fields, a privilege especially valued by the poor. As long as the peasant had few wants which his own industry could not satisfy, the traditional system afforded a subsistence to those who held sufficient land, provided the state, the church, and the landlord were moderate in their demands and the region was not afflicted by plague, famine, or the devastation of war.

But by the eighteenth century there were everywhere many countrymen who did not hold enough land to support them. The Malthusian pressure of increasing population on the means of subsistence was increasingly felt in the more thickly populated regions, such as France and parts of the valleys of the Po and Rhine. There appear to have been in France (and at Laxton in England, according to the Orwins) more peasants with too little land than with no land at all. The man who held too little land might become a *métayer*, or sharecropper, on land held by a town dweller as an investment of capital accumulated in a trade or profession. Or he might become a worker for wages, a *journalier*, or supplement his resources by a craft he could carry on in his cottage or in the village, such as carpentry or weaving. What we now call "social security" depended very largely, not merely for the poor and underprivileged, but for the rich and the privileged as well, on holding land. The clue to the economic and social history of the Old Regime, and to the variations between the political and social development of different regions and countries, lies in their respective systems of land tenure, still quasi-feudal.

[4] For the "gates," see A. G. Ruston and Denis Witney, *Hooton Pagnell, the Agricultural Evolution of a Yorkshire Village* (New York, 1934), 141-158; also Orwin, *Open Fields*, 160, 161. They still exist in Hooton Pagnell, but this survival into the twentieth century is exceptional.

III. SYSTEMS OF LAND TENURE

The most baffling feature of eighteenth-century land tenure is the nature of property rights in agricultural land, which were nowhere absolute in fact or in law: "landholding was governed by complex rules which preserved most of the objectionable elements of feudal law and failed to achieve any of the advantages of a positive system of private property."[5]

Locke's emphasis on the "right of private property," which was repeated throughout the eighteenth century, as for instance in the French declaration of the Rights of Man and of the Citizen in 1789, was wholly subversive of the rural and agricultural organization of the Old Regime. Property, like liberty, connotes individualism; and the eighteenth-century countryside was communal, depending chiefly not on self-help but on mutual aid of a blindly traditional sort, almost like that of the bees and the ants. Since the rise of that vague complex of phenomena lumped under the term "capitalism" had made private property in funds theoretically absolute long before 1715, it has always been easy for city people to forget that land was not owned outright, even by English landlords, prior to the enclosure acts. In subsistence farming the object of production is use, not profit. The insistence of the French physiocrats on the necessity of private property in land if French agriculture was to become profitable to investors and to the nation was obviously essential to reform. But that came after 1750.[6]

The struggle for agrarian individualism in France culminated in the establishment of a "positive system of private property" at the time of the Revolution. But in England there was no such logically finished system until the Law of Property acts of 1922 and 1925 abolished copyhold and other feudal débris and provided for only two forms of tenure, freehold and lease. Yet since the act of 1660, which abolished feudal tenures, it had been customary to speak of property in land in England as though it were in law the simple "right" advocated by Locke.[7]

[5] Bowden, Karpovich, and Usher, *Economic History*, 63.

[6] On the physiocrats, see G. Weulersse, *Le mouvement physiocratique en France* (Paris, 1910); and H. Higgs, *The Physiocrats* (London, 1897).

[7] For the general history of land tenures, see article on "Land Tenure" in *Encyclopaedia of the Social Sciences*, IX, 73-127. On eighteenth-century France, Soulge, *Le régime féodal et la propriété paysanne* (Paris, 1923), an introduction to publication of *terriers* from Forez, sheds some light from the point of view of a royalist. H. Sée, *Les classes rurales en Bretagne du XVIᵉ siècle à la révolution* (Paris, 1906); F. Vermale, *Les classes rurales en Savoie* (then, of course, not part of France) *au XVIIIᵉ siècle* (Paris, 1911), by a pupil of Mathiez; and G. Lefebvre, *Les paysans du nord pendant la révolution* (Paris, 1924), give details on other

The modern and Lockeian concept "property" does not fit the facts of agricultural history in Europe prior to the shift from production for use to production for a local or a distant market. Prior to that capitalistic development, some sort of tenure in commonalty prevailed almost everywhere. But in the eighteenth century such commodities as wool and wheat were, and long had been, produced for markets, sometimes for distant markets. The cities had to be fed and clothed, as well as the provincial market towns. Some farmers in many regions, and most farmers in a few regions, were already by 1715 producing agricultural commodities primarily for profit and for more or less distant sale. Only a great number of detailed regional surveys would enable historians to determine just how far the change from medieval local subsistence to modern commercial agriculture had progressed and just how obsolete and unworkable the old tenures in commonalty had become.

Local surveys would show conditions ranging from the barbaric quasi-nomadic and pastoral Highland clans of Scotland to the highly developed and specialized agriculture of Belgium and of the region around Turin. For agriculture and for everything else the difficulty in understanding the Old Regime is the infinite variations between regions and localities. What was true in one county, one *pays*, was not true at all twenty miles away in the next river valley. Thus it is hard to measure trends. Complete data and a refined statistical procedure would be necessary for anything like scientific accuracy, and the historian of the early eighteenth century can command neither. The published data are too meager to afford samples sufficient to avoid a high probability of error.

The land tenures in general remained seignorial or manorial in character in the early eighteenth century. To be sure, there were a considerable number of alodial tenures in certain regions such as parts of southern France and of northwestern Germany. Some peasants at least had escaped from payment of any form of feudal dues or of rent to a landlord. Probably some had always been able to avoid being drawn into feudal obligations. In eighteenth-century France the royal authorities tried to include these free holdings in the domain of the kind, so as to collect the *lods et ventes*.[8] But such tenures were at best exceptional. In many cases they escaped the usual obligations because of their insignificance.

---

regions. Further regional studies would be necessary before a definitive general treatment could be made. For England the monumental work of Beatrice and Sidney Webb on *English Local Government* (London, 1912-1927) is a useful source, but again there is no definitive treatment of land tenure from the point of view of economic policy and social development.

[8] See Soulge, *Le régime féodal et la propriété paysanne*, 125, 129.

The more usual types of tenure may be considered, first from the point of view of the peasant, then from that of the recipients of the various dues which he had to pay. The proverb that "possession is nine points of the law," and Burke's remark that prescription gives the best possible title to land, supply the key to peasant tenure. What the eighteenth-century subsistence farmer wanted was the right to use land. The right to transfer his holding, to sell it, or to buy other land was less important to him. The pasture and the wood lot were common to citizens of the village or dwellers on the manor. Whether the payment made in money or in kind for the use of land was legally rent or a feudal due mattered little to the subsistence farmer. The surviving records show clearly that frequently the same family occupied the same holding for centuries. Such occupancy became a kind of property right. Few attempts were made to evict such occupants except in connection with capitalist ventures, like the establishment of sheep pasture in Tudor England or commercial wheat raising in the eighteenth century. It was not the old nobility and gentry, but the bourgeois capitalist who tried to make the land pay and thereby did most to disturb the traditional social security of the peasant under the Old Regime. Land was then almost universally regarded as the safest investment, and the social standing associated with landholding was so superior that most successful business and professional men invested their savings in holdings of land, to which they were anxious to establish as clear a title as that to their property in "the funds," i.e. in what we call stocks and bonds.

The peasant in the eighteenth century might hold his land subject to payment of a rent charge, the feudal *cens*, usually small in amount, and to various other feudal survivals, often commuted into small annual fixed charges. The smallness of the amount was partly owing to the decrease in the value of money in the centuries since the sum was fixed. It is well known that many of the French peasantry enjoyed what amounted to freehold proprietorship of their lands subject to these payments. English freeholders, despite the name, still paid similar charges of feudal origin to the lord of the manor in the eighteenth century. Copyholders, of course, paid more.

At Hooton Pagnell (in the West Riding of Yorkshire), to cite a typical case, the freeholders of the manors of Hooton Pagnell, Clayton, and Frickley paid to the lord of the manor under the name of "chief rent" in the half year ending at Martinmas, 1731, sums of which the largest was ten shillings and eightpence and the smallest twopence. At Clayton there was a curious item, "Waken silver," explained as probably monetary commutation for services due under an ancient military tenure in connection with guarding the beacon at Watchley Crag. The amount is 15*d*. The manor of Hooton Pagnell had been conveyed "by fine" in 1704 to Sir John Warde and his son, Patience Warde. Sir John had been Lord Mayor of London. In the deed of 1704 the

tythes, feedings, moores, marishes, woods, underwoods, wastes, commons; Mynes, Quarries, Watercourses, Mills, Fishings, Fishing Places; Rents, Reversions, Services; *Courts Leete, Courts Baron, perquisities and proffittees of Courtes, Waifes, Strayes, goods and chattels of Felons, Fugitives, Deodands, Fines, Amerciaments and all other Rights, Royalties, Jurisdictions, Privileges, proffitts* and commodities

were conveyed to the self-made London merchant and his family. This enumeration indicates the chief features of the seignory as it still survived in most of Europe in the early eighteenth century.[9]

The lord of the manor, or the seigneur, might purchase his position. He might be of bourgeois or even of peasant origin. But as owner of a manor or seigneury he became the responsible leader of a self-contained and still largely self-supporting rural community. He did not own any of the land (except what had been enclosed) free from the restrictions on its use common to all the manor. His holdings, like those of yeoman or peasant freeholders, might be subject to dues owed to another lord of a manor, or to the king, or to a religious corporation. The Pierrepont family at Laxton, or their agents, had often been fined by their own court-baron in the past three hundred years, for example. Even the most favored tenures, in short, whether held by privileged or by unprivileged persons, were not, despite their superficial resemblances to a modern estate, private property in land as we think of it today.

The peasant might hold his property by one of a baffling variety of tenures which were restricted to descendants of a particular person or to a limited number of lives. If the line failed, the holding reverted to the lord of the manor or the seigneur. These tenures amounted to perpetual leases to specified families, but there were many local variations in the terms of the contract, which was not a written document, but a customary right enforceable at law and a matter of record. These restricted tenures, of the type represented in England by copyhold, differed from freehold in that the land might revert by escheat to the lord of the manor in default of direct heirs and in the requirement that a fine be paid at each transfer of the holding or of the manor. In the eighteenth century this fine amounted as a rule to much more than the annual fixed rent charge. It

---

[9] Ruston and Witney, *Hooton Pagnell*, 268, 302-304.

had to be paid if a new tenant inherited the holding or if the manor changed hands. It resembled modern transfer and inheritance taxes levied by the state.

English copyhold tenants were obligated to pay a money rent "of assize," payable semiannually and usually a fixed sum which by the eighteenth century had become very small through the decrease in the value of money. They had to attend the manorial court and might be impaneled to serve on its jury. Their interest in the timber and minerals on their holding was usually sharply restricted. They had to pay fines on the death of the lord, or on the alienation of the land. They had also to give reliefs and heriots (the best horse or ox or its value in money). Frequently they had to agree that all their grain would be ground at the lord's mill. It was, for instance, not until the year 1853 that the "resiants" of Wakefield, Sandel, and Ossett bought off for eighteen thousand pounds the manorial restriction which obliged them not merely to grind all their grain at the Soke mill, but also to consume no flour which had not been ground there. Under Queen Victoria this particular feudal survival was an exception. In the early eighteenth century such conditions were certainly far more frequent, how frequent only much further investigation by historians could determine. Squire Purefoy at Shalstone, Bucks, for example, had a mill for which a quitrent had to be paid to the lord of a neighboring manor, not in money but in cuminseed. Purefoy himself, as lord of the manor of Shalstone, held a court-baron, with the aid of his family lawyer, at regular intervals. He, with the jury or "hommage," drew up rules for the cultivation of the open fields, the use of the common pasture, and so on, and as lord of the manor had power to "distrain the goods and chattels of every defaulter of keeping the same orders and to sell the said goods in like manner as goods distrained for rent."[10]

But Squire Purefoy, like most other English landlords in the period 1715-1740, also had tenants who leased their land for short terms of years, with no permanence of tenure. When these leases ran out, the landlord could raise the rent, especially if he had invested capital in draining, enclosing, or otherwise improving the land. More research would be necessary for any determination of the proportion of English tenants whose holdings were by these leases of modern type as compared with the freeholders or the copyholders. Since some have mistakenly assumed that only freeholders were yeomen, it is to be noted that any substantial tenant was called a yeoman, and if the annual rent charge in a lease for life exceeded 40s., had a vote for the county members of Parliament. All such

[10] *Purefoy Letters, 1735-1753*, ed. G. Eland (London, 1931), 36, 434 ff.

tenants had working capital, stock, tools, etc., and nearly all of them hired agricultural laborers. There was a similar class of prosperous peasants in France, in northern Italy, in the Low Countries, and in western Germany. The kulak is neither a new nor a peculiarly Russian character in history.

From the point of view of the eighteenth-century landlord in all parts of western Europe, it was desirable to increase the money income from his holding. The noble seigneur or lord of the manor had everywhere adopted luxurious and expensive ways of living for which his customary income was inadequate. No longer was he satisfied to live as his ancestors had done, chiefly at home on his estate, with most of his food home-grown and even his everyday clothing homespun. On the Continent the large number of nobles meant that the majority of them were too poor to come to court, and even the courtiers were often in desperate need of royal pensions and perquisites. In England the small number of nobles and great gentry meant that there were few really hopelessly impoverished landlords and many very wealthy ones. The Tudors had granted church lands to their newly created nobility on terms more favorable than those on which land on the Continent was held by the seigneurs.

The greater part of the English nobility and most of the country gentry were either of relatively recent bourgeois origins or had intermarried with the rising urban capitalist class. So they already took more nearly the entrepreneurial capitalist view of their estates than did most Continental landlords. They bought a manor as they would have bought a business concern and expected it to show a profit in money on the capital invested. This profit was lower than that from business, because land values were raised by the demand for land from newly rich aspirants to gentility, and also because land was a safer investment. But even the Wardes at Hooton Pagnell did not make much progress in eliminating feudal survivals, "manorial incidents," in the early eighteenth century. As long as the system of cultivation depended on open fields, any real improvement in agricultural technique was almost impossible. As long as quasi-feudal tenures survived, rents could not be raised. And any reform of the traditional system could be effected only over a long period of gradual change, such as that illustrated by the subsequent history of Hooton Pagnell. A revolution like that in France, or the despotic rule of Peter the Great or of the abler among the Hohenzollerns in Prussia, could result in more rapid change. But in most countries of eighteenth-century Europe, where legal property rights could be enforced in the courts as against decrees from the monarch (as was always in fact the

case in France under the Old Regime), no easy or rapid agricultural
reform or land reform was practicable. The cult of stability had its roots
in an almost unalterable social order which from time immemorial had
governed the lives of the rural majority of the population of all European
states.

IV. THE DEAD HAND

The position of the several established churches, Protestant as well as
Catholic, in Europe in the early eighteenth century made them high
priests of the cult of stability. Not merely did they still claim authority
co-ordinate with, but on certain points independent of that of the state;
they also held a great deal of property, most of it in land, by the "dead
hand" of mortmain. Many monarchs made persistent efforts to restrict
mortmain. Philip V of Spain, for example, annulled legacies to ecclesiastical persons by penitents in mortal sickness, and his concordat with the
Holy See in 1737 provided that lands thereafter acquired by the church
should be taxable, not tax exempt. Despite such persistent efforts to reduce
church property, clerical holdings in Catholic countries tended to increase.
Conservatives like Philip V did not object to mortmain as such, but to
the exemption of church lands from taxes and from feudal dues, and to
the excessive extent of such lands. In Protestant countries the church
holdings had been in large part, but by no means wholly, confiscated at
the Reformation.

The justification for endowing the regular clergy with land was that
under the Old Regime education, public health, and charity were the
concern of the church and largely of the monastic orders, rather than that
of the state. The glebe lands of the secular parish priests, Protestant as
well as Catholic, provided a large part of their support, either because
they themselves farmed them like the other peasants, or because the lands
were rented to peasants. The church also had its own system of taxation,
the tithes, collected in rural districts in kind, not in cash. The amount
taken of the peasant's crops varied according to local custom. In Brittany,
according to Henri Sée, it might be as little as a thirtieth or as much as a
sixth of the wheat. For Prussia, Pariset does not venture any generalization.
For England no generalization is possible either, but in some instances
at least the burden of tithe payments was heavier there than in either
France or Prussia.[11]

[11] See Georges Pariset, *L'état et les églises en Prusse sous Frédéric Guillaume I* (Paris,
1897), 322-367. This is the most detailed and careful study of the institutional history of the
church in any country for the period covered, 1713-1740. See also Ruston and Witney,
Hooton Pagnell, chap. ix, and Sée, *Les classes rurales en Bretagne*.

A portion of the tithes, the French *portion congrue*, was devoted to the support of the parish priest and the maintenance of the parish church. The rest went to a variety of other uses, including education, public health, various charities, and the incomes of royal appointees to abbeys, held *in commendam* contrary to the decrees of the Council of Trent which, in this respect as in some others, were not enforced in France until after 1789. In England the king had taken over a large part of the so-called "great tithes," or rectorial tithes, at the Reformation, and they had frequently been granted or leased to individuals in search of a good investment. In the eighteenth century the English landed gentry often leased or purchased these tithes for their estates. The small or vicarial tithes, the *portion congrue,* were still often collected in kind by the incumbent. At Hooton Pagnell, for example, these tithes in 1764 and therefore also in this period, were the following:

Hay . . . a tenth part of hay throughout the Parish.
Rape & Line (—flax), Turnips, Clover & all small seeds . . . tith (*sic*).
Wool & Lamb . . . tithe; one lamb in six, allowing 3*d.* for every one under Ten.
Pigs . . . Tyth (*sic*), one in six, allowing 1*d.* for every one under ten.
Geese . . . The same rule observed.
Dove-coats (*sic*) . . . Composition of 2*s. 6d.*
Agistment of unprofitable Cattle.

> One foal 4*d.*; Bees 1*d.* per swarm; one pig of the first litter without allowing anything.

There follows a list of "Easter Reckonings," corresponding to the Prussian calendes, or *Vier Zeiten Pfenning.*

Offerings two pence, House Duties two pence halfpenny.
Cows 2½*d.* & 1½*d.*; Eggs 6*d.* a year for a Great Farm, 4*d.* for a lesser, and 2*d.* a Cottage.
Servants' Wages. 5*d.* per pound. . . .[12]

It will be noted in the above list that some of the parson's share of the tithes had been commuted into a money payment, but that much of what he needed for his own use or to stock his glebe farm he still took in kind. The Easter reckonings show the customary origin of the payments. They had probably once been voluntary, but had become a right. Similarly, the fees paid to the French judiciary were still in the eighteenth century called *épices*, or spices, because their origin was in medieval gifts of spices.

---

[12] Ruston and Witney, *Hooton Pagnell*, 412-413. See Orwin, *Open Fields*, 183-184, for similar eighteenth-century lists of vicarial tithes.

In 1743 the Vicar of Hooton Pagnell had forty-two acres of open field glebe lands, in strips scattered through the common fields, and nineteen acres of enclosed land, probably grass, besides his croft or close. He farmed this himself and probably collected his own tithes, either in person or by one of his servants. Some parsons already leased their glebe, and others made an arrangement for collection of small tithes like the "tax farms" in France, selling for a sum of money the right to collect them. The vexations and disputes these arrangements occasioned may easily be imagined, especially when dissenters also had to pay. Yet in terms of a self-contained rural subsistence economy these small tithes were not really unreasonable or unjust.

The English great tithes were, however, far less justifiable and far more resented. At Hooton Pagnell, to cite once more an individual case which appears to be reasonably typical despite local peculiarities, the great tithes had before the Protestant Reformation belonged to the Prior and Convent of Holy Trinity, York, and to the Chapel of the Blessed Mary and Holy Angels in St. Sepulchres, York, in equal shares. After the Reformation the king leased these tithes to various persons not otherwise connected with Hooton Pagnell, and one third of them were given to Wakefield Grammar School as an endowment. In the early eighteenth century the Warde family, who had bought the manor in 1703, leased two thirds of the "Great or Corn Tithes" of Hooton from the crown and the other third from Wakefield Grammar School, so that they could add this tithe to their rents. The lease from the crown in 1704 was at the rate of £11, 6s. 8d., which appears to have been much less than the value of the grain that was collected and stored in the tithe barn awaiting a market. Yet the Wardes already owned far more than half the land, and did not collect the grain tithe in kind. Instead they exacted a money payment. It would be interesting to know what proportion of the income of the English landed gentry in the eighteenth century was derived from the "impropriation of great tithes," but the whole subject of tithes has been too much neglected by historians of the Old Regime to make conjectures possible.[13]

The persistence of the ecclesiastical courts in England in the eighteenth century is another topic which, like the tithes, is in need of further investigation. These courts retained jurisdiction not merely over church discipline and over certain offenses against public morals, but also in a

[13] Such standard works as the *Encyclopaedia of the Social Sciences*; Lipson, *Economic History of England*; Sykes, *Church and State in England*; Trevelyan, *England under Queen Anne*; and Williams, *Whig Supremacy*, virtually ignore the subject of tithes. The best brief account I have found is in Lord Ernle, *English Farming, Past and Present* (London, 1936), chap. xvi, 332-348.

variety of civil cases concerning tithes, church dues, and dilapidations. Cases concerning advowsons belonged, however, not to church courts but to common law. In Protestant countries like Prussia, where the church did not have an episcopal form of organization, the church courts had disappeared. In Catholic countries like France they retained jurisdiction and powers which also require further study to be clearly understood. From the point of view of the eighteenth-century Spaniard the governmental functions of the church seem to have been more important and more conspicuous than those of the state. Except for Pariset's painstaking work on Prussia, really thorough studies of the institutional history of the church in the early eighteenth century by trained historians appear to be lacking. But the inadequate data available indicate clearly that even in Protestant lands the church had retained much of its medieval power, especially in rural districts. Yet even in Catholic France, after the rise of the dynastic states, the king had become the central authority, not the pope. It was the king who appointed the bishops. It was also the king who diverted church funds from their appointed uses into the pockets of his favorites. The concordat between Napoleon and the papacy was in some ways less unfavorable to the church than the prevailing arrangements of the French *ancien régime*.

Religious institutions of all sorts have usually been conservative upholders of the *status quo*. Reformations in religious matters usually begin, like Methodism and German Pietism in this period, not as revolts, but as attempts at purging the establishment of corrupt deviations from its original purity. It is natural, then, to find the established churches acting as high priests of the cult of stability. Their involvement in the traditional social order which, it must be repeated, was still primarily agricultural and predominantly rural, made stability as necessary to the churches as to the nobles and to the less prosperous of the peasants. The property rights of the churches were mostly in quasi-feudal dues of which tithes were the most important. On many manors the church, through one of its constituent bodies, was itself the feudal lord. That changes of a radical character would result in financial loss to the church is clear from the royal confiscations in Protestant countries at the Reformation, and from what happened during the French Revolution. Neither political individualism nor entrepreneurial capitalism has ever really been favored by the Catholic church in any land. And with all due respect to the late Max Weber, the chief difference in this respect between Catholicism and Calvinism was that Calvinism proved in practice somewhat less unfavorable to capitalistic developments, most of which took place not in accord with the spirit of any Christian church, but in the face of constant opposition, until a *fait accompli* had perforce to be more or less grudgingly accepted.

V. THE BOURGEOISIE

A question even more difficult to answer than those we have already discussed is the extent to which the urban *bourgeoisie* in Europe between 1715 and 1740 had already the characteristics of the stock-figure "bourgeois" condemned by the Marxists. Factories, some of them with machinery run by water power, others mere collective workshops, already existed. There was already on the one hand an employing class and on the other a working class which in no sense owned or controlled instruments of production. There were considerable accumulations of capital seeking investment, and a rapidly developing commerce of world-wide scope. One would expect that between 1715 and 1740 any city dependent on manufacturing, commerce, and banking would already have what the nineteenth century considered a really "progressive" and "modern" attitude, resembling that of Manchester in the palmy days of oratory at the Free Trade Hall.

In writers like Defoe, not to mention professed economists, such an attitude was indeed already manifest, and many tradesmen in countries other than England acted in the spirit of Defoe's advice to British business people. But such forerunners of the nineteenth century as the Lembe's silk mill at Derby, or the Blackwell Hall factors, were probably far from typical or representative. What was a city dependent on trade, manufacture, and banking really like in the early eighteenth century? The answer is that every such European city at that time had local traditions, local peculiarities, and local institutions which, as in the case of the manors, make generalization peculiarly risky. The safest thing is perhaps to discuss not "the city" but a single city for which reasonably full data are to be had. Frankfurt am Main will provide a not untypical sample.[14]

Frankfurt was a free city, maintaining its own army of about thirty-five officers and from seven hundred to eight hundred men, coining money, administering justice according to its own laws as codified in the "Erneute Reformation" of 1578 with additions dating from 1611, governing itself in accordance with its traditional institutions, with senior and junior burgomasters as chief executives, and with a council or *Rat* as legislative

[14] Full details on Frankfurt may be found in *Die Stadt Goethes. Frankfurt am Main im XVIII Jahrhundert*, published by the city of Frankfurt to celebrate the centenary of Goethe's death, and edited by H. Voelcker, whose contributions to the collective work are especially important (Frankfurt am Main, 1932).

and administrative board. It had a bureaucracy of about five hundred members, out of a total population estimated to have been thirty-two thousand in 1700 and thirty-nine thousand in 1800. But it was also part of the Holy Roman Empire, the place indeed where the emperors were crowned. From its courts appeals could be taken by those able and willing to pay heavy fees to the imperial courts or to the emperor. In time of war seven of the eleven companies of Frankfurt's army joined the Nassau-Weilburg regiment of the imperial army, and the local militia replaced them on garrison duty at Frankfurt, still defended (rather inadequately) by its medieval walls and turrets. Frankfurt was part of an imperial circle and was represented in the *Corpus Evangelicorum*, guardian of the rights of German Protestants in the Holy Roman Empire, by its senior Lutheran minister, an important personage in the city who was always chosen from outside the city.

The ties binding the Imperial City to the Empire were not mere matters of form. In the early eighteenth century the repeated intervention of the emperor guided a reorganization of the city's administration, which between 1705 and 1732 took the form it retained until the nineteenth century. The burghers had appealed to the emperor against the financial mismanagement and the concentration of power in the hands of a patriciate which monopolized the administration. The patricians, who had long since been ennobled, claimed that the other burghers were their subjects and hence without political rights. But after prolonged and bitter disputes, the government was re-established on quasi-medieval corporate lines and the suzerainty of the emperor again recognized.[15]

The burghers of Frankfurt were not a single group or class. On the contrary, they were divided according to status, as indicated by birth and by occupation, into five *Stände* or ranks. According to medieval ordinances, renewed for the last time, as it proved, in 1731, the members of each rank were supposed to wear a distinctive and traditional style of dress. The Jews, of whom there were between two thousand and three thousand in Frankfurt's ghetto, the *Judengasse*, were also required to wear a costume identifying them on sight. They could not become burghers, but by imperial decree were protected in the limited rights allowed them. Religion, rather than any notion of "race," seems to have set the Jews apart.

Christians, too, were divided politically as well as socially by religious differences. Only Lutherans were eligible for municipal office in Frankfurt.

---

[15] See Paul Hohenemser, *Frankfurter Verfassungsstreit, 1705-1732* (Frankfurt am Main, 1920).

The numerous Calvinists of either French Huguenot or Reformed faith were not even permitted to hold religious services. Luckily the adjacent village of Bockenheim belonged not to Frankfurt but to Hesse-Cassel, and the Calvinists could go there for their church services. The smaller Roman Catholic minority in Frankfurt was under the protection of the Elector-Archbishop of Mainz, enjoying a kind of extraterritoriality which permitted several religious and charitable foundations in the city to remain in Catholic hands, and left the Catholics several churches and chapels in which they could hold services, as these places were not under the control of the city authorities. Religious processions of any sort, however, were strictly forbidden to the Catholics.

The composition of the five *Stände* is fairly typical of commercial cities like Frankfurt, where manufacturing, though not unimportant, was less important than wholesale trade and banking. The topmost rank included the *Schultheiss* (who, like the French *échevin*, was the link between the central and local authorities), the aldermen (the first bench in the *Rat*), the members of the second bench of the *Rat* and some other administrative officers, doctors of laws and divinity, the syndics, and those belonging to noble families which for at least a century had held positions in the city government. To the second rank belonged the remaining council members of the third bench, chosen from the guilds, outstanding citizens, and all wholesale merchants with fortunes of at least twenty thousand thaler. The third rank included lawyers, artists (including some craftsmen like jewel cutters), and retail shopkeepers. To the fourth belonged ordinary poor retailers, employees of merchants, handicraftsmen; and to the lowest, the fifth rank, day laborers, servants, and suchlike. This grouping into *Stände* with a requirement, apparently not rigidly enforced, of distinctive costumes, had no reference to religion or to being a burgher (freeman). The real distinction was between the upper two classes and the lower orders.

The well to do, the nobility and gentry, and the holders of university degrees formed a patriciate which after the reforms still controlled the government, since it had a majority of the *Rat* as well as leadership in business and the professions. By the eighteenth century such an urban aristocracy or oligarchy existed in most of the older Continental cities, such as Genoa, Venice, and Amsterdam, which had grown rich through trade.[16]

[16] For Amsterdam, see J. E. Elias, *Geschiedenis van het Amsterdamsche regentenpatriciaat* (Gravenhage, 1923); for Bordeaux, A. Nicolai, "La population de Bordeaux au XVIII° siècle," *Revue économique de Bordeaux*, XVIII (1908), 76-102; for Lille, M. Braure, *Lille et la Flandre wallonne au XVIII° siècle* (Lille, 1932); for Bristol, John Latimer, *The Annals of Bristol in the Eighteenth Century* (Frome and London, 1893); for Nantes, Martin, *Nantes au XVIII° siècle*.

The members of the Frankfurt *Rat* were chosen after the reform by committees of the *Rat*, but near relatives by blood or marriage of members might no longer be selected. Once chosen, the members served for life subject to good behavior. Only eight of the existing thirty-four guilds were represented on the third bench, but the two memberships formerly belonging to the woolen weavers, who no longer existed, were given to members of the remaining guilds.

The political power of the guilds in Frankfurt had been lost before the Thirty Years' War. The eighteenth-century reforms did nothing to restore it. Charles VI as suzerain of the Imperial City merely insisted on the breaking up of the small clique of families which had completely dominated the Frankfurt regime, by the new rule excluding relatives of members, and provided several commissions to supervise finances, so chosen as to represent the whole of the propertied classes, Jews not included.

The guilds of craftsmen and retailers were kept alive chiefly as a means of excluding outsiders and competitors from all occupations so organized. Newcomers to the city, if Lutherans, could obtain admission to a guild, but in practice this could be effected only by marrying the widow or the daughter of a member. The policy of the ruling patriciate was to encourage small independent retailers and craftsmen. They refused to permit the establishment of factories or workshops employing large numbers of wage earners within the territory belonging to the city. But foreign merchants with substantial capital could establish themselves in the city without much difficulty, even after an ordinance of 1708 had restricted their right to trade outside fair time, by requiring them to be registered with the municipality, and to engage only in wholesale trade. After ten years' residence the payment of a substantial fee would in fact suffice to win admission as a burgher for almost any Christian capitalist willing to conform nominally to the Lutheran church.

Resident aliens paid heavier taxes, as did the Jews, who in their self-governing ghetto enjoyed a kind of extraterritoriality. The Jews had an imposing synagogue in the *Judengasse* long before the Calvinist Protestants were permitted a church in Lutheran Frankfurt. But no Jew could ever become a burgher, or live outside the ghetto, or compete openly with guild members. By the eighteenth century, however, there were a number of trades which were without guild organization, and so more readily open to newcomers. The spirit of the Frankfurt guilds in the eighteenth century reminds one of the craft unions of the American Federation of Labor today. The restriction on membership, the preference given to sons of members, represent merely a clinging to a means of livelihood. In the eighteenth century the craft guilds in many, perhaps in most cities where they survived, resembled those at Frankfurt.[17]

A rather cursory examination of the political, social, and economic organization of eighteenth-century Frankfurt indicates that in urban and bourgeois life the cult of stability was almost as strong as in rural areas. Newcomers, innovators, dissenters of all sorts were sharply restricted. Traditional ways were followed and defended by the great majority, not merely because they were traditional, but because they offered a satisfactory life to each of the subdivisions of the *bourgeoisie*.

And yet there was a career open to talent in Frankfurt, as there was nearly everywhere under the Old Regime. This is shown by the case of the Goethe family. Goethe's grandfather, son of a blacksmith in rural Thuringia, had become a journeyman tailor, had lived in Paris whence he was driven by the revocation of the Edict of Nantes, had come to Frankfurt, married the daughter of a master tailor, been admitted as a burgher, prospered as a "ladies' tailor," and eventually, after a second marriage with the widow of an innkeeper, set up in that business, in which he accumulated a small fortune. Goethe's father was sent to the university, became a doctor of laws, purchased an imperial councilorship, built or rather rebuilt a fine house, and lived as a *rentier*. Goethe's mother was the daughter of the *Stadtschultheiss* Texter, of an old bourgeois family in Frankfurt. Goethe himself, by becoming a minister to the Duke of Saxe-Weimar, followed the career of a professional bureaucrat which was frequently entered upon by sons of families in the first rank in such cities as Frankfurt. Only through the ducal connection, however, was Goethe finally accepted as a social equal by the Frankfurt noble families of long descent, though his parents belonged to the first of the five *Stände* and had greater wealth than many of the old first families.

VI. THE CORPORATE IDEAL

The institutions and the stability of the Old Regime were based on a corporate ideal which differed markedly not only from the individualism of the capitalist entrepreneur and of the nineteenth-century liberal, but also from the much-discussed "corporate state" of the totalitarian regimes in Germany, Italy, and Russia.

For most men under the Old Regime personal, family, and group ties

[17] See for England, Lipson, *Economic History of England*, III, 330-351; for France, H. Sée, *Histoire économique de la France* (Paris, 1939), and Olivier-Martin, *L'organisation corporative de la France d'ancien régime* (Paris, 1938).

were what bound them to society and entitled them to their appointed share in the commonwealth. The whole spirit of the Old Regime is expressed in two well-known passages of Burke: the eloquent passage, perhaps the best known that he wrote, which tells us that "Society is indeed a contract," between past, present, and future, a partnership in all art and in all science, the aims of which are not to be attained in a single generation; and the simpler one, also from the *Reflections on the French Revolution*, which says that each man

has a right to a fair portion of all which society, with all its combinations of skill and force, can do in his favor. In this partnership all men have equal rights, but not to equal things. He that has but five shillings in the partnership, has as good a right to it as he that has five hundred pounds has to the larger proportion. But he has not a right to an equal dividend in the product of the joint stock.

Or, as Burke goes on to say, to any share of power or authority and direction in the management of the state, "a thing to be settled by convention," that is, by tradition and custom.

The Old Regime did not believe in political or in social equality. It did not think in terms of individualism. The tie binding the individual to the community was not an impersonal citizenship in an impersonal state, but a status in a social hierarchy with innumerable gradations from the peasant or artisan at the bottom to the king at the top. The concept "class" does not, as Marx himself recognized, really fit the facts of the Old Regime. Still less the class struggle. The *bourgeoisie*, by which Marx means the entrepreneurial capitalist, has "simplified the class antagonisms," "put an end to all feudal, idyllic patriarchal relations," "pitilessly torn asunder the motley feudal ties that bound man to his 'natural superiors,'" and has left no bond between man and man other "than naked self interest, than callous 'cash payment.'" "In place of the numberless indefeasible chartered freedoms" it has set up "that single unconscionable freedom—Free Trade." In the opening paragraphs of the *Communist Manifesto* of 1848 from which all the above quotations are taken, Marx, of course, concluded that "for exploitation, veiled by religious and political illusions," the *bourgeoisie* has "substituted naked, shameless, direct brutal exploitation." For a professed materialist like Marx all ideals were naturally "religious and political illusions." And it is certainly true that under the Old Regime, as under all regimes, there was not a little exploitation of the underprivileged by the overprivileged. But the noteworthy thing is Marx's clear preference for the Old Regime over the nineteenth century.

It is in the "numberless chartered freedoms" that the ideals of the Old Regime centered. In theory, everyone had a place in the commonwealth with a charter to some portion, however small, of indefeasible freedom. It might be no more than the right of a peasant to pasture a cow on the manorial common, to gather dead branches in the woods, or to let his pigs forage there for acorns. But this right was as indefeasible as any the king or the pope possessed. Perhaps the hardest point for the modern reader to grasp about these indefeasible rights is that none of them were uniform, even within a single country, despite many analogies. In the eighteenth century they were everywhere enforced by law and by custom. Nobody but a despot could really shatter the Old Regime and substitute a "planned economy," or a laissez-faire economy. Peter the Great and Frederick the Great were less successful than Napoleon in imposing uniformities dictated by "the light of reason," and sanctioned by the wishes of the businessman, not merely because those monarchs came earlier, but because, being rulers by heredity, they were themselves more bound to the Old Regime than a dictator coming after a revolution could be.

The extent to which this corporate ideal was attained in practice by the Europe of 1715-1740 may be judged by the provisions made for the orphan, the vagrant, the person without a status entailing on him its privileges as well as its restrictions. These provisions in theory consisted in reintegrating the unfortunate individual into the commonwealth by providing for him a status, unless his crimes were such that the galleys, or the scaffold, or banishment from the European world to a colony beyond the seas appeared justified. Religious heresy as well as theft or murder was still almost everywhere legally felonious, though by 1715 heretics in the more "enlightened" countries were in fact more frequently ignored and thus tolerated than sent to the scaffold or even into exile.

The urban orphan was by law apprenticed to learn a trade which would not merely fit him to earn a living, but would also gain him membership in a guild and entitle him to freedom of the city. The rural pauper in England had in theory the right of "settlement," gained by birth. If he belonged in a parish, that parish had to make some provision for him and for his widow and minor children in case of need. The assumption was that any able-bodied man could get a living from the land and prior to the enclosures it was usually not difficult for him to get a cottage and a little land under some form of tenure. An Elizabethan act, still unrepealed but not actively enforced, provided that every household in a rural parish should have a cottage and four acres of land. If a man was found tramping about the country or loafing instead of working, the law assumed what was probably usually the fact, that he was "a sturdy beggar," willfully idle. There was a series of acts repressing such vagrants. They were first to be stripped to the waist, women as well as men, publicly whipped until the blood ran, then returned to the parish where they belonged. For the incorrigibly idle and disorderly, houses of correction were provided, where, in theory, such persons would be forced to earn their keep.[18]

The Act of Settlement and of Removal, passed in 1662, provided for the forcible removal to the parish of settlement of all persons likely to become public charges. In practice, able-bodied single men were not usually interfered with. If they left home to work elsewhere they could generally without difficulty obtain from their own parish a certificate that it would be responsible for them, and this ensured them against molestation elsewhere. The effect of the act was that the local officers of the fifteen thousand English parishes inflicted harsh treatment on widows with small children and especially on unmarried mothers who were always sent back to their original parish. In eighteenth-century England the central government left poor relief, like the rest of local government, almost entirely in the hands of local authorities, in this case of parish authorities, who were empowered to levy a special tax, the poor rate, to pay the cost of relieving the indigent poor. A poorhouse was usually provided in which feeble-minded, insane, aged, orphans, prostitutes, drunks, and tramps were all grouped with no separation of sexes and with no distinction of innocent from vicious persons. Meat six times a week and beer three times a day seem also to have been usually given. The lazy and the rowdy poor probably enjoyed these rather lively and hearty, if invariably dirty and lousy conditions, just as they did the similar life in the eighteenth-century prisons when their vices had gotten them committed to jail. But for the quiet and decent poor the conditions were almost intolerable, not merely in the primitive rural cottage poorhouse, but in the elaborate institutional housing which by the 1720's was beginning to be provided in some parishes.

In London, which already had a population of nearly a million, the majority of the poor were immigrants from rural England, or from Scotland, Ireland, or the Continent. Those who remember Hogarth's "Gin Lane" will not need to be told that there was an urban proletariat in the great city, with housing conditions, sanitation, education, and

---

[18] See Webb, *English Local Government*, VII: *The Old Poor Law;* and Dorothy Marshall, *The English Poor in the Eighteenth Century* (London, 1926).

public morals at a level far below that of the East End today, or even, it would appear, of the worst days of the nineteenth century.[19]

The oft-repeated story of the sign which read "drunk for a penny, dead drunk for tuppence" seen in a gin-shop window cannot be proved true. Yet it sums up accurately enough the horrible conditions of the London poor. The metropolis had outgrown its bounds, so that by far the greater number of Londoners did not live in the City of London, but in parishes once rural and still under a local government adapted only to rural conditions. In such parishes guild restrictions either did not exist or did little to alleviate the condition of the wage earners. Some trades were relatively well paid and not unprosperous, others were, to use a modern term, "sweated." There was no governmental provision for education, no control of sanitation or of overcrowding, no police force, no regulation of wages or of hours of labor, no interference with child labor. The assumption was that those who did not like London, or became distressed there, could and should return to their country homes. As the London death rate exceeded the birth rate, and the metropolis was growing rapidly, it was true that many, probably a majority of the London poor, were not natives but immigrants from country parishes, or from Ireland or Scotland.

Judged by modern standards, there were few other great cities in Europe. Paris alone seems to have been almost as populous as London, with half a million inhabitants. Vienna had about 250,000, Berlin about 150,000. But for all great towns of 100,000 or more the corporate ideal as exemplified by Frankfurt am Main had already broken down completely. At Frankfurt the entrepreneurs were rugged individualists on the make, but they did not yet dominate the political, economic, or social life of the city. In London the "City" with its traditional medieval liberties and its liveried companies was a richer and greater Frankfurt, but the population of the sprawling suburbs, except for the limited area inhabited by the nobility and gentry who came to town for a few months each year, was a mob easily roused to rioting. Such instances as the Sacheverell riots in 1709, the demonstrations against Walpole's excise bill, and the Gordon riots of 1780 were without parallel in Paris or in other great cities in Europe, until 1789. It was London which made England the *pays classique de l'émeute*, the traditional home of mob violence to eighteenth-century observers. The cult of stability failed in the end, partly because it did

[19] See M. Dorothy George, *London Life in the Eighteenth Century* (London, 1925). For the view that the proletariat was worse off after the so-called industrial revolution, see J. L. and Barbara Hammond, *The Town Labourer, 1760-1832* (London, 1925). The weight of expert opinion, such as that of J. H. Clapham, would seem to favor Mrs. George's view that conditions in the period 1720-1750 were at their worst.

nothing to better the condition of the London mob beyond raising the price of gin by heavy taxation and so somewhat reducing public drunkenness. Neither manor nor guild were institutions with any real bearing on the actual state of the urban wage earners of the metropolis. The humanitarian provision of orphan asylums and hospitals, both usually not well administered, had little effect beyond keeping alive persons probably better dead. The origin of the word "bedlam" for an unendurable noise and bustle is significant. It comes from the Bethlehem Hospital for the Insane, one of the sights shown to tourists in eighteenth-century London, most of whom found the maniacs as laughable as drunks are still supposed to be in farces.

The actual working in such cities as London of the provision in the English poor law which required parish authorities to arrange apprenticeship for children when necessary, is indicated by a comment published in 1738.

A most unhappy practice prevails in most places to apprentice poor children, no matter to what master, provided he lives out of the parish, if the child serves the first forty days we are rid of him for ever. The master may be a tiger in cruelty, he may beat, abuse, strip naked, starve or do what he will to the poor innocent lad, few people take much notice, and the officers who put him out the least of anybody. For they rest satisfied with the merit of having shifted him off to a neighbouring parish for three or four pounds and the duty they owe to every poor child in the parish is no further laid to heart. The greatest part of those who now take poor apprentices are the most indigent and dishonest, in a word, the very dregs of the poor of England, by whom it is the fate of many a poor child, not only to be half-starved and sometimes bred up in no trade, but to be forced to thieve and steal for his master, and so is brought up for the gallows into the bargain.[20]

Mrs. George has collected many case histories which appear to substantiate the accuracy of this comment. The treatment of poor apprentices who had relatives able to look out for them was somewhat better, since the courts would punish abuses if the evidence was clear and the case flagrant. Apprenticeship, often with the payment of a premium, remained in the eighteenth century the usual way of starting life in a business or a trade. Foundling children, put out to nurse by the parishes in London, seldom lived long. The parish in which they were born was legally responsible for them. The usual custom was to get from the putative father, if possible, a sum of ten pounds, the greater part of which was spent by

[20] *Enquiry into the Causes of the Encrease and Miseries of the Poor of England* (London, 1738), quoted by George, *London Life in the Eighteenth Century*, 227.

the parish officers on a "feast," and not devoted to the purpose of providing a nurse. Mrs. George was able to adduce detailed figures, and much other testimony indicates that about nine out of ten of these "bastard brats" died in infancy. By the end of the century numbers of them survived, only to be apprenticed in the cotton factories described by Mr. and Mrs. Hammond. Compared with the lot of the poor in Cambridgeshire and Northamptonshire, regions for which modern detailed surveys have appeared, the London poor were far worse off, simply because the quasi-medieval corporate ideal remained alive in rural parishes and in such towns as Wisbech, where those in distress were usually neighbors known personally to the parish officers.[21]

London municipal government and that of other English commercial cities, on the other hand, tended to be dominated by the ideas of the merchant class. Defoe's pamphlet, *Giving Alms no Charity*, published in 1703, stated what were already coming to be the prevalent notions of this class about poor relief.

The reason why so many pretend to want work is that they can live so well with the pretence of wanting work they would be mad to leave it and work in earnest. And I affirm of my own knowledge, when I have wanted a man for labouring work, and offered 9s. per week to strolling fellows at my door, they have frequently told me to my face they could get more a-begging.

These remarks were incidental to his main argument, directed against a proposal then before Parliament to establish "houses of industry" in which the unemployed poor could be given materials and tools and enabled to earn a living. As Defoe pointed out, unless the consumption of manufactured articles could be increased this could only mean competition with existing business, "putting a vagabond in an honest man's employment" and thus driving the honest man into difficulties caused by unfair state-aided competition.

The upshot of much discussion and many proposals was an act of Parliament in 1723, introduced by Sir Edward Knatchbull, enabling the officers of individual parishes to hire premises and maintain them as workhouses for the poor. Those who would not go into the workhouses were then to be refused all relief. This was suggested by an experiment already tried at Bristol. Within a decade about a hundred parishes, mostly urban, were imposing under this act what was later called "the workhouse

---

[21] See Miss E. M. Hampson's careful study, "The Treatment of Poverty in Cambridgeshire, 1597-1834," in *Cambridge Studies in Economic History*, ed. J. H. Clapham (Cambridge, Eng., 1934); and J. D. Chambers, *Nottinghamshire in the Eighteenth Century* (London, 1932), esp. chap. viii.

test." As the work was purposely made disagreeable, the poor preferred to refuse to enter the workhouses, and the poor rate fell. Since neither efficient management, nor any attempt to separate the paupers into such obvious classifications as the feeble-minded, the aged, the orphans, and the able-bodied, characterized these workhouses, they were later abandoned for the outdoor relief of the Speenhamland system. To the merchant class, poverty seemed if not a crime at least a misdemeanor, to be punished not remedied.

In Catholic countries on the Continent the church still took care of the poor and provided institutions, often largely endowed, for the care of the sick, the orphans, and the insane. The doing of good works aided in the salvation of the souls of pious and charitable donors, and the management, nursing, and other care was done by religious orders like the Sisters of Charity (founded by St. Vincent de Paul in 1633). The work of these orders, despite its faults, was certainly more successful in alleviating the sufferings of the poor than the English poor law of the eighteenth century.[22]

In Prussia the church retained a large part of its traditional position as the giver of alms to the needy. But as the Lutheran and Calvinist churches, after the Reformation, did not possess resources sufficient for their needs, or retain a hierarchy, the king, partly as head of the state and partly in a quasi-episcopal capacity as head of the church, allocated money to supplement church income from tithes and poor boxes. Poor relief, like every other activity of the state, was controlled by the bureaucracy under the personal supervision of the monarch. As the Hohenzollerns were Calvinists ruling a country in which the vast majority of the population was Lutheran, the position of the minority religions, even the Catholics, was better than that of English dissenters, not because the Hohenzollerns before Frederick the Great were tolerant, but for the reasons which impelled James II as Catholic king of Protestant England to favor increased tolerance of dissenters. State funds were given to both Calvinist and Lutheran churches.

The general economic and social policy of Prussia favored social security for every man according to his rank, so there was none of Defoe's dis-

[22] See Léon Lallemand, *Histoire de la charité* (Paris, 1902-1912), for the general history. For eighteenth-century France, see G. Valran, *Misère & charité en Provence au XVIIIe siècle* (Paris, 1899), mostly about conditions at Aix. E. Chaudron, *L'assistance publique à Troyes, 1770-1800* (Paris, 1923), and Camille Bloch, *L'assistance & l'état en France à la veille de la révolution* (Paris, 1908), give some details about earlier periods. State intervention on a large scale began only in the time of Turgot. For Spain, see Desdevises du Dézert, *L'Espagne de l'ancien régime*, II, 207-214.

position to let the poor starve on the ground that they were undeserving. The situation in other Protestant countries where the state did not interfere was more or less like that at Montbéliard, an enclave in French territory belonging to the Duke of Württemberg, with a Protestant population. Here there were trust funds, some of them established long ago by pious donors to aid the poor, but the municipal authorities who administered them tended to borrow the income in times of stress and delay or neglect repayment.[23]

The provision made for the destitute by private and public charity was, in the Europe of the early eighteenth century, then, not merely the giving of alms, but in most cases a recognition that the distressed belonged to some more or less corporate group which was responsible for them. Only in English commercial cities like London and Bristol was "cash payment the sole nexus between man and man." Here the beginnings of the nineteenth-century *bourgeoisie* and the nineteenth-century proletariat can be traced. What we now call "social security" is not a new ideal but a traditional ideal.

It is not possible in a brief and cursory treatment to discuss in detail other examples of the corporate ideal of the Old Regime in theory and practice. The universities were one of many instances that could be elaborated upon. The French government's attempt in the eighteenth century to revive and broaden the trade and craft guilds so they should include all workingmen was plainly inspired by the corporate ideal. But, as we shall see, the current of ideas was already strongly in the direction of individualism, liberty, equality, and *laissez faire*, all equally contrary to the corporate tradition inherited by the eighteenth century.[24]

VII. PATRONAGE AND LEADERSHIP

The relationship between man and man under the Old Regime was still as a rule a personal bond, often quasi-feudal in character. The corporate ideal was not an impersonal and impartially disciplined group of men like the Prussian army or the Jesuit order, both exceptional and

[23] See Pariset, *L'état et les églises*, for Prussia; and for Montbéliard, Madeleine Fortin, *La charité et l'assistance publique à Montbéliard sous l'ancien régime* (Besançon, 1933).

[24] See the cautious and tentative approach to the Old Regime in terms of the corporate ideal by Olivier-Martin, *L'organisation corporative de la France d'ancien régime*, and the somewhat more theoretical and, in my judgment, less sound and scholarly attitude of some of the writers in the studies under the auspices of the "Commission internationale pour l'histoire des assemblées d'états" entitled: *L'organisation corporative du moyen âge à la fin de l'ancien régime* (Louvain, 1937-1939), written in terms of political theory rather than of history.

still relatively novel developments, but was an extension of the family. Society was everywhere organized into small local units, manors, seigneurys, parishes, cities, New England townships, Virginia plantations, under a leadership which was personal and traditional, respecting the vested interests of the humblest subject. The Chinese empire as it existed until 1911 has been called "an autocracy superimposed on a democracy." The emperor and his agents, the mandarins, did not interfere with local administration, carried on by groups which resembled both guilds and clans. They merely insisted that taxes and "squeeze" (traditional perquisites of the mandarins) be paid. The European Old Regime was also in some ways an autocracy superimposed on democracy, if by democracy one understands the kind of government favored by most of the members of the American Constitutional Convention of 1787 and not that later advocated by Andrew Jackson.

The dynastic state at first merely wished to collect taxes regularly in order to support the army, defend the realm, and, when the royal patrimony was inadequate, maintain the king and his court in the luxury appropriate to their exalted station. The beneficent despotism of the French intendants and of the Hohenzollerns in the eighteenth century was a modern innovation often subversive of the old order of things. The success or failure of the cult of stability, its preservation under the altered conditions of the eighteenth century, with its commercial expansion and its wars of the Old Regime, depended chiefly on the character of the leadership in the country and the provincial cities, not on the courtiers and bureaucrats as such. The personal qualities of the monarchs themselves were, however, of immense importance. The power of all the lesser leaders depended on that of the crown, to which they owed a personal quasi-feudal allegiance. The local leaders, obviously, were the link between crown and subjects.

The work of Beatrice and Sidney Webb on English local government and that of L. B. Namier on the structure of English politics has shown clearly the unreality of what Namier describes as "the first article of constitutional cant," namely the description of "the right of freely choosing representatives as 'the most valuable privilege of every English freeholder.' " In reality, as Namier points out,

neither in counties nor in boroughs was the least attempt made to hide or disguise the methods of compulsion and intimidation by which votes were secured; the resultant of social forces was thus obtained without recourse to election stunts. It was taken for granted that the tenants would vote as instructed by their landlord or his agent . . . the political position of a man in his county, and even to some extent the claim which he could urge for appearing as a candidate for its representation in Parliament, was measured by his rental.

These conditions were "the inevitable result of open voting by people in dependent positions." It will be remembered by readers of Dickens or of Trollope that English parliamentary elections in the nineteenth century were still, despite "reform bills," subject to the influence of the leading gentry both in boroughs and in counties.[25]

In the eighteenth century contested elections were rare. For example, no election was contested for the county of Nottingham from 1722 to the beginning of the nineteenth century. In Nottingham borough, where the franchise was wide, so that most men had votes, "there appears to have been no real political issue at stake outside the manoeuvring of aristocratic factions" in eighteenth-century elections prior to 1776, when the framework knitters secured representatives pledged to advance a bill on their behalf in the House of Commons. The Duke of Newcastle was usually able to secure the election of four of the eight members from Nottinghamshire (two for the county and two for each of the boroughs of Nottingham, Newark, and East Retford). He sometimes had to spend a good deal of money from his private fortune, which was greatly reduced by his half century of electioneering. He nominated to only one seat in each pair, leaving the other member, as a rule, to be chosen by the local gentry.[26]

In England the administration of justice remained largely in the hands of the gentry in each locality, who served without pay by appointment from the crown as justices of the peace. Their jurisdiction did not extend to felonies, which were tried by the judges on circuit, but they initiated all criminal proceedings by issuing warrants for the arrest of accused persons. Petty offenses were tried before justices of the peace. This judicial power was sometimes gravely abused. It gave all of the gentry a means of control over the lower orders in society, since those gentlemen who were not themselves justices always were friends and neighbors of justices. The Webbs refer in this connection to a passage in Fielding's *Joseph Andrews*, written by a member of a county family who later himself became a London magistrate:

Lady Booby, whom the virtuous Joseph (in parody of Richardson's

[25] The quoted phrases are all from L. B. Namier, *The Structure of Politics at the Accession of George III* (London, 1929), I, 87-88.

[26] Chambers, *Nottinghamshire in the Eighteenth Century*, 30-35. See also, Namier, *Structure of Politics*, I.

Pamela) has spurned, is furious because Joseph, whom she has dismissed from her service, wishes to marry a pretty girl in his own humble walk of life. So she tries to make trouble by appealing to a justice for a warrant against the pair, on a trumped-up charge. They are saved by the intervention of Joseph's brother-in-law, Pamela's husband, who of course is one of the gentry himself. The dialogue is a sidelight on history.

"Would you commit two persons to Bridewell for a twig?"

"Yes," said the lawyer, "and with great lenity too; for if we had called it a young tree, they would have been both hanged."

"Harkee," says the justice, talking aside to the squire; "I should not have been so severe on this occasion, but Lady Booby desires to get them out of the parish; so lawyer Scout will give the constable orders to let them run away, if they please: but it seems they intend to marry together, and the lady hath no other means, as they are legally settled there, to prevent their bringing an incumbrance on her own parish."[27]

Joseph and Fanny were what the eighteenth century often called "foreigners," that is, persons from another part of the country, who had, under the Act of Settlement discussed above, become legally settled by being servants for more than a year in the Booby household. As they were unlikely to acquire a holding of land, there was real danger that they and their children would "come on the parish," so that there is some excuse for the severity of the justice from a parochial point of view. Had they been natives and tenants, justice and squire would have been their patrons and defenders, just as Parson Adams, whom they encounter on the way from the justice's, is prepared to be.

Patronage, indeed, was an inevitable accompaniment of the corporate ideal. The successful leader, great or small, was under the Old Regime in a quasi-patriarchal relationship to his dependents. It is significant that his entire household was usually called his family, though it invariably included many persons not related by blood or by marriage. In French the word *maison* had a similar use, meaning both family in the biological sense and household. One way to get on in the world was to find a patron and enter his household. Of this innumerable instances could be cited. Members of the governing classes had a far greater number of dependents, clients in the Roman sense of the word, who were not in their immediate household, but whose claim on them for protection and aid was still quasi-feudal. These personal relationships ran from top to bottom of the social hierarchy, in a complex pattern. Only the urban entrepreneur and

[27] Henry Fielding, *Joseph Andrews* (first published in 1742), Bk. IV, chap. v.

the urban proletariat of such great commercial cities as London were not involved in the web. Only for these two groups was "individualism," to use a nineteenth-century word for it, already the prevailing attitude.[28]

Namier's study of English politics has shown the extent to which members of the House of Commons were involved in these personal ties, to which they frequently owed their election. It was much more by a careful distribution of patronage in Parliament and the constituencies, resembling that carried out by United States senators today, than by bribery or corruption that the Duke of Newcastle, chief political manager for the Whigs through the two reigns when they were "supreme," collected majorities for Walpole and subsequent prime ministers.

As the Duke of Wellington later remarked, there was "No damned nonsense about merit" in appointments to government positions. George I and George II, however, favored merit in army promotions to the upper ranks. It was a standing grievance with Newcastle that he never could get army patronage into his hands. That the eighteenth century saw nothing wrong in patronage is illustrated by an epitaph quoted by Trevelyan.

> Here rest all that was mortal of Mrs. Elizabeth Bate,
> Relict of the Reverend Richard Bate,
> A woman of unaffected piety
> And exemplary virtue
>
> **********
>
> She was honourably descended
> And by means of her Alliance to
> The illustrious family of Stanhope
> She had the merit to obtain
> For her husband and children
> Twelve separate employments
> In Church and State.
> She died June 9, 1751, in the 75th year of her age.[29]

Yet the Parliament and the administration so constituted were more than adequate to the task of ruling England and her empire. They

[28] The earliest recorded use of the word "individualism" is in the English translation of A. de Tocqueville's *Democracy in America* (London, 1840). Tocqueville, who apparently coined the term "individualisme," says that it is "a novel expression to which a novel idea has given birth." See article on "Individualism" by A. D. Lindsay in *Encyclopaedia of the Social Sciences*, VII, 674-680; and *Oxford English Dictionary*, ed. J. A. H. Murray and others (Oxford, 1888-1928).

[29] Trevelyan, *England under Queen Anne*, III, 317, quoting John Nichols, *Literary Anecdotes of the Eighteenth Century* (London, 1812-1816), III, 52.

preserved and extended the checks against royal despotism secured at the 1688 Revolution. They maintained the favorable position in the world which Britain had won in Marlborough's wars. The prestige of Parliament as an institution, according to Basil Williams, has never been greater than between 1714 and 1760, nor its debates more brilliant or more statesmanlike. Contemporaries discounted as merely political opposition the complaints of Bolingbroke's followers about "corruption," as historians are again learning to·do. Nobody wanted the government to interfere in merely local affairs, after the fashion of the French intendants and the Prussian autocrats.

A good test of the personal and human quality of French eighteenth-century administration is furnished by the way in which the *lettres de cachet* were actually used. It is hardly necessary to say that the nineteenth-century fairy tales about Louis XV giving his mistresses *lettres de cachet* with the name of the person to be imprisoned left blank do not correspond with the facts as revealed by modern research. A *lettre de cachet* was a royal warrant to arrest a person who would then be held in custody at the pleasure of the administration. Its secrecy·and its swiftness made it the usual method adopted by persons wishing to restrain a member of their family from disgracing it. Young men who wished to marry unsuitably, or who were idle˙and disorderly, could by this means be put in custody without being given a criminal record. Though it is obvious that so arbitrary a procedure might easily be abused, especially if employed, as it seldom was in fact, against political offenders, the *lettre de cachet* often did more good than harm. The surviving records, which in the eighteenth century were kept rigidly secret, prove not merely that the officials responsible were usually very careful to investigate before issuing a *lettre de cachet*, but that they showed remarkable patience in studying the full details of the family quarrels of quite humble persons.[30]

Thus even in apparently despotic and authoritarian governments the Old Regime was characterized by a personal quasi-feudal leadership. The economic organization of the manor and the seigneury in the apparently unchanging countryside and the persistence of corporate traditions in urban life made for a local self-sufficiency and independence which was diminishing, but not necessarily vanishing, as the dynastic states grew strong and commerce became world-wide. If wars could have been localized so that they were not costly enough and dangerous

---

[30] See F. Funck-Brentano, *The Old Regime in France* (New York, 1929), 201-231, a readable and semipopular account, but in accordance with the numerous monographs.

enough to necessitate great national efforts at concentrating economic and military power against a foreign foe, the Old Regime might have continued almost indefinitely, provided that the problem of reconciling a central control of the state with a large degree of local autonomy had been solved elsewhere as effectively as it actually was in England.

The problem of leadership under the Old Regime had two phases, local leadership by squires, parsons, burgomasters, and urban patricians, and national leadership under royal, imperial, or papal authority. If, as in Italy, there were no national leadership, the country was constantly menaced by foreign domination dangerous not merely to its pride but to its economic security. It is no accident that so many of the wars of the Old Regime were fought on Italian and German soil. The Rhineland, Belgium, and much of Italy were in this period not merely centers of culture and of the arts, but also both in agriculture and in manufactures fully as advanced as England and France.

The industrial backwardness of Italy, for instance, dates only from the introduction of steam power. Until the coal and iron she lacks became indispensable to industrial success Italy was relatively rich and progressive. Her painting and her literature in the early eighteenth century were not of the same high standard of excellence that had obtained in earlier centuries, but her music was still unexcelled, if one omit two great geniuses, Bach and Handel, both strongly under Italian influence. Her great cities, Genoa, Venice, Milan, Florence, Rome, Naples, and the rest were still important financial and commercial centers.

For an understanding of the Old Regime it is necessary to remember that in some of the most highly civilized parts of Europe the growth of the leviathan state did not occur until the nineteenth century. Italy is even more typical of the Old Regime than France. A rich field of historical investigation, with abundant source material, has so far remained uncultivated by the "new historians" to whom it ought to make a strong appeal. Italian national unification was necessary not so much for internal stability and order, which was attained in such city-states as Genoa and in Tuscany under the Hapsburgs, as for protection against aggressors.

Turning to problems of local leadership, one is faced by the obvious fact that under the Old Regime this tended to become hereditary in families, although ability is not necessarily inherited. The biologists are not in agreement on the question, but there is a good deal of evidence to support the view that a boy born of an able father is rather more likely to be able himself than the son of a mediocre father. Local leadership in ordinary times does not demand transcendent genius. What is needed are men of no more than ordinary gifts guided by a tradition which crystallizes the wisdom of experience, and opportunity for a limited number of exceptionally able men to rise from humble origins into the ruling class. To demand more than this in any social and political system is to expect Plato's "Republic" to be attained. The eighteenth century did not make its philosophers (rather unplatonic ones) kings, but it eventually came to expect that its kings would be philosophers. For example, in the case of Joseph II the ideal of beneficent despotism was to prove not merely subversive of the Old Regime, but wholly impracticable.

It would be hard to prove that the kind of life lived by the population of Europe in 1740, at the end of the era when the cult of stability dominated, was less satisfactory in terms of human needs and desires than the kind of life lived in Europe in the year 1940. Both were war years, so that the comparison is not unfair. In 1740 the problems confronting the leaders were so much simpler, and the situation was so much more stable, at least in appearance, that there seemed no danger of collapse or chaos. But the intellectuals were already actively dissatisfied with stability and all for progress, reason, and other new notions, most of them dangerous to the existing regime.

Chapter Six

THE APPEAL TO NATURE AND REASON

1. TABULA RASA

THE cult of stability of conservatives after 1715 was menaced by the opinions held by the intelligentsia, especially in England. The ideas of Locke, Shaftesbury, Mandeville, Hutcheson, and the deists were, from the point of view of supporters of the established order, "dangerous thoughts"; should they become generally accepted among the governing class, they were bound to subvert the Old Regime. The immense prestige of Sir Isaac Newton, whose work in physics and mechanics had been completed but not popularized before 1715, had encouraged hopes that all branches of knowledge could be reduced to a few simple, uniform laws which any educated man could understand and every reasonable man must accept. The search for such laws of nature and of human nature was expected to reveal that a few simple principles of uniform and universal application underlay all the apparent complexity and contradiction of man and of human society. Reason would then enable an enlightened world to make its institutions conform to natural law.

Even David Hume, whose later skepticism is well known, as a young man consciously set out to become the Newton of human nature. "There is no question of importance whose decision is not comprised in the science of man." "It is evident that all the sciences have a relation, greater or less, to human nature," he wrote.[1] More indebted to Locke's *Essay Concerning Human Understanding* than he acknowledged, Hume undertook to work out on Newtonian principles a scientific psychology.

We must glean up our experiments from a cautious observation of human life, and take them as they appear in the common course of the world, by men's behavior in company, in affairs, and in their pleasures. Where experiments of this kind are judiciously collected and compared, we may hope to establish

---

[1] Hume, *A Treatise of Human Nature*, Everyman ed. (London, 1911; first published in 1739), I, 405. See also J. Laird, *Hume's Philosophy of Human Nature* (New York, 1932), 20-24.

on them a science, which will not be inferior in certainty, and will be much superior in utility to any other of human comprehension.[2]

This point of view was also that of Shaftesbury, an earlier disciple of Locke. Hume however admitted, as Locke had also done, that "any hypothesis that pretends to discover the ultimate original qualities of human nature ought . . . to be rejected as presumptuous and chimerical." He was, then, relying more on experience than on experiment. If his work resembles in tone and content *Les Caractères* of La Bruyère or the *Maximes* of La Rochefoucauld more closely than it does a modern treatise on psychology, one must remember that in his day the biological sciences such as physiology, on which modern psychology has so largely built, were in their infancy. Despite his professed avoidance of introspection, there is in Hume much that he could only have derived from examination of his own mental processes. His psychology is important historically not as a constructive achievement, but as a corrosive solvent of the received opinions of the Old Regime. His belief that without a science of psychology no social science is really possible is shared by many in the twentieth century.

Like Locke before him, Hume rejected the notion of innate ideas of moral or mathematical truth and started from sense data. The mind was a *tabula rasa*, a blank sheet of paper, on which the environment and experience worked. It is impossible to give an adequate brief summary of the subtle and ingenious arguments by which Hume accounted for the complexity of mental phenomena, and for their relationship to the external world. What the average educated man got from these subtleties was not their intellectual content so much as a blind faith in human reason, human goodness, and human perfectibility. Hume, indeed, was not much read at first, nor would an attentive reader glean from him optimism about human perfectibility. His influence was greatest upon the associationists in psychology like Hartley, upon Bentham, who professed to find the basis for his utilitarianism in Hume, and on the French *philosophes* of the 1760's. In this period it was still Locke whose influence was paramount in psychology.

The *tabula rasa* view of the human mind was really advanced by Locke as an argument against the Platonist view that there are beliefs immune to criticism. What he wanted was freedom of thought, by which he deemed it possible to defend his beliefs in the reasonableness of Christianity, the educability of the governing classes, the necessity of religious

[2] Hume, *Treatise of Human Nature*, 7-8. See also Shaftesbury, *Characteristics of Men, Manners, Opinions, Times* (London, 1723), III, 156.

toleration for Protestant dissenters (of whom he was one), and the wisdom of the leaders of the Revolution of 1688. In religion and in politics he held views contrary to those sanctioned by tradition and sustained by the majority of his contemporaries. Among his friends were scientists, Boyle and Newton the best known of them. Locke was a moderate and a man of common sense; but ideas which Locke could be trusted to use with a humble and a moderate temperament were inflammatory when adopted by enthusiasts like Rousseau, and as we have intimated in Hume's case, corrosive in the hands of skeptical casuists. Open Locke's works almost where you will, and the gist of his teaching is likely to be found in a paragraph interjected into the argument or exposition.

For example, take this from the *Essay Concerning Human Understanding*:

The idea of a supreme being, infinite in power, goodness, and wisdom, whose workmanship we are, and on whom we depend; and the idea of our selves, as understanding, rational beings, being such as are clear in us, would, I suppose, if duly considered and pursued afford such foundations for our duty and rules of action, as might place morality among the sciences, capable of demonstration; wherein I doubt not but from self-evident proposition, by necessary consequences, as incontestable as those in mathematicks, the measures of right and wrong might be made out, to any one that will apply himself with the same indifference and attention to the one, as he does to the other of these sciences. The relation of other modes may certainly be perceived, as well as those of number and extention: and I cannot see, why they should not also be capable of demonstration, if due methods were thought on to examine or pursue their agreement or disagreement. Where there is no property, there is no injustice, is a proposition as certain as any demonstration in Euclid: for the idea of property being a right to anything; and the idea to which the name injustice is given being the invasion, or violation of that right; it is evident that, these ideas being thus established, and these names annexed to them, I can as certainly know this proposition to be true as that a triangle has three angles equal to two right ones. Again, no government allows absolute liberty; the idea of government being the establishment of society upon certain rules, or laws, which require conformity to them: and the idea of absolute liberty being for anyone to do whatever he pleases; I am as capable of being certain of the truth of this proposition as of any in the mathematicks.[3]

Morality is here made to depend not on an immortal soul and innate ideas, not on an enthusiasm for the right, nor on the love of God; but on

[3] John Locke, *Essay Concerning Human Understanding* (Bk. IV, chap. iii), in *Works*, 5th ed. (London, 1751), I, 257-258.

standards to be observed with "the indifference and attention" bestowed on mathematics. Locke himself remained a firm believer in Christianity; but the scientific method in the hands of Hume reduced the distinction between virtue and vice to a choice between pleasure and pain. It led La Mettrie in the 1740's to his view of the "man machine."

Locke's *tabula rasa* had obviated not merely original sin, but the human soul. His science of man, though professedly empirical, tended to disregard tradition and custom, which are crystallized experience. Its worst flaw was a preference, sanctioned by Newton, for simple and uniform principles of explanation, whose very simplicity was supposed to guarantee their validity.

II. THE LAW OF PARSIMONY

Newton, in a famous passage in his *Principia,* gave several rules for scientific reasoning. Most of them, rightly understood, are still valid in the natural sciences. But the first one, stating what has been called the law of parsimony, is not beyond question. Its ill-considered application to the science of man as an individual and as a socius was responsible for much of the superficiality of which posterity has accused eighteenth-century enlightened writers. Newton's rule or law of parsimony was this:

We are to admit no more causes of natural things than such as are both true and sufficient to explain their appearances. To this purpose the philosophers say that Nature does nothing in vain, and more is in vain when less will serve; for Nature is pleased with simplicity, and affects not the pomp of superfluous causes.

A modern scientist would say merely that the simplest explanation fitting the observed facts is obviously the most convenient one to use in scientific work. Like Newton, he would leave to the philosophers such assertions as that "Nature is pleased with simplicity" and "does nothing in vain," and feel free (as Newton himself in his actual work would probably have felt) to "use the wave theory of light Mondays, Wednesdays and Fridays, and the corpuscular theory Tuesdays, Thursdays and Saturdays," not teaching that either was true. Newton was no dogmatist. He spent much effort on experiments, parallel to those of Boyle, on the old puzzle of the alchemists about transmuting base metal into gold. He wrote, but did not publish, an elaborate treatise on the fulfillment in history of the prophecies contained in the Bible. But the Newtonianism of the eighteenth-century Enlightenment was largely based on an uncritical acceptance of simple, uniform rules, incapable of laboratory or mathematical verification.[4]

What the Newtonians in this period were doing with the law of parsimony may be illustrated from Pope's poem *An Essay on Man* (first published in 1784, begun in 1732), which Voltaire regarded as "the most beautiful, useful and sublime didactic poem ever composed in any tongue."[5] Pope's preface says that

The Science of Human Nature is, like all other sciences, reduced to a few clear points: there are not many certain truths in this world. . . . If I could flatter myself that this Essay has any merit, it is in steering betwixt the extremes of doctrines seemingly opposite, in passing over terms utterly unintelligible, and in forming a temperate, yet not inconsistent, and a short, yet not imperfect, system of ethics.

The basic principles of human nature, for Pope, following Shaftesbury, were two in number:

Two principles in Human Nature reign,
Self love to urge, and reason to restrain. . . .

Modes of self love the passions we may call. . . .

Suffice that Reason keep to Nature's road:
Subject, compound them, follow her and God. . . .

It is not wholly clear why God is brought in at all; probably merely because Pope was a Roman Catholic who never renounced his faith. It is to "Unerring Nature still divinely bright" that the poet seems really to owe allegiance, not God or the church. Yet in Pope's system, as in Locke's and in Voltaire's, God was still wanted as a first cause, as the starter of what Professor Randall has called the "Newtonian World Machine."[6] Pope had set out in his *Essay on Man* to "vindicate the ways

---

[4] See L. T. More, "Boyle as an Alchemist," *Journal of the History of Ideas*, II (1941), 61-76, and the volume prepared under the auspices of the History of Science Society as a "bicentenary evaluation" of Newton's work, entitled *Sir Isaac Newton, 1727-1927* (Baltimore, 1928).

[5] Voltaire, *Lettres philosophiques*, no. 22, in *Oeuvres*, ed. Beuchot, XXXVII, 260-261. The quoted passage was not in the first edition, but added later. Voltaire goes on to remark that since the gist of it is to be found in Shaftesbury, "the pupil of the celebrated Locke," he doesn't see why Pope gave so much credit to Bolingbroke instead of to the *Characteristics*. But Shaftesbury was dead, and Bolingbroke was the offstage leader of the political opposition to Walpole, to which Pope was an adherent.

[6] See J. H. Randall, *The Making of the Modern Mind*, rev. ed. (Boston, 1940), chap. xi. This gives an admirable introductory treatment of the Enlightenment in chaps. xi-xv. See also Carl Becker, *The Heavenly City of the Eighteenth-Century Philosophers* (New Haven, 1932); and E. Cassirer, *Die Philosophie der Aufklärung* (Tübingen, 1932). The best comprehensive treatment in English is Preserved Smith, *A History of Modern Culture* (New York, 1934), II.

of God to man." The conclusion at which he arrived was, as Carl Becker
has pointed out, in substance that of St. Thomas Aquinas.

> All Nature is but Art unknown to thee,
> All chance direction which thou canst not see
> All discord, harmony not understood;
> All partial evil, universal good
> And spite of Pride, in erring Reason's spite,
> One truth is clear, Whatever is, is right.

Milton, too, had set out in *Paradise Lost* to

> Assert Eternal Providence
> And justify the ways of God to men.

His conclusion, expressed best, perhaps, in the final chorus of *Samson
Agonistes,* had also been that

> All is best, though we oft doubt
> What the unsearchable dispose
> Of Highest Wisdom brings about.

The difference between Pope and his predecessors was merely that for
St. Thomas and for Milton life in this world mattered far less than the
future life, in heaven or in hell. Pope had forgotten hell, because he had
got rid of sin.

> Whether with Reason or with Instinct blest
> Know all enjoy that power which suits them best;
> To bliss alike by that direction tend,
> And find the means proportioned to their end.
> Say, where full Instinct is th'unerring guide,
> What Pope or Council can they need beside?

By instinct Pope apparently meant self-love, and he explained that
both in the state of nature prior to the social contract and in civilized
society

> God and Nature linked the gen'ral frame,
> And bade Self-love and Social be the same.

Private vices are public benefits, as the ironical and cynical Mandeville
had already pointed out. The self-interest of the individual will lead
him to acts promoting the greatest happiness of the greatest number, as
the favorite writers of the English middle classes were to reiterate almost
to our own day. Pope, borrowing from Shaftesbury and Hutcheson,
supported this notion with the added idea of a spontaneous philanthropic

humanitarian impulse implanted in man by his Creator, which would
lead to universal peace and brotherhood.

> For forms of government, let fools contest
> Whate'r is best administered is best:
> For modes of faith let graceless zealots fight
> His can't be wrong whose life is in the right.
> In Faith and Hope the world will disagree,
> But all mankind's concern is Charity.

These enlightened ideas are commonplaces now. But in Pope's time they
were novel truths to a whole generation of cultivated men and women,
not merely in England but all over Europe. Voltaire's praise, quoted
above, was merely an especially influential Continental tribute to the
art and the ideas of *An Essay on Man.*

Pope, it will be noted in the passages given above, made no clear
distinction between what is and what ought to be. He assumes that the
laws of human nature and of human society are "reduced to a few
clear points," in accordance with the law of parsimony. The moral law is
of the same kind and susceptible of the same verification as Newton's
laws. Revelation, the authority of the church, the traditions of past
ages, are no longer needed as guides to moral truth. Only a passionate
desire to reject what Protestants and Catholics alike had previously
deemed the essential elements of Christianity can explain so curious a
confusion, from which few leaders of thought in the early eighteenth
century escaped. It ought to be obvious, as Bishop Berkeley pointed out,
that if the external world is made up of atoms governed by Newtonian
physics and mechanics, as Locke and his disciples asserted, and if our
knowledge depends upon the impingement of these atoms on the
tabula rasa, that is our mind, as Locke and his psychological school also
claimed, then the logical conclusions would be materialism, determinism,
and an atheism of the type eventually worked out in France by La
Mettrie and Holbach.

Berkeley in his *Principles of Human Knowledge* (of which the first
version was published in 1710 and the final one in 1734) therefore denied
the existence of matter and argued that *esse est percipi,* to be is to be
perceived. Kant's *Critique of Pure Reason* later vindicated this tran-
scendental road of escape from materialism and universal mechanism, but
in this period Berkeley's argument was taken hardly more seriously
than was his advocacy of "Tar Water" as a specific for all bodily ills.
Hume took another way out, the skeptical denial that any laws we can

ascertain, or any experiences we may have of the external world, are more than provisional and probable, even at best, since absolute truth is not only unknown but unknowable.

It was easy for the first generation of the Enlightenment to fall into these errors and confusions. Most people had retained, often without fully realizing it, a great deal of the essentially traditional and medieval point of view in which they had been brought up; and, naturally enough, they regarded the dazzling achievements of "the incomparable Mr. Newton" in physics and mechanics as only the beginning of new discoveries to be made by the same method. Not only Pope, but (by way of Hooker and his *Ecclesiastical Polity*) also Locke was an unconscious follower of St. Thomas Aquinas.[7] But for Aquinas there was divine purpose in everything and explanation of any phenomenon, showing the working out of God's design, of divine providence, enabled man to partake of "a share of providence by being provident" for himself and for others.

The Enlightenment, however, was not really justified in assuming that, in the words of Addison's familiar hymn,

> The spacious firmament on high . . .
> And all the planets in their turn,
> Confirm the tidings as they roll,
> And spread the truth from pole to pole.

The world machine, like the man machine, might far more plausibly be regarded as unmoral. The natural laws of the allegedly exact sciences had no necessary connection with any moral law, and none with God, unless time was assumed to be absolute and a creator therefore necessary as maker.

III. LIBERTY AND LAW

From the standpoint of the Old Regime, the most dangerous notion advanced by the enlightened intellectuals was that of liberty. Since, however, these intellectuals were well aware that, as they were fond of remarking, "where there is no law, there is no liberty," they had to reconcile freedom for the individual with both natural law and positive law. In the traditional theological and legal notion of natural law they found a theoretical justification for curbing interference with the individual either by society or by the state. They confused this kind of

---

[7] On Locke's indebtedness to Aquinas see George Sabine, *A History of Political Theory* (New York, 1937), 523.

natural law with natural law in a very different sense, namely the Newtonian law of parsimony, *a rule of scientific procedure,* which they hoped to establish for psychology and the social sciences. In the place of the positive law enforced in the courts, still largely an illogical and often merely parochial custom or tradition, exemplified by French *coutumes* and by the English Common Law, they wished to substitute logical, uniform, rational codes, backed later on by written constitutions and bills of right, based on a few simple, natural rights, and principles of equity. As both "law" and "nature" are peculiarly slippery terms, habitually used in the eighteenth century in a baffling variety of ambiguous ways, and surcharged for our own day also with powerful emotional overtones, it is extremely difficult to sort out and classify eighteenth-century notions about them.

For the historian the chief consideration is the nature of the opinions prevalent at a given period and the effect of these opinions on events and on institutions. In a general survey of a period the main emphasis must necessarily be placed on a few of the most significant current opinions and on their effects.

Back of the new psychology of the *tabula rasa,* and back of the attempts to substitute what in a later period was called "ethical culture" for traditional Christianity, was a revolt against the authority of the church. The struggles which had filled so much of the seventeenth century, the Thirty Years' War in central Europe, the *Fronde* in France, the Puritan Commonwealth in Great Britain, for example, were blamed on the church by enlightened intellectuals at the beginning of the next century. "For modes of faith let graceless zealots fight," as Pope put it. Civilized man ought to take his religion more reasonably and more moderately. Liberty meant, at first, freedom from ecclesiastical control. "Enthusiast" became a term of reproach. Only for the common man did the blood and tears of the long series of martyrs for Christian faiths, or even the sufferings of Christ on the Cross, retain an emotional appeal. Such fervor, according to the intellectuals, had led only to misery, to an impoverished and depopulated Germany, to an England torn by civil strife, and finally to a France seriously menaced by it and escaping into the absolutism of Louis XIV only to be driven into years of dynastic war that ended in the Treaty of Utrecht, without a victory.

Liberty for the early eighteenth century meant, accordingly, not merely emancipation from ecclesiastical authority, but also escape from the authority of absolute monarchs, whose claim to rule by divine right was no longer conceded by the enlightened. In the age of Walpole and

Fleury the generation whose youth had been spent in the wars of Louis XIV wanted "liberty and property," chiefly because it had learned to distrust the authority of church and king, the sanction for those years of fruitless struggle. The squire, the *hobereau*, wanted to go back to his estate and live there peaceably among his dependents. The great nobleman did not withdraw from court, but his zeal for church and king had notably diminished. The intellectual, like the other dissenters, wanted toleration for unorthodox opinion. The entrepreneur, from the prosperous peasant capitalist to the great city merchant or banker, wanted to be free to make a profit from anything he could find for his money and his energies to make fruitful.

For all of them, squire, peasant, nobleman, dissenter, and money-maker, liberty meant *laissez faire*. They all wanted freedom from interference by the king and by the church. They sought to win and preserve their liberties by appealing to reason, to natural law, to rights of man. The divine right of kings and the authority of the several established churches had been invoked to justify dynastic and religious war. A generation with a cult of stability was therefore impelled to reject the authority of the church, and to oppose at least passive resistance to any attempt to exert or to extend royal authority.

This attempted "return to normalcy," or to a quasi-medieval society, meant a blind reliance on what Bagehot called "the cake of custom." But the intellectual arguments used to defend it by leaders of the Enlightenment were bound in time to prove corrosive solvents of that cake of custom. They could also be used, as they were to be later in the century, to defend either the beneficent despotisms or the various Utopian schemes of the intellectuals like Condorcet and Robespierre in the French Revolution, to cite two contrasting examples. Until after 1740 this reaction against centralized authority, lay and ecclesiastical, was largely spontaneous, unintellectual, and conservative, as has been seen in Chapter III. Rulers like Walpole and Fleury used the authority of the crown and of the church so cautiously, so mildly, and in many ways so wisely that the ordinary gentleman did not find himself sufficiently thwarted to turn to the intellectuals for arguments, since he had few deep or serious grievances to complain of.

When the pacification of Europe had been completed by the Treaty of Nystadt, stability seemed reasonably secure, and the average gentleman was no longer greatly concerned with affairs of state. In England, for example, it was difficult for leaders like Walpole and Bolingbroke to

secure the attendance of their professed followers in the two houses of
Parliament because these gentlemen preferred to remain on their estates
or enjoy the pleasures of the town. In France, Louis XV was not at
Versailles at all during his minority, and even after he came of age he
was much less anxious to hold the principal members of the nobility to
constant attendance at court than Louis XIV had been until the last
years of his long reign. In Russia one of the grievances of the nobles
against Peter the Great had always been that he insisted on taking them
away from their estates to go to war, or to his court. One of the topics
on which monographic research might profitably be done is the pursuits
of the Continental nobility away from court and from the army during
the years of peace after 1715. It would probably show that on the Continent, as well as in England, the gentry devoted much more attention
to their landed estates and much less to court intrigue and army life
during these years than has usually been assumed by historians. The
courts of kings tended everywhere to be peopled largely by impoverished
and ambitious intriguers, and deserted for most of the year by many of
the most influential of the gentry. The history of France, in particular,
stands in need of reinterpretation for this period in this respect.

The notions of law which the intellectuals already held, and to which
the gentry as a group still paid very little attention, can be gathered from
that "dangerous" work, Voltaire's *Lettres philosophiques sur les Anglais*,
condemned and burnt publicly by order of the *Parlement* of Paris, June
10, 1734. Voltaire did not discuss law directly, nor make a frontal attack
on church and king. He began by praising the Quakers because they
had courageously rejected the authority of church and state, and lauding
the English for tolerating such stubbon dissenters. He then explained
that this toleration in England was possible because ever since Magna
Charta the English Parliament had checked royal absolutism. The fruit
of England's internal troubles had been liberty.

The English nation is the only one on earth which has succeeded in regulat-
ing the power of its kings by resisting them; and which after repeated efforts
has finally established that wise government under which the prince, all
powerful for good, is restrained from doing ill; in which the nobility are
great without insolence, and without vassals, and in which the people shares
in the government without confusion.

Voltaire explained in a footnote that in England, as in Sweden and
Poland, the king was merely the *premier magistrat*, since he did not
rule by right of inheritance but by choice of Parliament (under the Act

of Settlement).[8] Although the "idol of despotic power was drowned in seas of blood," the English did not believe that they had paid too dearly for their good laws, and for their dearly bought liberty.

Voltaire's admiration for English merchants, whom he praised at the expense of self-styled French *marquis* from the provinces "who know at precisely what time the king gets up, and just when he goes to bed, and who give themselves airs while playing a slave's role in a minister's antechamber," like his praise of Lady Mary Wortley Montagu for introducing inoculation against smallpox, is not to our present purpose. His discussion of English science and of scientific method, however, is relevant, since it illustrates the shift in the meaning of natural law. Bacon, though ignorant of nature, expressed in his *Novum Organum* the proper method of approach, the experimental method. Locke, rejecting the ancient illusion that ideas are innate, which had been held by the Greeks, by the scholastics, by Descartes, and by Malebranche (about whom Voltaire later admitted he had been wrong), had studied the mind and soul of man in true Baconian fashion.

Instead of defining at the outset something of which we are ignorant he examines step by step what he wishes to learn. He takes a child at the moment of birth, follows step by step the progress of his understanding—he consults especially his own personal evidence, the consciousness of his thought.[9]

Neither Voltaire nor anyone else at this time seems to have felt that introspection was not a valid method of experiment in psychology. He explained that although Locke's statement that we shall perhaps never be capable of knowing whether a purely material being can think or not had been taken as a denial of the immortality of the soul, it was really "a purely philosophical speculation, quite independent of faith and of revelation." He concluded the letter devoted to Locke with the famous passage:

Divide the human race into twenty parts, and nineteen of them will be composed of those who work with their hands and remain ignorant that such a man as Locke ever lived. . . . The number of those who think is excessively small, and these persons do not even try to disturb the world. It is not Montaigne, nor Locke, nor Bayle, nor Spinoza, nor Hobbes, nor mylord Shaftesbury, who have caused discord in their respective countries, it is, for the most part, the theologians.

[8] Voltaire, *Lettres philosophiques*, no. 8, in *Oeuvres*, ed. Beuchot, XXXVII, 148-150.
[9] Voltaire, *Lettres philosophiques*, no. 13, 179-180.

His discussion of Newton and of his predecessors in mathematics and physics emphasized, as one would expect, the simplicity and the sublimity of Newton's laws, of which he gave a superficial and inaccurate discussion. The details of the exact sciences hardly mattered. It was the emancipation from authority, from innate ideas, from revelation, the substitution of a reason and a method by which a few simple principles of explanation could be made to account for everything explicable (and the rest dismissed as unknowable and insignificant to men) which counted.

Locke's ideas about government Voltaire did not venture to discuss in the *Lettres philosophiques*. But they were implicit in his work, as for instance in the remark already quoted about kings as chief magistrates instead of hereditary absolute monarchs, and in his admiration for liberty and toleration. Though they had been published in 1690, Locke's views were still not widely disseminated outside Great Britain. Their greatest influence was, of course, not felt until the French and the American revolutions. What Professor Sabine has aptly called "the reception of Locke" is the most important fact, at least for the historian, in the intellectual history of the early eighteenth century. It is therefore relevant to discuss Locke's views here.

M. Mornet has shown how difficult it is to determine the extent of the influence of Locke and other enlightened writers in France before 1750. A French translation of the *Treatises of Government* had appeared in 1691, and there were in all six editions. But the intellectual class, as Voltaire indicated, was not numerous. Men like Barbier and Marais, whom we know to have read much not merely of the published radical writers, but also of the atheist and cynical literature like the "Testament" of Meslier which was circulated in manuscript copies, read these works in the critical spirit inculcated by Bayle, not accepting the new ideas, but no longer afraid of them.[10]

In Germany the Enlightenment was more indebted to Leibnitz and to his disciple and popularizer Christian Wolff than to English thinkers. But Leibnitz, for some years before his death in 1716, had lived in relative obscurity, and Wolff's position was not firmly established, nor his influence wide until after he was recalled to Halle by Frederick the Great. Cassirer regards Leibnitz as "the true originator and founder of the philosophy of the Enlightenment." But this really means that Leibnitz' conception of the monads and of a pre-established harmony

---

[10] D. Mornet, *Les origines intellectuelles de la révolution française,* 3rd ed. (Paris, 1938), 1-70. See also G. Lanson, "Questions diverses sur l'histoire de l'ésprit philosophique en France avant 1750," *Revue d'histoire littéraire de la France,* XIX (1912), 1-29.

offered the soundest and most consistent philosophical basis for the faith in intellectual and moral progress which animated eighteenth-century intellectuals; and not that Leibnitz actually as a matter of historical fact was among the most influential thinkers of his time. (His later influence was, of course, considerable.)[11]

In estimating international exchanges of ideas one must also bear in mind eighteenth-century intellectual cosmopolitanism. Queen Caroline of England, wife of George II, like her husband's grandmother, the Electress Sophia, was under Leibnitz' influence as well as under that of English deists and rationalists in religion, like Clarke and Hoadley. Leibnitz may perhaps even be credited through her with an indirect influence on appointments to bishoprics of the Church of England in the reign of George II. Dr. Pangloss in Voltaire's *Candide* (1757) is to some modern readers a still better-known disciple of Leibnitz. But there is no evidence that Voltaire (before his sojourn at the court of Frederick the Great) knew much about the German philosopher.

What enlightenment meant to Caroline and her bishops, and to Voltaire, was freedom from "prone submission to the heavenly will." They claimed moral autonomy for man, since morality was becoming a science enabling man to "serve the only God" without the "fear" Milton had assumed as necessary. God's laws had become intelligible, and his ways not past finding out.

The notion of natural law was thus basic in eighteenth-century ethics, and even more so in eighteenth-century politics and jurisprudence. Here again Locke provided a reservoir of arguments. Despite his excellent technique as a debater, he was not the builder of a philosophical system. Most of his works were written not to establish allegedly eternal verities, but to show that what he did, or what the English government did when in the hands of his friends, was in accord with sound principles. In reading Locke one must remember that common sense, not logic, was his great intellectual gift, and that he always chose his principles to fit the facts of a given situation, rather than his facts to fit a purely theoretical system. Locke was certainly a great and good man, but he was not a great philosopher. As Newton was not a Newtonian, so Locke was not a Lockeian. On the immediate question at issue, Locke's view was almost invariably sane and prudent. But too often he justified it by arguments which later in other hands became dangerous thoughts.

[11] See Cassirer, *Philosophie der Aufklärung.* His view is conveniently summarized in his article "Enlightenment" in *Encyclopaedia of the Social Sciences,* V, 547-552. My quotation is from Cassirer's article "Leibniz" in the same work, IX, 401.

Locke, a Calvinist by inheritance though an Arminian in theology, was influenced by the Calvinist use of natural law, as Troeltsch has shown.[12] He was also, through Hooker, influenced by the scholastic view of Thomas Aquinas. He must have known the way in which Grotius and Roman jurists had employed the concept, though he had not the type of mind apt to discriminate between these different antecedents of the idea. He also used the notion of a state of nature supposed to be prior to the establishment of organized society and government. He thought that travelers' tales about American savages showed that Hobbes had been wrong in thinking man's life in this state "solitary, nasty, brutish, and short."

Citation of equally familiar passages from Locke's second *Treatise of Government*, the famous "Essay concerning the true original, extent, and end of civil government," perhaps the most influential essay ever written, may clarify the use made of these notions about nature, law, and reason by eighteenth-century political theorists.

To understand Political Power a right, and derive it from its Original, we must consider what State all Men are naturally in, and that is, a State of perfect Freedom to order their Actions, and dispose of their Possessions, and Persons as they think fit, within the bounds of the Law of Nature, without asking leave, or depending upon the Will of any other Man. . . .

The State of Nature, has a Law of Nature to govern it, which obliges every one, and Reason, which is that Law, teaches all Mankind, who will but consult it; That being all equal and independent, no one ought to harm another in his Life, Health, Liberty or Possessions; for Men being all the Workmanship of one Omnipotent, and infinitely wise maker; All the Servants of one Sovereign Master, sent into the World by his order and about his business, they are his Property. . . .

What concerns us here is not the rest of the argument of the second chapter, near the beginning of which the passages quoted may be found, but the assumed "Law of Nature" which a faculty called "reason," assumed to be possessed by every man, or at least by every Englishman, enables men to understand and to follow.

The two natural rights which Locke wished governments to recognize are liberty and property. What he understood by liberty is clear from the opening paragraphs of the short fourth chapter entitled "Of Slavery." It will be apparent that his ideal corresponds to that professed down to our own day in democratic countries.

[12] E. Troeltsch, *The Social Teaching of the Christian Churches* (New York, 1931), II, 636-639.

The Natural Liberty of Man is to be free from any Superior Power on Earth, and not to be under the Will or Legislative Authority of Man, but to have only the Law of Nature for his Rule. The Liberty of Man, in Society, is to be under no other Legislative Power, but that established, by consent, in the Commonwealth, not under the Dominion of any Will, or Restraint of any Law, but what that Legislative shall enact, according to the Trust put in it. Freedom then is not what Sir R.[obert] F.[ilmer] tells us, . . . *A Liberty for every one to do what he lists, to live as he pleases, and not to be tyed by any Laws:* But Freedom of Men under Government, is, to have a standing Rule to live by, common to every one of that Society, and made by the Legislative Power erected in it. A Liberty to follow my own Will in all things, where that Rule prescribes not, not to be subject to the inconstant, uncertain, unknown, Arbitrary Will of another Man. As Freedom of Nature is to be under no other restraint but the Law of Nature.

This Freedom from Absolute, Arbitrary Power, is so necessary to, and closely joyned with a Man's Preservation, that he cannot part with it, but by what forfeits his Preservation and Life together.

King James II of England had done his best to make Locke's own life forfeit by demanding his extradition of the Netherlands government after he fled thither in voluntary exile. The essay quoted from above was written not as a calm scientific study of the true nature of government, but to justify the Revolution of 1688, by which James II was dethroned. It is one of the most remarkable bits of special pleading on record. Parliament, led by a group of prominent persons dissatisfied with James because he was a Catholic, and because he tried to revive the absolute power of the monarch, rebelled. William and Mary were called in, and the Prince of Orange, a foreign ruler with a little Stuart blood, was placed on the English throne with the aid of foreign troops. Those who thus violated the constitution were careful to make a bargain with the new rulers, by which the power of the monarchy was limited and that of Parliament preserved. Hence Locke in defending such a revolution could not appeal to tradition, or to the existing unwritten constitution, or to the Common Law. Therefore he had to assume that a rather unrepresentative legislature expressed the will of the majority of Englishmen, though it seems clear that what happened in 1688 was at first approved only by a minority of the nation.

Hence, also, the legislative power of Parliament, by which alone these changes were sanctioned, had to be exalted and made to accord with a natural law anterior to and supreme over tradition. Hence the corporative ideal, by which the state included many constituent bodies with privileges sanctioned by tradition and justified by social utility, had to be abandoned.

Locke's "legislative," even though it came to represent in fact the will of the majority of the people, and not merely that of a politically active minority, could still be tyrannical from the point of view of minorities. His whole argument was theoretical, not in correspondence with the actual organization and working of the English government, either in his day or in our own. He wished to justify a revolution which effectually prevented in Britain the growth of institutions like those of France under Louis XIV or of Prussia under Frederick the Great.

It has been shown in earlier chapters of this book that England in the eighteenth century was not, for the most part, a nation of "rugged individuals" freely and rationally exercising their "natural rights to life, liberty and the pursuit of happiness." At least three quarters of the population were living in rural communities which were still primarily engaged in subsistence farming, despite some part-time weaving or other trade. The members of the House of Commons were most of them nominated in fact by the landed gentry, often by members of the House of Lords. Tradition and personal relationships still bound society into something more corporate than "free" or "atomic." The theories of Althusius, neglected, almost unknown, in Locke's day, would have been actually far more in keeping with England after 1688 than were the notions Locke so illogically combined from Hobbes and from Hooker. Althusius had argued for popular sovereignty without unduly exalting the national state, which was merely one of several political groups, and without dissolving these natural social groups or corps into atomic individuals. The federalistic elements in his theory, suggested by the United Netherlands and the Holy Roman Empire, might, after the Tudor unifications, have seemed unsuited to England.

But one of the fascinating though futile "ifs" of history is what might have happened if France under the Old Regime had adopted his ideas, avoided wars of conquest, and enlarged her political domain, as it is not inconceivable she might have done, by peaceful absorption of other lands into a Continental federation as extensive as her cultural domain was in the eighteenth century, when even Frederick the Great wrote his complete works, not in German, but in French. There were, in short, possible alternatives to a theory of national popular sovereignty, one of the ultimate results of Locke's influence, which inevitably led to nineteenth-century nationalism.[13]

[13] See on Althusius, Sabine, *History of Political Theory*, 416-420, and O. von Gierke, *Johannes Althusius und die Entwicklung der naturrechtlichen Staatstheorien*, 3rd ed. (Breslau, 1913), also his *Natural Law and the Theory of Society*, tr. E. Barker (Cambridge, Mass., 1934). Sabine's book is the best introduction to all the political theories discussed in this chapter. He is not kind to the eighteenth century, except to Hume and Burke.

A cosmopolitan like Voltaire, with a passionate hatred of war and of injustice, cannot really have wished to foster the growth of the leviathan, or, in Blackstone's phrase, of the "supreme, irresistible authority" of the state. When Voltaire used words like "citizen" instead of "subject," he was following Locke in trying to curb royal absolutism. But in the year 1946 it should be obvious to all that in no modern state are the citizens as free from interference with their private lives by state authority as were the subjects of Louis XV throughout his reign. Locke and the eighteenth-century Enlightenment tried to dissolve the traditional quasi-feudal organization of society, with its infinite and often irrational diversity, in order to establish certain uniformities, ostensibly dictated by reason, and sanctioned by an assumed law of nature. But liberty is not necessarily to be found in making every man obey the same impersonal rules. Experience, which, crystallized into quite illogical and complex traditions, had created the Old Regime, might conceivably prove that there must be great variety and considerable inconsistency in human institutions to fit them to the desires of different people in different places and different circumstances. Whatever the general blessings of uniformity and of standardization, when they were applied to the Old Regime the only result was inevitably the end of that regime, so essential to its continuance were its diversity, its lack of a "planned economy," and its personal ties.

Equality is an ideal implying uniformity and standardization. In Locke's hypothetical "state of nature" all men were equal, not in ability or in wealth, but in respect to their assumed natural rights. They had equal right to enjoy the fruits of their labors, though of course these fruits were unequal. Only in later times was the idea of equality developed into that of leveling, of the mass state. Montesquieu, in objecting that the result of Law's system, had it succeeded, would have been the worst of tyrannies, had a clear perception of the danger to human values that lurks in social uniformity, the sort of danger indicated by his somewhat fanciful argument that there are three forms of government, republican, monarchic, and despotic, with virtue, honor, and fear as their respective mainsprings or principles. The difference, in his view, between monarchy and despotism lies in the excessive uniformity and simplicity of the organization of a despotism, which lacks the "intermediate bodies" that in a monarchy lie between sovereign and subject, and guarantee security by their diversity. For him the France of Louis XV, in which he wrote, was in theory no despotism, but a monarchy. Locke, when dilating upon the horrors of despotism, even in the reign of Louis XIV, and while England was at war with France, had spoken of Russian tsars and of

Oriental potentates in Ceylon, but he had not called France a despotism. The passages he quoted with approval from James I of England, especially the remark of King James, "And therefore a king, governing in a settled kingdom, leaves to be a king, and degenerates into a tyrant, as soon as he leaves off to rule according to his laws," must have struck him as the theory and the practice of the Bourbon monarchy in France, where the jurists made a distinction between absolute and arbitrary power.[14]

Locke's remarks about tyrannical abuses of the royal prerogative were all directed, as his contemporary readers must at once have seen, against particular acts of James II. His appeal to natural law was made in order to limit the power of government. That the later influence of the idea of uniform rights and of individual citizenship tended to strengthen state authority, he could not have foreseen. The greatly enhanced prestige of the ideal of law, and of simple uniformities in the eighteenth century obviously owed their enhanced prestige not to the authority of Locke but to the prestige of what was understood to be science as exemplified by Newton. Yet despite lip service to Newton and not a little comment on alleged facts, the method of the eighteenth century in trying to found "social sciences" remained essentially more Cartesian than Newtonian, more deductive than experimental. The tendency was to start with one or two simple generalizations, analogous to Descartes' "Give me extension and motion, and I will construct the universe." Locke, in defending the Revolution of 1688, was not actually trying to establish political science on universal and simple foundations, but he did talk as though the policies he (probably rightly) deemed expedient for England at the time were to be deduced from universal laws.

IV. THE "RIGHT OF PROPERTY"

Locke's emphasis on the liberty of the individual as justified by natural law and guaranteed by a social contract was, as we have seen, subversive of the corporate ideal and the traditional social order of the Old Regime. He identified this liberty for each man with "his property, that is, his life, liberty, and estate," thus using the word "property" in a broad sense with connotations different from those the word has since acquired. The much-admired fifth chapter, "Of Property," was interpreted by the eighteenth century and by most later writers as justifying a simple, uniform, natural right to the individual possession of any kind of estate,

[14] Locke, *Second Treatise of Government,* chap. vii. See also chap. xviii.

real or personal. The "Right of Property" appeared in the French declaration of the Rights of Man and of the Citizen of 1789 coupled with liberty. Much of the legal and institutional history of the Western world in the past two centuries has been conditioned by this assumed right, without which the rather complex phenomena lumped crudely under the head of capitalism could hardly have developed as they did.[15]

Locke begins by stating that "natural reason . . . tells us that men being once born, have a right to their preservation, and consequently to meat and drink and such other things as Nature affords for their subsistence"; and that "revelation" (in ironical quotation marks) teaches " 'that God,' as King David says (Psalms cxv, 16) 'has given the earth to the children of men, given it to mankind in common.' " This was the received opinion, of course, handed down by tradition from the Middle Ages. "I shall endeavor to show," says Locke, "how men might come to have a property in several parts of that which God gave to mankind in common, and that without any express compact of all the commoners."

This property was based on labor, because "every man has a property in his own person." Locke illustrated from the use of common lands in the system of land tenure in England as it was when he wrote, "The grass my horse has bit, the turfs my servant has cut, and the ore I have digged in any place, where I have a right to them in common with others become my property without the assignation or consent of anybody. The labor that was mine, removing them out of that common state they were in, hath fixed my property in them." Under the usual tenure in commonalty the individual landholder had, in fact, the rights Locke mentioned to the extensive, uncultivated common lands of the manor. The reference to enclosure was also historically accurate. "We see in commons, which remain so by compact, that it is the taking any part of what is common, and removing it out of the state Nature leaves it in, begins the property, without which the common is of no use." Remember that, as has been already seen, individual tenure under the Old Regime was of arable land and of meadowland put under the plow, whether enclosed or in the common fields. It would appear from other incidental passages in his works that Locke thought, quite correctly, that the cultivation would be more efficient if in the hands of an entrepreneur raising crops for market than it would be if carried out by a subsistence

[15] See Locke, *Second Treatise of Government,* chap. v, and for modern criticism from widely different standpoints, P. Larkin, *Property in the Eighteenth Century, with Special Reference to England and Locke* (Dublin and Cork, 1930); W. M. Hamilton, "Property— According to Locke," *Yale Law Journal,* XLI (1931-1932), 864-880; E. Beaglehole, *Property* (London, 1931).

farmer.[16] But he nowhere gave a clear and distinct statement of his view of the existing economic and legal arrangements, with which he was on the whole apparently satisfied. As he said, "the chief matter of property" is "the earth itself." In Spain, suffering from depopulation, "a man may be permitted to plough, sow, and reap, without being disturbed upon land he has no other title to, but only his making use of it." In England, however,

or any other country where there are plenty of people under government who have money and commerce, no one can enclose or appropriate any part without the consent of all his fellow commoners; because this is left common by compact—i.e. by the law of the land, which is not to be violated. And though it be common in respect of some men, it is not so of all mankind but is the joint property of this country [i.e. *pays*, or district] or this parish. Besides, the remainder, after such enclosure, would not be as good to the rest of the commoners as the whole was, when they could all make use of the whole.

Again, Locke was referring to the actual situation in the primarily agricultural subsistence economy of his day. The final stage of en-closure, which eliminated common lands, had exactly the effects Locke indicated on "the rest of the commoners." But this stage was not reached until the reign of George III, when Locke had long been in his grave.

Locke's chief interest was in the position of the landholder, because before the creation of the national debt and of the Bank of England, both, as we have seen, later than 1690, there was no investment other than commerce open to money. It was a condition, not a theory, he was discussing. He was opposing royal absolutism as exemplified by James II, not justifying capitalism.

He went on to argue that any man has a natural right only to what he can use before it spoils or goes to waste. As money, meaning gold and silver, does not spoil by being stored up or hoarded, there is no limit to the amount of it a man may rightfully possess. Locke seemed to assume, without going into detail, that a man's wealth is all really the hoarded product of his or of his ancestors' labor, though he must have known that this is not demonstrably true of many forms of capital. He pointed out that without commerce and the use of money, nobody would bother to enclose and stock and cultivate land beyond what was needed for bare subsistence.

With these blessings, safeguarded by the law, "a man may rightfully

[16] See Locke, "Considerations of the Lowering of Interest and the Raising the Value of Money," *Works*, 5th ed. (London, 1751), II, esp. 19 ff. I have not space to quote the remarks on which I base this inference.

and without injury, possess more than by himself he can make use of by receiving gold and silver, which may continue long in a man's possession without decaying." The rise of commerce had not yet led to accumulations of holdings in stocks and bonds, to what Swift later called the "funded interest," opposed to the "landed interest." In Locke's discussion there was no reference to the position of the industrial worker under the "putting-out" or "domestic" system, much later comment to the contrary notwithstanding.[17] Most Englishmen still owned or controlled their means of production, and Locke did not discuss the exceptions. Like Defoe, he tended to regard the unemployed as undeserving "sturdy beggars," and to assume that the industrious and frugal poor man, or even woman, could set up in business on the capital he might reasonably save from his wages. As a small capital would suffice for some forms of shopkeeping and for the tools needed in most trades, this was not as inhumane a line to take as it would have been in the nineteenth century.

In order to understand the influence of Locke's ideas about property rights on the development of European thought and on the course of events in the eighteenth century, it would be necessary not merely to examine in detail the writings of his intellectual successors, but also to determine what the governing classes, the politically active minority under the Old Regime, understood by such terms as "property," "capital," "rent," and "profit." It is well known to historians that the words "nature" and "law" were used by eighteenth-century savants in a variety of senses, often inextricably confused with each other. But the layman, perhaps with an indiscriminating reverence for the assumed clarity on fundamental terms of economic theory, may mistakenly assume that the terms basic to a theory of property were and are used in definite and consistent ways by the social scientists. Twentieth-century economists, of course, know better.[18]

Locke himself repeatedly emphasized the "getting clear and determined ideas, and the employing our thoughts rather about them than about sounds put for them," and the necessity of "settling the signification of words which we use with ourselves in the search of truth, or with others

[17] See Larkin, *Property in the Eighteenth Century*, 67, and M. Beer, *History of British Socialism* (London, 1920-1921), I, 190.

[18] See the attempt of E. Cannan, known to historians as editor of the standard edition of Adam Smith's *Wealth of Nations*, to elucidate "The Early History of the Term 'Capital,'" *Quarterly Journal of Economics*, XXXV (1920-1921), 469-481, and the subsequent discussion of it in the same journal by R. D. Richards and by H. R. Hatfield, XL (1925-1926), 329-338, 547-548.

in discoursing about it."[19] But neither he nor succeeding social scientists (historians in this respect included) practiced what he preached. Semantics, or at least the need for this difficult discipline, is not as modern a discovery as some of its present-day popularizers perhaps imagine.

As the writers of monographs have not yet provided adequate materials for a semantics of the eighteenth-century Enlightenment, all that is here possible is an indication of some points in need of further study. When one tries to form one of Locke's "clear and determined ideas" of what the right of property meant to the early eighteenth century, a cursory investigation merely reveals confusions and perplexities. It is reasonably clear that the actual estates of eighteenth-century men of property, outside the merchant-entrepreneur group who engineered the so-called industrial revolution, consisted of claims to annual income, and that what they habitually thought of as their property rights were such claims, or "annuities," as they called them. In most cases the greatest amount of a man's annual income came from the various incidents of land tenure, feudal dues, tithes, and other charges lumped together under the term "rents." When, for example, the British government under George I confiscated the estates of the attainted Jacobites after 1715, the value of such property was stated, first in terms of the annual income, then in terms of sale "at twenty year's purchase," and, in a supplementary list, in terms of the annual value, and of a sale at "ten year's purchase" of estates in which attainted persons had a reversionary right.[20]

In legal terminology, the enumeration of what was included in these forfeited estates, under the act of Parliament, included all and every one of the

castles, honours, lordships, manors, messuages, lands, tenements, rents, reversions, services, remainders, possessions, royalties, franchises, jurisdictions and privileges whatsoever, and all appurtenances to them belonging; and all rights of entry, rights of action, titles, conditions, uses, trusts, powers, and authorities; and all leases for life, lives, or years, pensions, annuities, rents, charges, and hereditaments

of all persons convicted under the act. No discussion of the detail above enumerated is necessary to show that property was a complex, not a simple phenomenon, and that it was still entangled with power of a quasi-feudal kind.

If, however, we examine what was included in the estate left by a

[19] Locke, *The Conduct of the Understanding*, Sec. V.
[20] See the list as given in J. Stevens, *An Historical Account of All Taxes*, etc. (London, 1733), 364-366.

self-made man, in this case by Sir Isaac Newton, we find a more modern kind of property. According to the accounts of his executors, he left at his death in 1727 thirteen thousand pounds in bank stock; ditto bought October 7, 1726, one thousand pounds; South Sea stock five thousand pounds, South Sea annuity five thousand pounds; also an annuity of one hundred pounds in the Exchequer, on his own life.[21]

It is not altogether clear how Sir Isaac had accumulated this fortune (roughly equivalent to several hundred thousand dollars today). His post as Master of the Mint, which he held for about thirty years, was worth from one thousand two hundred pounds to one thousand five hundred pounds a year and, as a bachelor with simple tastes, he could no doubt make considerable savings. But he had invested, not in land but in "the funds," no doubt with the expert advice of such friends as Montagu, later Lord Halifax (not to be confused with the author of *The Character of a Trimmer*). Newton's fortune, like his fame, was evidently self-made. His father was a small freeholder who farmed his own land. His mother's second husband was a country clergyman. The creation of the national debt, which, as we have seen, originated with the founding of the Bank of England in 1694, had enabled Newton to invest his savings conveniently and, as it proved, safely. In 1727 he was receiving 4 per cent, but for some years before that the rate had been 5 per cent. Newton's possession of the South Sea stock does not, of course, necessarily imply that he was a speculator in the notorious boom. On this stock he received the same rate as on the Bank of England stock after 1711, i.e., 6 per cent to 1717 and 5 per cent thereafter until 1727. All these securities were government debts, and all were secured by the pledging of the revenue from specified sources of government incomes, as we have already seen.

The contrast between the simplicity of funded property, secured by the credit of the government, and the complexity of the sources of income of the attainted Jacobites is striking. It should not be assumed, however, that the landed gentry were not holders of government and other securities (which, it may be noted, were included in the enumeration of the forfeited properties under the term annuities and elsewhere). Although such scattered examples as these are not sufficient evidence upon which to base dogmatic conclusions, yet another English instance may indicate a further line of research to be pursued.

It is well known that the position of the squirearchy was very different

<hr />

[21] Historical Manuscripts Commission, *Report on the Manuscripts of the Late Reginald Rawdon Hastings, Esq.* (London, 1928-1934), I, 416.

from that of the nobility. Most historians content themselves with references to Squire Western (in Fielding's *Tom Jones*) to prove this point. Western, unlike Squire Allworthy in the same novel (meant as a rather flattering portrait of Ralph Allen), does not seem to be suggested by an actual individual. His fortune, three thousand pounds a year, and his uncouthness were scarcely typical of the class to which he belonged. We now have a surprising wealth of detail about an authentic squire, Henry Purefoy of Shalstone, also in some ways not wholly typical. From the *Purefoy Letters* an attentive reader may glean not merely a great deal of social history, but also a certain amount of economic history. Purefoy's estate, by his own estimate, was worth £382 a year in 1720. It was rated at £200 a year in the land-tax assessment made in the 1690's, and not subsequently revised. Part of it was enclosed, part held on leases of modern type, part on copyhold at what he called "old rents" (i.e. customary rather than economic rent charges). The editor surmises that fines and heriots as well as rents were part of the squire's income. But he also bought lottery tickets in the state lotteries. The blanks were usually redeemable for 75 per cent of the purchase price, and he won several prizes, though no large ones. He purchased annuities (i.e. government bonds) and considered buying other public stocks if government obligations were not to be had, rejecting insurance-company shares on the advice of a neighbor who had "lost considerably" by purchasing them. His mother owned a leasehold on a house in a good neighborhood in London, and had a mortgage on the Shalstone estate as well as her widow's jointure. Her father had been a London tradesman. She inherited a half interest in a freehold house in Grub Lane in London, which had been her grandmother's, but sold it.

The Purefoys invested the surplus from their rather miscellaneous annual income either in buying copyhold real estate (if they could get it at not over twenty-five years' purchase, which they usually failed to do), or in government obligations. Their investments must have been typical of what was going on all over eighteenth-century England. There was no sharp dividing line between the landed gentry and Swift's funded interest. But no town dweller living on his own investments could have lived half as well as the Purefoys did on their few hundreds a year supplemented by their garden, dairy, game, fish, and other rural produce. Those interested will find in the carefully edited letters full details of just how they managed it. They have left us written records of every penny they spent.[22]

[22] *Purefoy Letters, 1735-1753.*

It is only by the patient study of a great number of such cases as these that any generalizations about the right of property, the rise of capitalism, and the genesis of the industrial revolution can eventually be justified. English examples have been chosen here for discussion for the obvious reason that the political, intellectual, and economic revolutions of the eighteenth century originated in England. On the background of these momentous developments, all of which were under way between 1715 and 1740, there is an immense amount of material in manuscript and a great deal already in print which is in need of further study, classification, and interpretation. The economic historians have made a good beginning in the past twenty years at the inevitable reinterpretation. But the textbooks and the more ambitious general surveys do not yet fully reflect the result even of these preliminary revaluations.

It seems probable, but by no means certain, that Locke's view of property as a simple, uniform, natural right found as ready an acceptance among the English landed gentry as among the merchants and moneyed men, because it supplied to both classes a convenient excuse for following their own interests as they saw them. If one takes Sombart's description of the "Spirit of the Capitalist System" as dominated by "three ideas, acquisition, competition, and rationality," and applies it to the English phenomena we have been considering, rationality, which implies uniformity as well as good bookkeeping and standardized techniques, found its justification in Locke's concept of the right of property. But such a concept plainly did not fit the complex property rights actually held by the English governing classes when he wrote.[23]

According to Max Weber,

the factor which produced capitalism is the rational permanent enterprise, rational accounting, rational technology, and rational law. . . . Necessary complementary factors were the rational spirit, the rationalization of the conduct of life in general and a rationalistic economic ethic.[24]

At the beginning of all these rationalisms stands Locke's insistence on the right of property, in which he included "life, liberty, and estate," as justified by a natural law anterior to and more cogent than the law of the land. His conviction that reason rather than revelation enables

---

[23] Sombart's views are summarized in his important article "Capitalism" in *Encyclopaedia of the Social Sciences*, III, 195-208. See also W. Sombart, *Der moderne Kapitalismus* (Munich, 1921-1927); and for a briefer treatment avowedly based on it, F. L. Nussbaum, *A History of the Economic Institutions of Modern Europe* (New York, 1933).

[24] Weber, *General Economic History*, 354. See also M. Weber, *Gesammelte Aufsätze zur Religionssoziologie* (Tübingen, 1920-1921), I, 30 ff.

us to understand this natural law and the rights we possess under it, is more important than his belief, repudiated later by many of his successors, that God is the ultimate lawgiver, and that Christian morality is at bottom supremely rational. These notions, given enhanced prestige by a dubious analogy between Newtonian science and the social sciences, eventually subverted the Old Regime.

What has been aptly called "the reception of Locke," not merely in France through Voltaire and Montesquieu, but later in so much of the modern world, was thus of immense historical significance. Henceforth, in Sabine's words, "the principles of the Treatises of Government (supplemented of course by other English works) became axioms of political and social criticism." Henceforth the law of nature superseded all revealed or supernatural truth. Henceforth reason, not tradition, was to be followed. The content of this new law was "substantially, enlightened self-interest." Henceforth, there were determined, and in the long run successful, efforts "to create a society in which individual energy and capacity are the keys to power and wealth."[25]

For the historian trying to comprehend, not thought alone, but the whole of past experience within a given number of years, the problem of the "reception of Locke" is not merely to establish the well-known fact that he was accepted, but to determine how and why this happened. None of his ideas was really new, nor did he construct a new system of philosophy. He did not even mean by his writings to convey what the eighteenth century took from them.

Reason and self-interest would combine to bring about the acceptance of so convenient an economic philosophy as Locke's by lords and squires as well as by entrepreneurs turned gentlemen landholders. If the landholders had tacitly or openly rejected the traditional religious faith of their fathers, his new ethical individualism would be all the more readily acceptable. Whether the enlightened landlords were Protestant or Catholic, Lutheran or Calvinist, Jesuit or Jansenist, seems relatively unimportant, despite the attempts of theorists to prove Calvinism and capitalism especially congenial. The unsolved problem here is the extent to which traditional institutions retained their hold on the landholder. Until the middle of the century the medieval tradition of communal landholding appears, from the scattered evidence available, to have been a good deal stronger both in England and on the Continent than one might have supposed it, and, as has been pointed out by a recent student

[25] Sabine, *History of Political Theory*, 545-547.

of English common fields, a good deal less impractical under eighteenth-century conditions than reformers of the type of Jethro Tull believed.[26]

The position of the *rentier*, living on the interest of loans made to the government, depended on the stability and solvency of the particular regime which paid him his income. On the Continent the urban *bourgeoisie* ever since the Middle Ages had included a good many well-to-do patricians whose families, perhaps centuries earlier, had turned over some or all their wealth to the state in return for a rent charge, perpetual in character, secured not merely by the credit of the municipality but also by the pledging of specified receipts for its payment. The aristocracy at Rome and in other Italian cities, long before the eighteenth century, was largely composed of *rentiers* of this sort, who often also held land somewhere in the adjacent countryside. Locke's right of property merely gave this class a theoretical justification for what was already a customary and legal right to receive their annuity regularly. The property of the *noblesse de robe* in France often included *rentes sur l'hotel de ville de Paris,* once municipal, but now state obligations besides their purchased offices under the king, with a small salary and often rather large fees. The *rentes* were perpetual, and not like the English annuities created with the national debt in the 1690's for a limited term of years. There were also similar funded debts of the church in France and of the provincial Estates. The credit of municipalities, of the church, and of the provincial Estates was far better than that of the king. Louis XIV's taking over legal control of municipal administration was a fiscal rather more than an administrative measure. By it he might raise money for his wars, by sale of municipal offices and redemption of them by the city concerned, and by creation of *rentes.* Locke's notion of the sanctity of private property made an especial appeal to French *rentiers* in a century when, as Gaxotte has said, there was "a poor state in a rich land." But it was obviously to the entrepreneur, the capitalist of the period of early capitalism, that Locke's ideas about property and liberty especially appealed.

V. THE ENLIGHTENMENT AND THE "CAKE OF CUSTOM"

The proper task of the historian is not the effort to determine whether the Enlightenment had arrived at new and valuable truths concerning God, man, and society. Probably most of the readers of this book would be prepared to fight for many of the main principles of Locke, Pope,

[26] Orwin, *The Open Fields.*

and Voltaire, which have become cherished parts of our common cultural heritage. Those principles seem so obviously true that one wonders at the stress these eighteenth-century writers placed upon them and fails in sympathy for the eighteenth-century opposition. The Old Regime, particularly the period from 1715 to around the middle of the eighteenth century, has been neglected and misunderstood by historians largely because of a strong feeling that the triumph of the enlightened ideas, on which democracy today is still so largely based, meant a victory over effete medieval superstitions. The revolutions which after 1750 swept away so much that has been casually dismissed as "feudal débris" or "tyranny" were indeed so momentous that there is some excuse for neglecting, in the period immediately preceding them, everything neither directly preliminary to revolution nor material for dramatic narrative.

Yet the period between 1715 and 1740 is worth studying for its own sake, with only incidental reference to what came afterward. It was an age between two worlds: one world, as it proved, moribund; the other still powerless to be born; a period of relative peace; and perhaps consequently, of relatively great and increasing prosperity and security. The modern tourist can see with half an eye that the new towns then growing up, say Bath, England, or Williamsburg, Virginia, were comfortable and pleasant dwelling places. So also appear the eighteenth-century country houses (not the palaces, like Blenheim, but the English and Continental equivalents of the homes of Virginia's first families).

Compare these with the surviving medieval towns and castles, picturesque enough, but not places in which a modern man can imagine existence to have been sanitary, safe, or pleasant; and the nonrational but tangible basis for the eighteenth-century faith in enlightenment and progress is evident. After the pacification begun at Utrecht in 1713 had been completed, and the bubbles of the subsequent postwar credit inflation had burst, men resolved to live in the good old way, a stable, comfortable, prosperous, yet enlightened existence. They had got rid of the fervors of religious and of dynastic strife. They fell back on traditional ways, on local customs, relying, most of them, on "the cake of custom." They did not reject the church. They were still loyal to their kings and other constituted authorities. But they had no solid intellectual justification for thus reverting to traditional and often quite irrational ways of living. To weaken church and king, they had begun to use intellectual criticism like that of Bayle, and to exaggerate the philosophical and theological implications of Newtonian (or in many cases still of Cartesian) mathematics and physics. The arguments which began as attempts to limit the power of church and king would, if anyone were to begin to take them with emotional fervor, prove disruptive of the cake of custom. It was later said of Rousseau that though he invented nothing, he set everything on fire. The devotees of the eighteenth-century cult of stability had attained their stability by using arguments which could not possibly defend and preserve it. Those who wish to preserve the institutions of any country, when it and they are under attack, must have and use plausible arguments in its defense, arguments at once logical and not in open conflict with familiar facts.

The cake of custom by which men's lives from 1715 to the middle of the century were for the most part actually governed was old and indurated. At the base of society was the family. Both in fact and in theory membership in the family, and other personal ties to individuals and to groups, were for the vast majority what lent meaning to life and gave security. An eighteenth-century man was a landlord, or a tenant, sometimes both at once. He was not just a Christian, or a deist, but a parishioner, with duties to his fellow parishioners as such, which the state would aid the church in enforcing. He was not just an individual craftsman or tradesman; but still, in most cases, at least a nominal member of a guild. He was not an individual citizen of an impersonal state, but a subject of a ruler to whom he was an object of personal solicitude. In France, for instance, he could, if decently clothed, walk at will into the royal palace at Versailles and watch the king at his dinner.[27] The king would order ices and other delicacies handed around among the women present. But if he had a request to present to the king, he was actually less likely to do it by handing him a petition personally (as he had the right to do, and as many persons actually did), than to undertake to present it by means of a patron whom the king knew personally. Nearly all kings did heed and grant petitions from obscure and unknown persons, as Queen Caroline in Scott's *Heart of Midlothian* did in the case of Jeannie Deans. But, like Jeannie, such persons usually had, or found, friends at court able and willing to get them an opportunity to present their petitions, a thing which persons ignorant of the daily routine of the monarch might easily find hard to compass.

The fact that the Old Regime was based on inequality of rank and of privilege did not necessarily mean that the ruling class neglected or tyrannized over the common man. *Noblesse oblige* was not just a motto.

---

[27] On the way in which Versailles was open to all comers, see Funck-Brentano, *Old Regime*, 153-162. Throughout the Old Regime, from the early Middle Ages to Louis XVI, French kings were accessible to the public.

It was a fact to a greater extent than most modern democrats have been willing to admit. Anyone who has some degree of familiarity with material about the Old Regime written prior to 1789 will recall offhand countless instances of patience, tact, generosity, and long suffering on the part of the nobility toward their dependents. To cite a single, quite typical instance: when Maurepas was trying to arrange the almost hopeless financial tangle in which Saint-Simon, the author of the famous memoirs, had involved his affairs, his cotrustee and fellow minister of state Joly de Fleury sent him a petition from "the widow Matey, former postmistress at Brézolles," setting forth the wretched situation in which she found herself because the contractors for the post office had seized her furniture for nonpayment of one thousand one hundred francs due them. Saint-Simon owed her this sum for postage on his copious correspondence, and it could not be paid until his affairs were settled. Maurepas therefore took the trouble to write a personal appeal to Dufort, *Intendant des Postes*, because, in his words, "This woman seems to me in so sad a state, and the circumstances in which she finds herself so little her fault, that I have thought it my duty to write you about it to get you to obtain a delay," until Saint-Simon's affairs were settled and the one thousand one hundred francs paid.[28]

Maurepas, whose career as a minister of state rivaled in length that of Lord Palmerston, is commonly thought of as a typical eighteenth-century aristocrat, witty, cynical, depraved, heartless. Yet he took this trouble to help a poor woman in the provinces, whom he probably had never seen. *Noblesse oblige* still functioned, even for Regency wits grown into ministers of Louis XV. The trouble, and it was enormous, which he took with Saint-Simon's affairs was undertaken owing to old family ties, but his aid to poor Widow Matey was to a dependent of Saint-Simon, in whose stead Maurepas here acted as patron. Patronage was merely one expression of the way in which the customary relationships constituting society were based on personal ties; merely one characteristic instance of what Olivier-Martin has investigated as the "corporate organization" of the Old Regime.

Now, is not the corrosive effect of Locke's individualism and rationalism on all this hierarchy of personal relationships obvious? Man, according to Locke's theories, is an individual. He is to be restrained only by the minimum of law, by an impersonal and weak government. When to this we add the notions that "self-love and social are the same," that

---

[28] Saint-Simon, *Mémoires*, ed. Chéruel et Regnier, with supplement by A. de Boislisle, XXI, 270, prints Maurepas' letter to Dufort.

the miraculous effect of letting men obey selfish impulses for personal profit will spontaneously be the greatest good of the greatest number; and the belief that traditional and customary ways of behaving, in short, the whole cake of custom ought to be disregarded unless disintegrated, justified by reason, and classified as instances of a few simple principles of universal validity, the danger of enlightened ideas to the whole eighteenth-century social order is apparent. The danger was delayed in its action merely because ordinary men in everyday life do not in ordinary times really act upon the principles they profess, but are in fact guided by the prejudices with which they were brought up.

Finally, there must be recalled once more in connection with positive law what Heckscher has called "feudal disintegration." In the early eighteenth century the positive law by which men lived was customary, not rational or logical. Back of eighteenth-century law, as enforced in eighteenth-century courts, there may have been general principles derived in some cases from the Anglo-Saxons or the Franks, and in others from the Roman law, as eighteenth-century and later students of jurisprudence have tried to show. Great jurists in this period, the Chancellor Daguesseau in France and Sir Philip Yorke (later Lord Hardwicke) in England, were striving toward greater uniformity in legal principles, and for the even more important practical necessity of simplification and standardization of court procedure. Daguesseau's codification of the law, for instance, about gifts, wills, and entails was later embodied with little change in the Code Napoléon. He also strove, on the whole with success, to prevent corruption and bribery in the courts. Lord Hardwicke's great achievement was a clarification of the principles of equity. English court procedure in both civil and criminal cases remained almost incredibly cumbersome, but lawyers and judges were frequently ingenious in managing to evade the well-known excessive severity of the penal statutes, in actual court cases.

The law provided in England for the death penalty for all felonies. This had customarily been evaded by the provision for benefit of clergy. By the reign of Queen Anne all that was necessary to obtain benefit of clergy was to read, or even to recite with the book open at the wrong place, what was called the "neck verse," the first verse of the Fifty-first Psalm, "Have mercy upon me, O God, according to thy loving kindness: according unto the multitude of thy tender mercies blot out my transgressions." Parliament in the fifth year of Anne's reign passed an act by which the claim was allowed without the reading to anyone convicted of a clergyable felony. The effect was to restrict the death penalty for the future to offenses for which Parliament had enacted statutes containing the words "without benefit of clergy." But the harsher statutes of this kind were also evaded. In the case of the notorious law providing the death penalty for stealing from a shop goods to the value of five shillings, a modern English judge has pointed out that "jurors, in defiance of their oaths, and with the encouragement of many judges . . . constantly found that a valuable article stolen in a shop was worth less than 5s.: the thief might then claim the benefit of clergy, and depart, after being burned in the hand with an iron that (again by the judge's connivance) was only luke warm."[29]

Everywhere, even in England, the law and the administration of justice as they existed in the early eighteenth century illustrate feudal disintegration. The English Common Law is really customary law, the "custom of the realm" supplemented by judge-made case law and by parliamentary statutes, both largely clarification and application of Common Law. Parliament, of course, did not make statutes for all of the British possessions, nor did the English law rule in all British courts. Scottish law, the peculiar customary law with its many local variations of the Channel Islands, and the law of the Isle of Man were all distinct from English law, as they are today. Even in England local customary law still survived, as in the Kentish "gavel-kind" which governed inheritance by rules different from those for the rest of England. The hundreds of different systems of customary law in France, the *coutumes*, are well known, as are those in the rest of Continental Europe. The reception of the Roman law was nowhere complete and uniform.

English jurisdictions, like those on the Continent, were still in a medieval tangle. Besides the three Common Law courts—the King's Bench for criminal prosecution, the Court of Common Pleas for civil suits, and the Court of Exchequer for cases affecting the royal revenue—there was the Court of Chancery, with equity jurisdiction, and ecclesiastical and admiralty courts at Doctors' Commons. The justices in eyre who had formerly had jurisdiction over the forest laws still drew salaries, though their functions did not last beyond the reign of Charles II. Each

---

[29] Sir Frank MacKinnon (a judge in the King's Bench Division of the High Court of Justice) in *Johnson's England*, ed. A. S. Turberville (Oxford, 1933), II, 308. My remarks on English legal procedure are based on his account of it. See also William Blackstone, *Commentaries on the Laws of England* (Oxford, 1765-1769); and W. S. Holdsworth's monumental *History of English Law* (London, 1922-1938), X-XII. On Daguesseau see J. F. Monnier, *Le chancelier d'Aguesseau, sa conduite et ses idées politiques*, 2nd ed. (Paris, 1863). The chancellor himself spelled his name as I have done, without pretensions to the *particule*.

of the king's courts had encroached upon the provinces of the others. Fictitious suits appropriate to the court in question were begun, with a "rider" beginning *ac etiam* and leading to the real matter in litigation. Customary law and principles borrowed from Roman or canon law did not suffice for the often complicated and technical civil suits of eighteenth-century merchants and bankers, nor did the customary "law merchant" and arbitration of disputes by guilds, or arbiters, privately agreed upon, the means by which businessmen had avoided taking their financial disputes into the king's courts.

The real importance of Lord Hardwicke, and after him of Lord Mansfield, in English legal and administrative history is that they found in an elaboration of equity means of attracting business litigants to their courts. The laws governing property were thus clarified and strengthened by judge-made law. And the judges took their principles from Locke and the Enlightenment. As Roscoe Pound has said

> Jurists believed that a complete and perfect system of legal precepts could be built up upon principles of natural law discoverable by reason, and derived from the ideal of the abstract man. The fields of jurisprudence and of ethics were taken to be the same. It was sought to make law coincident with morals.[30]

As Pound points out, authority, ecclesiastical and classical, had previously been rejected as a basis for law, especially for legal systems. But to reject the customary law, based on the divergent experience of many men in particular regions over long periods, and to substitute for it simple, primarily ethical principles assumed to have universal validity for Man in the abstract, was an especially "dangerous thought." Luckily, the subsequent development of law and the later administration of the courts were sufficiently varied and nonrational to exempt the jurists from blame for Utopian rationalism.

The whole endeavor of the Enlightenment, then, may be summed up as a desire to make ethics scientific and simple, and to invent a psychological science which should prove that men are capable of profiting by such an ethics. This endeavor was bound to fail, but it could and did contribute not a little to the collapse of the Old Regime.

VI. A NOTE ON VICO

The inconveniences of the chronological subdivision of history come out clearly in the case of Giambattista Vico (1668-1744). The Neapolitan

---

[30] Roscoe Pound, "Jurisprudence," *Encyclopaedia of the Social Sciences*, VIII, 480.

author of the *Scienza nuova* (1725-1744) belongs squarely in the period of this book; yet he was quite out of tune with his age, and his work, not widely known in his lifetime, fell into complete neglect, not to be revived until in the romantic early nineteenth century the French historian Michelet rediscovered it in raptures of delight. Here was a contemporary of Locke and Pope who held "right reason" in as deep, if less vocal, contempt as ever any professional romanticist did.

Vico's work was essentially philosophy, and indeed of that kind often rather scornfully classed as "philosophy of history." Its starting point was a vigorous dissent from the intellectualist epistemology of Descartes and the fundamentally similar epistemology of Locke, which was intellectualism claiming a basis in physical "nature." For Vico, knowing was not just or not mainly thinking as a geometrician thinks, but above all doing. And doing involved the whole man, the man of feeling, dreaming, mythmaking. The test of truth is not in clear, simple ideas, but apparently —Vico does not answer this directly—in the sum total of rounded human life. History, and not mathematics, is thus man's primary teacher.

Vico felt so out of sympathy with his own time that he took revenge by working out a philosophy of history in which the advanced and enlightened eighteenth century appeared, not as the beginning of an age of perfectibility, but as the dried-up, dismal human end of a cycle that had begun with the divine presence of Jesus, and had gone on into the heroism of the Middle Ages. Now, according to Vico, in the eighteenth century, with all the refinements of a very self-conscious civilization, men were growing softer, losing their physical and spiritual energies, quarreling stupidly, not heroically, paving the way for the inevitable collapse, and for the inevitable new beginning of the cycle with a fresh and barbarous people. Vico was not quite "modern" enough to be sure where the barbarians were coming from; but he was as sure as any twentieth-century prophet of doom that they were coming.

This cyclical theory of history, in a three-stage framework (the age of the gods, and of myths; the age of the heroes, and of epics; the age of civilized men, and of prose and reason), may or may not have been in Vico's mind a simple recurring cycle. There are some signs that he felt that each cycle benefits from the experience of the previous ones, that, indeed, the cycles are part of an upward spiral. Vico was a Christian, and a purely mechanical sequence of cycles was a conception quite foreign to his temperament. It is, at any rate, very clear that his notion of man's destiny was poles apart from the simple unilinear notion of progress which in the early eighteenth century was just beginning to establish itself as the faith of most educated men.[31]

The list of Vico's quarrels with his time could be made very long. He admired the Middle Ages, which the fashionable world would not do for another hundred years. He liked Homer *because* Homer was a primitive, and he actually held that Homer and Dante represented parallel stages in their respective cycles. He preferred the mythmakers to the geometricians, and he disliked contemporaries who patronized earlier times and sought to explain men's behavior in those days as a kind of fumbling, infantile rationalism. He was, in short, a man born just about a century too soon.

And yet, Vico seems less out of place in the first half of the eighteenth century than he would have been in the second half. It is hard to think of him as a contemporary of Locke, but even harder to think of him as a contemporary of his fellow countryman of the next generation, the most enlightened jurist Filangieri. For there is a real distinction between the first generation of the Enlightenment, that of Locke and Montesquieu, and the second, that of Rousseau, Holbach, La Mettrie, Condorcet, and their fellow propagandists for a new world. As we have seen, Locke was no revolutionist. Reason was for him, as it was for Walpole, an instrument for adjusting, compromising, working with what one has; and even Nature was fairly mundane. It was the next generation that hypostatized Reason and Nature, and made them corrosive ideals—corrosive, that is, of things-as-they-were.

Vico, no doubt, was too queer a person ever to have adjusted himself to his contemporaries, or to have tried to influence them by talking their language. Had he been willing to do so, he might just possibly have made himself understandable to a Locke for whom knowing was, after all, a kind of doing. But he never could have made himself understood to Condorcet and his fellow dwellers in the "Heavenly City of the Eighteenth-Century Philosophers."[82]

[31] J. B. Bury, *The Idea of Progress* (London, 1928), 78-143.

[32] On Vico, see the excellent little article by B. Croce, *Encyclopaedia of the Social Sciences*, XV, 249-251, and the appended bibliography; also C. Brinton, "The Revolutions," *Encyclopaedia of the Social Sciences*, I, 139.

Chapter Seven

THE ARTS

I. INSTRUMENTS OF PROGRESS

IN THE early eighteenth century there was no rigid dividing line between the useful arts and the fine arts. Nor was the technology on which the useful arts were increasingly based sharply separated from "natural philosophy,' which we would now call "science." It therefore seems justifiable in sketching briefly and generally the progress of "the arts" from 1715 to 1740 to employ the term in a broader sense than it usually has for twentieth-century readers.[1]

To the eighteenth century the arts were the means or instruments by which civilization was to progress, to gain in comfort and in enlightenment. It is obvious that before the introduction of power machinery and the mass production of standardized wares for the world market, most of the consumers' goods of the economists were in a sense works of art, displaying the skill, or lack of skill, of an individual craftsman. A pair of shoes would be made by a single worker on lasts copied from the wearer's feet. Ready-made articles already existed, even in the case of cheap shoes, but they were not yet typical. The way to improve the art of shoemaking was not thought to be to standardize it, but to train better craftsmen. In some crafts, such as the making of nautical instruments, the advice of scientists was already sought. In others, the great majority, such advice still appeared wholly irrelevant. The sciences and the fine arts were, in fact, more indebted to the craftsmen who made their instruments than craftsmen in general were to scientists.

The orchestral music of Bach and Handel has a different instrumentation, except for the strings, from that of Wagner or of Richard Strauss, because in the eighteenth century the modern wood-wind and brass

---

[1] The name of the Society of Arts founded in London in the 1750's, and that of the French Conservatoire des Arts et Metiers founded in 1794, refer primarily to the useful arts. The titles of two of the earliest encyclopedias, E. Chambers, *Cyclopædia, or an Universal Dictionary of Art and Sciences* (London, 1728), and J. T. Jablonski, *Allgemeines Lexicon der Künste und Wissenschafften* (Leipzig, 1721), show a use of the term "art" which is inclusive rather than restrictive.

instruments had not been perfected. The trumpet parts, for example, in scores by Bach and Handel, were written for a natural trumpet, playing only a few notes in the single key. Those of Wagner and Strauss were conceived for a far more versatile and more sonorous modern instrument, which Bach and Handel would probably have been delighted to use had it existed in their day. Modern investigators have shown that the progress of the science of physics has been strongly influenced by the work of instrument makers. It is obvious that the telescope and microscope made astronomy and biology possible as exact experimental sciences.[2]

It has often been pointed out that the development of mining and metallurgy, which had reached a relatively advanced stage by the eighteenth century, was a necessary prerequisite for the whole later development of modern civilization. Coal and iron, the well-known bases of nineteenth-century industrial progress, began in the early eighteenth century to occupy the place they later held. The technique of mining remained substantially that described in the sixteenth century in Agricola's *De Re Metallica*, but a number of the mines had become so deep that the pumping out of water, and ventilation, as well as the hoisting of the minerals to the surface, presented almost insoluble problems. Many mines were still nothing but small holes or quarries in surface deposits, worked by individuals without much capital; but the deep mines, such as the coal mines around Newcastle-on-Tyne, had long since become capitalistic enterprises. Charcoal was still in general use for smelting. Consequently the metallurgical industries, especially those dealing with iron and steel, were everywhere hampered by the prevalent deforestation.

Two new developments in England marked the beginning of the industrial revolution: the use of Newcomen's pumping engine for coal mines, which by 1715 was becoming common, and the process, perfected by the Darbys at Coakbrookdale, for using coke instead of charcoal in making cast iron. In 1718 their firm made the first fire-engine castings (steam-engine cylinders) for Newcomen. From 1724 to 1760 the Darbys retained what amounted to a monopoly of this business. They also constructed one of the earliest railways, over which coal and ore were hauled by animal power.[3]

[2] For the development of musical instruments, see *Grove's Dictionary of Music and Musicians*, 3rd ed. (New York, 1927-1928), the standard reference work on all musical topics. For physics and instruments, see C. A. Crommelin, *Physics and the Art of Instrument Making at Leyden in the Seventeenth and Eighteenth Centuries* (Leyden, 1925).

[3] A. Wolf, *A History of Science, Technology, and Philosophy in the Eighteenth Century* (New York, 1939). See also Ashton, *Iron and Steel in the Industrial Revolution;* T. S. Ashton and J. Sykes, *The Coal Industry of the Eighteenth Century* (Manchester, Eng., 1929); T. A. Rickard, *Man and Metals* (New York, 1932), II; and numerous articles in the *Transactions* of the Newcomen Society.

For the historian the chief importance of these developments in mining and metallurgy was the emergence of the industrial entrepreneur demanding *laissez faire*. Minerals such as coal had been regarded as belonging to the king, to his vassals, or to merchants and adventurers leasing mineral rights from the crown or from a feudal lord. But no such lessee would invest the amount of capital necessary for the risky undertaking of developing a mine unless he were given what amounted to ownership. When the nobles themselves undertook to develop mines, as they did with the coal deposits round Newcastle, the usual result was that they exhausted their capital resources, that is their claims to annual income from various sources crudely lumped together as rents, and had to borrow. Then the creditors, frequently city merchants, would eventually take over the property. The legal right of landholders to mineral deposits other than gold and silver was not finally established by act of Parliament until 1688, though an Elizabethan court decision had recognized it for all minerals except metals like lead which are found in association with precious metals. The Stuarts, however, had tried to assert regal rights to mineral deposits and the Bourbons in France had maintained similar claims though they did not assert them in practice until 1744 in the case of coal. Before that time a variety of arrangements were tried which gave no chance for the capitalistic entrepreneur, whose concessions from the state date from a decree of 1744.[4] In Germany, where the Hapsburgs and many of the lesser princes claimed rights to varied and valuable deposits, the eighteenth-century cameralist theories supported state control, not *laissez faire*. Actually the state mines were often mortgaged to secure the debts incurred in wars.[5]

The entrepreneur, with the combination of business ability and willingness to attempt new methods of production, was a type found in most European countries in the early eighteenth century. One of the most interesting examples was a Swede, Christopher Polham (originally Polhammer), 1661-1751, educated at Upsala University, active as a mining engineer, then "Assessor" to the Swedish Board of Trade, who engaged in important public works, especially canals. He devised a rolling mill for iron bars, operated by water power, and invented wheel-cutting and file-cutting machinery, hoists, conveyors, textile machinery, and scientific instruments. Many of these inventions were later rediscovered inde-

[4] See J. U. Nef, *Rise of the British Coal Industry* (London, 1932); M. Rouff, *Les mines de charbon en France au XVIIIe siècle* (Paris, 1922); Lipson, *Economic History of England*, II, 112-183.

[5] See J. Srbik, *Der Staatliche Exporthandel Oesterreichs* (Vienna and Leipzig, 1907).

pendently. But in a poor country like Sweden Polham could not obtain capital enough to mechanize industry as thoroughly as his ideas would have made possible. Nor could he have found labor competent to apply ideas so far in advance of all contemporary technique. Furthermore, his rolling mill demanded an exceptional amount of water power, such as but few localities afforded.

The men capable of modernizing industry existed, but the instruments at their command were crude. The Newcomen engine, for instance, was so wasteful of fuel that its use was not commercially practicable except in coal mines. Watt's celebrated invention, of course, was merely an improvement on this earlier steam engine, and suggested itself to him when he was asked to repair a model belonging to Glasgow University. But even in Watt's day, in the 1760's, it was very difficult to get the parts made accurately enough to make his engine work properly. When malleable or wrought iron was needed, there was no cheap and effective way of removing impurities in the ore, nor was it understood which chemical reactions would produce the qualities desired. Sulphur, for instance, which is actually undesirable, was held responsible for the superior hardness of steel.

All industries requiring the transport of cheap and bulky materials were dependent on water transportation alone, since by land there was no better means than the pack horse, or, where the roads were not blocked by mudholes, clumsy and inefficient wagons. Yet Swedish iron was used extensively in England, and coal from Newcastle was sent to France and to other parts of the Continent in considerable amounts. It was the exceptionally high quality of these minerals as well as the enterprise of businessmen which overcame the obstacles to trade interposed by the extremely slow and costly methods of transport, even by water. For at least a century before 1715 London had been almost wholly dependent on Newcastle coal for fuel, brought thither by a fleet of several hundred vessels.

Paris after 1715, as its available wood supplies neared exhaustion, also became dependent on coal, so that mining in France had to be regulated and encouraged by the state. Again, as in the iron industry, the effects of deforestation made an increase in the supply of coal essential, and set a pressing problem for either private or state enterprise to solve. The whole development shows factors apparently unconnected dovetailing as causes for industrial revolution. Coal had to be used to smelt iron. It could not be mined without pumping engines, which in turn could best be made by improved methods of casting iron and of making steel.

The capital needed for these improvements was in part found by the bankers, whose methods of mobilizing the savings of the public were constantly improving. The use of bills of exchange and of other means of extending and transferring credit was not by any means created by the banks. Every eighteenth-century merchant (small retailers excepted) was in some respects a private banker, which explains why so many merchants left off other business for banking.

If one regards the entrepreneur as the chief instrument of progress, it is apparent that his efforts were most important historically in those undertakings which could not be carried on without considerable capital. In the early eighteenth century the most important of these, aside from mining and metallurgy, were shipping and the support of armies and navies. By shipping, not merely shipbuilding and ship operation, but foreign and coastwise commerce is to be understood. The support of armies and navies included not merely the provision of uniforms, weapons, and other supplies, but also the means of financing these transactions through government loans, the nature of which we have previously considered. Examples of the broad field for study here indicated may be found in the art of navigation and in the technique of making cannon, both of which clearly illustrate the interdependence of all the arts and sciences which may be called "useful" in the immediate and narrow sense of the term.

To determine accurately the position of a ship at sea it is necessary to know the altitude of celestial bodies above the horizon, or to ascertain their position relative to the neighboring stars. Instruments used for this purpose, such as the cross-staff and the astrolabe, had existed long before the eighteenth century. But they were greatly inferior to the modern nautical sextant, invented independently by an Englishman, John Hadley, and by an American, Thomas Godfrey, about 1730. Hadley's "new instrument for taking angles," described in a paper read before the Royal Society May 13, 1731, was an octant, but its design was essentially the same as that of the modern sextant. The astronomer Edmund Halley remembered vaguely that Sir Isaac Newton had suggested the possibility of an instrument of this type, a fact confirmed after Halley's death by the discovery of a memorandum in Newton's hand. It is also known today that Robert Hooke had suggested the same idea in 1666, but the credit for bringing the invention into actual use must go, not to these scientists, but to Hadley and Godfrey. Their new instrument made it easy for a ship's officer with the requisite mathematical training, not difficult for the average man to master, to take accurate observations, since the motion of the ship would not interfere with the use of the sextant. The determination of the latitude was thenceforth simple.

The determination of longitude, however, remained difficult until the perfection of the chronometer, largely the work of another Englishman, John Harrison, in 1735 and 1739. Harrison constructed chronometers for which he claimed a reward of twenty thousand pounds offered by Parliament in 1714 for any practicable method of determining longitude within half a degree. To ascertain longitude by the most practical method, it is necessary to compare the local time at the point of observation (which can be determined by use of the sextant) with the corresponding time at a standard meridian, such as Greenwich. Ordinary clocks with pendulums run at varying rates at sea, influenced by the motion of the ship, changes in moisture, etc. The merit of Harrison's chronometer was that it gained or lost at a fixed and known rate, so that it was capable of giving Greenwich time accurately once its gain or loss was ascertained. Harrison did not receive the full amount of the prize, one of the largest ever offered, until near his death in the reign of George III. But his chronometer, like the sextant, came gradually into general use. Both instruments are still used by navigators today, though radio time signals now afford a convenient check on the chronometer and a possible substitute for it.[6]

These new instruments, the sextant and chronometer, exemplify general tendencies of the time, which are also illustrated by the invention of instruments used almost daily in most households—like thermometers. The thermometer was not new, but in principle went back to Galileo and even further. Its modern form, however, was not perfected until the eighteenth century. Between 1720 and 1740, Fahrenheit, Réaumur, and Celsius, working independently, devised thermometers using mercury or alcohol, and measuring changes of temperature between fixed points by the use of conventional and arbitrary scales. The Fahrenheit, Réaumur, and centigrade scales now in use are perfected versions of these. The early instruments were still crude devices which were not standardized until the work of De Luc and others after 1750.[7]

The general adoption of improved scientific instruments like the sextant and the thermometer may be taken to measure both the progress made in a number of independent branches of science and technology and the

[6] Wolf, *Science, Technology, and Philosophy*, 146-160. See also R. T. Gould, *The Marine Chronometer, Its History and Development* (London, 1923); and for Harrison's career, S. Smiles, *Men of Invention and Industry* (New York, 1885).

[7] See Wolf, *Science, Technology, and Philosophy*, 306-313, and H. C. Bolton, *Evolution of the Thermometer, 1592-1743* (Easton, Pa., 1900).

advance in popular enlightenment. It is very doubtful whether most of Dante's contemporaries, or even Shakespeare's, would have been especially interested in exact measurement of temperature or time, or the exact position of a ship at sea. One can scarcely imagine a medieval knight looking at the thermometer before sallying forth to do battle. But by 1740 the *bourgeoisie* had already adopted the attitude of the present-day educated classes in such matters.

Hardly less important than the development of science and the improvement of techniques as a force making for change in the eighteenth-century world was the provision of munitions and supplies for armies and navies. For instance, a device invented by the ironmaster Wilkinson for boring cannon enabled his firm to make accurate parts for Watt's steam engine; without these parts, the engine would have failed to work in practice at Boulton's plant in Birmingham, as it had previously failed to give satisfaction in Scotland. The urge to make bigger and more lethal guns had not a little to do with the progress of metallurgy. As G. N. Clark has suggested, the growth of large-scale textile industries owed a good deal to the custom of putting armies into uniforms. As we have seen in an earlier chapter, it was war financing which created national debts and government banks. Sombart's thesis about *Krieg und Kapitalismus*, however, needs to be put to the test of further detailed monographic study before being unquestioningly adopted.

II. COMFORTS AND CONVENIENCES

The progress of the useful arts by 1715 had made living for the upper and middle classes more comfortable and more convenient than it had been since the decline of the Greco-Roman civilization, and people were beginning to think that it was possible to improve even upon that ideal. There was a striking contrast between the clumsiness and inefficiency of the earliest machines, such as Newcomen's engine, and the excellence and variety of the consumers' goods made by the multitude of skilled craftsmen in Europe and the Orient for the use of the well to do. Good machines were seldom made until the development of machine tools, nearly a century later. But good hand tools and admirable workmen produced a great variety of articles which commerce brought to such cities as London, Paris, and Frankfurt am Main from all parts of the world, and which the gentry introduced into their country houses as well as their city dwellings. The taste for luxuries spread abroad from European courts, all more or less imitators of Versailles, and did much to aid the development of what we rather loosely describe as "modern civilization." A family of means and taste in our own day could move into a house built and furnished in 1740 by a French, German, Italian or English upper-class family and find that most of the comforts and conveniences of the eighteenth century were still comfortable and convenient. The furnishings, draperies, silverware, pottery and so on would be admirable and enjoyable and in the "best of taste." It is only the more utilitarian and prosaic conveniences and comforts, such as central heating, plumbing, and lighting, which would be found painfully inadequate, or else lacking. The eighteenth-century craftsman, as a visit to any museum will show, turned out wares at best more beautiful and more durable than most of what our factories produce.[8]

The architecture of the dwellings of the middle and upper classes in England in this period is familiar through much imitation in twentieth-century America. When it did not become grandiose, as it did in the palace at Blenheim designed by Vanbrugh for the Duke of Marlborough, or ornate, as in the Zwinger Palace at Dresden, eighteenth-century architecture afforded comfort and convenience without undue expense. The Duchess of Marlborough in her old age is recorded as having said: "I never desire to see Blenheim again; in a lodge I have everything convenient and without trouble."[9] But Blenheim was intended as a palace, not as a home. Its baroque magnificence, like the rococo ornateness of the Zwinger, made a suitable stage setting for the ceremonial functions incumbent upon the eighteenth-century great man.

The nineteenth century used both baroque and rococo as terms of reproach, much as the early eighteenth used the term Gothic. But in recent years connoisseurs of architecture have again begun to praise the best specimens of both types as showing beauty and originality. Employed chiefly for great public buildings, the baroque is at least a sumptuous variation on the Renaissance style which it succeeded. It originated in Italy and by this period had spread over the rest of Europe. The rococo, which at its best depends on a structural pattern of broken curves and not on superficial ornament, seems to have originated in France, though many of the best examples are Spanish churches.[10]

[8] See Oliver Brackett, "The Interior of the House," *Johnson's England*, II, 125 ff. These two volumes, edited by A. S. Turberville, include a remarkable collection of expert opinion for the period covered by Johnson's life (1709-1784).

[9] *Memoirs of Sarah, Duchess of Marlborough*, ed. W. King (New York, 1930). The preface to this edition gives a careful discussion of the authenticity of writings attributed to the duchess.

[10] Sacheverell Sitwell, *Southern Baroque Art* (London, 1924), and *Spanish Baroque Art* (London, 1931); and W. Weisbach, *Die Kunst des Barock in Italien, Frankreich, Deutsch-*

III. CEREMONIAL AS A USEFUL ART

Everyone who knows anything about the Old Regime has read of the elaborate ceremonial which governed the daily lives of kings and princes from Louis XIV down to the autocrats of the hundreds of German petty states. Readers of such memoirs as those of Dangeau, Saint-Simon, and the Duc de Luynes have often rather wearily wondered why so many pages were devoted to apparently trivial and futile details of court etiquette, and why courtiers became so excited over disputes about precedence. Louis XV, unlike his great-grandfather, was himself obviously bored by all the fuss attending upon his getting up in the morning and his eating dinner and his going to bed again at night. Of all the ceremonial functions of the crown, only the royal hunting parties seem really to have given him pleasure.

Why, then, did he not, like Frederick the Great, ruthlessly eliminate most of these tedious formalities? It was partly, of course, that he seldom cared to exert himself to correct things that went wrong. All he actually did was to have built for his own daily use a convenient and comfortable suite of small rooms, easy to heat, and then exclude from them all save his family, a few intimates, and the inevitable servants. He spent a good deal of time away from Versailles, at smaller houses. But he still devoted much time and effort to the elaborate ritual perfected by Louis XIV, and went through it with dignity and self-possession. The same obligation to hold a levée while getting up and dressing in the morning, receiving all sorts of tradesmen, artists, suppliants, and dependents, was incumbent upon ladies and gentlemen of high rank everywhere. The Countess in Richard Strauss's operatic masterpiece, *Der Rosenkavalier*, is in this respect an authentic eighteenth-century great lady. One of the pictures in Hogarth's sequence "Marriage à la Mode" shows the heroine at her dressing table with as miscellaneous an array of company present as that in the famous scene in Strauss's opera. The formal entertainments, dinners, receptions, card parties, dances and so on, were elaborate affairs and were governed by etiquette punctilious beyond anything to be found in the modern world.

The grace and apparent ease with which the French upper classes went through all this business of ceremonial was inimitable, though

---

land, und Spanien (Berlin, 1924). The terms baroque and rococo are not clearly distinguished from each other in current usage. In so far as they mean successive periods of time, this period is that of transition between the two. German historians in the past few years have used both terms extensively and tried to generalize them.

the rest of Europe tried to copy it with results which in Russia under
Peter the Great were a rather sinister farce. When one notices the portraits of tiny children in elaborate court costumes, one realizes that the
nobility and gentry were conditioned to their roles in life from very early
childhood. The way in which Louis XV as a boy of eleven was shown
off to the Turkish ambassador by his governor, the Marshal de Villeroi,
is a typical instance. After praising the king's beauty and pointing out
that the golden hair which hung to his waist was genuine de Villeroi
said to the young ruler, according to the Turk's account of the scene,
"Walk as you do when people are watching you." The boy "with the
majestic gait of a partridge" went to the middle of the room and back.
"Go faster, so that he may see how lightly you run." And the king ran
as requested.[11]

What the French called *la vie en représentation* was then the universal
lot of the great. Manners and etiquette had been brought to a perfection
never attained before or since in Western society. The privileged classes
spent much of their time in the company of their dependents, their
peers, and their monarch. A little reflection will show that ceremonial
was not mere idle artifice, but a necessary duty, and that the squabbles
over precedence had a vital importance in fact.

The society of the Old Regime was, as we have already noted in other
connections, not individualistic, not egalitarian, but corporate. The position of its leaders depended on a hierarchical array of personal ties of
quasi-feudal character. It was thus very important to know your own
exact rank and the relative position of your superiors and your inferiors.
The protocol of ceremonial, the ranking of persons to be seated at a
formal dinner or ordered in a coronation procession, was no empty form.
In a society based on status, as the Old Regime so obviously was based,
one must have distinctions for the same reason that in the modern
world there are varying ranks among army officers and a known order
of precedence.

Granted the uses of precedence, it might still be argued by some that at
least the eighteenth-century gentry had insufferably formal manners.
They were not stiff, at least not in France, but there always was an
elaborate background of training. The French ease of manners was not
a natural and simple thing, but the last refinement of an exacting art.
The masters of the art no doubt enjoyed it, but, especially for the rising
bourgeoisie, it was rather too demanding. The romantics were shortly to

[11] Leclercq, *Régence*, II, 500, quoting the *Relation de l'ambassade de Mehemet Effendi à
la Cour de France en 1721* published as a translation from the Turkish in 1757.

rebel against this etiquette, as well as against more important kinds of formalism.

Many elaborate descriptions might be cited of the ceremonial the eighteenth century found so picturesque and so useful in asserting the status of participants. The coronation of George II and that of Louis XV, for instance, were impressive displays, meticulously recorded. But no abridgment could convey in a couple of sentences the full flavor of the original.[12]

The details of the court ceremonial at Versailles, and of the unconscious parody of them at petty German courts, could furnish material for many an amusing essay. Those of the pompous receptions accorded foreign embassies were often especially full of color. These displays served the purpose of impressing upon all beholders the power and wealth of the sovereigns concerned. When, for example, Ibrahim Pasha was sent from Constantinople to Vienna in 1719 for the exchange of ratifications of the Treaty of Passarowitz, his suite consisted of "763 men, 645 horses, 100 mules, 180 camels," all fed and housed by the Emperor Charles VI during their sojourn in his domains. The ambassador received "a gratification of 150 écus a day." His entry into Vienna resembled the circus parades so dear to nineteenth-century American small boys. Near the head of the long procession was a "Treasurer" with six four-horse chariots containing the gifts, seventy times seven in number, of the sultan to Charles VI.

The ambassador rode in a coach all scarlet and gold, richly painted with various scenes on the inside panels. To the right and left were a "cupbearer" and a "chief sharpshooter," in long scarlet robes, bonnets of white felt, and tiger skins draped over their shoulders. They carried silver-handled sabers in red velvet scabbards. There was a military band of chalumeaux (an ancestor of the modern clarinet), cymbals, trumpets, and a great many tambourines, making what eighteenth-century German composers sometimes imitated as "Turkish music." Charles VI reciprocated by an equally lavish embassy to Constantinople.[13]

[12] For George II's coronation, see the description in *A Foreign View of England in the Reigns of George I and George II. The Letters of Monsieur César De Saussure to His Family*, tr. and ed. Madame Van Muyden (London, 1902), 239-270. For that of Louis XV, see Saint-Simon, *Mémoires*, XIX, 61-77.

[13] See the full description in J. de Hammer Purgstall, *Histoire de l'Empire Ottoman* (Paris, 1835-1843), XIV, 14 ff.

IV. ARTIFICE, PATTERN, AND ELOQUENCE

When one turns from the useful arts to the fine arts of poetry, painting, music, and the rest, it is possible to discover certain characteristics common to most of the works of the first half of the eighteenth century which distinguish them from earlier and later productions. These may be summed up under the three heads, artifice, pattern, and eloquence. Artifice was a concentration on technique as an end in itself, a meticulous elaboration of style, a love of ornament for its own sake, a sharp separation of art from ordinary everyday life. Pattern was the confining of artistic creation within the often narrow bounds of conventional forms, such as the heroic couplet or the fugue. There are necessarily patterns of some sort in any work of art, even though it be called a rhapsody or free verse. But the eighteenth-century artist as a rule worked within strict conventions, like the three unities of neoclassic drama. Eloquence was a quality harder to explain than the other two, an emphasis on expressiveness independent of the thing expressed, an endeavor to arouse admiration rather than to stir deep emotion.[14] An example may help to explain this somewhat elusive quality. Bach and Handel were certainly the two greatest creative artists of this period. Neither of them hesitated to use musical settings originally employed in secular compositions in their most lofty and ambitious religious works, or vice versa. In *Esther*, an oratorio based on Racine's play and originally intended as an opera, Handel used for the scene in which Haman pleads for his life the same music he had used in *Brockes Passion* for Christ's agony in the garden. Similarly, Ahasuerus' love song was originally a lament sung by a believer for his crucified Saviour. This transferring of music from one work to another without regard for the particular emotion it originally was supposed to convey was a lifelong trait of Handel.[15] So also Bach, commonly regarded as a more spiritual musician, did not scruple to use in the cantata *Also hat Gott die Welt geliebt* an air which he had previously written for a hunting cantata given as an after-dinner entertainment at a princely country house. Similar transferences of secular music appear even in such masterpieces as the Christmas oratorio.[16]

Voltaire's conception of poetry stressed this same quality of expressive-

---

[14] I believe there is no exact term—no term even mildly free of semantic difficulties—for this quality. I use "eloquence" as a handy term, to which I am forced to give a special meaning.

[15] See R. A. Streatfeild, *Handel* (New York, 1909), 267, 268.

[16] See J. Combarieu, *Histoire de la musique des origines à la mort de Beethoven* (Paris, 1913-1919), II, 286.

ness divorced from particular significance. Poetry, he said, is a kind of music. Pope he thought "the most elegant, the most correct . . . the most harmonious poet England has had. . . . He can be translated, because he is extremely clear, and because most of his subjects are general." Poetry in short is harmonious eloquence.[17]

To discuss the application of these three qualities to each of the fine arts in detail would demand more space than can be spared in a cursory general survey of the state of the arts in the early eighteenth century. Of architecture we have already spoken briefly as a setting for ceremonial. The link between the crafts and the fine arts in the eighteenth century, if not in all periods, was the development of ornament from a mere incident to an end in itself.

For the eighteenth century the arts were all decorative in function, all meant to adorn the spacious and elegant leisure of the governing classes, and to enhance the pomp and solemnity of traditional ritual and essential ceremonial observance. Art was not thought of as a means to truth, or as a steppingstone toward the higher life. Not until the time of such romantics as Chateaubriand was the aesthetic approach believed to be a substitute for the ethical. For the eighteenth-century gentleman the arts added to the graces and the comforts of living. They had nothing to do with saving one's soul. Beauty was not yet confused, in Keatsian fashion, with truth.

It is obvious that in all the arts the early eighteenth century paid strict regard to conventions about forms and patterns. The regular repetition of motifs in architecture appears in the intricate curves of the rococo as well as in the Palladian style which was still more popular in England. The heroic couplet and the French Alexandrine in verse, especially in dramatic verse, the fugue in music, the careful composition in painting, all bear witness to this salient characteristic of the neoclassic era.

It is almost equally obvious that a great deal of ingenuity, a close attention to technique, was the rule among eighteenth-century artists. No English poet has ever wrought his verses more carefully than Pope, no English poet has ever attained a greater technical skill. Voltaire's epic, the *Henriade*, and his numerous tragedies seem artificial in the bad sense of the term today. *Zaïre* is still studied in courses in literature and still occasionally revived in French theaters, but its inferiority to Racine in imaginative intensity and in artistic perfection has long been a critical commonplace. Brunetière, whose sympathy with classicism in general

---

[17] Voltaire, *Lettres philosophiques*, no. 22, in *Oeuvres*, ed. Beuchot, XXXVII, 258-259.

caused him to make out as good a case as he could for Voltaire as a dramatist, pointed out that even his bad plays, such as *Rome sauvée*, represented effort as laborious as had ever gone into the making of a masterpiece. Voltaire's passion for the theater is well known to readers of his letters. The ingenuity he displayed in contriving plots, and in giving his plays settings then novel, such as Palestine during the Crusades (*Zaïre*), as well as the labor of making his verse smooth, elegant, and harmonious, are typical examples of the quality of artifice.[18]

Artifice in a more favorable sense of the term characterizes Swift's cunningly contrived *Gulliver's Travels* (1726). Every detail of the life in Lilliput and Brobdingnag is so carefully thought out that most of us read the book as children just for the story, without any notion of the real meaning. Another and quite different masterpiece, Marivaux's best comedy *Le jeu de l'amour et du hasard* (1730), still a standard repertory piece in French theaters and required reading in schools, exemplifies artifice both in its substance and in its style. A marriage between two young people has been arranged by their elders. The young gentleman and the young lady, who have not met before, each make the same plan, to change places with their servants so as better to observe the proposed betrothed. The struggles of the lady's maid and the valet to be genteel, and the unforced gentility of the real lady and the real gentleman, are admirably and subtly depicted. Of course the lady finds herself, to her horror, falling in love with the valet (as she supposes) and the gentleman prefers the lady's maid (as he supposes) to her mistress. After all the misunderstandings there is a happy ending. There are, of course, no hints of democracy or equality in the play. Rank is simply accepted as a fact of life.[19]

The popularity in this period of the mock-heroic and the pastoral, two of the most artificial of literary genres, is well known. Pope's *Rape of the Lock* (1712, much revised later), unsurpassed in the mock-heroic style, was much imitated, especially in Germany. The pastoral and Arcadian vein was especially cultivated in Italy, where numerous literary academies produced nothing comparable in merit to the seventeenth-century scientific ones, like the Lincei. But Pope, as well as "Namby-pamby" Ambrose Phillips, whom he ridiculed, wrote pastorals.

The two veins were combined in Gay's *Beggar's Opera* (1728) written, it is said, as a result of Swift's suggestion that a "Newgate pastoral" might

---

[18] F. Brunetière, *Histoire et littérature* (Paris, 1884-1886), III, 95-119.

[19] On Marivaux as an artificial writer, see C. A. Sainte-Beuve, "Marivaux," *Causeries du lundi* (Paris, 1851-1862), IX.

make "an odd pretty sort of thing." The bankruptcy of the Academy Italian Opera Company in London, which had given many of Handel's earlier operas, was an incidental result of the mock-heroic side of *The Beggar's Opera*. The failure of the company forced Handel to become an impresario himself. The charming popular tunes arranged by Dr. Pepusch, and the satire on Walpole's administration, had something to do with the unprecedented success of *The Beggar's Opera*, which beat all records by running for sixty-two nights, and then touring the country.[20]

In painting the element of artifice was also prominent. Portraits were commissioned by all families with social pretensions and means. But they were seldom photographic likenesses of the sitters. Sometimes the draperies and the elaborate background, an interior or a garden scene, were painted by another hand than the one that painted the head. The likenesses were not so much flattering as conventionalized. So also the portrait busts. In the portraits by Rigaud of French statesmen, for example, there is an improbable amount of resemblance between Orry and Chauvelin, or even between Dubois and Fleury, for which costumes and wigs do not wholly account. Hogarth, whose style was realistic, was unsuccessful in winning favor as a portrait painter, and had to fall back on the famous quasi-narrative series, "The Rake's Progress," "Marriage à la Mode," and the rest, of which the prints were very popular. The spirit of the age was perhaps best represented in painting by Watteau's familiar "Embarcation for Cythera," a masterpiece never surpassed in its kind.

The quality of eloquence is to be noted at its best in the poetry of Pope, when, in his own words, he is saying "What oft was thought, but ne'er so well expressed," and in the well-known lines written as an attack on Addison but embodying truths as old as human nature.

> Peace to all such! but were there One whose fires
> True Genius kindles, and fair Fame inspires,
> Blest with each Talent and each Art to please,
> And born to write, converse, and live with ease:
> Shou'd such a man, too fond to rule alone,
> Bear, like the *Turk*, no brother near the throne,
> View him with scornful, yet with jealous eyes,

[20] Full details on the Italian literature and academies are given in G. Natali's two admirable volumes on the *Settecento* (Milan, 1929) in the *Storia Letteraria d'Italia.* The English writers mentioned are discussed in *Cambridge History of English Literature,* ed. A. W. Ward and A. R. Waller (Cambridge, Eng., 1907-1927). The best brief account is E. Legouis and L. Cazamian, *A History of English Literature* (New York, 1927), a translation of a manual used in French schools. On Handel and opera in London, see Newman Flower, *Handel* (London, 1923), 171-187.

And hate for Arts that caus'd himself to rise;
Damn with faint praise, assent with civil leer,
And without sneering, teach the rest to sneer;
Willing to wound, and yet afraid to strike,
Just hint a fault, and hesitate dislike;
Alike reserv'd to blame, or to commend,
A tim'rous foe, and a suspicious friend,
Dreading ev'n fools, by Flatterers besieg'd,
And so obliging that he ne'er obliged;
Like *Cato,* give his little Senate laws,
And sit attentive to his own applause. . . .[21]

This is not merely Addison, it is Pope himself, it is any gifted and
sensitive writer who has become an authority on his art. The perfect
felicity of expression in this passage should be obvious to the dullest ear.
Scrutinize it line by line, word by word, and it is clear that any change
would be for the worse.

Now "eloquence" as exemplified by Pope's lines on Addison is plainly
not bombast or fustian like that too often spouted by Daniel Webster,
and even by Cicero. Rather it is the use of what Flaubert called the *mot
juste,* the inevitable one right word in the right place, but to convey not
sense impressions as much as clear ideas. To worshipers of the romantic
"strangeness added to beauty" of Pater's famous phrase, clarity no doubt
may seem a prosaic quality. To the eighteenth-century artist, it was the
highest excellence for which he strove. Without ordered and formal
patterns, without meticulous craftsmanship, it could not be attained.
Without something of universality it was impossible. A unique experience
cannot be communicated from one imagination to another. Observation
of life and of the classics, not introspection, was the proper preparation
for artistic expression.

It is probably in music that this impersonal, generalized eloquence of
the neoclassic eighteenth century was most perfectly realized, partly
because in that century there flourished an unusual number of great
composers. Mozart, whose art has at its best the perfection of the
Parthenon, or of the *Antigone* of Sophocles, belongs, like Haydn, Gluck,
and the early Beethoven, to the latter part of the century, but such great
musicians as Rameau, Domenico Scarlatti, Pergolesi, Bach, and Handel
were in this period. It is, therefore, with Bach and Handel that our
discussion of music as exemplifying artifice, pattern, and eloquence must
chiefly be concerned. Their works represent the culminating point of a

[21] *Epistle to Dr. Arbuthnot* (London, 1734), lines 188-205.

development which had begun in Italy at the end of the sixteenth century and foreshadowed new trends which were to govern their art until the death of Brahms in 1897.

Music, unlike poetry and architecture, had no masterpieces surviving from the Greco-Roman civilization to influence its development. Opera, to be sure, had begun in an attempt to recreate Greek tragedy, but the music known to have accompanied the works of Sophocles and the rest has been lost, or rather its notation in surviving copies is interpreted differently by different scholars. Music, again unlike its sister arts, is a world in itself, not a representation of the external world. Its language and conventions are its own. They are based on acoustical principles, but adapted to the needs of performers and the creative imagination of composers, and conditioned by the instruments, including the human voice, which are to convey the music to the listening ear. The development of the art of music presents more differences than resemblances with that of the sister arts. Its relationship to the general development of civilization, to the course of historic events, is less close than is the case with poetry, for example.

These rather obvious general truths about the nature of music must be borne in mind in considering the place in its history of Bach and Handel. The first point to note is that in the early eighteenth century the language of music became stabilized, the rules of harmony were definitely codified, and the technique of the art of composition was perfected within a somewhat arbitrary set of limitations which are still elementary rules taught to beginning students of musical theory, though in the past fifty years they have had less and less relationship to the actual practice of modern composers. Rameau's *Traité de l'harmonie,* published in 1722, was a precise formulation of notions already current about the importance of the major scale (the old Ionian mode), of chords built up in thirds, and of tonality. For the twelve modes henceforth were substituted our familiar major and minor scales. Bach's *Well Tempered Clavichord*, of which the first part also appeared in 1722, is a set of twenty-four preludes and fugues, in each of the twelve major and minor keys which are musically feasible. It was written to show that the use of the tempered scale (in which a single note represents F sharp in one context, and G flat, which is acoustically and theoretically a different note, in another context) would facilitate writing music in major and minor keys, with definite tonality and practicable modulations. To musicians, the greatness of the changes which the work of Rameau and of Bach brought to completion will be obvious. However much the narrowing down of the harmonic possibilities of music to those correct in Rameau's view may be regretted by modernist musicians, who for half a century have gone back to modal harmonics in some ways akin to those of Renaissance music, it represented in the eighteenth century an advance which made possible not merely the achievement of Bach and of Handel, but after them that of Mozart and Beethoven. It is only the apparent exhaustion of the possibilities for original and powerful creative expression in terms of strict tonality and orthodox harmony which has caused the innovations of Ravel, Debussy, Schönberg, Stravinsky, and the rest.

To nonmusicians it is perhaps necessary to say that the familiar do-re-mi scale they learnt in school and can pick out by ear on the piano was used in this early eighteenth-century period by Bach and Rameau as preferable to numerous other possible scales, of which only the minor (in its several forms) was retained along with it. The significance of the change they will have to take on faith.[22] What the historians of music now describe as the "monodic revolution" at the close of the sixteenth century, the substitution of a single melody with an accompaniment of chords for the older convention of polyphony, had been necessary for the development of tonality and of harmony. This revolution had been associated with the beginnings of opera, which originally was intended as a revival of Greek dramatic art in Renaissance Italian guise. Seventeenth-century operatic composers, like Lully, had already written airs with accompaniment which had definite tonality and harmonization correct according to modern textbooks. Handel was merely the greatest and the best known of the composers contemporary with Rameau who wrote what the modern untrained listener will readily accept as the kind of tune with accompaniment to which his limited musical experience has accustomed him. What Rameau did was, therefore, not to innovate so much as to provide a logical theory for innovations previously developed simply and spontaneously.

The monodic revolution had not, however, been complete. Revolutions seldom are. Polyphonic music had gone on, to reach its culmination in the work of J. S. Bach, not merely the greatest musician of the period, but according to a number of admirers, the greatest of all time. Finally, in the work of Haydn, Mozart, and Beethoven, after 1780, classic forms for instrumental music were perfected which depended on tonality as a basis for unity and for the necessary contrast. In their work, as already in Handel and in Bach, monody and polyphony were reunited.

[22] Combarieu, *Histoire de la musique,* II, 272-296.

It should be added that not all musical historians divide the history of music into periods determined by purely musical considerations. One might group the standard works in musical history which have appeared in the present century into three classes. Besides those which employ a purely musical classification, in terms of the language and the style of the art of music, there are works which are akin to chronicles rather than histories, mere lists of composers, often grouped by types of composition as well as by chronology and by the nationality of composers. These have chapters, for example, on "The French Instrumental School in the Eighteenth Century," followed by "Music in Great Britain" (from the sixteenth through the eighteenth century).[23] The best of them, like the one here cited, by a noted French musicologist, also devote some consideration to purely musical developments, such as the monodic revolution.

A third class of histories of music endeavors to integrate the development of the art with the general stream of political, social, and cultural history. Short and, to the historian, often rather conventional and superficial discussions of "The Age of Absolutism" or of "The Enlightenment" are interspersed among often highly detailed and technical accounts of the music contemporary with these nonmusical periods. Many German and some non-German writers have in recent years tried to apply to the music of the seventeenth and eighteenth centuries Friedrich von Schlegel's well-known remark that "architecture is frozen music" by assuming that music is fluid architecture, and that, accordingly, periods of architectural history are also appropriate to transfer to the history of music. It is certainly true, as Adler has pointed out, that the analogy between baroque architecture and the music of Bach is full of imaginative insight, if not taken too literally or pushed too far. But on the whole, attempts to connect the development of the art of music with nonmusical developments have not so far given conclusive results.[24]

A second point which must be grasped as a preliminary to an understanding of the creative achievement of Bach and of Handel is the nature of the instruments, including the human voice, at their command. Bach was all his life an organist. His reputation among his contemporaries depended on his unusual mastery of that instrument, rather than on the great choral works rediscovered for posterity long after his death by

[23] H. Prunières, *Nouvelle histoire de la musique* (Paris, 1934-1936), II, chaps. xi-xii.

[24] See G. Adler on the "Periodisierung der abendländlichen Musik" in the excellent *Handbuch der Musik-Geschichte,* 2nd ed. (Berlin, 1930), I, 68-71, of which he is the editor. Further references in bibliographical essay, *infra.*

Mendelssohn and other nineteenth-century musicians. The organs for which Bach wrote the finest music ever composed for that instrument did not, like those in modern movie houses and in many modern churches, ape the orchestra. They were sonorous instruments, admirably adapted to the performance of polyphonic music because the several keyboards, and the pedals which supplemented the manuals, enabled the performer to interweave independent parts, and to ornament them with florid and elaborate figuration. For centuries the organ had been associated with church music, and the works written for it by Bach continued in many respects the ecclesiastical tradition. Music, of course, when it advanced beyond the primitive stage of song tunes and dance tunes unaccompanied, had done so not by providing such tunes with a harmonic accompaniment, but by weaving together independent parts. Only gradually were the chords, the harmonies, thus produced regarded for their own sake. It is difficult in the modern world, even for amateur musicians, to remember this elementary fact of musical history, that polyphony and counterpoint preceded harmony. Bach, whose use of the tempered scale favored the development of homophonic music, music with a melody and a harmonic background, represented the culmination, the highest point attained by the centuries of development of polyphony, as well as the transition to the style represented by Haydn and Mozart, and by Bach's sons, of whom several were composers of note. It is the fact that Bach was pre-eminently a performer on keyboard instruments, especially the organ, that explains his essentially polyphonic style and the character of the numerous and important vocal compositions he wrote for his various church choirs.

Bach could also play the violin, for which he composed a number of works, some of them masterpieces. This instrument had been perfected by such makers as Stradivarius (1644-1737) who, aided by his sons, was turning out not only violins but also violoncellos of unparalleled excellence. But the violin had not yet wholly displaced the numerous now obsolete inferior instruments of the same general type, the viols, such as the *viola da gamba, viola d'amore*, etc., for which Bach also wrote. Bach's chief primarily orchestral work, the six Brandenburg concertos, accordingly contains a good deal of music not practicable for the usual modern symphony orchestra. Although such Italian composer-violinists as Tartini and Corelli had already written essentially violinistic music, Bach did not markedly differentiate his musical idiom when writing for violin from that which he employed in works for keyboard instruments.

The wood-wind and brass instruments of Bach's day were primitive and crude compared to their modern successors. Much of what Bach wrote for them in the accompaniments to his choral works sounds to a modern listener as if intended rather to add tonal color to the background, to supplement the organ or clavier accompaniment than to be important for its own sake. But to Bach it was all probably part of a polyphonic pattern. He loved loud and brilliant music, noisy music as much, perhaps, as his successors, Wagner or Richard Strauss. In dramatic passages he obviously strove to get the utmost possible volume of sound. But his partiality for the almost inaudible clavichord, because of its expressive quality, and much of his chamber music show an equal or even greater love for calm and quietly contemplative music. His writing for voices, especially in the motets (where the accompaniment was either absent or relatively subdued) demanded of singers probably not of remarkable competence a command of vocal technique and a facility in florid song which must have seemed to them exacting. We do not know how adequately Bach's works were performed. It is certain that some of the greatest of them like the *B Minor Mass* were not performed at all in his lifetime.

Bach did not write for the male sopranos and contraltos who sang in Handel's operas. Their technique, to judge by the music written for them and by contemporary comment, must have surpassed that of any modern singers, male or female. The tone produced by these *castrati* is said to have had a brilliance and power the female voice cannot equal. One of these male sopranos, Farinelli, may well have been the most admirable singer ever known. The extraordinary story of his becoming a favorite of the King of Spain, Philip V, to whom he sang the same six songs every night for ten years, is well known. His favor persisted under Philip V's successor, Ferdinand VI. The remarkable simplicity and pathos of his vocal style was attributed in his mature years, perhaps flatteringly, to the advice of another royal musician, the Emperor Charles VI. He had previously excelled in florid song. Our modern coloratura sopranos often vie publicly with a flute. Farinelli as a young man used to compete with a trumpet player. He could sustain and swell a tone more powerfully than the trumpeter, besides ornamenting his vocal passages with elaborations quite beyond the rather limited possibilities of the eighteenth-century trumpet. It may have been age and relative loss of vocal power as well as the imperial advice which caused him to change to a less florid style. The unanimous praise given him by contemporary musicians would indicate that he was a phenomenal artist, as well as a phenomenal voice. He was, however, too tall and ungainly to be an effective actor in opera.[25]

The differences in style between the music of Bach and that of his contemporary, Handel, also born in 1685, were partly owing to the very different courses they took in life. Bach became a German *Kapellmeister*, at Weimar and Cöthen, and finally *Cantor* (organist and choirmaster) of the Thomas-Schule at Leipzig, where he was responsible for the music used in the services of three other Lutheran churches besides his own Thomas Church. He was well known as a virtuoso player on keyboard instruments, and for his advocacy of the tempered scale in tuning them. Incidentally, his skill as a performer was enhanced by his improvements in the technique of fingering. He used the thumb as well as the fingers, then an innovation. Handel, born at Halle only a few miles from Bach's birthplace at Eisenach, went to Italy as a young man, and eventually became the impresario as well as the chief composer for Italian opera in London. When the popularity of opera waned, he turned to oratorio. Of the details of Bach's life we know almost as little as we do about Shakespeare, but on Handel's career after he came to London in 1712 we have a great deal of information, some of it of dubious accuracy.

Of Handel's operas, now very rarely performed, it is not necessary to speak at length. They contain a wealth of beautiful airs, some of which are familiar to all concertgoers, and one or two of which are known to all persons not born tone deaf. The beautiful *"Ombra mai fu"* from *Xerxes*, for example, was bloated by a nineteenth-century arranger into "Handel's Largo in G" (the original key is F), and it is now performed by every conceivable combination of instruments. It is quite possible that some of these operas if revived would, as Handelians like Streatfeild have claimed, seem no more archaic than those of Gluck who is still in the operatic repertory, despite the rigid and artificial conventions governing the succession of vocal numbers and the dramatis personae. One of the oratorios, on the other hand, *The Messiah*, has certainly been performed more often in England and the United States than any other musical masterpiece. In many cities it is given every Christmas season as a kind of ritual observance. It is Handel's career as an operatic composer which explains the predominance in much of his music of what the eighteenth century called "the Italian style" of flowing, often ornate melody with harmonic accompaniment. Bach could and not infrequently did write in this Italian style, and Handel often wrote

---

[25] For an eighteenth-century account of Farinelli, see Sir John Hawkins, *A General History of the Science and Practice of Music* (London, 1776), V, 318-327.

essentially polyphonic music, but the average untrained though sensitive listener will today find Handel's musical idiom much more familiar than that of Bach.

Both of these great composers exemplify artifice, pattern, and eloquence. The *Well Tempered Clavichord*, one of the supreme masterpieces of all time, as we have seen as a methodical illustration of the musical possibilities of a new system of tuning, has an element of artifice as obvious as that in the *Musical Offering*, one of the latest and most elaborate of Bach's works. He had been invited to visit Frederick the Great of Prussia. The king, who took flute playing very seriously and was, moreover, a composer not without genuine talent, gave Bach a theme upon which to improvise. Bach afterward wrote the *Musical Offering*, in which everything was based on a somewhat improved version of the royal theme. It contains a fugue in three parts, a fugue in six parts (a musical tour de force), a sonata, and a number of canons. The two fugues probably represent those which Bach had extemporized at Potsdam. He used an old word, *ricercar*, instead of fugue in their titles, partly because he could make it mean *Regis jussio cantio et reliqua canonica arte resuluta* by taking each letter of the word as an initial. This artificial work was a compliment to the King of Prussia, but that Bach delighted in such intricate and ingenious displays of technical skill is shown by his *Art of the Fugue*, composed shortly afterward, where everything is based on a theme of his own invention.

Handel's ingenious but rather naïve musical depiction of the plagues of Egypt in his *Israel in Egypt* is a rather trivial example, one among many, of his delight in musical artifice. The extraordinary hopping figuration of the orchestral accompaniment to "And the land brought forth frogs" is an almost ludicrous instance, paralleled later in Haydn's *Creation* by the orchestral roars of the newly created lions in the Garden of Eden, to mention only a single case. The ornate musical arabesques, with which the musical outlines of much of the music of both Bach and Handel are decorated, resemble the intricate curves of rococo architecture. But according to the great critic Hanslick, music is essentially nothing but "sounding arabesques."[26]

Neither Bach nor Handel showed any slavish devotion to conventional musical forms or patterns, preferring to create their own in accordance with their imaginative aims. The fugues in the *Well Tempered Clavichord*, for instance, are not strict in form. Sometimes a mere episode is elaborated at greater length than the subject itself. But there is always

[26] E. Hanslick, *The Beautiful in Music* (London, 1891).

a very definite musical skeleton underlying the body of any work by Bach or by Handel, which can be laid bare by musical analysts.

It is obvious that if the two composers had been mere artificers in music, mere jugglers with technical devices, their music would not have survived for two centuries. In a great deal of it there is an intense emotional drive, as in the *Well Tempered Clavichord*. Often there are dramatic outbursts which are still, even after repeated hearings, thrilling to many listeners. In Bach's *St. Matthew Passion*, for instance, when Pilate has asked the mob which culprit it wishes pardoned, the savage cry from the chorus, "Barabbas," rouses any sensitive listener to intense excitement.

At the first performance in London of Handel's *Messiah* (previously produced in Dublin), King George II was in the audience. His scorn for the other arts, "Bainting and Boetry," has been much ridiculed. But he was too good a German not to be sensitive to music. When the "Hallelujah" chorus came to the words "For the Lord God omnipotent reigneth," the king, and with him the audience, "started up and remained standing until the end." Audiences in many cities still stand during the performance of this chorus, as a kind of ritual observance. The soprano air, "I Know that My Redeemer Liveth," has from the first also moved audiences. The words and music of the opening line are inscribed on Handel's tomb in Westminster Abbey. But the beauty of the music is not really dependent on the words. Some German has said of the famous air of Orpheus, *"Che faro senza Euridice,"* in Gluck's opera that the words might just as well be *"Ach, ich habe sie gefunden,"* instead of *"verloren"* ("I've found her," instead of "I've lost her"). The eloquence of such music is generalized, independent of nonmusical meaning.

The variety of styles in which Handel and Bach excelled is a proof not merely of their virtuosity but of the wide scope of eighteenth-century music. Even such relatively minor figures as Domenico Scarlatti, Pergolesi, Rameau, and Couperin had a good deal of the same breadth of imaginative and technical range. The strictures of Madame Wanda Landowska, herself an admirable concert performer of eighteenth-century music for harpsichord, on the inadequate interpretation too often given by modern performers who play as though all such music were mere graceful tinkling, apply also to other instruments and to vocal solos.[27] The choral works are, on the other hand, nowadays too often distorted by an excessive number of singers. They were written for small professional

[27] See Wanda Landowska, *Musique ancienne* (Paris, 1921).

choirs, not for aggregations of hundreds of amateurs. Romain Rolland has stressed this point about Handel's oratorios.[28]

Artifice, pattern, and eloquence do not, of course, exhaust the characteristics of eighteenth-century art which would have to be considered in a full-length historical treatment. Its cosmopolitanism, exemplified by the career of Handel, German born, Italian trained, and resident for most of his creative life in London, or by that of Voltaire, is significant. An age in which a German national hero, Frederick the Great, could write in French the works by which he set most store was happily exempt from the narrow and sometimes absurd cultural nationalism so dear to nineteenth-century romanticists. Its emphasis on clarity and eloquence, its horror of bombast, its tendency to allow emotion to degenerate into sentimentality and form into formalism, are all sufficiently well known to need no explanation in a brief sketch of the period. Nor does the remarkable excellence of the best eighteenth-century prose, that of Voltaire and Swift, require more than a bare mention.

It is, however, important to notice that alongside the art we have been discussing, an art created for the most part to meet the desires of a cultivated and cosmopolitan aristocracy, there was developing in the first half of the eighteenth century a quite different kind of art intended for the shopkeeping middle classes. The only enduring masterpiece of this bourgeois art which has survived outside the textbooks and the scholarly monographs is perhaps Defoe's *Robinson Crusoe* (1719).

But a long list, including such productions as Lillo's play *George Barnwell*, could easily be compiled. Hogarth's almost nineteenth-century realism is in a sense a part of this same middle-class art. In fairness to the middle-class public it should be said that in many respects they aped the tastes of their social superiors, and also that the later vogue of such masterpieces as Handel's *Messiah* was a middle-class vogue. But by and large, the taste of the middle classes does not greatly concern the historian of the fine arts in the first half of the eighteenth century. This was, in its strength as in its weakness, the art of a privileged upper class.

[28] Romain Rolland, *Hændel* (Paris, 1910), in the very useful series: *Les maitres de la musique,* ed. Jean Chantavoine. Louis Laloy's *Rameau* (Paris, 1908) and André Pirro's *J. S. Bach* (Paris, 1907) are other volumes pertinent here. There is an English translation of Rolland's *Handel* (London, 1916).

Chapter Eight

THE COURSE OF POLITICS

I. "QUIETA NON MOVERE"

THE decade of the 1720's marked in international affairs the liquidation of most of the questions left unsettled at the end of the world wars of Louis XIV. The great financial crises were past. The adventurers, the disturbers, the men with daring ideas, had vanished from the stage. Law, Alberoni, Dubois, Goertz had gone. In the two greatest, or at least richest, of European countries, political power had fallen into the hands of able and cautious leaders, Walpole in Britain and Fleury in France, both destined to hold power until the world wars of the mid-century broke out in 1740. European international relations were in a state of comparative quiet. Domestically, most of the states of Europe had reached a stage of political equilibrium.

There was, however, only comparative quiet in international relations. These decades were filled with congresses, intrigues, treaties, mild wars mostly of marching and countermarching, with all the play of European balance of power at its most elaborate and most delicate. If Alberoni had gone, Elizabeth Farnese was in the 1720's at her most active, and still bent on a throne for Don Carlos. The manners, morals, and aims of European diplomacy underwent no change.

Similarly, domestic politics were by no means uneventful. Throughout this book, we have had to make much use of the term "security," "stability," "equilibrium," "formality," and the like, for they are terms that *must* be used of the early eighteenth century. But they should not be given overtones of fixity, death, decay. Do not understand by stable, "static," nor by formal, "cut and dried." Such disparaging overtones are echoes of the romantics of the nineteenth century, who had a great and misunderstanding contempt for the early eighteenth century. We should now have a better perspective than they.

Indeed, the kind of balance attained by a master politician like Robert Walpole was the balance of the tightrope walker or, better, the juggler.

It was nothing easy, automatic, effortless—though it appear so in the exercise. It was, with Walpole and indeed with most of its practitioners in that age, which was not an age of mass movements, a skill at handling individuals and small groups. It was therefore not a spectacular skill, not one that depended on oratory or on an appeal to great moral principles. But it was a real skill, and never altogether common. In practice it served as one of the threads that tie together the somewhat disparate course of history in the states of Europe in these years.[1]

II. BRITAIN UNDER WALPOLE

Under the first two Hanoverians, the modern constitution of Great Britain was blocked out in the form that has come to be known as parliamentary government—that of an executive committee (cabinet) responsible to a representative legislative body. But it was blocked out only in its broad lines; much remained to be filled in. Nevertheless, when allowance is made for the full power of the hereditary House of Lords, the undemocratic character of the constituency of the Commons, the considerable extent of the royal prerogative, it is still true that politically Walpole's England was not worlds apart from modern England. Whether Walpole was or was not the first prime minister remains a matter of definition. He had the kind of job prime ministers now have.

Walpole was by inheritance a country squire, of a family with considerable estates in Norfolk, at Walpole and Houghton, where they had certainly been landholders since the reign of Henry II, in the twelfth century, and quite possibly before the Norman Conquest. His grandfather and his father had both held the family seat for the borough of Castle Rising, which he occupied when he first entered the House of Commons in 1701. He married, however, the daughter of a Baltic timber merchant, John Shorter, whose father had been Lord Mayor of London. Walpole's grandfather had married the daughter of another Lord Mayor, and by this marriage with a Lord Mayor's granddaughter, Sir Robert was brought into close connection with the wealthy merchant class which was an essential element in the Whig party. Except for going to school with some of them at Eton and at Kings College, Cambridge, Walpole had no connection with the class of great nobles and of court officials who hitherto had governed England. And as a scholarship pupil, Walpole at school and college would not have been in the same

[1] For an excellent corrective to the conventional Victorian view of Walpole as a rather ignoble fellow, see F. S. Oliver, *The Endless Adventure* (Boston, 1931).

group as the gentlemen of wealth and rank. He began life as a third son and only inherited the family estates by the death of his brothers when he was already a young man. His background was thus a combination of the country squire class and the city merchants, and characteristically English. His sister presently married a Norfolk neighbor, Lord Townshend (afterward more famous for his turnip culture than he had been as a statesman), and it was Townshend's patronage which aided Walpole in entering the inner circles of the oligarchy of Whig nobles. His own conspicuous ability in debate, especially in financial matters, had attracted attention in the House of Commons almost from the first. Thus Walpole's background and training fitted him to mediate between the different groups or "interests" as the eighteenth century called them, of which the British governing class was in his day composed, the great nobles, the landed gentry, and the merchants and financiers, especially of London.

His virtues and his defects alike fitted him for this great and essential role of mediator between groups inclined to suspicion and jealousy. He had natural good humor, courage, self-control and patience, and an altogether exceptional sense of fact. He could not only see a course of action which would attain the end he desired, but could persuade others by sober and sensible arguments that both means and end were as reasonable and as practicable as he thought them. He never strove to attain perfection, or lost (in the pursuit of an ideal) his sense of proportion and of actuality. What he wanted was peace and prosperity for the British people, not conquests or glory, which his generation had seen in the world wars that raged in his youth to be futile and unprofitable.

Nineteenth-century romanticists have compared Walpole unfavorably with William Pitt, later Earl of Chatham, the national hero of the renewed world wars which Walpole had vainly striven to avert. They have echoed the accusations of his defeated rival Bolingbroke and his other enemies about bribery and corruption, though these charges were sufficiently disproved by the failure of the parliamentary investigation conducted by his enemies just after his fall to produce any evidence of Walpole's guilt. It is significant, however, that those nineteenth-century writers with actual experience of English politics, Sir Robert Peel, Lord Morley, and J. M. Robertson—also, more recently, F. S. Oliver—representing various shades of opinion, all agreed in ranking Walpole among the greatest of English statesmen.[2]

[2] For Peel's view, see Lord Stanhope's *Miscellanies*, 1st ser. (London, 1863), 68-80; also John Morley, *Walpole* (London, 1889), and J. M. Robertson, *Bolingbroke and Walpole* (London, 1919). Another treatment, G. R. Stirling Taylor, *Robert Walpole and His Age*

Walpole was as little sensitive as Frederick William of Prussia to the claims of the ideal, to intellectual abstractions. Then, too, he lacked refinement and culture. He had an intense interest in hunting and the other usual pursuits of the country gentry, but there is nothing to show that he ever read poetry or listened to music with any attention. In the magnificent new house he built on his ancestral estate at Houghton he did, to be sure, install a notable collection of paintings, afterward purchased from his heirs by the Empress Catherine the Great of Russia, and in part from her successors by the late Andrew Mellon. But these old masters were an example not so much of a genuine interest in the fine arts as of what Veblen called "conspicuous consumption." He did not patronize contemporary painters, except for the usual family portraits. His lack of refinement as well as his common sense is illustrated by his remark that when he found his dinner guests at one of his political dinners for men constrained or ill at ease, he always told a bawdy story to set things going.

The problem of Walpole's internal policy in his long administration (April, 1721, to February, 1742) was to establish and to preserve a balance of power between the nobility, the country gentry, and the businessmen so that the new and unpopular Hanoverian dynasty would be acceptable to each of the various elements of which the governing classes were composed. This was essential to avoid the peril of a civil war waged to restore the exiled Stuarts. That the Jacobite menace had not ceased to be a threat with the defeat of the rising in 1715 was shown by, among other vain attempts, the elaborate plot discovered in 1722, for which Layer was executed and Bishop Atterbury exiled.[3] The evidence against the bishop, the friend of Pope and Swift, produced at his trial was not conclusive, but Walpole, convinced that he was an active Jacobite and not just another sentimental well-wisher to the "King over the water," had used against him a parliamentary bill of pains and penalties not requiring proof as rigid as judicial procedure would have demanded. Walpole would presumably not have permitted Bolingbroke, after he left the service of James III, the Old Pretender, to return to England, could he have prevented it. Bolingbroke had married as a second wife a niece of

---

(London, 1931), which uses the mass of new material made available by the publications of the Historical Manuscripts Commission, is also highly laudatory. Of this new evidence, that contained in the three volumes of the *Diary of Lord Percival* (later Earl of Egmont) is especially noteworthy (London, 1920-1924).

[3] See Williams, *Whig Supremacy*, 174-176, for a succinct account of this plot. See also H. C. Beeching, *Francis Atterbury* (London, 1909). Atterbury's guilt is proved by the Stuart Papers.

Madame de Maintenon and with his wife's money had bribed the Duchess of Kendal, the most influential of George I's mistresses, to persuade the king to order Walpole to let him (Bolingbroke) come back. His estates were restored to him, but not his seat in the House of Lords, a typical example of Walpole's skill in making compromise arrangements which preserved essentials while making concessions on lesser points. Bolingbroke, however, was for some years the center of a vociferous opposition to Walpole in the name of "patriotism."

The agency through which Walpole effected a working compromise between the Whig oligarchy of great nobles and court favorites, the lesser landed gentry, and the new funded interest of merchants and *rentiers*, was the House of Commons. He had also to manage the king to whom, and not to Parliament, he was responsible as a minister of the crown, in fact as well as in name. He managed George I, whose good sense made him highly appreciative of Walpole's skill as finance minister, by the agency of the Duchess of Kendal. The king, whose reluctance to let Walpole resign with the other seceding Whigs in the party squabble in 1717 is well known, was glad to get him back again at the Treasury Board in 1721. It is also well known that Walpole alone among the leading politicians seeking office at the opening of the reign of George II in 1727 was shrewd enough to perceive that Queen Caroline, and not the royal mistress Lady Suffolk, had paramount influence with the new monarch. Even so, if George II's first choice, Sir Spencer Compton, had not at once proved his incompetence by his inability to draft the necessary speech from the throne without consulting Walpole, Sir Robert might not have continued as first minister. It was his promise, faithfully carried out, of an increase in the new king's civil list and the new queen's jointure which proved decisive. But George II promised Walpole permanence of tenure. "It is for my life and for yours." When Walpole finally was forced in 1742 to insist that his resignation be accepted, Sir Spencer Compton, now Lord Wilmington, was for a brief period prime minister.

Walpole, dependent on king and Parliament for support, was obviously not in a position to initiate changes which either might dislike, or to block measures on which either might choose to insist. His motto was thus almost necessarily *Quieta non movere*, "Let sleeping dogs lie." He refused to attempt to change the law so as to give equal political rights to dissenters, though his failure to enforce the acts against them showed where his sympathies lay. His financial measures were popular and successful until his proposed excise, which interfered with the profits of smugglers and the frauds on the customhouse, gave the opposition fomented by Bolingbroke a chance to rouse the rabble (always Tory in sympathy in the English eighteenth century) without offending the powerful merchant class, ordinarily Whig in politics.[4]

This struggle over the excise bill, the chief major reform proposed by Walpole, illustrates both his domestic and his colonial policy, as well as the numerous difficulties with which his administration of Great Britain and her empire had constantly to struggle. It therefore deserves examination, even though the bill was withdrawn by Walpole and never enacted. It is probable that the proposal for an excise on tobacco and wine was intended merely as the beginning of a comprehensive reform of the cumbersome and ineffective traditional fiscal methods of the English government. For existing customs duties on tobacco, amounting to 51s. 3d. per lb., a single duty of 4d. per lb., to be paid when the tobacco was withdrawn from a bonded warehouse for domestic consumption, was to have been substituted. Walpole believed that such a duty could be collected honestly and in full, and that the various frauds of smugglers and dishonest claimants of the "drawback," or rebate on re-exported tobacco, could be eliminated. He expected so great an increase in revenue that he contemplated reducing the land tax (really an income tax paid on rents). He argued that the new system would be to the advantage of the planters in the American colonies, because they were being defrauded by factors and agents in England. On all these points modern investigators are in substantial agreement that Walpole was right. He had the enthusiastic support of George II and of Queen Caroline, who probably knew what an excise had done to aid Prussian revenues, and supposedly led a large Whig majority in Parliament. Why, then, was so reasonable a proposal, made by a statesman seemingly so powerful, opposed and thwarted?[5]

The chief arguments advanced against the excise scheme were that, since it tended to increase the power of the crown, it would revive evils England had experienced in the seventeenth century; that "an army of revenue officers" would be needed to collect it; that unwarrantable searches of private premises would be made; that it would raise the price of tobacco and thus lessen consumption and injure both trade and the

---

[4] For the Tory sympathies of the eighteenth-century English mob, see Webb, *English Local Government*, IV, 415.

[5] See Paul Vaucher, *La crise du ministère Walpole en 1733-1734* (Paris, 1924); E. R. Turner, "The Excise Scheme of 1733," *English Historical Review*, XLII (1927), 34-57; *Proceedings and Debates of the British Parliaments Respecting North America*, ed. L. F. Stock (Washington, 1924-1941), IV, 197-224.

colonies. These arguments lacked substantial justification. They were primarily debating tricks employed in the hope of forcing Walpole out of office. He had, by two needless tactical errors, laid himself open to attack. He had used the hated word "excise," made odious by both the Stuarts and the Commonwealth, and he had brought in his bill before a parliamentary election campaign when the opposition was in search of a popular issue to play against him. If he had used another name for his scheme and not brought the matter up until after the election of 1734 (necessitated by the Septennial Act), it is quite possible that no real issue would have been made over so harmless and sensible a scheme. It was probably Walpole's conviction that his plan would save money and injure nobody but swindlers and smugglers which made him neglect common-sense precautions in proposing it. When he expected to meet opposition, he was generally far more adroit. The volume and vehemence of the opposition to the excise scheme seem to have taken him by surprise. When he found that a plain explanation of the facts in the House of Commons did not suffice to calm fears even among many of his usual following, he prudently withdrew the bill, following its second reading.

Back of the widespread opposition to the proposed excise on tobacco there was no doubt, as the late F. S. Oliver insists, fear that Walpole intended a general excise tax bearing on many if not most commodities as a means of raising revenue. There were already in 1733 excise duties levied on twenty-two such articles of commerce in England. Walpole had abolished the excise on salt in 1728, only to restore it in 1732. He admitted that he wished to reduce the land tax and was accused of meaning to abolish it altogether. Now although Adam Smith states that the land tax, introduced under William and Mary, was originally intended to tax also income from "stock" (by which he means not the stock on the land but "the stock or trade of the towns"), he explains that in the original assessment in the 1690's (never subsequently altered) this urban capital had been greatly undervalued. With the rapid growth of wealth in the great towns, the merchant and trading classes as such were not bearing their share of the tax burden; and, naturally, not anxious to assume it. Hence all city businessmen would oppose any proposal to reform the system of taxation, since they were almost certain to be forced to carry a larger share of it. This practical motive, which Oliver ignored, may have been quite as important as the British love of liberty and fear that an excise would endanger it which he alleges to explain the opposition to the excise of the more moderate and able members of the merchant classes.[6]

The fear of tyranny was aroused by every device known to modern high-pressure salesmanship and propaganda. A monograph on an eighteenth-century pressure group could perhaps be written to demonstrate exactly how the incongruous alliance of Bolingbroke and the London merchants went to work to stir up the agitation against Walpole and the excise, but the kind of turmoil they raised has been described by several students. Popular songs and ballads were advertised, sold in the streets, sung in the taverns. Emblems were on sale in the shops. Wooden shoes, imported from the Continent, were carried about on poles by paraders, to show the people the sad state of poverty to which they were about to be reduced. Pamphlets and newspaper articles reminded the public that in former times wicked prime ministers and royal favorites had been exiled, assassinated, imprisoned, or executed. A supporter of Walpole at the time described the agitation in terms which modern research has proved not to be greatly exaggerated.

Besides the regular Infatuation from daily and weekly papers, little Hand Bills were dispersed by thousands all over the City and Country, put in people's hands in the Streets and Highways, dropped at their Doors and thrown in at their windows; all asserting that Excisemen were (like a foreign Enemy) going to invade and devour them, and ready to enter their Houses; into all Houses private or public, at any time, by Day or by Night. . . .

Such as could not read were informed by such as could; and all were ready to inform, and mislead, and enrage one another. It was the Theme of Coffee-Houses, Taverns, and Gin-Shops, the Discourse of Artificers, the Cry of the Streets, the Entertainment of Lacquies, the Prate of Wenches, and the Bugbear of Children.[7]

It would be interesting to know how all this agitation was started, financed, and propagated. The ill-defined phenomenon now named "propaganda" obviously did not originate, as some people seem to assume, during the World War of 1914-1918.

Walpole, though obliged to withdraw the excise bill, and, if he had had any real intention of introducing a general excise, to abandon it once and for all, nonetheless used the incident to gain an important end. Members of the ministry, of whom Lord Chesterfield is the best known

---

[6] See the excellent discussion of the excise scheme in Oliver, *Endless Adventure*, II, 217-297, and Smith, *Wealth of Nations*, Bk. V, chap. ii, "Taxes upon Profit, or upon the Revenue Arising from Stock."

[7] From a contemporary pamphlet, quoted by Turner, "Excise Scheme of 1733," 38-39. This article includes a mass of data bearing out the quoted passage.

today, had agitated against Walpole's bill, and though they had done nothing then unusual, Walpole persuaded George II to dismiss them all from office. Walpole by this step greatly increased the power of the prime minister and party leader. Henceforth, ministers of the crown were responsible to the prime minister as well as to the king, a responsibility eventually to become a constitutional principle, and a milestone in the slow but steady growth of cabinet government by which the Hanoverian monarchs were eventually reduced to purely ceremonial functions.

The relation of the colonies to Parliament and to the crown was also involved in the excise bill, since tobacco was for several of them their chief crop, the basis of their whole economy. Burke's famous phrase, "salutary neglect," described accurately enough the facts of the relationship between Britain and her North American colonies in the era of Walpole, but the theory of British sovereignty was not one of neglect. The colonies had been established under varying royal grants to proprietors or companies. Their government in the early eighteenth century was, in Professor Labaree's phrase, "government by instruction," from the Board of Commissioners for Trade and Plantations to the royal governors. The Board of Trade, as it is usually called, was not under Parliament or the ministry, but an offshoot of the Privy Council. The Parliament at Westminster did not legislate for the colonies except for acts of trade like the Molasses Act of 1733, passed to further English rather than other British interests. George II like Louis XV and Charles VI ruled over a surprising variety of dominions, each with its own separate constitution, sanctioned by royal concessions and hallowed by tradition.

These accumulated possessions of the eighteenth-century monarchs came to him as wearer of a crown or, to be more accurate, of several crowns. His power over each of them varied according to its past history. The administration of these dominions was everywhere still largely in fact in the hands of local authorities. When the regal authority was exercised it was not by the king personally, but by bureaucrats, acting in the king's name and not subject to much interference from anyone else. The position of the Board of Trade and its royal governors and that of the French intendants and the *Controle Générale* was much more similar than historians have usually noticed it to be. Both tried to "govern by instruction," and neither was ever able really to get its instructions carried out. Distance and a long tradition of local autonomy made orders from London and Paris, or from Vienna or St. Petersburg, easy to evade and hard for governors and intendants to enforce, even when they wanted to do so.

The attitude of the bureaucrats in the Board of Trade was in the early eighteenth century an endeavor to enforce what it loved to call "the true principles of a provincial constitution," to maintain and to standardize the royal prerogative.[8] "True principles," as an attempt at standardization or rationalization, could prove corrosive of old habits and allegiances, as the American Revolution later proved. The royal governor was supposed to exercise in each province all those broad powers which various officials exercised in England in the name of the king. He was assisted by a group of councilors chosen for their loyalty and prominence. Provincial assemblies were supposed to have powers far more sharply limited than those of the English Parliament. The judiciary were assumed to be under the crown, not under the Assembly. The interests of the province were supposed to be subordinate, in case of conflict, to those of the mother country. The provincial government was "by royal grace and favor." Though the colonial assemblies were actually in possession of the "power of the purse," since they levied taxes and paid the salaries of royal officials in the colonies, the English Parliament never abandoned its theoretical claim to the right to tax the colonies. If Walpole had been in power in the 1760's, however, it is unlikely that Parliament would ever have tried to exercise its authority with a Stamp Act. Neglect of the "true principles of a provincial constitution" was too obviously salutary.

Walpole, in his speech defending the proposed excise on tobacco (March 14, 1733), alluded to some of the grievances of the American planters. "If they are to be believed," he said, "they are reduced to the utmost extremity, even almost to a state of despair, by the many frauds that have been committed in that trade, and by the ill usage they have sustained from their factors and correspondents in England, who from being their servants are become their tyrants." Walpole went on to allude to the "many representations of the bad state of their affairs" sent home from the colonies, and especially to the remonstrance then recently brought from Virginia by Sir John Randolph. He gave a clear explanation, backed by details of actual cases, as to how these frauds on the customs cheated both the government and the planters.

In the ensuing debate Mr. Alderman Perry, one of the alleged tyrants, retorted that none of the planters had ever thought of complaining "till they were put upon it by letters and applications from hence," and asserted that the "hardships the factors labour under are by much the most numerous and the most grievous." He threatened to give up his

---

[8] L. W. Labaree, *Royal Government in America* (New Haven, 1930), 426-427. See also C. M. Andrews, *Colonial Period of American History* (New Haven, 1934-1938), IV.

extensive business as a tobacco merchant and correspondent for planters in Virginia, if the excise bill were passed. Enough is known about Perry to prove that he was not exactly impartial in this matter. He had been for some years involved in a lawsuit in which the crown was trying to collect duties fraudulently evaded. He had also been engaged in a lawsuit with members of the Randolph family some years earlier, in which the executors of Micajah Perry the elder had finally obtained judgment against the heirs of William Randolph for £2,460 damages and £10 costs.

The size of Perry's business may be gathered from his statement to a parliamentary committee in 1723 that he was then paying thirty thousand pounds a year on his imports of tobacco as customs duties. He was a member of Parliament from 1727 to 1741 and Lord Mayor of London in 1738 and 1739. Either he or his predecessor, who died in 1721, had appeared as a witness before a committee of the House of Lords in 1718 to protest against a bill "for preventing the clandestine running of goods," or smuggling. He objected especially to a clause giving the right of search to customs officials on ships of over forty tons. He was also engaged in the slave trade and in many other colonial ventures. The Board of Trade frequently took his advice on commercial and colonial matters.[9] So did prominent people in the colonies, as his correspondence with Cadwallader Colden of New York shows. His statement to Colden, quoted by Miss Donnan from the Colden Papers, that "I shall always think my self obliged to support the interest (sic) of the Continent of America from whose favour and goodwill I very gratefully own, I owe the little fortune I am master of" is borne out by some of the facts of his career. That he was a respected and prosperous man of unusual ability and considerable wealth is obvious.

Walpole, in governing England, was dependent on the support of the London merchant-capitalist group, a rather small one, to which Perry belonged; just as he was also dependent on that of George II and of the country gentlemen who were in so large a majority in both houses of Parliament. Sir Robert was too wise and too moderate a man to press any point obnoxious to any essential element among his followers for the sake of any fine logical theory or blueprint plan of reform. His view

---

[9] See Elizabeth Donnan, "Eighteenth-Century Merchants: Micajah Perry," *Journal of Economic and Business History*, IV (1931), 70-98, and the numerous references to the Perrys in *Proceedings and Debates of the British Parliaments*, III-IV (indexed under the name Perry in each volume of this admirable collection of documents). For the debate on the excise, IV, 197 ff., gives useful excerpts.

of the art of government, judging from his actions, was that later
expressed by Madison in the famous "Tenth Paper" of *The Federalist*:

A landed interest, a manufacturing interest, a mercantile interest, a moneyed
interest, with many lesser interests, grow up of necessity in civilized nations,
and divide them into different classes, actuated by different sentiments and
views. The regulation of these various and interfering interests forms the
principal task of modern legislation, and involves the spirit of party and
faction in the necessary and ordinary operations of the government.

Walpole undertook, on the whole successfully, to mediate between
these "various and interfering interests," without ever carrying through
any measure thoroughly obnoxious to any of them. When forced to
permit an enactment unpalatable to the dissenters, for example, to go
unrepealed, or like the Molasses Act obnoxious to the North American
colonies to be passed, Walpole merely refrained from enforcing it. Perry,
and men like him, had so great an importance in eighteenth-century
England that it is peculiarly unfortunate that they have not more
frequently been studied by historians. Case histories of early capitalist
merchants could do much more than windy generalities about "capitalism"
and "class conflict" to illuminate the early course of events which has
so enormously altered the modern world since 1700. Walpole's policy
toward the merchant class was necessarily one of *laissez faire*. But he tried
to hold the balance even between merchants, colonists, landed gentry,
funded gentry, and the crown. His role in the great game of politics
was in some ways that of an umpire.

III. THE POLICY OF FLEURY

That French politics of this period should have produced a political
leader who, however unlike Walpole personally, could quite as well
have adopted the motto, "Let sleeping dogs lie," may well be an accident
of history. But it was a singularly congruous accident. Neither Fleury
nor Walpole could possibly have thrived so well a generation earlier or
a generation later.

Cardinal Fleury, prime minister of France in fact, though never in
name, from 1726 until his death in 1743, has shared in the general
indiscriminate condemnation of the Old Regime prevalent among
French and other modern historians. Only recently has he found in the
work of Vaucher, Gaxotte, and of an American scholar, Professor A. M.
Wilson, defenders, especially of his foreign policy, but also of his manage-

ment of internal affairs. These modern estimates of Fleury are in line with the opinion of many of his contemporaries.[10] The great Duchess of Marlborough, though she suspected Fleury of wishing to restore the Stuarts and make England Catholic, wrote in 1736 that he had "hitherto acted very wise and honestly for his own country, without putting it to any very extraordinary expense for himself." In 1738-1739 she said, "I wish we might have a minister that had power to the age of Cardinal Fleury, if they deserved from their country as well as he does from France."[11]

Voltaire, who had no reason to regard Fleury as a friend or a fellow philosopher, wrote of him some years after his death, when praise could not have served any immediate politic aim, a discriminating and yet highly favorable account, still the best brief description of the man and of his work:

If there has ever been a happy man on earth, it was certainly Cardinal Fleury. Up to the age of 73 he was regarded as one of the most amiable and congenial of men; and after, at that age, when so many old men withdraw from the world, he took charge of the government, he was regarded as one of the wisest. From 1726 to 1742 everything went well with him. He preserved almost to the age of 90 a clear and healthy mind, apt in business. . . . His administration was less contested and less envied than those of Richelieu and of Mazarin in the best days of their ministries. His place changed nothing in his manners. People were astonished to find in the premier minister the most amiable and the most disinterested man at court. The good of the state was for a long time in accord with his moderation. The peace he loved was needed, and all the foreign ministers thought it would not be broken while he lived. He hated every system because his mind was happily limited. Understanding absolutely nothing in any financial scheme, demanding only from his subordinates the most rigid economy, not fit to be a clerk in an office (he was) capable of ruling the state. He quietly permitted France to recover from her losses, and to grow rich through an immense commerce, without making a single innovation, treating the state like a powerful and robust body which would of itself regain health.[12]

Fleury, like Walpole, belonged to a family of country gentry of long descent, but of a rank definitely below and apart from the great nobility. His father was receiver of church tithes at Lodève. Fleury got his start

[10] See the generally favorable treatment accorded Fleury in Pierre Gaxotte, Le siècle de Louis XV (Paris, 1933); Paul Vaucher, Robert Walpole et la politique de Fleury, 1731-1742 (Paris, 1924); A. M. Wilson, French Foreign Policy during the Administration of Cardinal Fleury, 1726-1743 (Cambridge, Mass., 1936).

[11] Memoirs of Sarah, Duchess of Marlborough, 286, 326.

[12] Voltaire, Précis du siècle de Louis XV, in Oeuvres, ed. Beuchot, XXI, 37, 40.

in life by the patronage of the Cardinal de Bonzi. When Louis XIV, by the codicil added to his will in the last month of his life, named Fleury as preceptor to Louis XV, the future cardinal was Bishop of Fréjus, a poor diocese in the south of France, where he had been since 1698. He resigned the bishopric, which he had never liked, and returned to Paris. The regent made him chief of the *Conseil de Conscience* in succession to the Cardinal de Noailles, and Fleury's firmness and tact in imposing silence on the noisy disputants over the Bull Unigenitus condemning the Jansenists gave the first real proof of his great gifts. When the regent died, it was at Fleury's suggestion that the boy king granted the request of the Duc de Bourbon to succeed to the post of principal minister. Voltaire says that Fleury almost from the moment he became tutor to Louis XV planned to become a *de facto* prime minister, but this cannot be proved. His kindness to the boy king was unfailing. The anecdote that he catered to his pupil by playing games with him instead of making him do his lessons is, however, refuted by the existence in the Bibliothèque Nationale of numerous themes and exercises written or copied by Louis XV between 1717 and 1723. When in 1726 the Duc de Bourbon, his mistress Madame de Prie, and her friend the financier Pâris-Duverney undertook, with the aid of the queen whom they had picked out from eighty-nine possible princesses, Marie Leszczynska, to get rid of Fleury, his paramount influence with the king was shown. The sixteen-year-old boy insisted that his tutor, who had withdrawn from court, be called back. He had not previously shown any personal initiative in an important matter.

A few weeks later (June 11, 1726) the Duc de Bourbon was suddenly dismissed from office. Louis XV announced that the post of principal minister was abolished, and that henceforth he would himself govern as well as reign. But the announcement also stated that "the former Bishop of Fréjus" would assist at all council meetings. A special brevet soon gave orders from Fleury the same force as those from the king. A boy of sixteen could hardly govern alone. We do not know enough of the relation between Fleury and the king in subsequent years to be able to determine whether the cardinal's retention of control was complete, and whether he ever tried to get Louis XV to become the efficient kind of ruler Louis XIV had been. After Fleury's death, Louis again undertook to be his own prime minister, without conspicuous success. Fleury does not appear to have been unduly anxious to be made a cardinal. The excuse for the request in 1726 that the pope confer this honor on him was that without it the marshals and others in the councils would not give precedence to a mere ex-bishop. Clearly Fleury's position demanded that he take precedence over all other royal officers not themselves of the blood royal.

Few matters in modern history have been more misrepresented and, in consequence, more misunderstood than the nature of the French monarchy under the Old Regime. The many who condemn it damn it for being a tyranny, which it never was, rather than blame it for its inefficiency, a necessary consequence of its incomplete sovereignty over the innumerable stubborn vested interests of an essentially corporate regime. Modern French royalist writers on history, such as Louis Bertrand, Jacques Bainville, and Pierre Gaxotte, also exaggerate the extent of royal authority under the Old Regime. Gaxotte, for example, condemns the ideas of what he calls "feudalist and medieval royalism." He praises what he names "positive royalism," and paints rose-tinted pictures of Louis XV aided by strong, silent men like Machault and Maupeou, with able intendants, Trudaine, for example, each a king in his own *généralité*.

It is true that ultraroyalist theories, such as those of Bossuet, or of Louis XV's reproof to the *Parlement* of Paris in 1766, advanced under the Old Regime, might seem to show that it had indeed a positive royalism, a beneficent despotism. Louis XV said, "In my person alone resides sovereign authority whose especial characteristic is the spirit of counsel, of justice, and of reason. . . . To me alone belongs the legislative power, without dependence, and unshared. . . . All public order emanates from me." *L'état, c'est moi,* in short.

Joseph de Maistre, however, saw more clearly the true nature of the French monarchy in the eighteenth century:

The will of the king is infinitely far from doing everything in a monarchy. It is supposed to do everything . . . but in fact it does hardly more than centralize counsel and information. Religion, law, custom, opinion, the privileges of orders and of corps restrain the sovereign and prevent him from abusing his power; it is indeed especially noteworthy that kings are far more often accused of lacking will power than of abusing it. It is always the Council of the prince which rules.[13]

Fleury's power depended on his attendance at all council meetings, whether of individual secretaries of state, or of the controller general

---

[13] Paul Viollet, *Le roi et ses ministres* (Paris, 1912), 78, 160 ff. The quotation from Louis XV is from his answer to a remonstrance by the *Parlement* of Paris, March 3, 1766. That from Joseph de Maistre is from his *Etude sur la souveraineté,* composed in 1788, text first published in *La Quinzaine,* April 1, 1895, 278.

"working at fixed hours with the king," or sessions of the supreme council and other committees. From 1732 to 1737 Chauvelin, privy seal (*garde des sceaux*) and minister for foreign affairs, was associated with Fleury in these powers. He attended the king with Fleury and took the cardinal's place when absent, so that for these years there were in fact, though never in name, two joint prime ministers.[14]

Fleury's conception of his duties can only be gathered, like that of Walpole, from his demeanor and acts. But these make it plain that the cardinal, like his English contemporary, was a mediator, an umpire between different interests and factions. No conspicuous achievement is associated with his name. Like Walpole, he is to be praised rather for the misfortunes he averted than for any heroic deeds. Like Walpole, he wanted a peaceful and prosperous reign for his royal master. Like Walpole, he followed consistently, and often against strenuous opposition, a policy which actually did make for peace and prosperity.

Lady Mary Wortley Montagu has left us in her well-known *Letters* two comments on France as seen by an able and skeptical British aristocrat. In 1718 she wrote to a London friend after a journey through France with her husband, returning from the embassy to Constantinople:

I think nothing so terrible as objects of misery, except one had the God-like attribute of being capable to redress them; and all the country villages of France shew nothing else. While the post-horses are changed, the whole town comes out to beg, with such miserable starved faces, and thin tattered clothes, they need no other eloquence to persuade [one of] the wretchedness of their condition.

But in 1739, writing to her husband, after another journey through France, she says:

France is so much improved, it is not to be known to be the same country we passed through twenty years ago. Everything I see speaks in praise of Cardinal Fleury; the roads are all mended . . . and such good care taken against robbers, that you may cross the country with your purse in your hand. . . . The French are more changed than their roads; instead of pale, yellow faces, wrapped up in blankets, as we saw them, the villages are all filled with fresh-coloured lusty peasants, in good cloth and clean linen. It is incredible the air of plenty and content that is over the whole country.[15]

The good roads and the absence of highwaymen must have seemed strange to anyone coming from an England where, according to Defoe,

[14] Viollet, *Le roi et ses ministres*, 278-279.
[15] Lady Mary Wortley Montagu, *Letters*, Everyman ed. (New York, 1906), 195, 271-272.

there were sloughs and mudholes so deep in main highways that horses with their riders had been known to sink from view, and where highwaymen made the environs of London, as well as more remote regions, very unsafe for travelers.[16]

In both England and France the badness of the main roads had previously been owing to the fact that their maintenance depended on local parochial authorities. The peasant farmers (yeomen and cottagers if you prefer those terms for England) were obliged to furnish labor and materials, and carts and horses every year. They did little but patch up the worst places in a road network suited only for very sturdy wagons.

The eighteenth century in England saw the development of turnpike trusts, quasi-charitable corporations empowered by acts of Parliament to charge tolls and to improve the roads at their own discretion with the proceeds. But in France, instead of these irresponsible and too often incompetent private and more or less local organizations, the royal government itself undertook the improvement and maintenance of the main highways. The *Corps des Ponts et Chaussées* had been established in 1716, but the improvement of the main roads which Lady Mary noticed really began with the Controller General Orry (1730-1745). In 1738 he procured an edict providing for a *corvée royale* intended to supply labor for the state roads under reasonable restrictions. This was bitterly resented by the peasants throughout the rest of the Old Regime. It was, in effect, a new tax, payable not in money, but in labor. The more enlightened intendants in later years tried like Turgot to pacify the peasants by paying them a money wage for their road work. But part of the opposition to the *corvée royale* was caused by the interference of the state with what had before been a purely local matter. The loudest protests came not from those who had themselves to work with pick and shovel, but from prosperous farmers obliged to furnish men, horses, wagons, and materials, or else pay a money equivalent. The French policy of building state highways is of course now universal in the modern world. Its results were plainly, as Arthur Young later testified, better roads than the English turnpikes. But the roads were built in a way that added to the vast sum of grievances that helped make the French Revolution of 1789.

In France, formal technical training of the type given by modern engineering schools began in the reign of Louis XV. Although the schools of mines, *ponts et chaussées,* and so on were not established until

[16] See Daniel Defoe, *A Tour through the Whole Island of Great Britain,* with an introduction by G. D. H. Cole (London, 1927; first published in 1724), 515-533. See also Beatrice and Sidney Webb, *The Story of the King's Highway* (London, 1912).

after 1740, it would appear that French engineers in the government service were already applying, at least by the 1730's, sound engineering principles to such state undertakings as road building. The beginning of modern engineering as a discipline was associated with military engineering, and France under Louis XV had the best army in Europe. Lady Mary's "mended roads" were really a by-product of French army engineering.[17] Transport was important in war, as well as in peace, as the subsequent road building under Napoleon I also demonstrates.

The marked increase in prosperity, the "plenty and content" of which Lady Mary speaks so admiringly, was apparently a genuine phenomenon, confirmed in part by modern economic historians, though her picture of it may have been a bit overoptimistic. To it Fleury's administration contributed notably, as she implies.[18] In 1738 the government's budget was actually balanced, a state not again attained in France before 1789. Yet Fleury's economic policies were opportunist and not based on any philosophical theory or blueprint plan. He seems to have gotten Louis XV to overthrow the Duc de Bourbon and his all-powerful minister, the financier Pâris-Duverney, to block just such a plan, the *cinquantième*, or universal 2 per cent tax on all crops.[19]

Pâris-Duverney had insisted upon this 2 per cent tax, from which clergy and nobles were not to be exempt. Since it was to be collected in kind, and no person or group was to be allowed to evade it by a lump-sum payment (*abonnement*), this *cinquantième* might, had it been accepted, have put French government finances on a scientific and rational basis. The assessments were to be made impartially and, it was hoped, accurately, with no reduction for people with influence. Such a scheme, however reasonable in the abstract, was revolutionary. It roused violent opposition from nearly everyone, yet Pâris-Duverney insisted that the *cinquantième* should be levied on the harvest of 1726. In June, just before that harvest, Fleury engineered the well-known palace revolution by which he swung himself into the saddle.

Fleury's first, and perhaps his most important, fiscal measure was to stabilize the currency, following a recoinage. From 1726 until the revaluation of gold in terms of silver in 1785, there were no further changes

---

[17] See F. B. Artz, *L'éducation technique en France au dix-huitième siècle* (Paris, 1939; reprinted from *Revue d'histoire moderne*, XIII, 1938, 361-407).

[18] See, for example, in the well-known brief popular book by the late Henri Sée, in the Collection Armand Colin, *La France économique et sociale au XVIIIᵉ siècle*, 2nd ed. (Paris, 1933), 19, 113 ff., the statements that French peasants were better off than those elsewhere, and that there was a remarkable expansion of both domestic and foreign commerce, especially after 1730.

[19] Marion, *Histoire financière de la France depuis 1715*, I, 134.

in the bullion content of the coins, or in the number of livres (not a coin but a bookkeeping unit), which remained fixed at 24 livres to the louis d'or. Anyone familiar with the violent and baffling fluctuations of the previous years before, during, and after the system of John Law, will readily accept M. Marion's statement that this stabilization of the coinage was an inestimable benefit. Henceforth Frenchmen could make contracts with assurance that the value received would be what they anticipated. Fleury, with no violence to tradition, secured many of the benefits John Law had vainly hoped to attain from his *écu de banque*.

Pâris-Duverney had tried to have the state collect its own taxes, instead of contracting with businessmen, the so-called "farmers," for the collection of some of them. Fleury made an arrangement, called the *Bail Carlier* after the strawman who lent his name to the operation, which grouped all the various taxes and duties which had traditionally been farmed out into a "General Farm." These included excise taxes on salt, wines and other liquors, tobacco, and a variety of other articles of consumption (*gabelle* and *aides*), and a perplexing variety of transfer taxes and internal customs duties (*traites* and *domaines*). They were not uniform for all France, but varied widely according to locality. Neither Colbert nor anyone else under the Old Regime had succeeded in simplifying and standardizing these sources of royal revenue. The government, as Fleury realized, collected more revenue through private contractors, the farmers-general and their subcontractors in the provinces, than it could have done with its inadequate personnel.

Fleury's *Bail Carlier*, ceding to the farmers the right to collect these various taxes and duties for six years for eighty million livres a year, has been criticized as unduly favorable to the tax farmers, who are said to have made excessive profits, estimated by different contemporaries at all the way from two to sixteen millions a year. Marion thinks six million annual profit above the eighty million they contracted to pay to the crown a fair guess. But without the hope of large profits no contractors would bid for the tax farm. Furthermore, it was customary for prominent persons at court to have shares as silent partners in these tax farms. By thus conceding to contractors the rights to collection on terms favorable to them of from a third to a half of the government revenue, Fleury won the support of the merchant-financier class who had done so much to ruin Law and his system. These capitalists were a necessary group to the royal government, since it could not have waged eighteenth-century wars without their business ability and their fluid resources. No doubt there would be no tax farmers in Utopia, but Fleury never mistook France for Utopia.

Fleury conciliated the church by confirming once more by royal decree its exemption from royal taxation, to which Pâris-Duverney's *cinquantième* would have subjected it. The church, as we have seen, had its own system of taxation, by tithes. The proceeds of these tithes supported the clergy and religious services; and were at the same time used to finance education and the care of the sick and of the insane, now thought of as duties of the state.

Fleury did not succeed in reconciling all of the warring factions among the court nobility and the administrative and judicial nobles, but he seems to have come nearer than anyone else since the best days of Louis XIV to creating around the young king an atmosphere of universal good feeling and loyalty. His policy was to prevent disputes about such controversial matters as Jansenism. His most pertinacious opponents were the *Parlement* of Paris, whose Jansenism was largely a disguise for political ambition. Fleury by a combination of tact and firmness finally succeeded in repressing both Jansenism and the ambition of the *Parlement* to become, through its right of remonstrance and of registry of decrees, all powerful. In the 1730's the energies of the leading legal minds in France were diverted to the useful task of codifying the civil law, under the leadership of Daguesseau.

Although Fleury has been accused of neglecting the navy, Professor Wilson's investigation of his commercial, financial, and naval policy has shown that this charge against him is unjustified. The weakness of the French navy in the ensuing great wars was owing not to inferiority in ships so much as to a purely defensive strategy and tactics, for which the cardinal can hardly be held responsible.[20]

Fleury's domestic policy and his foreign policy were both conducted with more conscious attention to the promotion of commerce than Voltaire's remarks about his noninterference imply. The cardinal, answering in 1727 a complaint from the Chamber of Commerce of La Rochelle about British interloping trade with Martinique, wrote, "I interest myself too much in what concerns commerce not to do . . . all which can contribute to sustain it and make it flourish for the nation's advantage."[21] In returning, for example, to the old policy of alliance with Spain, in 1739, at the risk of war with England, Fleury was careful to make the conclusion of a commercial treaty favorable to French interests the prerequisite of a political alliance.

[20] Wilson, *French Foreign Policy*, 71-90.
[21] Quoted in Wilson, *French Foreign Policy*, 62, from E. Garnault, *Le commerce Rochelais au XVIII° siècle* (La Rochelle, 1888-1890), III, 43-44.

The maintenance of a just balance between the interests of church, nobles, peasants, merchants, not as individuals but in accordance with the various corps and groups on which the social order of the Old Regime depended, is exemplified by Fleury's administration as clearly as by that of Walpole. But Fleury, though the royal authority he controlled exceeded that of the British king, lacked a really workable instrument for learning what the country's governing classes wanted, that is, a House of Commons. His attention to petitions and complaints, from whatever source they came, and his disinterested sense of duty enabled him to rule, on the whole, wisely and well. But, as we shall presently see, he, like Walpole, could not avoid permanently the wars he disliked and dreaded because they would undo so much of his work.

IV. TWO FEDERAL STATES

Modern Europe has not been prolific of experiments in federalism. Switzerland continues to be the only federal state in Europe with a continuous experience of this form of government. In 1715 the Swiss Confederation was, in German terms not neatly translatable, a *Staatenbund* (league of states) and not yet a *Bundesstaat* (state composed of units with local autonomy). It was a kind of offensive and defensive alliance of thirteen independent states (cantons). Some of the member states were simple agricultural and handicraft democracies much like the early city-states among the ancient Greeks. Others, of which Berne is best known, were essentially urban oligarchies with a dependent agricultural area. Each state retained complete control of its internal affairs. Until the Treaties of Westphalia in 1648, these Swiss cantons remained nominally part of the Holy Roman Empire, though their confederacy had begun centuries before as a rebellion of Hapsburg vassals and the imperial title had become in fact an heirloom in another branch of the Hapsburg family. Even the democratic cantons ruled with absolute sway over the regions they had conquered, as the city-states like Zurich and Berne did over their rural hinterland and over their urban common people.

With the Swiss League were associated more or less loosely other adjacent small states, which sought, like the thirteen cantons, to have their neutrality recognized in all wars. Of these associated states, Strasbourg and Franche-Comté had by 1715 become subject to the Bourbons, and Neufchatel to the King of Prussia, as his share of the heritage of the House of Orange. Geneva, not yet a member of the Swiss Confederation, remained an independent republic relying on France for protection against Savoy-Piedmont. The Protestant cantons of Switzerland had all been accustomed to rely on the Bourbons for protection, so that they, like Calvinist Geneva, had been much disturbed by the revocation of the Edict of Nantes, after which Zurich made a kind of alliance with the Dutch. The Catholic cantons had relied to some extent on the sympathy of the pope and of the Hapsburgs.

The internal history of the Swiss Confederation is full of quarrels among the different religions and the different nationalities included in its membership. Its geographical situation and its lack of rich natural resources aided, perhaps, by the number of Swiss with professional military experience as mercenaries in most European armies, kept the Swiss League precariously neutral. An agreement of the Catholic cantons with Louis XIV in 1715 put France for the rest of the eighteenth century in an acknowledged position of protector of the Swiss, since the Protestant cantons had not found any alternative to their accustomed reliance on France. But until the French Revolution there was no interference in Swiss internal affairs. A civil war within the Confederation between Protestant and Catholic cantons ended in 1712 with a victory of the Protestants which checked the tendency shown previously for the Catholics to gain dominance.[22]

In the Dutch federation, which was an example of the *Bundesstaat* rather than, like the Swiss, of the *Staatenbund*, every decision of the central government had to be ratified by each of the provincial governments, and also by the local governments within the provinces, before it was valid. Hence the Dutch failure to ratify such treaties as the Quadruple Alliance of 1718, discussed in Chapter I. But when a stadholder had been chosen, as was customary in periods of national emergency, he had quasi-regal power and could act without the long delay always caused by reference to the provinces. The stadholder was, however, theoretically a provincial, not a national, official. William III, for example, had been stadholder of five provinces, and his cousin of Orange-Nassau stadholder of the remaining two, Friesland and Groningen. William's power was largely due to his being stadholder of Holland and Zeeland, which dominated the federation because of superior wealth and population and because they furnished the navy. The Orange-Nassau family remained stadholders of their two provinces after William III died, but were unable to control the federation.

[22] There is a good summary of Swiss history in this period in W. Oechsli, *History of Switzerland, 1499-1914*, tr. E. and C. Paul (London, 1922), by a distinguished Swiss scholar.

Dutch internal politics in the eighteenth century were conditioned by a rivalry between two groups or parties, the *Staatsgezinden*, or federalists, dominated by Amsterdam and the province of Holland and representing an urban patriciate enriched by commerce; and the *Oranjegezinden*, or unionists, strong in the other provinces and increasingly favored by the common people, to whom the stadholder and the nobility seemed likely to be more generous than the *Bewindehebbers* (directors of the East India Company, and, by interlocking, also often of the Bank of Amsterdam), who dominated the States-General. The States-General, as we have seen, tried its best to avoid further involvement in European wars. When it pursued an active foreign policy it was from a commercial aim, such as the suppression of Belgian rivals, which influenced the terms of the Barrier Treaty, and made the abandonment of Charles VI's Ostend Company the price for Dutch ratification of the Pragmatic Sanction. In the period with which we are concerned the Dutch were the only European people who were already living under capitalism, with "safety and 4 per cent" as their ideal. They were large holders of English stocks and bonds, for example, and since Amsterdam was until the latter part of the century still the financial center of Europe, in a position to profit by the varied flow of wealth which the increase in world commerce constantly accelerated. The internal free trade, *laissez faire*, and heavy taxation (to pay war debts) which characterized the United Netherlands remind one more of nineteenth-century England than of any other eighteenth-century power.

V. SPAIN AND ITALY

Most of the drama of Spanish politics in the years after Utrecht centered upon foreign affairs. The Bourbons, as we have seen, brought with them a talent for able administration, and even while the War of the Spanish Succession was going on their efforts began to bear fruit in bigger tax yields and a slowly rising tide of prosperity. At the same time they drew Spain into so many new entanglements, involved her in so many expensive if not bloody wars, that the net gain of the Spanish people was slight. The intrigues of Alberoni and Ripperdá, however, make good stories while the financial reforms, the steady administrative work of both of them make much less interesting reading. Indeed, the internal history of the Spanish Bourbon state lends itself much more readily to analysis than to narrative.[23]

[23] A. Ballesteros y Beretta, *Historia de España y su influencia en la historia universal* (Barcelona, 1918-1941), devotes two volumes (V-VI) to the eighteenth century, one almost entirely to foreign affairs, the other to social, economic, and cultural history.

The royal house did provide material for gossip, which seems to be one of the most useful functions of royalty. Philip V, in an age without benefit of psychiatry, was considered to be afflicted with melancholia. As, among many other peculiarities, he refused to cut his toenails until they had grown so long that he had to limp, he was certainly a bit queer. Out of a fairly clear sky he suddenly abdicated in 1724, hoping to go into semimonastic seclusion. His sixteen-year-old son, who succeeded him as Luis I, died after a seven-month reign, however, and Philip, pressed by his court—and by the French ambassador, de Tessé—reluctantly went back to the throne. This second part of his reign was dominated more clearly than ever by the queen, Elizabeth Farnese, who seems in fact to have acted as his psychiatrist as well as his wife. Elizabeth now chose as the instrument of her obsessive ambition for thrones for her two boys a man who was almost a caricature of Alberoni.

This minister and favorite was Ripperdá, a Dutchman by birth, though said to have been of Spanish descent. Like Alberoni, he is often dismissed as an "adventurer," one of the favorite words nineteenth-century historians had for resilient eighteenth-century cosmopolitans. Ripperdá was brought up a Catholic, and converted to Protestantism. He went into "business" and gained a great reputation as a practical man of affairs and as what we should now call an economic expert. Sent to Spain as diplomatic agent for the United Provinces, he pleased the queen, became again a Catholic, and stayed on in the Spanish service. After some diplomatic success, he fell under suspicion of having indiscreetly let out secret parts of the first Treaty of Vienna with the Austrians, and was put under arrest. He managed to escape via Portugal and England, returned to Holland, and was reconverted once more to Protestantism. He died in Tunis, where he was said to be planning to make himself King of Corsica. As he had in the meanwhile been converted to Islam, and served the Sultan of Morocco, it must be confessed that his career seems to make the epithet adventurer no great exaggeration. Yet Ripperdá had many administrative gifts, an ability to handle men and women, intelligence, and energy. He was in some senses a peer of Walpole and Fleury. But he lacked the gift of knowing when to stop; he lacked *mesure* in an age which sought to avoid extremes—in public, anyway.[24]

Ripperdá was succeeded by Patiño, who was born in Italy, but was

[24] It is surprising that no writer of romantic biography has seized upon Ripperdá. Save for a translation from the French, P. Massuet, *Memoirs of the Duke of Ripperdá* (London, 1740), there is nothing in English on him. Ballesteros, *Historia de España*, V, 120, gives a good bibliography of articles on Ripperdá. See also G. Syveton, *Une cour et un aventurier au XVIIIe siècle* (Paris, 1896).

actually a pure-blooded Spaniard—a *Gallego,* in fact. Galicia is purported
to breed in her sons much the same caution Missouri is said to breed in
hers. Patiño rose through the royal administration in a steady, unspectacular way. He was never quite to dominate court and administration as
a true prime minister should, but he managed to restrain Spanish foreign
policy, and, at home, play a major part in the organization of the Spanish
government and economy which was destined by the second half of the
century to restore that country to some of her old prestige and power.
Patiño worked well and naturally with Walpole and Fleury in carrying
out the cult of stability.

The history of the individual states of Italy in this period can hardly
be followed in anything less than a many-volumed work. There were, as
in Germany, too many of them. In general, it may be said that after
Utrecht as before, Italy remained the best source of small weights to move
back and forth in the balance of power. These "weights" were, of course,
lands and the people on them, and they were moved with no consultation
of their inhabitants. It it commonly said that 1715 marks the supplanting
of Spain by Austria in the hegemony of Italy. This is substantially true;
but under the spur of Elizabeth Farnese, Spain was to have dynastic, if
not national, aspirations in Italy for some time, and the French could
always be calculated to intervene directly in the affairs of the neighboring
peninsula.

If it is permissible to generalize about Italy as a whole, it may be said
that the peninsula enjoyed during the eighteenth century the same gradual
rise in material prosperity that characterized most of Europe. Intellectually
the Enlightenment brought to the upper and educated classes of Italy a
new breath of air, and, if it did not bring back the cultural glories of the
cinquecento, at least saw Italy once more in the main current of European
thought. Italy also shared in the advances in the art of administration
which was one of the main achievements of the century.

But all these advances were extremely spotty, by no means evenly
spread over the peninsula. Much depended on the ability of the rulers a
given Italian state got from the international lottery. On the whole, the
formula that still holds for united Italy held true in the early eighteenth
century: the complex of what we moderns esteem as the "goodness" of a
society diminishes fairly regularly from north to south.

In the north, the holdings of the House of Savoy, with their nucleus
in Piedmont, emerged from the wars strengthened in fact and in prestige.
The prestige, which counted greatly in international politics, came from
the attainment of a royal title. This was originally meant to lie in Sicily,

but the upshot of the disturbances raised by Alberoni was that Sicily and Naples went to the Hapsburgs, and the House of Savoy had to be content with the royal title for Sardinia. It may seem absurd that the House of Savoy should have been helped along the way to its eventual unification of Italy by becoming kings instead of mere dukes, or that the Hohenzollerns should have been similarly helped by becoming kings instead of electors (*Kurfürsten*). But political power is clearly not quite identical with material power. Savoy gained little materially, for Sardinia was a poor and barren island. The new kingdom was well governed, and its capital, Turin, one of the neatest of eighteenth-century towns.

What Savoy had really wanted was the Milanese, and this, in the general sharing of the spoils after the War of the Spanish Succession, went to the Hapsburgs. There is an interesting example of the sort of survival of medieval forms we have often noted in this book in the fact that the Milanese, as a duchy, was formally "enfieffed" to the Empire, much as if Frederick Barbarossa really had come back to life. It, with Mantua, was actually administered after 1715 largely by members of Charles VI's Spanish retinue who had followed him when he was forced to leave that country in 1711. Vienna, of course, continued to supervise what was done in Milan. The duchy was, however, one of the richest parts of Italy, and on the whole it shared fully the prosperity of the time.

For Venice, a patrician republic which controlled most of northeastern Italy, this was a period of steady decline. Its international greatness, as we have seen, had been dealt a heavy blow by the Turks at the beginning of the century. It was already a center of what later came to be called "tourism"; but the tourists of the eighteenth century were a more exclusive lot than their successors of the railroad era. Venice was a city of pleasure for the rich and noble; and its economic decay was by no means as great as its political decay.

Genoa, too, was a republic ruled by an oligarchy of trading and banking origins, but it was somewhat better ruled than Venice. Tuscany was under the rule of the last of the Medici, Gian Gastone, a sickly, tired, and childless man. Tuscany had been promised to Don Carlos, and in 1731 Spanish troops quietly installed the lad as heir apparent in Florence. "Baby Carlos" had his first appanage. He was shortly destined to promotion to the throne of Naples, where he made his entry in 1734. Tuscany then fell to the Hapsburgs; or more accurately, the Tuscan succession went to Francis, Duke of Lorraine, who had married Maria Theresa, the girl about whom all the trouble of the Pragmatic Sanction had centered.

Less prosperous than Tuscany were the other splinter states of northern

Italy, Parma, Piacenza, Modena, Massa, and Carrara, like Tuscany much tossed about as prizes in the game of balance and power. Moving southward in the Papal States, however, all travelers were agreed that economic and political standards fell off rapidly. The Papal States were not subjected to a tyrannical government, but rather to an inefficient, routine, and complex administrative body. Rome itself was still a center of pilgrimage, cultural and artistic as well as religious, but these were not years of great Roman prosperity. Finally, there was at the extreme south the joint kingdom of Naples and Sicily, territorially the largest of the Italian states, and the poorest. The kingdom of Naples, or the Two Sicilies, was shifted back and forth from Savoy to Hapsburg to Spanish Bourbons between 1715 and 1734, but finally came to rest as a secundogeniture of the Spanish Bourbons, under which regime it was to remain until the days of Garibaldi and Cavour. The kingdom was backward, and though the rays of the Enlightenment reached the city of Naples, the kingdom as a whole remained for the rest of its independent career one of the most scandalously poor and badly run states of Europe.

VI. THE GERMANIES AND THE HAPSBURG WORLD

The Hapsburg complex of states filled in the early eighteenth century almost all that territory we loosely call central Europe. Only the Swiss Confederation was outside it. The Germanies were not, it is true, part of the Hapsburg dominions. As emperor, Charles VI headed a sort of Germanic confederation so loose that it can hardly be called a sovereign state. The Empire did indeed have a central organization for judicial purposes, and it had an army. But the army was contributed by the members, and only after the central Diet, which represented the princes and the imperial cities, had declared war in the name of the Empire. The prestige of the imperial crown no doubt helped a Hapsburg ruler in foreign affairs, and, over the centuries, had helped build up the Hapsburg domain outside the old limits of Germany. It was this domain that gave the Hapsburg rulers their real power.

As we have seen, historical writing about the reign of Charles VI has inevitably focused on his attempt to secure, by means of the Pragmatic Sanction, the transmission of that domain intact to his daughter Maria Theresa. In retrospect, we can see that such transmission was clearly essential if the Hapsburg state that survived until 1918 was to exist at all. But Charles VI would have been greatly surprised had he been told that he was working for the creation of a *real* union of his peoples, that he was founding an Austrian, or even an Austro-Hungarian, nation-state. He was working to keep a dynastic inheritance of semifeudal possessions intact. The Pragmatic Sanction meant one thing to its founder, and another to those for whom it became a constitutional principle to aid in their task —never quite achieved—of making the Hapsburg realm a "real" state. The case is roughly like that of Magna Charta, which can hardly have meant to those who signed it in 1215 what it came to mean to later generations.[25]

The reign of Charles VI was actually bedeviled at least as much by rivalries among his confidants, advisers, and ministers as by the struggles to get the Pragmatic Sanction accepted at home and abroad. Under the extreme of "feudal disintegration" which characterized the components of his realm, Charles could not from the center do more than hold together the elements—army, treasury, foreign office—necessary to maintain his place among the rulers of Europe. It must be repeated that he can hardly have been expected to create an efficient nation-state when neither Maria Theresa nor Joseph II, working later and with the benefit of the whole climate of opinion we sum up as "enlightened despotism," quite succeeded in doing so.

Nevertheless, divided counsel and Charles's own failure to get the best out of his servants were partly responsible for the weakness of the Hapsburg realm in competition with other European powers—a weakness Frederick the Great was to exploit fully. The revenues of Charles were at no time more than half of those of the King of England, though the population of the Hapsburg lands, including the rich Austrian Netherlands, was two-and-a-half times that of Great Britain and Ireland. Charles could never muster from his twenty-five million subjects an effective army quite equal to its paper strength of one hundred thousand; Frederick William of Prussia had at the end of his reign fully eighty thousand first-class troops ready for the field from a population of two million, five hundred thousand.

It is true that, in the first decades of his reign, Charles tried to remedy this economic weakness. He tried to build up the Levant trade through the ports of Trieste and Fiume, he built a good road over the Semmering from Vienna to Trieste, and, as we have seen, he worked hard to make a going concern of the Ostend Company. He made efforts to fund the

[25] The title of the long-delayed seventh volume of the history of Austria, started in 1885 by A. Huber and continued by O. Redlich, is a good example of this problem of perspective. It covers the years 1702-1740, and is called *Das Werden einer Grossmacht* (Becoming a Great Power). Charles VI must have thought of his inheritance as having been "great" already for at least two centuries.

Hapsburg debts, and gain for his lands some of the benefits of the new financial magic. Nor did these efforts wholly fail. The Hapsburg dominions shared some of the material progress of the era.

But neither the government nor the people achieved such progress as was achieved in western Europe and in much of Germany. There were, as usual in such cases, multiple reasons. Charles's own preoccupation with getting the Pragmatic Sanction accepted was certainly one. Another was his somewhat premature aging—he died in 1740 at only fifty-five—a process which brought with it increasing attachment to form, ceremony, and externals generally. Another was the impossibility, under conditions of the settlement of Utrecht, of integrating the advanced industrial society of Belgium with the more backward central areas of the Hapsburg domains. Neither Belgium nor Austria got much out of their eighty-odd years of very incomplete union, though the fertilizing effect of Belgium enterprise on the Austrians might have been considerable. Here again, as the history of the Ostend Company shows, it is hard to see how the ablest of statesmen in a position like that of Charles could have done much more than he did. The maritime powers did not want Belgium and Austria to flourish in union, and they were in a position to lay down terms which prevented even a start toward such a union. Yet the Austrian Netherlands, like the Italian possessions, took up much of the time and energy of the high officials at Vienna. Finally, Charles never succeeded in getting himself served by an effective team, by advisers who could work together.

It is true that Charles himself brought back from Spain a group of Spanish exiles loyal to him, that he allowed them to run Austrian Italy and have great influence even on central affairs, that one of them, Realp, a Catalonian, became a very close adviser. Against these "foreigners" Prince Eugene, who was himself a Savoyard born, Starhemberg, and others defended "pro-German" interests. But the division was not as simple as one between foreigners and Germans. Altheim, until his death in 1722 most influential with Charles, used the Spaniards and Italians as an effective balance to Eugene, and played on Charles's dislike for a subject whose glory was so much greater than his own. Eugene himself, in these later years of his life, had become somewhat set in his ways, which were those of a successful but aging general. In spite of his oft-quoted advice to Charles about army and treasury, it seems very likely that he himself in these years, when he ran the war department personally, was by no means an efficient administrator. Starhemberg was an upright man, but jealous of Eugene as well as contemptuous of the foreigners. Zinzendorf, and later Seckendorf, on whom Charles relied greatly in foreign affairs, were somewhat overclever, and often succeeded in annoying rather than conciliating their colleagues.

No administration, in any form of government, can be without jealousies, bickerings, and inefficiencies. But there are degrees in such things, which amount in the total to the difference between good teamwork and bad teamwork. One gathers that, during these critical decades when men like Walpole, Fleury, Frederick William, and Patiño did somehow create teams, such a thing was lacking in the Hapsburg central administration. It was an important lack.

The course of politics even in Prussia ran by no means perfectly smoothly. There were rivalries, intrigues, and plenty of material for the lively writer of memoirs, such as Pöllnitz.[26] There were even two favorites, Prince Leopold of Anhalt-Dessau and General Count Grumbkow, who duly disliked one another and intrigued for the top place. Yet Frederick William always managed to keep both Leopold and Grumbkow in a rivalry useful to him, but not disruptive to Prussia. For the most part, and especially as he grew older, Frederick William relied on plebeian and professional help for his task of governing, but he did not actually alienate even the older nobility of the Mark of Brandenburg. His court cost him very little; his cheeseparing economies in daily living—especially in the more decorative side of living, for in the matter of food and drink Frederick William was never grudging to himself or others—have long been a favorite source of historical anecdotes.

Somehow, though many of the ingredients that in other circumstances have made for disunity and poor teamwork were present in Prussia in the period, there was in fact a good team and effective administration, and no very striking internal tensions. It has often been said, but will bear repeating: the Prussian system demanded a capable, hard-working ruler who kept the reins in his own hands. This Frederick William did. He never allowed any minister to become a favorite in the bad sense of the word. He never lost control of the team, never got lazy, as did another Frederick William in the 1790's.

VII. THE MUSCOVITE AUTOCRACY

The reforms of Peter the Great in Russia had been similar in their aims to those of Frederick William I in Prussia. Peter's intention had been originally merely to reorganize the armed forces and to increase the

---

[26] K. L. von Pöllnitz, *Mémoires* (London, 1739-1740). These are excellent reading, and psychologically not unsound. Pöllnitz loved a good story and undoubtedly invented many.

financial resources of Russia, so that he might maintain and extend the vast but thinly peopled realm he had been called to rule. He intended no revolution by his attempts to borrow the intellectual and material resources of western Europe. The result, however, was a revolutionary change in the constitution and the governing classes, from which after Peter's death in 1725 it was not possible to go back entirely to old traditional ways.[27] The opposition of established social groups, nobles, clergy, monks and the rest, forced Peter to break down the old order. When, after a period of what Miliukov calls "chaos," Peter in the last years of his reign (beginning with his visit to France in 1717) undertook to establish a new order, he began by trying to impose taxes suggested by the French *taille* and *dixième*. If he could get seventy-five kopecks from every adult male Russian, he thought he could maintain his army. Previously existing duties and taxes would pay for the navy, the imperial court, and other minor government expenses. To get this seventy-five kopecks per man collected, he tried to establish a collegiate administration, suggested by a Swedish or German advisor named Fick. But the basis of the Swedish system was the local unit, with local officials, each responsible for only a few hundred taxpayers, and in Russia there were no such traditional local cantonal or parochial units. Peter was therefore driven to get a census of the male peasants, or "souls," and a tax list from the local landholding gentry, who were made responsible for the payment of the sums demanded from the peasants on their estates.

The momentous and unforeseen result of these measures was the reduction of the mass of the Russian people to a state of serfdom, previously nonexistent in Russia, which was to last for almost a century and a half, until the emancipation edict of Alexander II in 1861. Peter himself in the last years of his life was deeply concerned over the unhappy condition of the serfs, who became not merely attached to the land, but susceptible of being bought and sold. He insisted that in the breakup of an estate families of serfs should not be separated.

Peter, primarily with military service in mind, insisted on the principle of universal service for all. As the old nobility had opposed and tried to thwart him, Peter had been throughout dependent on Russian parvenus, and even more on foreign experts. He finally established in 1722 a "table of ranks," grouping military services, civil service, and

[27] See Kluchevsky, *History of Russia*, IV, 227-228, a passage summarizing a lengthy discussion. The best discussion of these reforms of Peter the Great, omitting works in Russian not translated, is that by Miliukov, in Milioukov, Seignobos, et Eisenmann, *Histoire de Russie*, I, 267-427.

court officials in three allegedly parallel columns. This seemed like a democratic recognition of the "career open to talent," but actually Peter gave preference to military service, especially in the guards regiments, into which he had forced sons of the nobility to go. The eventual result, since most of the personages in the table of ranks were also landholders, was the creation of an aristocratic privileged class which became hereditary. Peter's rule was that every man must serve the state for twenty-five years. A landholder refusing or evading this very unpopular obligation was subject to the penalty of "civil death." A ukase of 1722 provided that anyone might take his property, or even kill him with impunity if he did not appear when summoned to the military review.

As most upper-class Russians were still completely illiterate, and no schools except a theological seminary existed in Russia, Peter began by sending turbulent and illiterate young noblemen abroad to study the useful arts, as Peter himself did that of shipbuilding in Holland. One of them wrote to the tsar about a comrade: "Your majesty has deigned to ask me how Stephen is getting on in the study of geography without knowing the alphabet. I know nothing about it. God enlightens even the blind."[28] He tried next to establish secondary and technical schools in Russia, such as the academy headed by Pastor Gluck, in whose household had resided the pretty peasant servant girl who was to become the tsar's mistress, then his second wife, and at his death the Empress Catherine I, autocrat of all the Russias. He had Russian translations of technical and mathematical books printed in Holland. The only publication which was at all widely sold and read was, however, one entitled *An Honourable Mirror for Youth, or a Guide to Deportment*, published by Peter's order in 1717. This taught the young noble, among other things, never to get drunk in the daytime, at all times to refrain from dancing in boots, not to spit into the middle of a group of people, but always to one side, and never to gobble food noisily like a pig.[29] It also contained the significant advice never to speak Russian before servants or peasants. The subsequent universal adoption of foreign tongues by the Russian gentry, familiar to readers of Tolstoi and Turgenev by the frequent remark in the English translations of their great nineteenth-century novels, "In French in the original," helped to make the upper classes descended from Peter's nobility a caste apart from and out of sympathy with the masses.

Peter had not merely absolute, but completely arbitrary authority, since

---

[28] Quoted by Milioukov, *Histoire de Russie*, I, 398, with several similar documents.
[29] See the summary of it in Kluchevsky, *History of Russia*, IV, 259-260.

in Russia the autocrat was not limited by any tradition of an impersonal and permanent law, like the Roman and the canon law of western Europe. Peter had broken down the customs and traditions which in countries like England and France were even more potent guarantees against arbitrary despotism. There was nothing too cruel, too grotesque, too obscene, or too unprecedented to be beyond the tsar's power. The amazement of Peter's ministers, Tolstoi and Mateiev, at the liberties enjoyed by the Venetians and the French is significant. In Venice, "Every man is free from abuse," with no cause to fear anyone, able to act according to his own will, to dwell in peace, without overburdensome dues. In France, the nobility have neither any reason nor any means of hating and putting to shame any of their fellows, even the humblest. The "autocrat ruler" in that country cannot take dues secretly or by force, but only "as the *Parlement* shall have adjudged the need" (i.e., registered the edict). Noblemen's sons in France suffer from no harsh treatment, either by parents or by teachers, but are "reared in forethought, will, and daring; and accordingly learn their tasks without difficulty."[30]

Peter the Great in 1722 issued an edict by which he and later tsars were to have the power to name their own successors. The traditional Russian way of choosing a tsar had been either by the will of the previous tsar, or by a council of the nobility, but there had been irregular and arbitrary choices before Peter. He had put his eldest son Alexis to death, and another son had died. There was a grandson, still a child, son of the dead Alexis, and a daughter by the mistress (afterward the Empress Catherine I). But when the tsar lay dying he could only mutter that he "left the empire to . . ." without naming any name.

After he was dead the senate, the new imperial council he had created, would probably if left to itself have chosen the infant grandson, the only unquestionably legitimate male heir of the great tsar. But the guards regiment and the numerous parvenu officials combined, as the favorite Menshikov wished, to choose the tsar's second wife, the former pretty peasant girl. No woman had previously reigned in Russia. The nobles hoped to be able to do more nearly as they liked under the new reign. Menshikov, whose mistress Catherine had been before she attracted Peter's notice, thought he could still control her public acts, though in her private life he had long since ceased to figure.

The peasant woman's reign lasted only two years. She was persuaded to choose as her successor Peter II, grandson of Peter the Great, the natural and normal heir. But his death in adolescence of smallpox in

[30] Quoted in Kluchevsky, *History of Russia*, IV, 279.

1730 raised once more the question of the succession. This time a group of nobles chose Anna, the widowed Duchess of Courland, a daughter of Peter's half brother, the Tsar Ivan V. A few of the more enlightened nobles, led by Prince L. M. Golitzin, members of a new imperial council established in 1726, tried to set up a limited monarchy. Anna was offered the throne on condition that she would not remarry, nominate a successor, or without the consent of her council declare war, impose new taxation, conclude peace, make any appointment or confer any title of nobility, or do any executive act at all. She accepted those "points," only to repudiate them with the approval of the guards regiments when the opposition of the mass of the nobles and of the people to what would have been an oligarchy controlled by a few great families had become plain. She, or rather her favorite, Biron, and her bureaucrats, mostly Baltic Germans, henceforth ruled autocratically until her death in 1740. The period of palace revolutions, in which the guards regiments of noblemen played the decisive part, lasted from the death of Peter the Great in 1725 at least until the accession of Catherine II, the Great, a personality strong enough to make her own will felt and obeyed. In all this, the parallel with the Byzantine empire is obvious. Golitzin had studied English history and read Locke. But Russia was in 1730 far from ready for a revolution on the English 1688 model.

VIII. THE OTTOMAN HERITAGE

The decline of the Turkish power in the seventeenth and eighteenth centuries was as spectacular as had been its phenomenal rise in the later Middle Ages. In the long line of sultans who followed Suleiman the Magnificent (died 1566) only Murad IV (1623-1640) was a man of statesmanship, and his reign was too short to establish any basic reform. Yet in the early eighteenth century the Ottoman Empire still sprawled over North Africa, over the entire Near East as far as Persia, and over all of southeastern Europe to the borders of Hungary. It was very much a part of Europe and must be considered as such, despite the fact that religiously and culturally it constituted an entirely different world.

The early sultans had succeeded in their far-reaching conquests not only because they were exceptionally able men and warriors, but because, so far as Europe was concerned, they were able to take full advantage of the feudal anarchy and religious conflicts of their time. In the seventeenth and eighteenth centuries the Turkish rulers were for the most part utter nonentities, but they and their peoples were nevertheless favored by the antagonisms and confusions of the Thirty Years' War and later by the closing phase of the Hapsburg-Bourbon rivalry. Indeed, the wars of Louis XIV had enabled the Turks, under the leadership of the great viziers of the Kiuprili family, to reopen the offensive on Christendom: in 1683 the Ottoman armies stood for the second and last time at the gates of Vienna.

In short, then, the Ottoman Empire in Europe had long since become an anachronism, albeit a very tenacious one. Time and again both popes and secular statesmen had preached the union of Europe as the necessary first step toward the expulsion of the heathen. In this period Cardinal Alberoni renewed the plea (1736) and called not only for a union of Catholic and Protestant states, but for the establishment of a "permanent Diet" to maintain the settlement once the spoils of the infidel had been divided.[31] Though the cardinal's appeal went unheeded, like those of his predecessors, it had much that was tempting about it. He argued that it would be easy for a united Europe to drive the Turks out and in this opinion he was undoubtedly correct. The Ottoman Empire was notoriously weak and backward; the marvel was that it managed to hold together at all, to say nothing of the fact that on occasion it could make a real if not sustained effort. Let us analyze briefly why this was so.

The Ottoman sultan was, in theory at least, an absolute monarch, a simple despot. Actually, however, he was restrained, like every other Moslem, by the teaching and precepts of the Islamic law, expounded and enforced by the *ulema* or teachers learned in the law, who in turn enjoyed the support of the backward and conservative Moslem population. A great sultan might, as many did, interpret the law in his own way—the Turks were never purists like the Arabs. But since the middle of the sixteenth century the sultans lacked entirely the ability, will power and authority to impose themselves. To avoid dynastic conflict they were brought up in seclusion, in fact in a sort of gilded imprisonment. They knew little of administration, government or law and were therefore at the mercy of their advisers (viziers) and of their officials. These were, aside from the members of the grand council (divan), the Moslem judges—the grand mufti or sheikh-ul-Islam and the kadis—the provincial governors and the chiefs of the armed services.

Originally the civil and military officials had all been drawn from the so-called Ruling Institution, which consisted of Christian boys taken by

---

[31] The details in W. Evans Darby, "Cardinal Alberoni's Proposed European Alliance for the Subjugation and Settlement of the Turkish Empire," Grotius Society, *Transactions*, V (1920), 7, 83.

way of tribute and, after conversion to Islam, carefully trained for service. But this system had long since been abandoned. The tribute in Christian children had been given up and favoritism or bribery rather than systematic training had become the key to advancement. The chief minister (grand vizier) himself had to depend on the favor of an often whimsical and vicious ruler, and had to defend himself by corruption against the intrigues of his rivals. The same held true all up and down the official scale. Only in time of dire crisis and necessity would some outstanding personality be called to the helm to save the ship from disaster.[32]

The worst element in a generally bad system was undoubtedly the Janizary Corps, which had degenerated from being an élite, highly disciplined and terrifyingly formidable body of infantry into being a closed caste of unruly gangsters. In 1637 Moslems had been admitted for the first time. Thereafter one privilege after another was lavished on the Janizaries, whose numbers shot up until in 1700 there were almost one hundred thousand of them. The sultans feared them above all others and tried to keep them out of the capital. Nonetheless they were always ready to raise the mob and start a palace revolution. At best they lived in the provincial towns making life miserable for the officials, engaging in "trade" and generally extorting from the local population all sorts of favors and tribute. Lady Mary Montagu had occasion to observe them in Serbia, where their insolence defied all description. They were, she remarked, "sworn brothers," an "inviolable league" against whom no one could contend.[33]

Of the Turks themselves very little is known for this period. In the Balkans the upper classes lived on the land in something like feudal fashion. In an emergency they supplied a sort of feudal cavalry levy (*sipahis*), while in normal times they led an easygoing existence. Many of them, as we learn from Lady Montagu, were wealthy and highly cultivated, but quite devoid of any interest in progress in the European sense and much more intent on the pursuit of poetry or of religious speculation. The lot of the peasants in the Balkan area was in all likelihood an unenviable one, but probably not worse than in any other part of eastern Europe. Indeed, the regime in Serbia, Bulgaria and Greece was probably less oppressive and more democratic than in Christian countries. The Turks showed but little fanaticism and permitted a large measure of self-government to the rural communities. The natural leaders in this entire

[32] The best discussion may be found in Walter L. Wright, Jr., *Ottoman Statecraft. The Book of Counsel for Vezirs and Governors* (*Princeton Oriental Texts*, II, 1935).

[33] Lady Mary Wortley and Montagu, *Letters from Constantinople, 1716-1718* (London, 1861).

region were the Greek Orthodox priests, who in many cases were more exacting than the Moslem landlords.

The central government in the early eighteenth century was an amiable and ineffectual institution. Ahmed III, who ruled from 1703 until 1730, cared nothing for administration or war, but was a refined and appreciative devoté of the beautiful. His chief minister, Damad Ibrahim (1718-1730), was enlightened and able. Like Walpole and Fleury he did his utmost to preserve the peace and in order to maintain his position kept the sultan amused by the construction of palaces and pavilions. He assembled in Constantinople a veritable galaxy of poets, including Ahmed Nedim, one of the greatest figures in Turkish literature. Illuminations, tulip-fetes, parties, excursions and banquets followed each other in endless procession, all of them gracefully recorded in the lovely verses of the poets.[34]

Very characteristic of this period of cultural enlightenment was the opening of the first Turkish printing press in 1727. Although the Jews and Greeks had had their own presses in Constantinople for a long time, efforts to print books in Turkish or Arabic had been blocked by the copyists' guild and by respect for "Holy Writ." It was the Grand Vizier Ibrahim who finally overruled the opposition. Although the printing of the Koran was still forbidden, the press that was set up by the Hungarian renegade, Ibrahim Muteffarika, published a number of historical and geographical works before the middle of the century.[35]

Both Ahmed III and his grand vizier fell victims to a mob rising in 1730, but the new sultan, Mahmud I (1730-1754), was also a man of peace and culture. It was during his reign that the French adventurer, Count Bonneval, arrived in Constantinople and embarked upon his extraordinary efforts to reform at least the military system of the empire. Bonneval exercised an almost incredible influence on Turkish diplomacy during the 1730's and at least set the example for later reformers. But the net result was not impressive. Like everyone else, the French adventurer found himself blocked by ignorance and prejudice, but above all, by vested interests and selfish ambition.[36]

Our analysis of the Ottoman system would not be complete without

[34] See esp. Elias J. W. Gibb, A History of Ottoman Poetry, ed. Edward G. Browne (London, 1905), IV, chap. i; also the Letters of Lady Mary Montagu, and the recent book by Mary L. Shay, The Ottoman Empire from 1720 to 1734, as Revealed in Despatches of the Venetian Baili (Illinois Studies in the Social Sciences, XXVII, no. 3, Urbana, 1944).

[35] Franz Babinger, Stambuler Buchwesen in 18ten Jahrhundert (Leipzig, 1919).

[36] See Claude A. Bonneval, Memoirs of the Bashaw Count Bonneval (London, 1750); Zinkeisen, Geschichte des osmanischen Reiches, V, 836-848; Albert Vandal, La Mission du Marquis de Villeneuve (Paris, 1887).

some reference to the economic aspect. The Turks themselves had never shown any interest either in trade or in industry. Small local industries such as coppersmithing, rug weaving, leather tooling were, to be sure, well established and flourishing, but there was nothing in the way of larger enterprise and such financial and commercial transactions as were needed were left to non-Moslems and foreigners. The western countries had already built up a substantial export trade to the Levant, where British, French, Dutch and other companies were engaged in hot competition. But these companies dealt not with Turks, but with Jews, Armenians and Greeks, all of them races which enjoyed the utmost toleration from the Turks not only in the religious but in the social and economic spheres.

The Jews, for example, had long held an influential position at court, first as physicians and then as bankers and go-betweens. Lady Montagu described them as being "an incredible power," enjoying many privileges beyond the Turks themselves:

They have formed a very considerable commonwealth, being judged by their own laws, and have drawn the whole trade of the empire into their hands, partly by firm union among themselves and prevailing on the idle temper and want of industry of the Turks. Every pasha has his Jew, who is his *homme d'affaires*; he is let into all his secrets and does all his business. No bargain is made, no bribe received, no merchandise disposed of, but what passes through their hands. They are the physicians, the stewards, and the interpreters of all the great men.

But, added Lady Mary, the Jews, though vastly rich, were very careful not to make a show or arouse cupidity.

The same was not true of the great Greek families which rose to prominence in this period and which, because of their residence near the lighthouse (Phanar) came to be known as Phanariots. Many of these Greeks claimed later that they were descendants of the old Byzantine aristocracy. Be that as it may, they had grown prosperous in the administration of the Orthodox church and through tax-collecting contracts with the government. In 1714 the Ottoman government decided to replace the native governors of what is now Rumania, suspecting them rightly of constant intrigue with Russia and Austria. Greeks were appointed in their place and during the eighteenth century the governors of Moldavia and Wallachia were chosen without exception from twelve Phanariot families. The spoils of appointment to these rich provinces were simply enormous, but for that very reason the places were much coveted and high in price. So the Greek aristocrats groveled before the sultan and his ministers for favor, only to reverse the situation in dealing with their subordinates. In Rumania they ruled as absolute lords, treating the local landowners and peasants as dirt and extorting in money all that the country would bear. The whole system was one of endless treachery and corruption which put a premium on exploitation. As a result a large-scale emigration into Hungary began to take place, and it was only then, at the very end of this period, that Constantine Mavrocordatos, perhaps the most statesmanlike of the Phanariots, began to introduce some basic reforms.

Even so casual a review of Ottoman affairs as this will indicate how great was the chasm between western Europe and the Near East, not only in religion but in general outlook and in social structure. Among the Turks there was nothing like the emergence of a middle class, nothing like the surge of enterprise and the development of scientific thought. The Ottoman Empire was already a backwater, without any of the lift that was characterizing eastern European countries like Russia. On the other hand, it was an easygoing despotism, no longer a threat to Europe, but soon to become an obstacle in the way of progress.

Chapter Nine

THE UNEASY BALANCE

I. THE QUADRUPLE ALLIANCE

THE world wars of Louis XIV did not end abruptly with the Treaty of Utrecht in 1713. As we have seen in the first two chapters of this book, the War of the Spanish Succession was followed by a series of disturbances in the Baltic, the Balkans, and Italy, disturbances which may be likened to what the pathologist calls sequelae, morbid conditions that follow upon serious disease. The appearance of such sequelae after each of the half-dozen major crises of modern European and world history which we call world wars is, indeed, one of the relatively secure generalizations the historian can make.

These disturbances arose, or rather, persisted in 1715 in spite of the universal war weariness of peoples and in spite of the very real desire of most governments for a general peace. They persisted because the attempted general settlement could not cope at once with all the problems, big and little, that confronted European diplomacy. Some sort of special machinery was necessary. Haltingly, by trial and error, and without apparently altering the methods and traditions of diplomacy in which they had grown up, the Dubois, Stanhopes, Zinzendorfs, and their colleagues —and royal masters—tried to set up some less imperfect methods for the pacification of Europe and the effective maintenance of peace. We should beware against too crude a reinterpretation of history in terms of our own experiences; these men of 1715 were not thinking like or behaving like the men of 1918, or even the men of 1815. They were, in particular, much less self-consciously aiming at some sort of organization, league, or international government by consultation. But they were at least facing problems roughly analogous to those men faced in 1814, in 1918, and today.

Their solution was a rudimentary and imperfect sort of Concert of Europe (or rather of the great powers of Europe) and an even more rudimentary system of consultation through diplomatic congresses. The form assumed by the Concert of Europe was the Quadruple Alliance, originally concluded in 1718 among Britain, France, Austria, and the United Provinces to check Alberoni's schemes. Philip V was forced in 1720 to accept by the Treaty of London what amounted to membership in this system of great powers, which thus became in a sense a Quintuple Alliance. With the settlements in the Balkans at Passarowitz (1718) and in the north at Nystadt (1721) these five great powers had apparently a clear field ahead of them.

As a matter of fact, there were still in the early 1720's two sore spots in Europe, Italy and Poland. The problems centering in these lands were never entirely solved in this period. Moreover, the great powers themselves were quite unused to acting as a Concert. They were divided among themselves by the memories of old quarrels and by new commercial and economic variants on the old rivalries. Before we trace the complex interweaving of these rivalries during the uneasy international stability of the 1720's and 1730's, we may survey briefly the habits, the inclinations, the purposes (not always conscious purposes) which sent the diplomatists of the great powers off on their several ways. These were conflicting or diverging and rarely genuinely common ways.

The chief architect of the Quadruple Alliance had been the British statesman, Lord Stanhope. British policy was now all for peace in Europe. Great Britain was, in a sense, the dominant great power. Her powerful merchant class, though still thoroughly indoctrinated with mercantilist notions of trade as essentially a form of economic warfare, had found prolonged world war quite unprofitable. But these same merchants were used to trading methods in the Indies, both East and West, which amounted to a sort of running war with Spain, France, and, until recently, Holland. They, and even more the rest of the British ruling classes—the nobles, gentry, and professional men—had grown up in the belief that France and Spain were "natural" enemies of Britain. In the long wars of Louis XIV just ended, France had definitely taken over from Spain in the minds of most Englishmen the role of villain in the drama of international relations. It would be hard for British statesmen, partly Gallicized in manners, taste, and language though they were in the early eighteenth century, to deal with even the most pacific Frenchman without feelings of fear and distrust. Toward the rest of Europe the Britisher of the ruling classes already exhibited that curious sense of detached superiority that reached its height in Victorian times. British statesmen were used to thinking of the emperor as a makeweight against France, used, in a sense, to co-operation with the Hapsburg power; they showed few signs of having seized on the true importance of Prussia and were annoyed at the degree to which the Hanoverian connection involved them in German politics; they were just beginning to feel that hostility toward Russia, roused as we have seen by Russian interference with British Baltic trade, which has been pretty constant in later British history. But, it must be insisted, these British diplomatists were old hands, used to the ways of European diplomacy, and accepting its standards. Though in a sense they were anxious to keep Britain from too definite commitments on the Continent, though they were aware of Britain's role as guardian of the balance of power, they did not explicitly think of their position in terms of "splendid isolation."

France had emerged the loser from a world war, but had lost no important territories (save Nova Scotia and Newfoundland in the New World), and had actually gained one of her war aims in the establishment of a Bourbon on the throne of Spain. Her statesmen showed no feeling of guilt over her aggressive actions and no very definite signs that they felt international relations needed reform. France had lost a round in the game —that was all. Other rounds would come. Nor, to be frank, were there any indications that her recent foes felt that she had sinned. There was, as we have seen, a general European desire to get back to normal in 1715, but no such clear revulsion against a power regarded as the guilty aggressor as one finds in 1814, 1918, and 1945. Hatred of France was strong in England, in much of Germany, and in some Spanish circles, and it was a hatred sharpened by an awareness of how dangerous the ambitions of Louis XIV had been. But it had not the explicit quality of outraged moral sentiment.

For French statesmen, England was in 1715 still perhaps the classic enemy, and the Anglo-French colonial and commercial rivalry was already full grown. Yet the House of Austria was almost as much the hereditary foe and, moreover, Frenchmen felt exposed toward the east as they did not toward the channel. French diplomatists were trained in the policy of making weight against Austria, first by getting what support they could from Prussia and the *Kleinstaaten,* or at least keeping the Germanies divided, and second by having an ally or friendly power on the east of the Hapsburgs. For some time this friendly power had been Turkey; only now, in the early eighteenth century, was Russia emerging as a power the French might wish to woo. In the Baltic there was a French tradition of co-operation with Sweden, and another one of sharing with the other powers in the bribery of Polish groups. The men who made French foreign policy after 1715 were to a certain extent sobered by earlier defeats in war. They wanted peace, as did their contemporary British counterparts. But they were neither chastened nor resigned, and they were brought up to regard France as the natural leader in European politics.

Spain, which was still considered a great power—and with her overseas dominions still had the resources to be one—had suffered badly in prestige in the last years of the Spanish Hapsburgs and had by the official settlements of 1713-1721 been shut out of the Netherlands and Italy. Spaniards of the ruling classes had still the habit of thinking in terms of direct Spanish expansion in Europe, and it was this persisting sentiment that enabled Elizabeth Farnese to get Don Carlos established in Italy. Persistent and determined as that legendary lady was, she did not single-handedly keep Spain involved in Italian politics. For the rest, Spain had for long fought a running battle, only a bit sharper during formal war than during formal peace, to preserve against British, French, and Dutch the large areas of the globe she had appropriated. These maritime powers were her traditional enemies. Religious differences no doubt sharpened Spanish hatred for the British; but there was plenty of hatred left over for the sister Latin and Catholic state of France.

The ruling groups who determined the policies of Hapsburg Austria had in 1715 by no means forgotten the not-so-remote days of Charles V. The deep feelings Charles VI had for Spain were no private eccentricities; they were merely another survival, a dynastic inheritance. The emperor took his gains in Italy and Belgium as, at bottom, mere installments. The Hapsburg drive was toward the universal state. France had long been the great obstacle in the way, and Britain a somewhat impermanent but not inconsistent ally. But the Hapsburgs also held the European bastion against the Turks, and had recently become aware that southeastward, too, the land was bright and expansion attractive. Just as France was always falling between the two stools of expansion overseas and expansion eastwards, so Austria was falling between the two stools of expansion in Europe proper and expansion in the lands of the now decaying Ottoman Empire.

Prussia was not yet accepted as a great power. Under Frederick William her foreign policy was timid—no doubt profitably timid, but hardly foreshadowing what was shortly to come. Prussian rivalry seemed almost as keen with Hanover as with Austria. Indeed, it seems doubtful whether Frederick William, who had a deep sense of *Obrigkeit*, ever really thought of himself as a rival of his imperial overlord. Prussia had, in the shuttles of past wars, not infrequently been an ally of France. Yet even in 1715 the faint beginnings of a feeling for Prussia's mystic role as the anointed agent of Germanness are discernible. For the rest, a Hohenzollern would pick up almost anyhow any bit of German or near-German territory; but he was not much interested in lands farther afield, nor in the balance of power save as it touched Brandenburg-Prussia directly—which sooner or later it always did.

Russia in the early eighteenth century had just barely joined the rondo of international politics. She had her own national aims—the older ones of expansion toward the south, chasing out Tartar and Turk, and, very recently indeed, penetration of the Baltic area. Very wise heads might guess that she would soon find a more serious western enemy than Sweden or Poland. But in this period, Peter the Great might almost be described as shopping around for allies—all great nations had to have allies—and not really finding any. Time was to remedy that.

II. THE ITALIAN TROUBLES

In this Europe crisscrossed by old and new lines of alliance and rivalry, the new Quadruple (or Quintuple) Alliance sought to act as a Concert of Europe. Since Italian affairs had not really calmed down with Alberoni's departure—the details of the appanage for Don Carlos had not been settled—and there were other outstanding disputes between Spain and Austria, a full-blown European Congress was gathered at Cambrai in 1722, and finally, after two years' work getting organized, met formally in session in 1724. On this Congress of Cambrai Carlyle poured his contempt in familiar rhetoric: "The most inane of Human Congresses, and memorable on that account, if on no other. There, in old stagnant Cambrai . . . for about four years, were these poor fellow-creatures busied, bailing out water with sieves."[1]

For once, Carlyle's rhetoric was not unfaithful to the facts. No one has tried to rehabilitate the memory of the Congress of Cambrai. Its members were tied by the orders of their superiors in the various foreign offices. Charles VI was still hoping to avoid carrying out the promises he had made the Spaniards as to lands in Italy. He was in the midst of launching his Ostend Company and in no mood to do what the commercial rivals of that company, the British and the Dutch, wanted him to do—that is, settle down and be quiet. Philip V himself had joined the Quadruple Alliance only with great reluctance; the undeclared economic war between Spain and the maritime powers still went on. Yet—and this is a classic instance of the kind of incident that, under dynastic politics, upsets a

[1] Thomas Carlyle, *History of Friedrich the Second, Called Frederick the Great* (New York, 1858-1866), Bk. V, chap. iii.

delicate balance—two very personal matters brought Europe to a crisis.

First, Elizabeth Farnese, impatient with the delays of the Congress of Cambrai and convinced, not without reason, that no one was pressing the cause of Don Carlos very hard, determined to go right to the heart of things and buy off Charles VI himself with an offer of a Spanish alliance. With this in mind, Ripperdá, whom we have already met, was sent to Vienna in November, 1724, with an offer that Don Carlos marry Maria Theresa and preserve intact the Hapsburg hereditary dominions. As reinsurance, Don Philip, Elizabeth's younger son, was to marry the Archduchess Maria Anna, younger sister of Maria Theresa, and put together a new kingdom in Italy, which would have been all Italy save Savoy, Venice, Genoa, and the Papal States. This is eighteenth-century diplomacy in the grand style: for at the time Ripperdá was in Vienna, Monteleone, another Spanish agent, had been sent by the Spanish sovereigns to try to get from the French and English armed assistance to set up Don Carlos in his promised Italian duchies of Parma and Piacenza. The armed forces would have been, of course, no more than tokens, and what Philip and Elizabeth were asking for, in modern terms, was international or collective action from the two chief guardians of the Concert of Europe. But at the same time they were through Ripperdá asking Charles VI to join them in upsetting this Concert of Europe. The methods the Spanish sovereigns used were not unique, and the general diplomatic situation was typical enough of the *facts* of international life at almost any time. The unique thing here was the driving force of Elizabeth's own personality, which lifted her hypochondriac husband and a tired country into the role of aggressor in a quiet Europe.

Charles VI was always to be lured by any prospect, however remote, of restoring the dominions of Charles V; he was, moreover, particularly annoyed in the winter of 1724-1725 with the western powers, his allies. The Dutch had almost succeeded in bringing the whole problem of the Ostend Company before the Congress of Cambrai, and only the quick action of the French foreign minister, Morville, prevented this breach of international decency. For the affairs of a great ruler were not to be brought up without his consent in a mere international congress. Yet Charles was cautious, and worried about his Pragmatic Sanction, and most uncertain about how much support he could really get from Spain were he to break up the Quadruple Alliance. A second very personal matter acted here as a catalyst.

In February, 1725, the French government under Bourbon decided to send back to Spain the Infanta Maria Anna Victoria, a seven-year-old

child affianced to the fifteen-year-old Louis XV. There have been ingenious explanations of this act as part of an elaborate scheme of Bourbon
and his mistress, Madame de Prie, to get a particularly pliable consort
for the king; actually the evidence shows that the French court and its
advisers were unanimous, and that they were moved primarily by the
desire to have a queen who could bear children as soon as possible
and thereby remove the threat of a disputed succession, were Louis
to die. The Infanta could hardly bear a child in less than a decade.[2]
The French were, however, brusque and tactless in what seemed a dismissal of the Infanta. Spanish pride, not hard to wound, was quick to
take offense. And it was not only government circles who were affected;
the people of Madrid took to stoning Frenchmen in the streets, and there
clearly was what, in later times of newspapers and rapid communications,
came to be called a wave of popular indignation.

Spain had now a plausible excuse for withdrawing from the Quadruple
Alliance. Her delegates left the Congress of Cambrai, which shortly after
broke up. Encouraged by these definite acts of Spain, Charles signed in
April, 1725, a first Treaty of Vienna, setting up something new in the
politics of the time, an Austro-Spanish alliance. Charles gave up his claim
to Spain (not permanently, as a matter of fact), agreed that Don Carlos
was to have the reversion of the much-discussed duchies, and promised
to help get Gibraltar back in Spanish hands. Philip agreed to help out
the Ostend Company.

News of this "unnatural" alliance between Hapsburg Austria and
Bourbon Spain, so recently enemies, started a European war scare. The
Spaniards began strengthening and equipping their much-reduced fleet
and getting their armies on a war footing. France and Britain acted
quickly. They put together at Herrenhausen in September, 1725, the
League of Hanover, a combination of France, Britain, and Prussia, to
which were added finally Sweden, Denmark, and Holland. Later, in
1726, Austria added a somewhat tenuous alliance with Russia, which
ended with the death of Catherine I shortly after. It was the old
phenomenon once more; two rival coalitions were formed, each against
the other. Yet no general war broke out.

No general war broke out because the major powers were so afraid
of such a war that they began to withdraw from the challenging positions
they had assumed. This withdrawal was not, however, immediate. Both
Austrians and Spanish replied to the Treaty of Hanover with the proper
proud indignation, and in November wrote secret additions to the Treaty

[2] H. Gauthier-Villars, *Le mariage de Louis XV* (Paris, 1900).

of Vienna, which included among other things a fine plan for the partitioning of France. Charles also definitely accepted the proposed double marriage between the two sons of Philip and Elizabeth and his own two daughters. Spain was to get Gibraltar from a beaten England, and the Ostend Company was to be aided by Spain on the seven seas. These "secret" provisions were soon known, guessed, or merely exaggerated in all the chancelleries of Europe. The excuse for Ripperdá's dismissal was that he had indiscreetly boasted about these secret provisions.

This winter of 1725-1726 was the high point of the crisis. By the end of the summer of 1726, the necessary withdrawals had begun. Frederick William of Prussia, who had joined the western powers in the Treaty of Hanover, signed in October, 1726, the Treaty of Wüsterhausen with their opponent Emperor Charles VI. In this treaty Prussia promised to defend Austria against attack by the powers allied at Hanover. Frederick William's German conscience had troubled him over his action in joining the Hanover group; furthermore, the Austrian ambassador to Prussia, Seckendorf, was an able man with great influence on Frederick William; and finally, Charles was induced to give his imperial opinion that the Hohenzollern claims to the succession in Jülich and Berg were just. The full rounding out of their holdings in this rich lower Rhineland had long been a Hohenzollern aim. The net effect of Wüsterhausen was to encourage Charles VI toward peaceful measures, since he now felt protected on the north.

The Austrian-Spanish alliance now began to show signs of weakness. Charles had never really wanted the Spanish marriage for Maria Theresa; he still hoped to keep Bourbon Spain out of Italy; he soon realized that he could not hope to get any money out of Spain, which was no longer as fabulously wealthy in bullion as she had been and was often still supposed to be. Charles began late in 1727 to show himself more conciliatory toward France, where Fleury now had full power, and toward England.

The Spaniards also drew back. Ripperdá was dismissed, and the moderate Patiño gradually assumed the essential powers of a prime minister. It is true that Spain got herself into a touch of war by besieging the British in Gibraltar, a siege that dragged out for months after its beginning in February, 1727, in good eighteenth-century style, most unbloodily. But there was a state of war between Spain and Britain, and had Charles VI come actively to the aid of his Spanish ally, or had the French backed up Britain by force, general war might have ensued.

The initial positive steps in localizing this Anglo-Spanish war were taken by Fleury, who succeeded in restraining the strong pro-Spanish and anti-British party at the French court. This party, led by the able intriguer Chauvelin, a violent Anglophobe, actually seems to have proposed a Franco-Spanish alliance, which would have given a more fantastic turn to the kaleidoscope of European alignments than even the Vienna and Herrenhausen combinations of the year before. But Fleury lived up to the compliment Voltaire was later to make him:

> O vieillard vénérable, à qui les destinées
> Ont de l'heureux Nestor accordé les années,
> Sage que rien n'alarme et que rien n'éblouit. . . .[3]

The preliminaries of Vienna, signed by France, Spain, Holland, and Austria in May, 1727, were not the foundations of a combination against Great Britain, but the basis for a general European settlement. Charles agreed to suspend his Ostend Company for seven years (as we have seen in Chapter IV, this was its death sentence), and the Spanish agreed to raise the siege of Gibraltar. The still unsettled affair of Parma and Piacenza and other matters were to be dealt with in another European congress. Meanwhile Walpole had much the same trouble with the British fire-eaters of the war party as Fleury had had with his, but finally managed to quiet them. With both Fleury and the able Austrian diplomatist Königsegg urging Elizabeth to make peace, Spain and England were finally brought together in the Convention of the Pardo of March, 1728. The "war" was over.

The Congress of Soissons, called to meet in 1728 as a result of the preliminaries of Vienna, has had as bad a reputation as the previous Congress of Cambrai. It is true that from neither of them did there issue the practical conclusions and treaties by which the powers guided their actions. But both, and especially that of Soissons, acted as delaying mechanisms, allowed the real business of diplomacy to be done with less immediate pressure for action. Though the Anglo-Spanish war had been stopped, the unstable equilibrium produced by the sudden alliance between Austria and Spain had still by no means settled down. Elizabeth, for one thing, had as yet no sure throne for Don Carlos.

The winter of 1728-1729 was not an easy one. Chauvelin in France had now become Minister of Foreign Affairs in succession to the Anglophile Morville. Fleury was probably deliberately using Chauvelin's brusque energies to regain initiatives for France; but Chauvelin was a dangerous

[3] Ode XII, "A la Reine de Hongrie" (written in 1742), Voltaire, Oeuvres, ed. Beuchot, XII, 448.

tool.[4] Fleury did himself prevent a break with England and an active alliance with Spain. Charles VI helped redress the balance by telling Elizabeth in the winter of 1728 that the marriage of Maria Theresa and Don Carlos could not take place. Elizabeth characteristically decided to try once more to get through the friendly offices of England *and* France what she had not got through Charles VI. The brief alliance of Spain and Austria was over. The ghost of Charles V was laid.

Louis XV had been married in 1725 to Maria Leszczynska, daughter of ex-king Stanislaus of Poland. And now the birth of a male heir to the throne made the French succession secure, and put an end to whatever notions of a French crown for himself still existed in the clouded brain of Philip V. By the Treaty of Seville, signed by Spain, France, and Great Britain on November 9, 1729, Spain too abandoned the Ostend Company, restored to legal status the asiento and other Anglo-Spanish trade arrangements (that is, in fact, Spain agreed to take some smuggling by the British in the New World as an inescapable fact of nature) and resigned herself for the moment to the loss of Gibraltar. But Elizabeth got her duchies; six thousand Spanish troops were to go into Livorno and Porto Ferraio in Tuscany and into Parma and Piacenza to hold them for Don Carlos.

All was not quite settled. The Spanish troops could go in peacefully only if the imperial Austrian troops were withdrawn. And Charles refused to withdraw them unless he got his price—the formal guarantee of the Pragmatic Sanction by the maritime powers (Britain and Holland) and even by France herself. Treaty of Seville or no Treaty of Seville, Baby Carlos, now quite a lad, made as yet no entry into Parma and Piacenza. The sense of crisis flared up once more in January, 1731, when the last male Farnese, the Duke of Parma, died. Once more, a general war seemed about to break out should the Spanish infantry march into the Italian cities. Here again Walpole and Fleury as a team came to the rescue, though this time Walpole bore the brunt of the decision. He agreed to give Charles the guarantee of Britain and Holland to the Pragmatic Sanction—a guarantee which in Walpole's opinion would cost Britain nothing at all. The whole long tension of 1724-1731, mostly centered in the Italian duchies and the Ostend Company, was relieved by the second Treaty of Vienna, actually two treaties, one between Britain and Holland on the one side and Austria on the other (March, 1731), the second between Spain and Austria (July, 1731). By the first the

---

[4] Such is the conclusion of Wilson, *French Foreign Policy, 1726-1743*, 188. It seems unlikely that Chauvelin was in any way "foisted upon" Fleury.

maritime powers accepted the Pragmatic Sanction, and Charles agreed to let Spanish troops march in to hold the duchies for Carlos. The second implemented the Italian arrangement, though Spanish guarantee of the Pragmatic Sanction was not directly made. In 1732 Spanish troops occupied Parma. Don Carlos was on the road which took him through Florence and Naples to the crown of Spain as Charles III.

Elizabeth had prevailed at last, and without benefit of an Alberoni or a Ripperdá. The unspectacular Patiño had served her more successfully than his brilliant predecessors; or perhaps he had harvested where they had sown. Europe—the Concert of Europe—clearly had wanted peace ever since Utrecht, and until just this moment Elizabeth could not have had her duchies for Carlos without the defeat of Austria—something that could not, in the early eighteenth century, be accomplished save as part of a general European war. The Concert of Europe did not handle Elizabeth very skillfully, perhaps, but it did not let her bully Europe into a general war.[5]

Yet the serenity of 1731 was not to last long. Just as the Italian troubles displayed one sort of threat to peace in this period—dynastic ambitions, coupled with such mercantilist complications as those provided by the question of the Ostend Company—so the Polish crisis and the ensuing war showed another sort of threat, that of disputed succession in an area of chronic social and political instability.

III. THE WAR OF THE POLISH SUCCESSION

The war over the succession in Poland proved not to be a real general conflict. But it was very nearly such, and it settled very little. It sprang from the sort of disputed succession we have noted was especially dangerous to peace in this dynastic age; but it also sprang up in a problem area. For Poland presented to the eighteenth century the kind of problem Turkey presented to the nineteenth. The parallel is not of course exact, but the Polish question, like the Eastern Question as it shortly came to be, was essentially a problem of how to distribute among ambitious competing states territories not actually loyal to the weak central authority over them, and not effectively governed. Poland in the early eighteenth century still held thousands of square miles of her former great empire, lands where a very few Polish and allied Lithuanian landlords ruled over

[5] The reader who would like a neat guide through the confusion of these Italian troubles should look at Carlyle's "Travail-throes of Nature for Baby Carlos's Italian Appanage" at the end of Bk. V, chap. iii, of *Frederick the Great*. Carlyle here sums up very neatly the seven crises, 1717-1731, and without too pungent a Carlylean vocabulary.

White Russians, Lithuanians, Letts, Ukrainians, Germans, and other peoples, not perhaps yet "nationalistic," but certainly never Polish.[6]

The partitions of Poland were, however, yet to come. This War of the Polish Succession, once it began, had very little to do with Poland. It was fought mainly in Italy and in the upper Rhineland, and its chief result was a temporary increase in French prestige. The war did once more demonstrate the helplessness of Poland before her neighbors and enemies (the terms are in this instance synonymous) and the difficulties in the way of her neighbors' agreeing on a policy toward Poland.

The Polish king was the elected head of a republic—a paradox less sharp in the eighteenth century than it would be today, for the word "republic" had then much vaguer connotations. He was chosen for life by the Diet, a bicameral legislative body wholly recruited from the upper classes. Augustus II, called the Strong, had been elected to the Polish throne in 1697. He was also Elector of Saxony, and as such head of one of the rival German houses—Bavaria, Hanover, Brandenburg, and such— competing still on apparently even terms for wealth, power, and prestige. For the Wettins of Saxony, the Polish throne was just the kind of additional increment of wealth, power, and prestige that might enable them to keep up with the Brunswicks of Hanover and the Hohenzollerns of Brandenburg—and, who knows, even with the Hapsburgs of Austria. Indeed, since the heir of Augustus the Strong had married the *eldest* daughter of the Emperor Joseph I, the House of Saxony aspired, by repudiating the Pragmatic Sanction of 1713 and going back to older Hapsburg house law, to acquisition of the Hapsburg lands and perhaps the imperial crown. Therefore Augustus worked very hard to ensure the succession of his son in Poland. This succession involved the election of his son by the Polish Diet.

Many members of the Diet were won over to one or more of the numerous foreign powers who played Polish politics; there were pro-Russian, pro-Swedish, pro-French, pro-Austrian, even pro-Prussian groups, mostly paid from slush funds which every great power earmarked for Poland, but often (as was said of Mirabeau) paid to act in accord with their opinions. But there was always an undercurrent of Polish nationalism among these nobles, and one that might sweep to the top, especially as a protest against German or Russian influence. This happened

[6] For the internal state of Poland, the most modern treatment is by W. Konopczynski in *The Cambridge History of Poland from Augustus II to Pilsudski* (Cambridge, Eng., 1941), chap. ii. This somewhat unsatisfactory narrative should be supplemented by the excellent institutional summary of Lord, *The Second Partition of Poland*, 3-55, and chaps. iii-iv of the above-noted *Cambridge History of Poland*.

in 1733, when the death of Augustus the Strong left the Polish throne vacant.

There was a wave of resentment against the foreigner—a wave heightened by several millions of livres spent by the French ambassador in Poland, de Monti—which swept the Diet for a Pole, Stanislaus Leszczynski, proclaimed king in Warsaw on September 12, 1733. Leszczynski had already been chosen King of Poland in 1704 by a rump meeting of noblemen after the Swedes had demanded the dethronement of Augustus II. In the confused struggles of the Baltic theater of this world war, Augustus had finally triumphed, and Leszczynski had gone into exile. But he had had the extraordinary luck of having his daughter, Maria Leszczynska, chosen as consort for the young King Louis XV of France, and thereby became inevitably a protégé of the court of France. Yet in all fairness it must be admitted that Leszczynski would probably have been chosen King of Poland in 1733 even without de Monti's bribes; indeed, Polish historians have regretted that those millions were not spent rather on hiring soldiers and munitions for the new king.[7]

While Leszczynski was being elected, a group of dissenters were gathered in Praga, the trans-Vistula suburb of Warsaw, awaiting the Russian army of thirty thousand marching in from the east to see that Leszczynski did *not* become King of Poland. The Russians came with the full support of the Austrians, who had been massing troops in Silesia. Charles VI had decided to back Augustus III, son of Augustus the Strong, in return for Saxon acceptance of the Pragmatic Sanction, an acceptance particularly important in view of the fact that that document deprived the wife of Augustus III of her normal rights to the Hapsburg inheritance. Moreover, Charles was glad to back the Catholic Wettin (Augustus the Strong, born a Protestant, had been converted to Catholicism when he accepted the Polish throne in 1697) against his rival Protestant Hohenzollern. Frederick William to be sure had no aspirations to any such unsubstantial, indeed almost metaphysical, thing as the crown of Poland, but he had very concrete aspirations to Polish western lands. He had come out vigorously as protector of Protestants in Poland, mostly German burghers, after the so-called "bloody assizes" (*Bluturtheil*) of Thorn in 1724, when Protestants who had taken part in a riotous attack on a Jesuit college were condemned to death by what Protestants regarded as judicial murder.[8] But, though he let Stanislaus Leszczynski slip through Prussian

---

[7] Konopczynski in *Cambridge History of Poland*, 25.

[8] Droysen, *Geschichte der preussischen Politik*, Pt. IV, Vol. II, 361 ff., gives a sublimely prejudiced account.

territory on his way to Warsaw, Frederick William was not the man to attack the Hapsburg over the Polish succession.

Leszczynski was helpless against the Russian army; there was no need for the Austrians to move. He withdrew to the Free City of Danzig, hoping for help from France. Under Russian protection, a rump Diet elected Augustus III of the House of Saxony at Praga. The small French expeditionary force to the Baltic turned back without landing, but at Copenhagen the French ambassador to Denmark, Plélo, on his own authority assumed command of the fleet and the landing force, went to the Danzig region, and made a desperate and quite futile attempt to redeem the honor of his country by coming to the relief of Leszczynski. The attack failed, and Plélo was killed, an almost unnoticed hero in an unheroic age.

For, though Fleury could not accept this Russian and Austrian aggression in Poland, he was clearly determined not to unleash a general war. And this meant that Great Britain must be kept out of it, for if Britain attacked France while France was fighting Austria, the war would become a world war. Fleury probably had other reasons for not coming actively to the aid of Leszczynski; but one determining reason was that he did not want to challenge the British navy by sending a large French fleet into Baltic waters.

The actual sequence of events is clear. France had declared by royal proclamation that she would not tolerate any foreign interference in Polish elections. The proclamation of Augustus III as King of Poland on October 5, 1733, was followed by a French declaration of war against the Empire on October 16, 1733. Fleury built up in the next year a coalition of Sardinia (i.e. the House of Savoy) and Spain; French armies held the imperial troops even, or slightly better, in the old battlegrounds of the Baden bank of the Rhine; armies of the coalition waged a real war in Italy, marked by two important battles, Parma on June 29, 1734, and Guastalla on September 19, 1734, in which the Austrians were beaten, but by no means annihilated.

The trouble with Fleury's coalition—not a unique trouble in the history of European combinations—was that both of his major allies wanted the same thing. Both Sardinia and Spain wanted to expand in Italy, and specifically, both wanted the key fortress of Mantua, possession of which was essential for the control of the Milanese, and indeed, of all northern Italy. Neither wanted Mantua in the hands of the other, and both began to hold off militarily when it became clear that Fleury would promise it to neither.

Meanwhile Fleury had been having trouble restraining his own war party, which wanted as usual a war with England, and Walpole had been having trouble with the always considerable group in England that was eager for a war with France and Spain at almost any time. It may well be that the preoccupation of both government and opposition in England in 1733-1734 with the hot dispute over the excise bill and with other domestic matters was just sufficient to swing the balance away from war. At any rate it is clear that by the end of 1734 most of the active participants in the war were willing to compromise.

The materials from which a compromise could be worked out were fortunately abundant. Charles VI had now rounded up almost all the guarantees of the Pragmatic Sanction he wanted, save that of the greatest European power of the time, France. He had by the second Treaty of Vienna consented to share Italian hegemony with the Spanish Bourbons, and would not lose prestige by a readjustment of the particular areas in Italy controlled by Bourbons and by Hapsburgs. Philip V and his queen were quite willing to consent to such readjustments. As for Fleury, he was by now, at least, planning to gain one of those precious bits of territory on the Franco-German frontier for which generations of Capetian monarchs had schemed and fought. He was planning to bring the Duchy of Lorraine and Bar under direct French sovereignty, and for that he was even willing to guarantee the Pragmatic Sanction.[9]

Preliminaries of peace were signed at Vienna on October 3, 1735, and after some very complex negotiations over details, were embodied in what is usually known as the third Treaty of Vienna. By this settlement Leszczynski renounced his claim to the throne of Poland, but kept the courtesy title of king. He received the Duchy of Bar at once. On the completion of the arrangements by which Duke Francis of Lorraine, husband of Maria Theresa, and prospective successor to Charles as emperor, took over Tuscany, Leszczynski received Lorraine. On his death Lorraine and Bar were to go to his daughter and her heirs. Since his daughter Maria Leszczynska was Queen of France and her heir the King of France to-be, Lorraine was thus incorporated in the French state. France guaranteed the Pragmatic Sanction.

[9] A. M. Wilson presents the rather daring hypothesis that Fleury had from the very start planned to use Leszczynski's candidacy for the Polish throne in order to get the disappointed king "compensated" with Lorraine, that he therefore failed to back Leszczynski with French arms, not only and not chiefly out of timid fear of the British, but actually because he *did not want* Leszczynski to succeed in holding the Polish crown. Professor Wilson, admitting that no absolute proof of this hypothesis is possible, nevertheless makes out an excellent case. Wilson, *French Foreign Policy, 1726-1743*, 252.

In Italy there was a swapping of lands between Spanish Bourbons and the Hapsburgs. Don Carlos took over Naples (the Two Sicilies) with the royal title, but as a secundogeniture—that is, as a holding independent of, and not to be united with, the crown of Spain. The famous duchies for which Elizabeth Farnese had struggled so long, Parma, Piacenza, and now Tuscany, went to the Hapsburgs, where with the Milanese they rounded out a neat contiguous Hapsburg area. Tuscany, which went first to Francis, recently of Lorraine, and after he became emperor was erected into a Hapsburg secundogeniture, was to become one of the prize exhibits of enlightened despotism. In this Bourbon-Hapsburg exchange, the Bourbons got more, but the Hapsburgs better, land. The poor King of Sardinia had to put up with a very small "rectification" of his frontier toward the Milanese, where Austria begrudgingly ceded him two towns.

This was a peace that gave some satisfaction to everybody—except the Poles, over whom the war had started. The War of the Polish Succession settled nothing at all in Poland, save that a second Saxon king was to rule—or rather, occupy the throne. The fundamental constitutional weakness of Poland was not mended, and was, indeed, advertised more clearly than ever to the world. Now that a Russian army of thirty thousand had been enough to undo the work of the wholly legal Diet that had elected Leszczynski, it was clear that any really effective agreement among the three great neighbors of Poland would make possible the seizure and distribution of any part of the still extensive Polish state.

IV. WAR IN THE EAST

Hardly had the War of the Polish Succession ended when a new war broke out, this time on the eastern margins of Europe. The Turks had been since 1727 engaged in a sporadic war against Nadir Shah of Persia over some Transcaucasian lands into which the Russians had encouraged the Turks to expand after Passarowitz. Now, in the mid-thirties, the war began to go badly for the Turks, who were driven back into the Tigris-Euphrates valley. This was the classic opportunity for the Russians, and in 1735 they put an army into the field under Münnich and began an attack against the Crimea and adjacent areas, still under Turkish suzerainty. In the campaign of 1736 the Russians were spectacularly successful, taking Azov and sweeping across the Perekop peninsula into the heart of the Crimea. Now came another of the classic situations in the Eastern Question—though it was a situation not by any means always repeated in the long history of that question. Austria and Russia agreed to attack the sultan together and share the spoils. True to current habits, a diplomatic congress was called at Niemirov, a much less pleasant place than either Cambrai or Soissons, and true to pattern accomplished nothing. Austrian armies entered the field, and in the campaign of 1736-1737 carried on the earlier triumphs of Eugene in the Eastern War of 1714-1718. They swept on up the age-old routes to Constantinople and Athens, took Nish, a key city in almost all Balkan wars, and entered Bulgaria.

At this point something happened. The war had never, indeed, been quite a simple affair between Turkey and an Austro-Russian alliance. France, through her ambassador to Constantinople, the Marquis de Villeneuve, had exercised a subtle but continuous pressure on Turkey to go to war with Russia, and to back up French policy in Poland. In these fairly quiet years after the third Treaty of Vienna, French diplomacy had once more taken the initiative, and French self-esteem was being heightened by what seemed to be a return to the good old days of the Sun King. One area of this reassertion of French prestige was the Baltic, where the French had managed to get Arvid Horn out of office in Sweden, and had thereby brought England and Russia briefly together. France was also pro-Polish, or at least against the kind of control Russia now exercised in Poland.

So the Eastern War had not been wholly the product of Russian and Austrian ambition for Turkish territory. Nor was its end wholly a military matter. French historians have long claimed credit for the turn of the military tide in 1737-1738 for a Frenchman, Bonneval, in the Turkish service. Bonneval Pasha undoubtedly helped reorganize and modernize the Turkish armies, but he had much help from native Turkish soldiers like Yegen Mohammed.[10] The most important factor in the reversal was peace with Persia, concluded by the sultan in October, 1736, which enabled him to turn his full forces into Europe. In Serbia, the Turkish counteroffensive drove the Austrians back toward the Danube. In south Russia, too, the Turks were successful, and Münnich, driven perhaps as much by the heat of a very dry summer as by the Turks, retreated from the Crimea.

What finally brought peace seems really to have been the great new successes of the Russians in the campaign of 1739, when Münnich, turning westward, broke through to Jassy in what is now Rumania. The Austrians, who had been singularly unsuccessful in the field, and whose finances were worse and worse confounded, now grew alarmed at Russian

[10] S. Gorceix, "Bonneval-Pacha et le jeune Rakoczi," in *Mélanges Iorga* (Paris, 1933), 341-363.

successes—again a classic part of the Balkan pattern for the next few centuries. Charles VI made a separate peace with Turkey at Belgrade on September 18, 1739.

By this peace Austria lost all that she had gained at Passarowitz. Her frontiers went back to the Danube and the Save, and the banat of Temesvar. Turkey had made a slight surge forward. The Russians, already committed to policies in the Baltic and in Poland that might bring military involvement at any time, found it unwise to face alone the undoubtedly strengthened power of Turkey, and also made peace. This time, they kept the elusive town of Azov, but only on condition of razing its fortifications. Russia also promised not to build a fleet in the Black Sea.

Like the War of the Polish Succession, this Eastern War really decided nothing, and certainly not in the east. Turkey's decline, not yet the established fact in European consciousness that it came to be in the next century, seemed for the moment arrested. The appetites of neither Russia nor Austria were appeased. Austria, indeed, had squandered men and money at a time when she could ill afford to do so, as Maria Theresa was soon to discover. If anyone had gained, it was France; and France's gain had been in that real but immeasurable currency of diplomacy, prestige. Once more France had appeared in her old role as the protector of Turkey; once more, from Stockholm to Constantinople, her diplomatists seemed to be pulling the strings that actually moved things. Yet prestige is also a currency subject to violent inflation and deflation. The real power of France had by no means increased as rapidly as her prestige. This fact was to be made clear in the world war which broke out in 1740.

V. THE WAR OF JENKINS' EAR

As the thirties drew to a close, something like a war hysteria seemed to break over Europe. If Fleury had been unable to resist a combination of bureaucrats and glory seekers pushing him into war over the Polish succession, Walpole (who in England had at the time resisted a similar warmongering group) was presently pushed by a combination of entrepreneurs and glory seekers into a war with Spain, named picturesquely after "Jenkins' Ear." The profit motive seems to have been the most powerful warlike urge, but it was the insistence of the Duke of Newcastle, and the bellicose spirit of the king, neither of them at all likely to profit personally, which finally thwarted Walpole's efforts for peace. His power depended on managing king, lords, and commons, and holding a balance between all the vested interests of the privileged classes. He might perhaps have held out against the merchants, but he could not make headway against merchants and his royal master both. Nor could he control Newcastle's management of diplomatic relations with Spain when the king chose to support the duke instead of Sir Robert.

This Duke of Newcastle (Thomas Pelham Holles, 1693-1768) is usually spoken of by historians as a nonentity who owed his long continuance in high office to his mediocrity and to his immense fortune, freely spent on bribery and corruption. It is certainly true that he lacked the wit of Chesterfield, the eloquence of Chatham, the hearty common sense and imperturbable good humor of Walpole, the shrewdness of Hardwicke. It is also true that, as he was only too fond of complaining, nobody among his fellow leaders really understood or liked him, so that their recorded comments on him give an unpleasant picture of a muddle-headed, whining nincompoop. The mass of his papers preserved in the British Museum has so appalled research students that nobody is yet known to have thoroughly explored them all. Basil Williams has pointed out the lack, and the need, of a study of Newcastle and his work. Some of the important facts such a study would reveal have been shown in recent monographs. Professor Namier's remarkably illuminating work has made plain the difference between control of patronage and actual bribery. Newcastle was not, in the light of these revelations, a rich fool inexplicably buying up rotten boroughs, but a sort of eighteenth-century English Mark Hanna, a political boss of great industry and notable achievement. Professor Vaucher has shown that in 1739 and 1740 Newcastle took an independent line, and with royal backing got the better of Walpole in provoking a Spanish war. A revised estimate of Newcastle is overdue.[11]

The influence of the merchant class, especially of the British merchant class, in this period is well known and has been widely regarded, both by conscious and by unconscious Marxists, as paramount. In this war of 1739 with Spain, the merchant class, the "moneyed interest," played an unmistakable part, and served to mark this war off from the recent dynastic wars on the Continent.

The facts about Captain Jenkins and his ear are not clearly shown by the surviving records of the House of Commons. They merely reveal that when on February 19, 1736, additional papers "relating to any losses . . . by depradations committed by the Spaniards since 1725" were laid before

[11] Namier, *Structure of Politics at the Accession of George III;* Vaucher, *Walpole et la politique de Fleury,* 325, 335, 337, and *passim;* Williams, *Whig Supremacy,* 415. [Since Mr. Roberts wrote the above, Mr. Basil Williams, one of the great authorities on the period, has published his *Carteret and Newcastle: a Contrast in Contemporaries* (Cambridge, Eng., and New York, 1943)—editor.]

the House, "pursuant to their address to His Majesty" asking for all papers besides the 236 documents already laid before the House January 23, among the several hundred additional documents was an "extract of a Letter from the Duke of Newcastle to Mr. Keene" (ambassador at Madrid), June 18, 1731, enclosing a copy of the deposition of Robert Jenkins and others; and that March 16, 1738, just after additional papers on the negotiations with Spain had been submitted, covering matters since "midsummer last," it was "ordered, that Captain Robert Jenkins do attend this House upon Tuesday morning next, the Committee of the Whole House" to whom petitions from merchants trading to America complaining of Spanish interference with their trade had been referred.[12]

From other sources we know that Jenkins had returned from a voyage to Jamaica June 11, 1731, with a story, which seems to have grown in the telling, of seizure and search of his ship by Spanish officers, and a mistreatment involving in all versions some damage to his ear. Walpole sent for Jenkins and had him tell his story to Newcastle and Delafaye, so that Newcastle might write the letter to Keene at Madrid enclosing a deposition, June 18, 1731 (produced in the House of Commons later, as above mentioned). Walpole also procured for Jenkins command of an East Indiaman trading to China. The *Craftsman*, Bolingbroke's organ, first took up the sad case of Jenkins in its number of July 10, 1731, a circumstance which probably explains the selection of this case to publicize in 1738, seven years later. The *Gentleman's Magazine* published in 1738 a "Debate in the Senate of Magna Lilliputia" on "Spanish Depradations," being then forbidden by act of Parliament to publish proceedings in the House of Commons. Jenkins was reported to have said that when his ship was attacked "I commended my soul to God and my cause to my country." "These words, and shewing the Piece of his Ear which wrapt in Cotton he carries about with him in a Box, made a great impression on the whole assembly."[13]

This is the familiar story of Jenkins' ear, which was repeated throughout the country and aided so greatly in stirring up anti-Spanish and prowar feeling. Even after the declaration of war in October, 1739, we find *Common Sense*, Lord Chesterfield's organ, still arguing that this tale be used to rouse war spirit in the country. Here again we find the opposition to Walpole willing to use dubious means and to ally themselves with the

---

[12] *Proceedings and Debates of the British Parliaments*, IV, 281, 426, 430. Note also his comment in the introduction, p. v, on the disappointing scantiness of evidence about Jenkins.

[13] Laprade, *Public Opinion and Politics in Eighteenth Century England*, 332 ff., 393 ff. See also H. W. Temperley, "Causes of the War of Jenkins' Ear," Royal Historical Society, *Transactions*, 3rd ser., III (1909), 197-236.

merchants to turn him out. But the desire for military as well as for the civil glory of holding cabinet office played its part in this move in the political game. What the whole opposition kept repeating was that there must be no search of British ships by Spanish or other customs officials under any circumstances, something the merchant Micajah Perry and his friends would obviously have had practical reasons for wishing to obtain. Perry's speech in the House of Commons, in a debate on letting petitioners be represented by counsel, however, is full, as imperfectly reported, of fine phrases about British "liberties."[14]

To all this opposition clamor Walpole made repeated answers showing how unfounded the claim to unrestricted freedom for British ships in the Caribbean was. For example, in the debate on the compromise he had effected with Spain, the Convention of the Pardo, he told the House after a long debate that the existing treaties, the observance of which they had all been demanding, "provide absolutely that the navigation to the Spanish West Indies shall be reserved to the Spaniards alone, except in the case of our South Sea Company's trade." Yet, he went on,

they insist that our ships ought never to be searched wherever they are to be found, and let them be ever so near the Spanish coasts. Pray, Sir, what is the plain English of this but that the trade to the Spanish West Indies ought to be open to every interloper of ours . . . This, Sir, is the plain English of what those who are for a war with Spain advance.[15]

Walpole's position is so entirely in accord with the facts of the case that it is small wonder that Pitt and other opponents in later years admitted that he had been right and they wrong. Since England had no intention of abandoning her own navigation acts and other acts of trade and opening her trade to foreign interlopers, she could hardly expect to win from Spain greater concessions than those given by the treaties of which Walpole spoke.

The quarrel with Spain came to a head in 1739 over the interpretation of the Convention of the Pardo of that year, in which a real attempt had been made to settle by compromise a number of specific financial and trade difficulties between the two nations. The wise Spanish statesman, Patiño, had died in 1736; but on the whole the Spanish in 1739 were not unduly intransigent. English public opinion—or at least the public opinion of the coffeehouses—reflected the atmosphere of parliamentary debates.

---

[14] *Proceedings and Debates of the British Parliaments*, IV, 670-672. On the role of contraband trade in provoking war, see G. H. Nelson, "Contraband Trade under the Asiento, 1730-1739," *American Historical Review*, LI (1945), 55-67.

[15] *Proceedings and Debates of the British Parliaments*, IV, 779 (speech of March 8, 1739).

English pride, as the pamphlet literature of the time clearly shows, was involved in a situation where compromise seemed knuckling down to Spanish grandees. The British fleet, which had been recalled from the Mediterranean, was now ordered to concentrate at Gibraltar. In August the British ambassador Keene was recalled from Spain, and in October, 1739, George II formally declared that war with Spain had begun.

This was one of those wars which begin with rejoicing. As he heard the bells ring out in celebration, Walpole, who had worked so hard to keep the difficult balance he now saw destroyed, responded with a characteristic epigram: "They are ringing their bells now; they will be wringing their hands soon."[16]

VI. THE BALANCE UPSET

It is just possible that this Anglo-Spanish war might have been localized, though there is every sign that France would sooner or later have entered the conflict on the side of Spain. The question is, however, purely academic, for a much greater war was brewing. Frederick William died in May, 1740, and was succeeded by his son, the brilliant, intellectual, and apparently quite un-Hohenzollern Frederick II, who was to out-Hohenzollern the whole family. And in October, 1740, Charles VI, still only fifty-five, died suddenly. The Pragmatic Sanction was put to its first test, and failed. When Frederick in the winter of 1740-1741 marched into the Austrian province of Silesia, he unleashed a general war which Philip V, or Augustus III of Saxony and Poland, or Charles Albert of Bavaria, all claimants to the throne which Charles VI had tried so hard to secure undisputed for his daughter, might—indeed almost certainly would—have begun within the next few months.

With the world war known as the War of the Austrian Succession, into which the War of Jenkins' Ear was absorbed, we are not here concerned.[17] In retrospect, it is obvious that the uneasy balance of the two decades before the death of Charles VI was growing harder and harder to maintain. Though some of the men who had worked hardest to maintain it, and notably Walpole and Fleury, were still in power in 1740, they had been obliged to yield to complex pressures—in fact, to what we now call pressure groups—and go unwillingly to war.

In simplest terms, the tentative, uncertain international public order

---

[16] Lecky, *England in the Eighteenth Century*, I, 418.

[17] It is dealt with in the subsequent volume of this series, Dorn, *Competition for Empire, 1740-1763*, 130-177.

of the early eighteenth century could not stand the shock of so unsettling a condition as a disputed inheritance in a major dynastic state. A Polish succession might be settled in a partial war, but not a Spanish, not an Austrian, succession. There were, of course, many other contributing factors in the upsetting of the balance. A single determined and persistent figure—especially a royal personage—could in those days of dynastic politics act as a constant prod toward war. Elizabeth Farnese is a stock example. Just so, the dominating personality of Frederick the Great forced, if it did not produce, the crisis of 1740. The current, simple mercantilist belief that trade is really a form of war—a belief that must seem to us less odd than it did to our Victorian ancestors—was, especially in England, another constant goad toward war. The nobles and the upper classes, trained to the career of arms, needed war to keep busy and to provide properly for their sons. They would, no doubt, have preferred little wars, with pickings here and there in Italy or the Germanies. But their little wars helped pave the way for big wars. Finally, the great and thinly settled Spanish and Portuguese empires, the vast empty spaces of the New World, were a constant temptation to France, England, and Holland, which had the organized navies and the trading companies necessary to reach out into the world Pope Alexander VI had obligingly divided between Spain and Portugal. To the possible spoils of Europe, increasingly limited as nation-states grew, were now added possible spoils all over the world.

In fact, neither an institutional framework for peaceful international consultation, nor the habits and traditions of peaceful compromise, nor indeed the will to peace, really existed in the Europe of the eighteenth century. In the light of the rivalries of the time, the precarious peace that followed for a generation after Utrecht seems more surprising than does its dissolution in the wars of the mid-century. In view of the difficulties of maintaining in balance the three-hundred-odd states, great and minuscule, of the European state system, the comparative stability of the time may well be attributed more to general exhaustion after the wars of Louis XIV than to the efforts, skilled though they were, of peacemakers like Stanhope, Dubois, Walpole, Fleury, Patiño, and their fellows.[18]

Thus the cult of stability was undermined, internationally as well as nationally. In international relations stability demanded from peace-loving statesmen the exercise of such skills as could not humanly be made

[18] The number of independent states is raised to about eighteen hundred if the areas ruled by imperial Knights of the Holy Roman Empire are considered to be "independent." Actually, such small fiefs were not real participants in international politics.

effective over a long period. Within nations stability demanded from these same statesmen a perpetual series of compromises among nobles, bureaucrats, and merchants, compromises that, again, could not be of long duration. For what kept breaking through these compromises, in domestic as in foreign affairs, was the fierce human energy that has made the modern world. We today think of this energy first in economic terms, if not in Marxian terms, as the drive of the entrepreneur, the industrialist, the capitalist. Though its deeper psychological and sociological sources still escape us, we recognize in modern science, pure and applied, one of the great manifestations of this energy. The nineteenth century had a simple blanket term for it—progress.

The period we have been studying has this tenuous unity: during these years there was a brief and never complete fusion of the old and the new, tradition and experimentation, subordination and rebellion, faith and doubt. For generations, certainly, what we now abstractly sum up as "medieval" had been gradually growing into what we abstractly sum up as "modern." This process was not an even, uniform one. It varied both in time and space, so that no one part of Europe was at any given moment ever quite at the same stage in the process as another. Yet, though such generalizations are always risky, it would seem that the early eighteenth century marks in many ways the mid-term in this long transition. Then, if ever, men lived in a world half-medieval, half-modern.

BIBLIOGRAPHY*

(Revised as of January, 1959, with a Supplement, October, 1962)

No DIVISION of the history of the eighteenth century into chronological periods can possibly put in neat compartments all work previously done in the field. Many of the works listed in the preceding and the subsequent volumes of this series will be found germane in the study of European history from 1715 to 1740. The student should consult especially W. L. Dorn, *Competition for Empire, 1740-1763* (New York, 1940), and Leo Gershoy, *From Despotism to Revolution, 1763-1789* (New York, 1944). For Europe overseas, not treated in detail in this volume, consult the Dorn volume. Any system of classification —as libraries know to their sorrow—must be imperfect. The following bibliography is based on a distinction between *general* (i.e., dealing with all Europe, or at least with several countries) and *national* (i.e., focused on one political unit). Within each of the national subdivisions works are classified as dealing with "all" history, or primarily with political, or economic, or social, or intellectual history. Finally, diplomatic and military history are given a separate classification. In border-line cases—and there are many—a work is classified in the group in which its major emphasis lies.

Bibliographical Aids

For historians the most useful of the bibliographies of Bibliography is E. M. Coulter and M. Gerstenfeld, *Historical Bibliographies* (Berkeley, 1935). A valuable recent tool is P. Caron and M. Jaryc, *World List of Historical Periodicals and Bibliographies* (Oxford, 1939).

For books published before 1930, consult first *A Guide to Historical Literature,* ed. by W. H. Allison, S. B. Fay, G. M. Dutcher, and others (New York, 1931). A revised edition of this *Guide,* covering works published through 1956, prepared under auspices of the American Historical Association, is promised for late 1959. For current literature, the standard work is the *International Bibliography of Historical Sciences,* ed. by the International Committee of Historical Sciences (Zurich, New York, etc., 1926-), of which there are now 23 volumes. For special works, articles, and the rich resources of local periodicals, one must have recourse to national bibliographies. For Germany, F. C. Dahlmann and G. Waitz, *Quellenkunde der deutschen Geschichte,* 2

---

* In this 1959 revision, the requirements of space have made it necessary to omit certain works included in the original edition of 1947. Students wishing fuller coverage are referred to that edition, for many works there cited are still useful.

vols., 9th ed. (Leipzig, 1931-1932), is supplemented by W. Holtzmann and
G. Ritter, *Deutsche Geschichtswissenschaft im 2ten Weltkrieg*, 2 vols. (Marburg,
1951). For France, see A. Martin, *Bibliographie des travaux publiés de 1866 à
1879 sur l'histoire de France de 1500 à 1789*, 2 vols. (Paris, 1932-1938); G.
Brière and P. Caron, *Répertoire méthodique de l'histoire moderne et contem-
poraine de la France*, 9 vols. (Paris, 1899-1924); P. Caron and H. Stein, *Répertoire bibliographique de l'histoire de France*, 6 vols. (Paris 1923-1938); and,
currently, the *Bibliographie annuelle de l'histoire de France* (Paris, 1956-   ).
For Great Britain, there is an admirable guide for this period, S. Pargellis
and D. J. Medley, *Bibliography of British History: The Eighteenth Century,
1714-1789* (Oxford, 1951); J. C. Lancaster, *Bibliography of Historical Works
issued in the United Kingdom, 1946-1956*, supplements the above, and covers
all fields of historical writing. For Spain, there is B. Sanchez Alonzo, *Fuentes
de la historia española y hispanoamericana*, 2nd ed. (Madrid, 1927), and the
bibliographies (inserted as a series of footnotes to the text) in A. Ballesteros y
Beretta, *Historia de España*, 9 vols. in 10 (Barcelona, 1918-1941). For Portugal,
aside from the general works, the best tool available is A. J. Anselmo, *Bibliografia das bibliografias portuguesas* (Lisbon, 1923). For the Low Countries
there is the admirable bibliography of H. Pirenne, *Bibliographie de l'histoire
de Belgique* (Brussels, 1931), unfortunately covering Dutch history only to
1598. The best available historical bibliographies for Italy in this period are
a series of articles in the *Revue historique*, by L. G. Pélissier in vol. CVII
(1911), by J. Alazard in vols. CXXV (1917), CXXVI (1917), and CXXVII
(1918), by C. Morandi in vol. CLXIX (1932) and by G. L. Lesage in vol.
CXCVII (1947). R. Gragger, *Bibliographia Hungariae*, 2 vols. (Berlin, 1923-
1926), gives a list of works in non-Hungarian languages on the history of
Hungary. In Scandinavian history there are B. V. A. Erichsen and A. Krarup,
Dansk historisk bibliografi, 3 vols. (Copenhagen, 1917-1927), and K. Setterwall,
Svensk historisk bibliografi, 2 vols. (Stockholm, 1907; Upsala, 1923), with
current bibliographies in the *Historisk tidskrift*. In Russian, there is a good
introduction to the national historical bibliography in *V. I. Picheta, Vvedenie v
russkuiu Istoriiu* (Moscow, 1923); in Czech, C. Zirbt, *Bibliografie české
historie*, 5 vols. (Prague, 1900-1912); in Polish, L. Finkel, *Bibliografia historyi
polskiej*, a facsimile edition of an old and thorough work, 2 vols. (Warsaw,
1955).

The general collaborative histories are an excellent bibliographical source.
For this period the *Cambridge Modern History*, VI (Cambridge, Eng., 1909),
is quite complete up to its date, though uncritical and unanalytical. The *New
Cambridge Modern History* (Cambridge, 1957-   ) has no bibliographies in its
individual volumes, but promises a "companion volume" of aids to study. Good
bibliographies may be found in P. Muret, *La prépondérance anglaise, 1714-1763*
(Paris, 1937), vol. XI of the series *Peuples et Civilisations*, ed. by L. Halphen
and P. Sagnac.

Almost all historical periodicals contain reviews or bibliographies, or both.

Perhaps the most useful for a general coverage of Europe in this period are the *Revue historique* (its periodic surveys of writing on a given subject, under the title of *Bulletin historique*, are excellent), the *Jahresberichte für deutsche Geschichte*, the *English Historical Review*, the *American Historical Review*, the *Journal of Modern History*, the *Nuova rivista storica*, the *Istorik Marksist*.

For special bibliographies, the historian will find most useful H. Higgs, *Economic Bibliography* (London, 1935); J. Tramond and others, *Bibliographie d'histoire coloniale* (Paris, 1932); J. B. Williams, *Guide to the Printed Materials for English Social and Economic History*, 2 vols. (New York, 1926); A. Wolf, *A History of Science, Technology and Philosophy in the Eighteenth Century* (New York, 1939); and P. Smith, *A History of Modern Culture*, 2 vols. (New York, 1930-1934), II.

European History

The following deal with Europe as a whole or, at any rate, with more than one nation or with more than a small geographical area, such as Scandinavia.

General. With the specialization of historical studies of the past generation, professional historians confronted with the need for general histories have turned to the collaborative work. The latest of these, the *New Cambridge Modern History*, covers this period with one of its first volumes, J. O. Lindsay, ed., *The Old Regime, 1713-63* (Cambridge, 1957) scholarly, encyclopedic, most useful for the smaller countries and Europe overseas. The appropriate volume in the series *Peuples et Civilisations*, P. Muret, *La prépondérance anglaise* (Paris, 1937), deals chiefly with international relations and political history. The German collaborative work, *Propyläen Weltgeschichte*, 10 vols., is less detailed and aimed rather at the general reader than the student. The pertinent volume, W. Goertz, ed., *Das Zeitalter des Absolutismus* (Berlin, 1931), is generally competent and beautifully illustrated with contemporary materials. See also A. Bombaci and others, "Uebergang zur Moderne," vol. VII of *Historia Mundi* (Bern, 1957).

Economic. A recent general economic history is S. B. Clough and C. W. Cole, *Economic History of Europe*, 3rd ed. (Boston, 1952). More detailed are J. Kullischer, *Allgemeine Wirtschaftsgeschichte des Mittelalters und der Neuzeit*, 2 vols. (Munich, 1928-1929), and W. Sombart, *Die Entstehung des modernen Kapitalismus*, 6 vols. (Berlin, 1927). F. L. Nussbaum, *History of the Economic Institutions of Modern Europe* (New York, 1933), makes Sombart available to English readers in a digested form. Other economic histories of all or large parts of Europe are: G. Renard and G. Weulersse, *Life and Work in Modern Europe*, tr. from the French (New York, 1936); H. Heaton, *Economic History of Europe*, rev. ed. (New York, 1948); and H. Sée, *Esquisse d'une histoire du régime agraire en Europe aux XVIIIe et XIXe siècles* (Paris, 1921).

For the important subject of banking, see the excellent trilingual collaborative work J. G. Van Dillen, ed., *History of the Principal Public Banks* (The Hague, 1934). The little book of L. B. Packard, *The Commercial Revolution,*

1400-1776 (New York, 1927), is a good introduction to an important phase of economic history in this period. The English and French "bubbles" are so closely related that they are grouped together in the following bibliographical suggestions, in addition to the general economic histories above: H. Soudois, "Les difficultés monétaires au début du XVIII⁰ siècle," *Journal des économistes,* III (1924), 178-190; V. Brown, "The South Sea Company and Contraband Trade," *American Historical Review,* XXXI (1926), 662-678; Elizabeth Donnan, "The Early Days of the South Sea Company," *Journal of Economic and Business History,* II (1930), 419-450; E. F. Heckscher, "A Note on South Sea Finance," *Journal of Economic and Business History,* III (1931), 321-328; R. D. Richards, "The Bank of England and the South Sea Company," *Economic History,* II (1932), 348-374; and H. Hauser, "Crises de crédit et de spéculation en France et en Angleterre au lendemain de la paix d'Utrecht," *Revue d'histoire moderne,* IX (1934), 435-439. The great work on Law is P. Harsin, *Les doctrines monétaires et financières en France du XVI⁰ au XVIII⁰ siècle* (Paris, 1928), 115-210. Other works include C. J. Gignoux and F. F. Legueu, *Le bureau de rêveries, 1715-1759* (Paris, 1926)—a somewhat enigmatic title concealing a hostile, sound-money account of Law's work, and an appeal to Frenchmen not to try the same thing in 1925—and M. J. Wasserman and F. H. Beach, "Monetary Theories of John Law," *American Economic Review,* XXIV (1934), 646-657. Law's own writings have been brought together and edited by Paul Harsin in the excellent collection of *Oeuvres,* 3 vols. (Paris, 1934).

Mercantilism is another subject that goes beyond national histories. The indispensable work here is E. F. Heckscher, *Mercantilism* (London, 1935), one of the great historical works of our time. See also the following: F. K. Mann, *Der Marschall Vauban und die Volkswirtschaftslehre des Absolutismus; eine Kritik des Merkantilsystems* (Munich, 1914); E. S. Furniss, *The Position of the Laborer in a System of Nationalism, a Study of the Labor Theories of the Later English Mercantilists* (Boston, 1920); E. F. Heckscher, "Mercantilism," *Economic History Review,* VII (1936-1937), 44-54; C. R. Fay, *Imperial Economy and Its Place in the Formation of Economic Doctrine, 1600-1932* (Oxford, 1934); and A. V. Judges, "The Idea of a Mercantile State," *Royal Historical Society, Transactions,* 4th ser., XXI (1939), 41-69. P. W. Buck, *The Politics of Mercantilism* (New York, 1942), in spite of its title, is wholly concerned with British politics of the period.

Social. R. B. Mowat, *The Age of Reason* (New York, 1934), touches on a great variety of eighteenth-century ways. Social history in a more limited sense is covered by M. von Boehm, *Modes and Manners: the Eighteenth Century,* tr. from the German (London, 1935), A. Blum, *Les modes au XVII⁰ et au XVIII⁰ siècle* (Paris, 1928), and the same author's *Histoire du costume* (Paris, 1925). A. Goodwin, ed., *The European Nobility in the Eighteenth Century* (London, 1953), is suggestive. Two recent demographic studies are M. R. Reinhard, *Histoire de la population mondiale de 1700 à 1948* (Paris, 1949),

and R. Mols, *Introduction à la démographie des villes de l'Europe du XIV*
au XVIII siècle,* 3 vols. (Louvain, 1954-1956).

Intellectual. Much of the Enlightenment comes after 1740; but no clear division exists at that point, and the reader is here urged particularly to consult the very full bibliography of the Enlightenment in Dorn, *Competition for Empire,* 402-406, many titles of which refer to the period 1715-1740. This can be supplemented for France, at least, by a recent bibliographical article of G. Zeller in *Revue historique,* CXCV (1945), 339-357. Smith, *History of Modern Culture* (cited earlier), in his second volume, *The Enlightenment, 1687-1776,* gives a most useful map of the whole field. J. H. Randall, Jr., *Making of the Modern Mind,* rev. ed. (New York, 1940), Bk. III, and Basil Willey, *The Eighteenth Century Background* (New York, 1940), are good short accounts. For the field its title indicates, Wolf, *History of Science, Technology, and Philosophy* (already mentioned), is encyclopedic as to detail, accurate, but not successful as a synthesis. E. Cassirer, *The Philosophy of the Enlightenment,* trans. Koelln and Pettegrove (Boston, 1955), is a classic; so too are Carl Becker, *The Heavenly City of the Eighteenth-Century Philosophers* (New Haven, 1932), and J. B. Bury, *The Idea of Progress,* new ed. (New York, 1955). Recent work includes P. Hazard, *European Thought in the Eighteenth Century,* English trans. (London, 1954); G. S. Havens, *The Age of Ideas* (New York, 1955); F. E. Manuel, *The Age of Reason* (Ithaca, 1951); C. Frankel, *The Faith of Reason* (New York, 1948); H. Vyverberg, *Historical Pessimism in the French Enlightenment* (Cambridge, Mass., 1958). On the origins of nationalism, there is the pioneering work of H. Kohn, *The Idea of Nationalism* (New York, 1944), much of which comes within this chronological period. The best general work in English on the physiocrats is still H. Higgs, *The Physiocrats* (London, 1897). The authoritative work is G. Weulersse, *Les physiocrates* (Paris, 1930). For early economic theory in general, consult A. E. Monroe, *Monetary Theory before Adam Smith* (Cambridge, Mass., 1923). On political theory the indispensable preliminary view can be got from the very good survey, G. H. Sabine, *A History of Political Theory* (New York, 1937). For Althusius and the federative-corporative theories, see O. von Gierke, *Johannes Althusius und die Entwicklung der naturrechtlichen Staatstheorien,* 3rd ed. (Breslau, 1913); and the excellent introduction by C. J. Friedrich in his edition of Althusius, *Politica methodice digesta* (Cambridge, Mass., 1932). For more on the institutional side of the corporative state, see under French national history in this bibliography. On Locke, consult S. P. Lamprecht, *The Moral and Political Philosophy of John Locke* (New York, 1918), and the standard life, M. Cranston, *John Locke* (New York, 1957). For a special phase of Locke, there is the stimulating essay W. M. Hamilton, "Property—According to Locke," *Yale Law Journal,* XLI (1931-1932), 864-880, and a somewhat unorthodoxly democratic interpretation, *John Locke and the Doctrine of Majority Rule,* by W. Kendall (Urbana, Ill., 1941). On Hume, consult C. W. Hendel, Jr., *Studies in the Philosophy of David Hume*

(Princeton, 1925), and J. Laird, *Hume's Philosophy of Human Nature* (New York, 1932).

On science, invention, and technology, there are the general study of Wolf listed earlier, A. R. Hall, *The Scientific Revolution, 1500-1800*, 2nd ed. (Boston, 1956), and W. C. D. Dampier (formerly Whetham), *A History of Science in Its Relations with Philosophy and Religion*, 3rd ed. (Cambridge, Eng., 1942). On more specialized subjects, there are A. P. M. Fleming and H. J. Brocklehurst, *A History of Engineering* (London, 1925); A. P. Usher, *A History of Mechanical Inventions* (New York, 1929), a most suggestive book; H. C. Bolton, *Evolution of the Thermometer, 1592-1743* (Easton, Pa., 1900); C. A. Crommelin, *Physics and the Art of Instrument Making at Leyden in the Seventeeth and Eighteenth Centuries* (Leyden, 1925). On Newton, there is a modern collaborative estimate, *Sir Isaac Newton, 1727-1927* (Baltimore, 1928), a bicentenary evaluation of his work prepared under the auspices of the History of Science Society. See also the interesting study on the "reception" of Newton in France, P. Brunet, *L'introduction des théories de Newton en France au XVIIIᵉ Siècle* (Paris, 1931), Henry Guerlac on "Newton" in R. O. Rockwood, ed., *Carl Becker's Heavenly City Revisited* (Ithaca, 1958), and I. B. Cohen, *Franklin and Newton* (Philadelphia, 1956).

For the history of art, two collaborative works offer the results of modern scholarship: A. Michel, ed., *Histoire de l'art: l'art en Europe au XVIIIᵉ siècle*, 2 parts (Paris, 1925), and a volume in *Propyläen-Kunstgeschichte*, M. Osborn, *Die Kunst des Rococo* (Berlin, 1929). On the baroque there are W. Weisbach, *Die Kunst des Barock in Italien, Frankreich, Deutschland und Spanien* (Berlin, 1924), two books by a British intellectual of the period between the wars, Sacheverell Sitwell, *Southern Baroque Art* (London, 1924), and *Spanish Baroque Art* (London, 1931), and F. Fosca, *The Eighteenth Century: From Watteau to Tiepolo* (New York, 1953).

In music, the best single authority for the point of view of musicology is J. Combarieu, *Histoire de la musique des origines à la mort de Beethoven*, 3 vols. (Paris, 1913-1919), of which vol. II is here germane. Indispensable is *Grove's Dictionary of Music and Musicians*, ed. by H. C. Colles, 5 vols. (New York, 1927-1928). For further work the following are recommended: H. Prunières, *Nouvelle histoire de la musique*, 2 vols. (Paris, 1934-1936), II; M. F. Bukofzer, *Music in the Baroque Era* (New York, 1947). Wanda Landowska, *Musique ancienne* (Paris, 1921); Louis Laloy, *Rameau* (Paris, 1908); André Pirro, *J. S. Bach*, 2nd ed. (Paris, 1907); Romain Rolland, *Hændel* (Paris, 1910), with an English translation by A. E. Hull (London, 1916); R. A. Streatfeild, *Handel* (New York, 1909); and Newman Flower, *Handel* (London, 1923).

Diplomatic History. Many of the general works, and also many national histories, are to a great extent preoccupied with international relations. The following is but a choice from the rich literature of this special field during one of the great periods of "balance of power." The first volume of A. Sorel,

L'Europe et la révolution française, 8 vols. (Paris, 1885-1904), still the best introduction to eighteenth-century diplomacy, is now translated as *Europe under the Old Regime* (Los Angeles, 1947). Max Immich, *Geschichte des europäischen Staatensystems von 1660 bis 1789* (Munich and Berlin, 1905), is also basic. R. B. Mowat, *A History of European Diplomacy, 1451-1789* (New York, 1928), covers the ground at the textbook level. Emile Bourgeois devoted much special study to this era. His *Le secret des Farnèse* (Paris, 1909) and *Le secret du Régent et la politique de l'abbé Dubois* (Paris, 1909) are conventional diplomatic histories and somewhat exaggerate deliberate British aims at a European hegemony after Utrecht, but they are well documented and not too strongly biased on the French side. M. Braubach, *Versailles und Wien von Ludwig XIV bis Kaunitz* (Bonn, 1952), is a careful study of the origins in this period of the "diplomatic revolution" of 1756. There are several good monographic studies: J. F. Chance, *The Alliance of Hanover, 1725-1727* (London, 1923), presumably the definitive treatment; Sir R. Lodge, *Great Britain and Prussia in the Eighteenth Century* (Oxford, 1923), the authoritative work on the subject; L. Wiesener, *Le régent, l'abbé Dubois et les anglais,* 3 vols. (Paris, 1891), a good solid book, based largely on British sources; Roderick Geikie and Isabel A. Montgomery, *The Dutch Barrier, 1705-1719* (Cambridge, Eng., 1930), which helps clarify a very complicated matter; Dietrich Gerhard, *England und der Aufstieg Russlands* (Munich, 1933), good economic as well as diplomatic history; and S. Conn, *Gibraltar in British Diplomacy in the Eighteenth Century* (New Haven, 1942). J. A. R. Marriott, *Anglo-Russian Relations, 1689-1943,* 2nd ed. (London, 1944), adds little to Gerhard in this period and is interesting chiefly for the light it throws on current British conservative opinion. See also the A. M. Wilson book, below, p. 276.

Two good recent monographs on phases of economic and diplomatic relations between countries are D. K. Reading, *The Anglo-Russian Commercial Treaty of 1734* (New Haven, 1938), and C. Wilson, *Anglo-Dutch Commerce and Finance in the Eighteenth Century* (Cambridge, Eng., 1941). A. Sorel, *The Eastern Question in the Eighteenth Century* (London, 1898), is somewhat outdated as to facts, but still worth reading in view of the lack of general works on the subject. In the periodical literature, the following have not altogether been taken up into the general works: Mil. R. Vesnitch, "Le Cardinal Alberoni Pacifiste," *Revue d'histoire diplomatique,* XXVI (1912), 352-388; F. Stoerk, "Das Greifswalder Bündniss," *Pommersche Jahrbücher,* II (1901), 1-90; Sir Richard Lodge, "The Anglo-French Alliance, 1716-1731," *Studies in Anglo-French History,* ed. by A. Coville and H. W. Temperley (Cambridge, Eng., 1935), 1-18; J. L. Murray, "Baltic Commerce and Power Politics in the Early Eighteenth Century," *Huntington Library Quarterly,* VI 1942-1943), 293-312; J. J. Murray, "Scania and the End of the Northern Alliance (1716)," *Journal of Modern History,* XVI (1944), 81-92; G. H. Nelson, "Contraband Trade under the Asiento, 1730-1739," *American Historical Review,* LI (1945), 55-67; H. W. Temperley, "Causes of the War of Jenkins' Ear,"

Royal Historical Society, *Transactions,* 3rd ser., III (1909); 197-236; and P. Boyé, *Le mariage de Marie Leszczynska et l'Europe* (Nancy, 1939).

Military History. The years 1715-1740 marked a lull between two great wars and therefore present little of interest to the military historian. Here again the thorough bibliography in Dorn, *Competition for Empire,* 394-397, can stand with few additions. E. M. Earle, ed., *The Makers of Modern Strategy. Military Thought from Machiavelli to Hitler* (Princeton, 1943), deals in chap. ii, "Vauban: the Impact of Science on War," and chap iii, "Frederick the Great, Guibert, Bülow: from Dynastic to National War," with matters important to an understanding of this period. There are very full bibliographies. Lynn Montrose, *War through the Ages* (New York, 1944), is rather slight on this period. In a somewhat special field, note should be taken of an able monograph, R. G. Albion, *Forests and Sea Power* (Cambridge, Mass., 1929), of which chap. iv deals with this period. That part of Prince Eugene's field career included in the Turkish War can be followed in the official publication: L. Matuschka, *Der Türken-krieg, 1716-1718,* vols. VII and VIII of the *Feldzuege des Prinzen Eugen von Savoyen,* 21 vols., 2nd ser. (Vienna, 1876-1892). The best narrative accounts of the other wars between 1715 and 1740 are also somewhat old: the Persian-Turkish War of Nadir Shah, J. W. Zinkeisen, *Geschichte des osmanischen Reiches in Europa,* 7 vols. (Hamburg and Gotha, 1840-1863), V; the War of the Polish Succession, C. P. V. Pajol, *Les guerres sous Louis XV,* 7 vols. (Paris, 1881-1891), I, chap. vii, and A. von Arneth, *Prinz Eugen von Savoyen* (Vienna, 1864); the war of Turkey against Austria and Russia (1736-1739), M. E. von Angeli, *Der Krieg mit der Pforte, 1736-1739* (Vienna, 1880). On militarism in the sense of intellectual history, consult A. Vagts, *History of Militarism* (New York, 1937), and H. Speier, "Militarism in the Eighteenth Century," *Social Research,* III (1936), 304-336.

National Histories

It goes without saying that the literature of the history of the major countries of western and central Europe is more abundant in English and in other languages commonly read by Anglo-Saxon students than is that of the history of smaller countries of the west, and of all countries, large and small, of eastern and southeastern Europe. This is a fact of life. Increasing attention is certainly being given in the west to Russia, to the Slavic languages and countries in general, and to the Ottoman Empire; but it will be some time before such attention is focused back on the early eighteenth century. The following bibliography is, therefore, stronger for countries like Britain, France, Prussia, Austria, Spain, and Italy than for countries like Sweden, Hungary, Russia, Poland, or Turkey. An attempt has been made to secure as complete a "coverage" as possible. But in view of the present state of linguistic achievement in the west, it has not been deemed advisable to include works in the Slavic, Magyar, or Turkish tongues.

Great Britain

General and Political. Basil Williams, *The Whig Supremacy, 1714-1760* (Oxford, 1939), a volume in the *Oxford History of England*, the product of Mr. Williams' lifelong study of the period, is by all odds the best single volume available. Its very complete bibliographies are up-to-date and analytical. Mr. Williams, a professional historian in the great British tradition, is more at home with politics than with science, society, and the arts, but he bravely does his duty by these last. C. G. Robertson, *England under the Hanoverians* (London, 1922), is still a useful advanced textbook, almost wholly political. The classic W. E. H. Lecky, *History of England in the Eighteenth Century,* 8 vols. (London, 1878-1890), is mainly focused on the last two thirds of the century, but is still very good on cultural and social history. The following specialized histories contain useful treatments of law, foreign policy, and colonial expansion: M. A. Thomson, *A Constitutional History of England, 1642-1801,* ed. by R. F. Treharne (London, 1938); A. S. Turberville, *The House of Lords in the Eighteenth Century* (Oxford, 1927); J. H. Rose and others, eds., *Cambridge History of the British Empire,* 8 vols. (Cambridge, Eng., 1929-1940), I; W. S. Holdsworth, *A History of English Law,* 12 vols. (London, 1922-1938), the standard work on the subject; and J. R. Seeley, *The Growth of British Policy,* 2 vols. in 1 (Cambridge, Eng., 1930), a nineteenth-century book still read, as the new edition proves. The great work on this period, a work on the many-volumed scale of the classics, is Wolfgang Michael, *Englische Geschichte im 18ten Jahrhundert,* 5 vols. (Berlin, 1920-1955). At present the first two volumes are available in an English translation, somewhat abridged, *England under George I,* 2 vols. (London, 1936-1939). Professor Michael is amazingly thorough and detailed, and true to the best traditions of the school of Ranke. The work is an indispensable quarry in which anyone may gather materials, but it will probably not be read for itself. L. B. Namier, *The Structure of Politics at the Accession of George III,* 2 vols. (London, 1929), is almost as necessary for the early as for the later part of the century. An important analysis by an American scholar is W. T. Laprade, *Public Opinion and Politics in Eighteenth-Century England to the Fall of Walpole* (New York, 1936). R. Walcott's suggestive study of politics in Queen Anne's day throws light on those of George I. His "English Party Politics, 1688-1714," as well as the useful essay of W. T. Morgan, "Some Sidelights on the General Election of 1715," are to be found in *Essays in Modern English History in Honor of W. C. Abbott* (Cambridge, Mass., 1941). Basil Williams, *Stanhope* (Oxford, 1932), is the definitive book on Stanhope's administration. William Coxe, *Memoirs of the Life and Administration of Sir Robert Walpole,* 3 vols. (London, 1798), is not first-rate history, and is of course dated, but it remains a major source of much of our knowledge of

Walpole. F. S. Oliver, *The Endless Adventure,* 2 vols. in 1 (Boston, 1931), is a study of Walpole's techniques in the management of men, written by a very intelligent conservative. The distinguished English historian J. H. Plumb has begun an authoritative study of Walpole, of which the first volume, *Sir Robert Walpole: The Making of a Statesman* (New York, 1956), has appeared. Plumb's *The First Four Georges* (New York, 1957) is delightful popularization. E. R. Turner, "The Excise Scheme of 1733," *English Historical Review,* XLII (1927), 34-57, deals with one of Walpole's greatest crises. Two books by a French scholar add to high scholarship a foreigner's detached view: Paul Vaucher, *La crise du ministère Walpole en 1733-1734* (Paris, 1924), and *Robert Walpole et la politique de Fleury, 1731-1742* (Paris, 1924). Another recent French scholar throws light on Walpole's great rival: P. Baratier, *Lettres inédites de Bolingbroke à Lord Stair, 1716-1720* (Trévoux, 1939), and *Lord Bolingbroke: ses écrits politiques* (Paris, 1939). J. M. Robertson, *Bolingbroke and Walpole* (London, 1919), emphasizes their contrasting political ideas and programs. Still very useful is W. Sichel, *Bolingbroke and His Times,* 2 vols. (London, 1901-1902). Keith Feiling, *The Second Tory Party, 1714-1832* (London, 1938), is a study by a philosophical Tory of a party not on the whole philosophically inclined. Basil Williams, *Carteret and Newcastle: a Contrast in Contemporaries* (Cambridge, Eng., and New York, 1943), is somewhat disappointing, since it is not based on new research, but comes rather as an overflow from Mr. Williams' accumulated knowledge. J. F. Chance, *George I and the Northern War* (London, 1909), is a well-known monograph, somewhat heavy going. R. L. Arkell, *Caroline of Ansbach, George the Second's Queen* (New York, 1939), is a good new biography; more literary is Peter Quennell, *Caroline of England* (New York, 1940). There are three good modern works on the "Fifteen" by A. and H. Tayler: *The Old Chevalier* (London, 1934), *Seventeen-fifteen: the Story of the Rising* (London, 1936), and *The Jacobite Epilogue* (London, 1941).

Economic History. The best general survey is E. Lipson, *Economic History of England,* 3 vols. (London, 1931), III. T. S. Ashton, *An Economic History of England: The Eighteenth Century* (New York), is recent and authoritative. Earlier work on the Bank of England has been superseded by W. M. Acres, *The Bank of England from Within, 1694-1900,* 2 vols. (London, 1931), and the two hundred and fiftieth anniversary work, Sir John Harold Clapham, *The Bank of England, a History,* 2 vols. (Cambridge, Eng., 1944), an official study by one of the leading economic historians of our time. All bibliographies of eighteenth-century England must list J. L. and B. Hammond, *The Village Labourer,* new ed. (London, 1920), *The Town Labourer,* new ed. London, 1920), and *The Rise of Modern Industry* (New York, 1926); and S. and B. Webb, *English Local Government from the Revolution to the Municipal Corporations Act,* 9 vols. (London, 1906-1929). It should be noted that these great, painstaking works are admirable for detail, but present a total picture darkened by the contrasting Fabian hopes of their kindly authors. For rural matters, consult: Lord Ernle (R. E. Prothero), *English Farming, Past and Present*, 5th ed. (London, 1936), the best general work; A. G. Ruston and Denis Witney, *Hooton Pagnell, the Agricultural Evolution of a Yorkshire Village* (New York, 1934), a model study of a single village. On ideas of property, see E. Beaglehole, *Property* (London, 1931), and P. Larkin, *Property in the Eighteenth Century, with Special Reference to England and Locke* (Dublin and Cork, 1930). E. K. C. Gonner, *Common Land and Inclosure* (London, 1912), A. H. Johnson, *The Disappearance of the Small Land-owner* (London, 1905), and D. G. Barnes, *A History of the English Corn Laws* (London, 1930), give contrasting views on the subject of enclosures and the disappearing yeoman. G. N. Clark, *Guide to English Commercial Statistics, 1696-1782* (London, 1938), is a useful handbook. E. W. Gilboy, *Wages in Eighteenth Century England* (Cambridge, Mass., 1934), is a good monographic study. A small supplement to Mrs. Gilboy's work is T. S. Willan, "Some Bedfordshire and Huntingtonshire Wage Rates, 1697-1730," *English Historical Review*, LXI (1946), 244-250. For commercial methods and urban economy, see W. R. Scott, *Constitution and Finance of English, Scottish and Irish Joint-Stock Companies to 1720*, 3 vols. (Cambridge, Eng., 1910-1912); A. B. DuBois, *The English Business Company after the Bubble Act* (New York, 1938); Elizabeth Donnan, "Eighteenth-Century Merchants: Micajah Perry," *Journal of Economic and Business History*, IV (1931), 70-98; J. F. Rees, "The Phases of British Commercial Policy in the Eighteenth Century," *Economica*, V (1925), 130-150; E. Lipson, "England in the Age of Mercantilism," *Journal of Economic and Business History*, IV (1932), 691-707; and G. S. Thomson, *The Russells in Bloomsbury, 1669-1771* (London, 1939), a useful study of an eighteenth-century urban real-estate "development." For industry on the eve of the industrial revolution, see T. S. Ashton and Joseph Sykes, *Coal Industry of the Eighteenth Century* (Manchester, 1929); T. S. Ashton, *Iron and Steel in the Industrial Revolution* (Manchester, 1924); A. P. Wadsworth and J. DeL. Mann, *The Cotton Trade and Industrial Lancashire* (Manchester, 1931); and J. U. Nef, *Rise of the British Coal Industry* (London, 1932). T. S. Willan, *River Navigation in England, 1600-1750* (London, 1936), and his *English Coasting Trade, 1600-1750* (Manchester, 1938), are pioneering monographs. Thomas Watts, *An Essay on the Proper Method of Forming the Man of Business, 1716*, ed. by A. H. Cole (Boston, 1946), and J. J. Hecht, *The Domestic Servant Class in Eighteenth Century England* (London, 1956), are suggestive on socio-economic topics.

Social and Intellectual History. For a general view, there is the readable G. M. Trevelyan, *English Social History: a Survey of Six Centuries. Chaucer to Queen Victoria* (New York, 1942), very good on the eighteenth century. A. S. Turberville, ed., *Johnson's England*, 2 vols. (Oxford, 1933), is the standard students' manual. Daniel Defoe, *A Tour through the Whole Island of Great Britain*, ed. by G. D. H. Cole, 2 vols. (London, 1927), deserves in this modern edition to rank with Arthur Young's *Travels in France* as an historical classic.

G. Eland, ed., *Purefoy Letters, 1735-1753*, 2 vols. (London, 1931), is an invaluable microcosmic view of the life and workings of a small landed estate. A. S. Turberville, *English Men and Manners in the Eighteenth Century* (London, 1926), is a good general survey. E. B. Chancellor, *Eighteenth Century in England* (London, 1920), deals primarily with the life of the people, the arts, etc., and is very well illustrated. Dorothy Marshall, *The English Poor in the Eighteenth Century* (London, 1926), is the standard work. See also for a local survey, E. M. Hampson, "The Treatment of Poverty in Cambridgeshire, 1597-1834," J. H. Clapham, ed., *Cambridge Studies in Economic History* (Cambridge, Eng., 1934). L. Kronenberger, *Kings and Desperate Men: Life in Eighteenth Century England* (New York, 1942), is most readable; W. Sypher, *Guinea's Captive Kings: British Anti-Slavery Literature of the Eighteenth Century* (Chapel Hill, 1942), treats the literary side of the antislavery movement, but rather at the expense of full historical accuracy. M. Dorothy George, *London Life in the Eighteenth Century* (London, 1925), is readable social history, as are D. Marshall, *English People in the Eighteenth Century* (New York, 1956), and M. Plant, *Domestic Life of Scotland in the Eighteenth Century.* (Edinburgh, 1952). On religious history the following will provide an introduction: N. Sykes, *Church and State in England in the Eighteenth Century* (Cambridge, Eng., 1935); L. M. Hawkins, *Allegiance in Church and State: the Problem of the Non-Jurors in the English Revolution* (London, 1928); H. Broxap, "Jacobites and Non-Jurors," F. J. C. Hearnshaw, ed., *The Social and Political Ideas of Some English Thinkers of the Augustan Age* (London, 1928). D. C. Douglas, *English Scholars* (London, 1939), deals with scholars like Dugdale, Madox, Hearne, flourishing from 1660 to 1730. For the arts and literature the following are introductory for this period: C. H. Collins, *British Painting* (London, 1933); R. Blomfield, *History of Renaissance Architecture in England, 1500-1800*, 2 vols. (London, 1897); R. Quintana, *The Mind and Art of Swift* (London, 1936); and E. Sitwell, *Alexander Pope* (London, 1936). For purely historical details, the best source is A. W. Ward and A. R. Waller, eds., *The Cambridge History of English Literature*, 15 vols. (Cambridge, Eng., 1907-1927), IX-X. Leslie Stephen, *History of English Thought in the Eighteenth Century*, 2 vols., 3rd ed. (London, 1902), is a classic, best in this period for the origins of deism and for moral and religious rather than political thought. J. M. Robertson, *A Short History of Freethought*, 2 vols., 2nd ed. (London, 1906), is by a very fair-minded freethinker. On Bolingbroke's ideas, see the work of P. Baratier listed above under British political history.

France

  General and Political. The standard manual for advanced study remains E. Lavisse, ed., *Histoire de France depuis les origines jusqu'à la révolution,* 9 vols., of which vol. VIII, H. Carré, *Le règne de Louis XV* (Paris, 1911), is here pertinent. It needs supplementing on foreign affairs. The eighteenth-century volume in the series *L'histoire de France racontée à tous*, C. Stryienski, *Le dix-huitième siècle* (Paris, 1909; English trans., New York, 1916), is thin and anecdotal. G. Hanotaux, ed., *Histoire de la nation française*, 15 vols. (Paris, 1920-1929), is an ambitious collaborative work subdivided, not chronologically, but by subjects—i.e. political history, military history, diplomatic history, geography, etc. Unfortunately, it did not live up to its promise. It has very little to offer in this period, though its first two volumes (on the geography of France) are first-rate. The skillful Rightist propagandist, Pierre Gaxotte, has perhaps made out too good a case for the *ancien régime* in his *Siècle de Louis XV*, rev. ed. (Paris, 1956). The best monographic study is Dom H. Leclercq, *Histoire de la Régence*, 3 vols. (Paris, 1921-1922), somewhat conventional in its judgment of eighteenth-century political morals. P. E. Lémontey, *Histoire de la Régence et de la minorité de Louis XV*, 2 vols. (Paris, 1832), still contains much useful material. The famous essay of A. de Tocqueville, *L'ancien régime et la révolution* (Paris, 1856), is necessary for any study of eighteenth-century France. F. Funck-Brentano, *La Régence* (Paris, 1931), though anecdotal and prejudiced on the conservative side, is the work of a trained scholar. The same author's *The Old Regime in France*, tr. from the French (New York, 1929), is an excellent summary of modern French conservative—or reactionary—views. The best longer treatment in English is still to be found in the two books of J. B. Perkins, *France under the Regency* (Boston, 1892) and *France under Louis XV*, 2 vols. (Boston, 1897). For the period from 1726 to 1740, the admirable monograph of A. M. Wilson, *French Foreign Policy during the Administration of Cardinal Fleury* (Cambridge, Mass., 1936), though chiefly concerned with foreign relations, does give also a good picture of Fleury's main domestic problems and policies. Also mainly focused on foreign relations are P. de Nolhac, *Louis XV et Marie Leszczinska* (Paris, 1902); H. Gauthier-Villars, *Le mariage de Louis XV* (Paris, 1900); and M. Santai, *Les préliminaires de la guerre de la Succession d'Autriche* (Paris, 1907). On French constitutional history, the best manual is Joseph Déclareuil, *Histoire générale du droit français des origines à 1789 à l'usage des étudiants des facultés de droit* (Paris, 1925).

The problem of the *Ständestaat* or corporative state in France and its neighboring countries assumed considerable importance in the 1930's, and formed one of the prodromes of Vichy. There follows a brief list of books on this subject: F. Olivier-Martin, *L'organisation corporative de la France d'ancien régime* (Paris, 1938), the ablest and one of the earliest of these studies and one which had much influence in France, especially in scholarly circles; Emile Lousse, ed., *L'organisation corporative du moyen âge à la fin de l'ancien régime*, 2 vols. (Louvain, 1937-1939), containing twelve articles by various hands on phases of the *Ständestaat* or *état corporatif*; E. Coornaert, *Les corporations en France avant 1789* (Paris, 1941); E. Jordan, "Les corporations en France avant 1789," *Revue historique*, CXCIII (1942-1943); G. Espinasse, "La société d'ancien régime: la situation corporative," *Mélanges d'histoire sociale*, no. 5 (Paris, 1944); and F. Piétri, *La réforme de l'état au XVIII* siècle*

(Paris, 1935). In contrast with the above works, G. Pagès, *La monarchie d'ancien régime* (Paris, 1928), seems refreshingly old-fashioned. Two contemporary works are rather to be read in their own right than as mere sources: Voltaire, *Siècle de Louis XV*, numerous editions, and Saint-Simon, *Mémoires*, 20 vols. (Paris, 1908-1924). Recent monographs: J. Ellul, *Institutions française du Moyen Age à 1789* (Paris, 1956), Part III; G. T. Matthews, *Royal General Farms in the Eighteenth Century* (New York, 1958); P. Gessler, *D'Argenson, 1694-1757* (Basel, 1957). Martin Goehring, *Die Aemterkäuflickeit im Ancien Régime* (Berlin, 1938), is pioneering research in the documents, a very important monograph. H. Carré, *La noblesse de France et l'opinion publique au XVIIIᵉ siècle* (Paris, 1920), is an important study in a field that can still be worked profitably. L. Gottschalk, "The French Parlements and Judicial Review," *Journal of the History of Ideas*, V (1944), 105-112, presents a good critical summary of a subject often treated in vague analogies with American practices. E. Carcassonne, *Montesquieu et le problème de la constitution française au XVIIIᵉ siècle* (Paris, 1926), is an interesting essay. J. F. Monnier, *Le chancelier d'Aguesseau, sa conduite et ses idées politiques*, 2nd ed. (Paris, 1863), though an old book, remains the best available on this important jurist. Gaston Martin, *Nantes au XVIIIᵉ siècle*, 2 vols. (Paris, 1928-1931), is a very good local history, seen in the light of a thorough knowledge of national history. For France overseas, a start can be made in H. I. Priestley, *France Overseas through the Old Regime* (New York, 1939), with bibliographical suggestions in the notes.

Economic History. The best general sketch is H. Sée, *Histoire économique de la France* (Paris, 1939). More specialized is the same author's *La France économique et sociale au XVIIIᵉ siècle*, 2nd ed. (Paris, 1933). The first volume of Marcel Marion, *Histoire financière de la France depuis 1715*, 6 vols. (Paris, 1914-1931), contains a sketch of French finances in this period. The author is hostile to paper money and very critical of Law. M. Marion has put his ideas into popular form in a little book *Ce qu'il faut connaître des crises financières de notre histoire* (Paris, 1926). C. E. Labrousse, *Esquisse du mouvement des prix et des revenus en France au XVIIIᵉ siècle* (Paris, 1932), is a careful study, the main emphasis of which falls on the second part of the century. It is in the great French current of thought favorable to the Revolution, and hostile to the *ancien régime*. Marc Bloch, *Les caractères originaux de l'histoire rurale française* (Paris, 1931), is the masterpiece of a great economic historian, unfortunately a victim of the war of 1939-1945. It is fundamental to an understanding of French agriculture at any period. Other agrarian studies are Soulge, *Le régime féodal et la propriété paysanne* (Paris, 1923), and M. Fougères, "Les régimes agraires: recherches convergentes," *Annales d'histoire sociale*, III (1941), 118-124.

Harsin, *Les doctrines monétaires et financières*, already mentioned, has relevant discussions of French mercantilism and most useful bibliographies. See also the following studies: E. J. Hamilton, "Prices and Wages in Southern

France under John Law's System," *Economic History,* III (1934-1937), 441-461; Paul Harsin, *Crédit public et banque d'état en France du XVIe au XVIIIe siècle* (Paris, 1933); Léon Vignols, "La course maritime," *Revue d'histoire économique et sociale,* XV (1927), 196-230; E. Garnault, *Le commerce Rochelais au XVIIIe siècle,* 5 vols. (La Rochelle, 1888-1890); and M. Rouff, *Les mines de charbon en France au XVIIIe siècle* (Paris, 1922). W. C. Scoville, "Labor and Labor Conditions in the French Glass Industry, 1643-1789," *Journal of Modern History,* XV, (1943), 275-294, is of far more general interest in its account of the "gentlemen glassmakers" than its title would indicate. R. Romano, *Commerce et prix du blé à Marseille au XVIIIe siècle* (Paris, 1956), is a thorough technical study.

Social and Intellectual History. Sée, *La France économique et sociale au XVIIIe siècle,* mentioned above, is the best treatment of social history in its more serious phases. F. C. Green, *The Ancien Régime: French Institutions and Social Classes* (Edinburgh, 1958), is a fine brief introduction. As throughout modern French history, memoirs of contemporaries are usually both interesting and important. There is a good list of the really key memoirs for this period in J. R. M. MacDonald, *A History of France,* 3 vols. (New York, 1915), II, 307, 352. Of modern books, the soberest and best are perhaps Comte Fleury, *Louis XV intime* (Paris, 1899), and E. Rouveyre (R. de Parnès, *pseud.*), *La Régence: Portefeuille d'un roué* (Paris, 1881).

P. Sagnac, *La formation de la société française moderne,* Vol. II, 1715-1788 (Paris, 1946), is essential. On the nobility: Paul de Rousiers, *Une famille de hobereaux pendant six siècles* (Paris, 1935); Pierre de Vaissiere, *Gentilhommes campagnards de l'ancienne France,* 2nd ed. (Paris, 1925); M. Le Neufbourg, "Projet d'une enquête sur la noblesse française," *Annales d'histoire économique et sociale,* VIII (1936), 243-256; Marc Bloch, "Sur le passé de la noblesse française: quelques jalons de recherche," *Annales d'histoire économique et sociale,* VIII (1936), 366-378; and H. Brocher, *Le rang et l'étiquette sous l'ancien régime* (Paris, 1934), a convenient summary. Much of the important work of G. Lefebvre, *Les paysans du nord pendant la révolution* (Paris, 1924), is valid for the early eighteenth century. Two good regional studies are F. Vermale, *Les classes rurales en Savoie au XVIIIe siècle* (Paris, 1911), and H. Sée, *Les classes rurales en Bretagne du XVIe siècle à la révolution* (Paris, 1906). Two monographs by S. T. McCloy sum up their fields: *Government Assistance in Eighteenth Century France* (Durham, N. C., 1946), and *The Humanitarian Movement in Eighteenth Century France* (Lexington, Ky., 1957). F. L. Ford, *Robe and Sword* (Cambridge, Mass., 1953), E. G. Barber, *The Bourgeoisie in Eighteenth Century France* (Princeton, 1955), and J. F. Bluche, *L'origine des magistrats du parlement de Paris au XVIIIme siècle* (Paris, 1956), are new and suggestive.

On church history, consult A. Le Roy, *Le Gallicanisme au XVIIIe siècle* (Paris, 1892); A. Gazier, *Histoire général du mouvement Janséniste* (Paris,

1922); G. Hardy, *Le Cardinal de Fleury et le mouvement Janséniste* (Paris, 1925); E. Préclin, *Les Jansénistes du XVIII° siècle* (Paris, 1929). D. Mornet, *Les origines intellectuelles de la révolution française,* 3rd ed. (Paris, 1938), is a useful study of opinion among ordinary people, as well as of the ideas of the *philosophes* themselves. K. Martin, *French Liberal Thought in the Eighteenth Century* (Boston, 1929), is sympathetically liberal. Best of all are the relevant chapters of G. H. Sabine, *A History of Political Theory* (New York, 1937). I. O. Wade, *The Clandestine. . . . diffusion of philosophie ideas in France, 1700-1750* (London, 1938), is important. E. V. Souleyman, *The Vision of World Peace in Seventeenth and Eighteenth Century France* (New York, 1941), provides a useful summary, especially of Abbé de St. Pierre's proposals for a League of Nations, 76-99. The abbé's original proposal, *Projet pour rendre la paix perpetuelle en Europe,* 2 vols. (Utrecht, 1713), was translated into English and published in London in 1714. F. B. Artz, "L'éducation technique en France au XVIII° siécle (1700-1789)," *Revue d'histoire moderne,* XIII (1938), 361-407, breaks new ground. G. Lanson, "Questions diverses sur l'histoire de l'esprit philosophique en France avant 1750," *Revue d'histoire littéraire dè la France,* XIX (1912), 1-29, is still useful. There is a good recent study, R. V. Sampson, *Progress in the Age of Reason* (Cambridge, Mass., 1956). The magistral study by A. M. Wilson, *Diderot: the Testing Years* (New York, 1957), barely concerns this period.

The Low Countries

The latest long history of Holland is the handsome work of H. Brugmans, *Geschiedenis van Nederland,* 8 vols. (Amsterdam, 1935-1936). The substance of the old work of Blok is still, however, very useful, and moreover there is an English translation, P. J. Blok, *History of the People of the Netherlands,* 5 vols. (New York, 1898-1912).

For special aspects, consult E. Baasch, *Holländische Wirtschaftsgeschichte* (Jena, 1927); T. Bussemaker, "De Republick der Vereenigde Nederlanden . . . na den vrede van Utrecht, 1713-1721," *De Gids,* LXVIII (1899), 32-88; H. T. Colenbrander, *De Patriottentijd,* 3 vols. (The Hague, 1897-1899); J. E. Elias, *Geschiedenis van het Amsterdamsche regentenpatriciaat* (The Hague, 1923); F. P. Groeneveld, *De economische crisis van het jaar 1720* (Groningen, 1940); T. Bussemaker, "Die Triple Alliantie van 1717," *Bijdragen voor vaderlandsche geschiedenis* (1902), 158-271; and H. J. Tiele, *De zending van Pesters naar Hannover* (The Hague, 1921).

H. Pirenne, *Histoire de Belgique,* 9 vols. (Brussels, 1902-1932), is now clearly a classic, and indispensable here. L. P. Gachard, *Histoire de la Belgique au commencement du XVIII° siècle* (Brussels, 1880), is also useful. Michel Huisman, *La Belgique commerciale sous l'empereur Charles VI: la Compagnie d'Ostende* (Brussels and Paris, 1902), is the most complete and authoritative study of a subject that transcends Belgian history; it corrects some of Carlyle's most colossal mistakes in his study of Frederick the Great. G. B. Hertz,

"England and the Ostend Company," *English Historical Review,* XXII (1907), 255-279, gives the English point of view. M. Braure, *Lille et la Flandre wallonne au XVIII° siècle* (Lille, 1932), is a good monograph. R. Dollot, *Les origines de la neutralité de Belgique* (Paris, 1902), is again a matter of European rather than purely Belgian history.

Spain and Portugal

General and Political History. There is a good general history of the whole Iberian peninsula in German, R. Konetzske, *Geschichte des spanischen und portugiesischen Volkes* (Leipzig, 1939). This is nicely illustrated, and has good succinct bibliographies. A. Ballesteros y Beretta, *Historia de España y su influencia en la historia universal,* 9 vols. (Barcelona, 1918-1941), is a large-scale history. Vol. V deals with the narrative of eighteenth-century history, vol. VI with social, economic, and cultural history. Both are sprinkled with up-to-date bibliographical footnotes. J. Regla and S. Alcolea, *Historia de la cultura española: el siglo XVIII* (Barcelona, 1957), is a copiously illustrated survey. P. Zabala y Lera, *España bajo los Borbones,* 3rd ed. (Barcelona, 1936), is a good modern standard work. G. Desdevises du Dézert, *L'Espagne de l'ancien régime,* 3 vols. (Paris, 1897-1904), remains the classic analysis of institutions and culture. A. Baudrillart, *Philippe V et la cour de France,* 5 vols. (Paris, 1890-1901), the late cardinal's masterpiece, is essentially diplomatic history, and classifiable either under Spain or France. The book makes no concession to modern demands for liveliness. E. Armstrong, *Elizabeth Farnese* (London, 1892), is good sound history of the old school. On Alberoni there are Pietro Castagnoli, *Il Cardinale Giulio Alberoni,* 3 vols. (Piacenza and Rome, 1929-1932), a warm defense, but based on thorough documentary study, and S. Harcourt-Smith, *Cardinal of Spain: The Life and Strange Career of Alberoni* (New York, 1944), with a good bibliography. On Ripperdá there are G. Syveton, *Une cour et un aventurier au XVIII° siècle: Le Baron de Ripperdá* (Paris, 1896), and L. de Taxonera, *El Duque de Riperda* (Madrid, 1945). Two recent studies: A. Danvila, *El reinado rélámpago: 1707-1742* (Madrid, 1952); D. Gomez Molleda, *Gibraltar: Una contienda diplomatico en el reinado de Felipe V* (Madrid, 1953).

Economic History. Some special studies are: G. Desdevises du Dézert, "La richesse et la civilisation espagnoles au XVIII° siècle, "*Revue hispanique,* LXXIII (1928), 1-320; E. J. Hamilton, "Money and Economic Recovery in Spain under the First Bourbon," *Journal of Modern History,* XV (1943), 192-206; and J. O. McLachlan, *Trade and Peace with Old Spain, 1667-1750* (New York, 1940). The huge subject of the Spanish colonies can be studied in Ballesteros, mentioned above, and in broader generalizations in the interesting one-volume study by R. Altamira, *Historia de España y de la civilización española,* 5th ed. (Barcelona, 1935). Of the long (25 volumes), still-unfinished collaborative work, A. Ballesteros y Beretta, ed., *Historia de America* (Barcelona, 1936-), Vol. XIII, *Los virreinatos en el siglo XVIII* by C. Alcazar Molina, (1945) is most useful.

Social and Intellectual History. These fields are well covered in the general works cited above, especially Ballesteros, III, and Desdevises du Dézert, III. But see also Paul Marimée, *L'influence française en Espagne au XVIII° siècle* (Paris, 1936), a good study in cultural history; Sitwell, *Southern Baroque Art*, previously listed; G. Desdevises du Dézert, "Madrid au XVIII° siècle," *Revue des Pyrénées*, IX (1897), 1-31; A. Morel-Fatio, *Etudes sur l'Espagne*, 2nd ser. (Paris, 1890), containing many details of daily life in the eighteenth century; J. Hurtado and J. de la Serna, *Historia de la literatura Española*, 2nd ed. (Madrid, 1925); J. Pijoan, *History of Art*, tr. from the Spanish, 3 vols. (New York, 1933), III; and V. Lampérez y Romea, *Arquitectura civil españalo de los siglos I al XVIII*, 2 vols. (Madrid, 1922).

Portugal

T. Legrand, *Histoire du Portugal* (Paris, 1928), and G. Young, *Portugal, an Historical Study* (Oxford, 1917), are good general surveys, in which this period does not bulk very large.

Italy

General and Political. There is an admirable single-volume survey of modern Italy, L. Salvatorelli, *A Concise History of Italy*, tr. from the Italian (New York, 1940). E. M. Jamison and others, *Italy: Mediaeval and Modern* (Oxford, 1917), is brief but comprehensive in this period. A. Solmi, ed., *Storia politica d'Italia dalle origini ai giorni nostri*, is the latest great co-operative venture. For this period, the two volumes in this series by E. Rota, *Le origini del risorgimento (1700-1800)* (Millan, 1938), are detailed and authoritative. Though the *risorgimento* bedevils Italian histories of the eighteenth century much as the Revolution bedevils French histories of the same period, this work does succeed in analyzing the eighteenth century in and of itself. E. Callegari, *Preponderanze straniere, 1530-1789* (Milan, 1895), a volume in the *Storia Politica d'Italia*, an older co-operative history, is occasionally useful. P. F. Kirby, *The Grand Tour in Italy, 1700-1800* (New York, 1952), has interesting material. Consult also the bibliographies at the end of each chapter in E. Rota, above. Some studies of especial importance in this period are: H. Kretschmayr, *Geschichte von Venedig*, 3 vols. (Gotha and Stuttgart, 1905-1934), III, *Der Niedergang;* A. von Reumont, *Geschichte Toskana's seit dem Ende des florentinischen Freistaates*, 2 vols. (Gotha, 1876-1877); E. Robiony, *Gli ultimi Medici e la successione al Granducato di Toscana* (Florence, 1905); A. Anzilotti, *Le riforme in Toscana* (Pisa, 1924); C. Morandi, "La fine del dominio spagnuolo in Lombardia," *Archivio storico Italiana* (1936), II, 181-200; S. Pugliese, *Le prime strette dell' Austria in Italia* (Milan, 1932); H. Benedikt, *Das Königreich Neapel unter Kaiser Karl VI* (Vienna, 1927); B. Croce, *Storia del regno di Napoli* (Bari, 1925), more purely narrative history than most of his works;

H. Bédarida and others, *L'Italie au XVIII° siècle* (Paris, 1929), an uneven symposium, in which G. Ortolani, "Italie et France au XVIII° siècle," and G. Maugain, "Rome et le gouvernement pontifical au XVIII° siècle, d'après des voyageurs français," are especially suggestive; and I. Lameire, *Les déplacements de souveraineté en Italie pendant les guerres du XVIII° siècle* (Paris, 1911), almost unreadably technical and detailed, but with valuable information not elsewhere available. E. Viarana, *Carlo Emanuele di Sovoia, signore di Milano* (Milan, 1939), is an account of the brief expansion of Savoy during the War of the Polish Succession.

Social and Intellectual History. G. de Ruggiero, *Il pensiero politico meridionale dei secoli 18 e 19* (Bari, 1922), shows the strength and originality of Italian thought in a period sometimes held to have been "stagnant." Other studies primarily in intellectual history are: A. M. Ghisalberti, *Gli albori del risorgimento italiano* (Rome, 1931); and H. Bédarida and P. Hazard, *L'influence française en Italie* (Paris, 1935). On Vico, consult B. Croce, "La filosofia di Giovanni Battista Vico," in his *Saggi filosofici,* 3rd ed. (Bari, 1933); C. E. Vaughan, *Studies in the History of Political Philosophy,* 2 vols. (Manchester, 1925), I, 205-253; and F. Nicolini, *La giovinezza di Giambattista Vico* (Bari, 1932). G. Natali, *Il Settecento,* 2 vols. (Milan, 1929), is an admirable literary history. See also E. Codignola, *Illuministi, Giasenisti e Giacobini nell' Italia del Settecento* (Florence, 1947); F. Venturi, *Saggi sull' Europa illuminista; Albert Radicati di Passerano* (Turin, 1954).

Economic History. There is no adequate work for the period, and the general works pay little attention to economic history. A. Doren, *Italienische Wirtschaftsgeschichte* (Jena, 1934), I, is realy Italian economic history in the Middle Ages. Since its author is dead, vol. II, as yet unannounced, will have to be by a different hand. Some valid bibliographical aids for this period can be got from Doren's very full bibliography, 696-715. There is a chapter on Italy in G. Renard and G. Weulersse, *Life and Work in Modern Europe,* already mentioned.

Germany

General and Political. Historians of this period have been traditionally preoccupied with the struggle between Austria and Prussia which was about to break out in 1740, and they have generally felt that German political history in the eighteenth century was somehow "pre-national." These feelings penetrate two generally good and detailed late nineteenth-century histories: Bernhard Erdmannsdörffer, *Deutsche Geschichte vom Westfälischen Frieden bis zum Regierungsantritt Friedrichs des Grossen,* 2 vols. (Berlin, 1892-1893); and H. von Zwiedeneck-Südenhorst, *Deutsche Geschichte im Zeitraum der Gründung des preussischen Königtums,* 2 vols. (Stuttgart, 1894). There is a good short survey of German affairs as a whole in this period in A. von Hofmann, *Politische Geschichte der Deutschen,* IV (Berlin, 1925), 634-688; and some good generalizations about this period in the little book of H.

Pinnow, *History of Germany,* tr. from the German (New York, 1933). C. T. Atkinson, *A History of Germany, 1715-1815* (London, 1908), is as detailed a textbook treatment as can be found in English. The standard manual of constitutional history is F. Hartung, *Deutsche Verfassungsgeschichte von 15. Jahrhundert bis zur Gegenwart,* 2nd ed. (Leipzig and Berlin, 1922). O. Hintze, "Der oesterreichische und der preussische Beamtenstaat," *Historische Zeitschrift,* LXXXVI (1901), 402-444, is a useful comparative study. But the bulk of political history in this period is either concerned primarily with Austria or primarily with Prussia, for which see below.

Economic. There is no single general economic history of Germany as a whole in this period. Sombart, *Die Enstehung des modernen Kapitalismus,* mentioned before, is more than German and more than straightforward economic history. G. van Below, *Preblem der Wirtschaftsgeschichte* (Tübingen, 1920), has an interesting chapter (viii), "Der Untergang der mittelalterlichen Stadtwirtschaft (über den Begriff der Territorialwirtschaft)." An old book (1874), W. Roscher, *Geschichte der National-Oekonomik in Deutschland,* 2nd ed. (Munich, 1924), discusses policies of this period. There is a detailed study of agriculture, T. von der Goltz, *Geschichte der deutschen Landwirtschaft,* 2 vols. (Stuttgart and Berlin, 1902-1903), I. There are very many special studies, for which the student is referred to the bibliography of Dahlmann-Waitz, mentioned earlier.

Social and Intellectual History. There is an excellent general survey in English, W. H. Bruford, *Germany in the Eighteenth Century* (Cambridge, Eng., 1935). See also E. Ermatinger, *Deutsche Kulture im Zeitalter der Aufklärung* (Potsdam, 1935); Karl Biedermann, *Deutschland im 18ten Jahrhundert,* 4 vols. (Leipzig, 1867-1880), still most readable; and R. Du Moulin-Eckart, *Geschichte der deutschen Universitäten* (Stuttgart, 1929), a useful survey. For general histories of arts and letters, consult A. Koester, *Die deutsche Literatur der Aufklärungzeit* (Heidelberg, 1925); G. G. Dehio, *Geschichte der deutschen Kunst,* 4 vols., rev. ed. (Berlin, 1919-1934), III; and A. Feulner, *Skulptur und Malerei des 18. Jahrhunderts in Deutschland* (Potsdam, 1929). H. Cysarz, *Deutsche Barockdichtung* (Leipzig, 1924), though mostly concerned with earlier periods, has some admirable discussion of the relation of baroque art to the Enlightenment, to the rococo, and to classicism. K. Pinson, *Pietism as a Factor in the Rise of German Nationalism* (New York, 1934), and K. Borgmann, *Der deutsche Religionsstreit der Jahre 1719-1720* (Berlin, 1937), are good studies of special phases of religious and intellectual history. A. Small, *The Cameralists, the Pioneers of German Social Polity,* Chicago, 1909), deals with early German social and economic thought.

Prussia

The best introduction is the compact S. B. Fay, *The Rise of Brandenburg-Prussia to 1786* (New York, 1937). L. Tümpel, *Entstehung des brandenburgisch-preussischen Einheitsstaates im Zeitalter des Absolutismus* (Berlin,

1915), is an important general work. One of the classics of the "Prussian school," J. G. Droysen, *Geschichte der preussischen Politik*, 5 pts. in 14 vols. (Leipzig, 1868-1886), has by now been attacked so much that there is little danger of its being read uncritically. Actually it has a great deal of material not elsewhere available. Thomas Carlyle, *History of Friedrich the Second, Called Frederick the Great*, 6 vols. (New York, 1858-1866), is another famous work, biased and imperfect, and to some people quite unreadable. But again, it is a work full of very interesting detail. Much of it is Prussian, and indeed European history of this period, 1715-1740. Albert Waddington, *Histoire de Prusse*, 2 vols. (Paris, 1911-1922), can certainly be read as an antidote to German treatment of the subject. It is not a very interesting book, but it is sober, scholarly, and quite obviously French. O. Hintze, *Die Hohenzollern und ihr Werk* (Berlin, 1915), is predominantly institutional history, and is the authoritative work. Georges Pariset, *L'état et les églises en Prusse sous Frédéric Guillaume I* (Paris, 1897), is a good monographic study. W. L. Dorn, "The Prussian Bureaucracy in the Eighteenth Century," *Political Science Quarterly*, XLVI (1931), 403-423; XLVII (1932), 75-94, contains a more detailed treatment than was possible in the author's *Competition for Empire*. R. A. Dorwart, *The Administrative Reforms of Frederick William I of Prussia* (Cambridge, Mass., 1953) is a solid monograph. Gordon Craig, *The Politics of the Prussian Army, 1640-1945* (New York, 1955) is an original study partly concerned with this period. Robert Ergang, *The Potsdam Führer* (New York, 1941), is a substantial, fair-minded account of the life of Frederick William I, with a very good bibliography of this period of Prussian history. Pierre Gaxotte, *Frederick the Great*, tr. from the French (New Haven, 1942), over half of which is devoted to background and reign of Frederick William I, and is much less obviously prejudiced than Gaxotte's works on the French eighteenth century, and E. Lavisse, *Youth of Frederick the Great* (London, 1891), are useful.

Two recent studies of special phases of Prussian history are H. Wendorf, "Die 'Considerations sur l'état present du corps politique de l'Europe': Friederich des Grossens erster Versuch in der Aussenpolitik," *Historische Zeitschrift*, CLXIII (1941), and G. Rohde, *Brandenburg-Preussen und die Protestanten in Polen, 1640-1740: Ein Jahrhundert preussische Schutzpolitik für eine unterdrückte Minderheit* (Leipzig, 1941), a special study to which current events have given an ironic twist.

Useful studies on economic and social subjects are: E. Wolff, *Grundriss der preussisch-deutschen sozialpolitischen und Volkswirtschaftsgeschichte* (Berlin, 1909); G. Schmoller, *Umrisse und Untersuchungen zur Verfassungs-, Verwaltungs-, und Wirtschaftsgeschichte besonders des preussischen Staates im 17. und 18. Jahrhundert* (Leipzig, 1898; new ed., Berlin, 1921), the gleanings of a lifetime of study; M. Beheim-Schwarzbach, *Friedrich Wilhelms I. Colonisationswerk in Lithauen* (Königsberg, 1879); A Hundsdörffer, *Emigration der Salzburger Protestanten 1731-32* (Königsberg, 1932), a good general treatment of the exodus of the Protestants and their subsequent resettling; H.

Rachel, *Das Berliner Wirtschaftsleben im Zeitalter des Frühkapitalismus* (Berlin, 1931); S. Stern-Täubler, *Der preussische Staat und die Juden* (Berlin, 1925); W. Görlitz, *Die Junker* (Glücksburg, 1956); H. J. Schoeps, *Das War Preussen,* a nostalgic anthology (Honnef, 1955); and A. Moeller van den Bruck, *Der preussische Stil,* 2nd ed. (Munich, 1922).

Smaller German States

It is even more impossible, in a work of this scope, to cover the small states of Germany than to cover those of Italy in this period. There follows a sampling which, supplementing the general histories, will aid the student to understand the Germany of this period; for further work, consultation of Dahlmann-Waitz is necessary: H. Voelcker, ed., *Die Stadt Goethes. Frankfurt am Main im XVIII Jahrhundert* (Frankfurt am Main, 1932); A. Wohlwill, *Neuere Geschichte der Freien und Hansestadt Hamburg* (Gotha, 1914), with an introductory chapter on the eighteenth century; E. Finder, *Hamburgisches Bürgertum in der Vergangenheit* (Hamburg, 1930); A. Schulte, ed., *Tausend Jahre deutscher Geschichte und deutscher Kultur am Rhein* (Düsseldorf, 1925), for what became the Prussian Rhine province; A von Boroviczény, *Graf von Brühl* (Zurich, 1930), a good life of the Saxon statesman, defending him from Prussian attacks; G. Rüthning, *Oldenburgische Geschichte,* 2 vols. (Bremen, 1911), II; M. Doeberl, *Entwickelungsgeschichte Bayerns,* 3 vols. (Munich, 1912), II.

Austria and Other Hapsburg Lands

K. and M. Uhlirz, *Handbuch der Geschichte Oesterreichs und seiner Nachbarländer Böhmen und Ungarn,* 3 vols. (Graz, 1927-1939), is the best general treatment for the advanced student. On Austria proper, consult F. M. Mayer, R. F. Kaindl, and H. Pirchegger, *Geschichte und Kulturleben Deutschösterreichs,* 3 vols. (Vienna, 1929-1937). Two recent works of synthesis are somewhat more favorable to Charles VI than older historians had been. They are O. Redlich, *Das Werden einer Grossmacht: Oesterreich von 1700 bis 1740* (Leipzig, 1938), technically a continuation of the history of Austria begun by H. Huber in the late nineteenth century, but actually an independent, modern work; and H. Hantsch, *Die Geschichte Oesterreichs, 1648-1918* (Graz, 1950). William Coxe, *History of the House of Austria,* 4 vols., new impression (London, 1893-1895), III, is still to be read for details of diplomatic and administrative history, though it seems now a very old-fashioned work indeed. J. Redlich, *Das oesterreichische Staats-und Reichsproblem* (Leipzig, 1920), in its early chapters gives a brief general view of the Hapsburg dominions at this time, but perhaps underestimates the dynastic, as opposed to national, aims of Charles VI. A. Arneth, *Prinz Eugen von Savoyen,* 3 vols. (Vienna, 1858), is the old standard on Eugene and his campaigns. Paul Frischauer, *Prince Eugene; a Man and a Hundred Years of History* (London, 1934), is readable and fair. V. Bibl, *Prinz Eugen, ein Heldenleben* (Vienna, 1941), a recent German treatment, has been well reviewed. Hans Kohn, "AEIOU: Some Reflections on the Meaning and Mission of Austria," *Journal of Modern History*, XI (1939), 513-527, is a review article mainly focused on later periods, but with much of interest for the student of Charles VI. H. Hantsch, *Friedrich Karl, Graf von Schönborn, 1674-1746* (Augsburg, 1929), a very thorough study from original sources of an important imperial official, throws light on many phases of Hapsburg administration. W. Michael, *Das Original der Pragmatischen Sanktion Karls VI* (Berlin, 1929), is a controversial treatment. J. Srbik, *Der Staatliche Exporthandel Oesterreichs* (Vienna and Leipzig, 1907), covers a field little studied in detail.

On parts of the Hapsburg dominions later attaining to nationhood, there is, for Bohemia, R. Kerner, *Bohemia in the Eighteenth Century* (New York, 1932), which is, however, almost wholly concerned with the later part of the century; E. Denis, *La Bohême depuis la Montagne-Blanche*, 2 vols. (Paris, 1930); and B. Bretholz, *Geschichte Böhmens und Mährens*, 4 vols. (Reichenberg, 1924), pro-German as Denis is pro-Czech. S. H. Thomson, *Czechoslovakia in European History* (Princeton, 1943), is very brief on this period. E. Winter, *Tausend Jahre Geisteskampf im Sudetenland* (Salzburg and Leipzig, 1938), is a good account of religious troubles in Bohemia, and under the heading "Barock" has a good bibliography for this period. For Hungary, H. Marczali, *Hungary in the Eighteenth Century* (Cambridge, Eng., 1910), again deals with the later part of the century. F. Eckart, *A Short History of Hungary* (London, 1934), and D. G. Kosáry, *A History of Hungary* (Cleveland, 1941), are both very brief on this period. These two are the most objective of modern Hungarian histories in English, often a fertile field for propaganda. In German there is available A. Domanovsky, *Die Geschichte Ungarns* (Munich, 1923), and a translation of Marczali's constitutional history, F. Marczali, *Ungarische Varfassungsgeschichte* (Tübingen, 1910). In French there is E. Sayous, *Histoire générale des Hongrois,* 2nd ed. (Budapest, Vienna, and Paris, 1900), now somewhat old-fashioned.

Scandanavia

B. J. Hovde, *The Scandinavian Countries, 1720-1865* (Boston, 1944), treats all the countries, and mostly deals with economic and social history, and with politics as "determined" by economic and social conditions. Diplomatic history is almost wholly neglected. Still, it is a most useful book. In the older tradition of general histories of Scandinavia as a whole may be mentioned J. Stefansson, *Denmark and Sweden* (New York, 1917), in the *Story of the Nations* series. This is a bit brief on the early eighteenth century. See also R. M. Hatton, "Scandinavia and the Baltic" in *New Cambridge Modern History: The Old Régime, 1713-1763,* chap. XV.

Denmark. Aage Friis and others, eds., *Det Danske Folks Historie,* 8 vols. (Copenhagen, 1926-1929), V, *Det Danske Folk under den Aeldre Enevaelde,* is standard and very full; its bibliographies at the end of chapters cover all phases of Danish history, political, social, economic, cultural. Many entries are in German or French. A. Nielsen, *Dänische Wirtschaftsgeschichte* (Jena, 1933), in the series *Handbuch der Wirtschaftsgeschichte,* is modern and authoritative. *Sweden.* Carl Hallendorff and Adolph Schueck, *History of Sweden* (London, 1939), and R. Svanström and C. F. Palmstierna, *A Short History of Sweden* (Oxford, 1934), are largely superseded by I. Anderson, *A History of Sweden,* trans. Hannay (New York, 1956). L. Stavenow, *Geschichte Schwedens, 1718-1772* (Gotha, 1908), is monographic. C. G. Malmström, *Sveriges politiska historia från konung Karl XII's död till statshvälfningen 1772,* 6 vols. (Stockholm, 1893-1901), is a standard detailed study. The general work in Swedish, covering all aspects of history, and with modern bibliographical notes, is E. Hildebrand and L. Stavenow, eds., *Sveriges Historia till Våra Dagar,* 13 vols. (Stockholm, 1919-1926), IX.

Switzerland

There is a good short general history, W. Oechsli, *A History of Switzerland, 1499-1914,* tr. E. and C. Paul (London, 1922), but inevitably brief on this period. There is a suggestive chapter, "The Patriciate, 1718-1789," in W. Martin, *A History of Switzerland,* tr. G. W. Booth (London, 1931). More detailed treatment is in J. Dierauer, *Geschichte der Schweizerischen Eidgenossenschaft,* 5 vols. (Gotha, 1887-1919), IV. The overwhelming stress on Swiss history is, of course, political and constitutional. There is a recent collection of documents, Nabholz and Kläui, *Quellenbuch zur Verfassungsgeschichte der Schweizerischen Eidgenossenschaft und der Kantone von den Anfängen bis zur Gegenwart* (Aarau, 1940). Swiss local—that is, cantonal—history probably brings out more devotion than federal history, but goes beyond the scope of this book. For an example of an excellent cantonal history, see D. K. Gauss and others, *Geschichte der Landschaft Basel und des Kantons Basellandschaft,* 2 vols. (Liestal, 1932).

Poland

W. F. Reddaway and others, eds., *The Cambridge History of Poland from Augustus II to Pilsudski* (Cambridge, Eng., 1941), is the latest and most useful general history. The narrative chapters by W. Konopczynski covering this period suffer from too much compression and allusiveness. Chapters iii-v present a picture of Polish society, culture, and political institutions in the Saxon period which is very good indeed. The single volume by O. Halecki, *A History of Poland* (New York, 1943), gives a useful brief account of this period. The opening analytical chapter of R. H. Lord, *The Second Partition of Poland* (Cambridge, Mass., 1915), is a good institutional survey of pre-partition Poland. For a German nationalistic view, see W. Schlegel, *August der Starke, Kurfürst von Sachsen, König von Polen* (Berlin, 1938). There is an older and more scholarly German work, C. Gurlitt, *August der Starke,* 2 vols. (Dresden, 1924). Three books by Pierre Boyé, though based on research in the sources, deal rather with the personal affairs of Leszczynski and with European politics than with Polish history proper: *Stanislas Leszczynski et le troisième traité de Vienne* (Paris, 1898), a very detailed monograph; *Le roi Stanislas grand-père* (Nancy, 1922), a collection of the letters of the old ex-king; and *La cour polonaise de Lunéville* (Nancy, 1926), again mostly dealing with the period after 1740.

Russia

V. O. Kluchevsky, *A History of Russia,* tr. by C. J. Hogarth, 5 vols. (London, 1911-1931), IV, is the standard detailed treatment available in English. The translation is an awkward one. E. Hanisch, *Geschichte Russlands, I, Von den Anfangen bis zum Ausgang des 18. Jahrhunderts* (Freiburg im Breisgau, 1940), and M. Florinsky, *Russia: A History and an Interpretation* (New York, 1953), are good general studies. An excellent older German treatment is Karl Staehlin, *Geschichte Russlands,* 4 vols. (Berlin, 1923-1939). There is an excellent collaborative study in French, definitely not sympathetic with the current Communist point of view, but written by trained historians who avoid the obvious forms of subjectivity: P. Milioukov, C. Seignobos, and L. Eisenmann, *Histoire de Russie,* 3 vols. (Paris, 1932-1933). M. N. Pokrovsky, *History of Russia from Earliest Times to the Rise of Commercial Capitalism,* tr. from the Russian (New York, 1931), is the best available orthodox Marxist work, but its scale does not permit detailed treatment of this period. G. Vernadsky, *A History of Russia* (New Haven, 1929), provides in chaps. vi-viii a valuable *précis* of political, economic, and cultural history of the eighteenth century. The work of R. N. Bain, *The Pupils of Peter the Great, 1697-1740* (London, 1897), like most of the writings of this British specialist in Scandinavian and north Slavic history, is now outdated, and is held in low repute by contemporary Slavic specialists, but goes into greater political and personal detail than anything in English. The work of K. Waliszewski, *L'héritage de Pierre le Grand* (Paris, 1900), is similarly somewhat outdated, but is more scholarly than Bain's work. Among the few source materials available in western languages is A. I. Turgenev, ed., *La cour de Russie il y a cent ans 1725-1783: Extraits des dépêches des ambassadeurs anglais et français* (Berlin, 1858). It lacks, however, any scholarly apparatus. James Mavor, *An Economic History of Russia,* 2 vols. (London, 1914), I, is a thorough job, which leans heavily on Kluchevsky. J. Kulischer, *Russische Wirtschaftsgeschichte,* I (Jena, 1925), one of the admirable series *Handbuch der Wirtschaftsgeschichte,* ed. by George Brodnitz, unfortunately goes only to the reign of Peter the Great, but some of its bibliographical citations go on into later periods. Vol. II has not yet appeared. C. Marsden, *Palmyra of the North: the First Days of St. Petersburg* (London, 1942), is a pleasant and somewhat patronizing English essay. W. E. D. Allen, *The Ukraine* (Cambridge, Eng., 1940), gives a good bird's-eye view. Students who possess Russian can use the current bibliographies in the Russian historical review, *Istorik Marksist.*

For Russian literature, consult D. S. Mirsky, *A History of Russian Literature* (New York, 1927), necessarily brief on this period, not a major one in Russian literature. A longer treatment is in M. Hofmann, *Histoire de la littérature russe des origines jusqu' à nos jours* (Paris, 1934). For an interesting general cultural history, see P. Miliukov, *Outlines of Russian Culture*, 3 vols., ed. by M. Karpovich (Philadelphia, 1942). This is an able abridgment of the voluminous original study. The forthcoming Hans Rogger, *National Consciousness in Eighteenth Century Russia* (Cambridge, Mass., 1959), is a pioneer study.

Ottoman Empire

Josef von Hammer-Purgstall's *Geschichte des osmanischen Reiches*, 4 vols., 2nd ed. (Pest, 1936); also French translation in 3 vols. (Paris, 1840-1842), is a detailed, uncritical narrative which has, however, the great merit of being based on extensive use of Oriental materials. As such it is still an indispensable work. J. W. Zinkeisen, *Geschichte des osmanischen Reiches in Europa*, 7 vols. (Gotha, 1840-1863), is also basic, inasmuch as it deals in great detail with the European part of the empire and uses Greek and other Balkan materials. The work of the great Rumanian historian, Nicolas Iorga, *Geschichte des osmanischen Reiches*, 5 vols. (Gotha, 1908), is the most modern treatment, but is poorly arranged and crammed with unassimilated facts. The numerous shorter works of which the Vicomte de La Jonquière's *Histoire de l'Empire Ottoman*, 2 vols., new ed. (Paris, 1914), Sir Edward S. Creasy's *History of the Ottoman Turks*, 2 vols. (London, 1854-1856), new ed. by A. C. Coolidge and W. H. Claflin (New York, 1936), and George J. S. L. Eversley's *The Turkish Empire*, 2nd ed. (London, 1923), are perhaps best known, are mostly condensations of Hammer and Zinkeisen, and tend to stress the diplomatic aspects of Near Eastern affairs. An exception is Carl Ritter von Sax, *Geschichte des Machtverfalls der Türkei* (Vienna, 1908), which is an excellent short analysis of the decline of the empire internally as well as externally.

Still the best over-all description of the empire in the eighteenth century is the encyclopedic work of Ignatius Mouradgea d'Ohsson, *Tableau général de l'Empire Ottoman*, 4 vols. (Paris, 1787-1791). The introduction of Walter L. Wright, Jr., *Ottoman Statecraft. The Book of Counsel for Vezirs and Governors* (Princeton Oriental Texts, II, 1935), is far and away the most careful scholarly analysis of the governmental machinery in the time of Ahmed III. Lady Mary Wortley Montagu's *Letters and Works*, 2 vols., new ed. (London, 1887), contain her letters from Constantinople, 1716-1718, which have been frequently published in separate form. They are gems of English literature written by the wife of the British ambassador. Lady Mary made the journey to Constantinople overland, which was unusual. Her picture of life in Belgrade, Adrianople, and Constantinople is as fascinating as it is instructive and cannot be recommended too highly.

The diplomatic side of the Near Eastern question is dealt with in all the standard texts such as Edouard Driault, *La question d'Orient*, 5th ed. (Paris, 1912), and Sir John A. R. Marriott, *The Eastern Question*, 3rd ed. (Oxford, 1930). These very sketchy accounts should be supplemented for the early eighteenth century, by more detailed studies such as the classic book of Albert Vandal, *Une ambassade française en Orient sous Louis XV. La mission du marquis de Villeneuve* (Paris, 1887), and Hans Uebersperger's *Russlands Orientpolitik in den letzen zwei Jahrhunderten*, I (Stuttgart, 1913). Mary Lucille Shay, *The Ottoman Empire from 1720 to 1734 as Revealed in Despatches of the Venetian Baili (Illinois Studies in the Social Sciences*, XXVII, no. 3, Urbana, 1944), throws interesting new light on Turkish relations with Russia and on the development of Turkish-Persian relations. Mohammed-Ali Hekmat, *Essai sur l'histoire des relations politiques irano-ottomanes de 1722 à 1747* (Paris, 1937), is an important contribution to the history of the Turkish-Persian conflict, and makes use of unpublished French, Turkish, and Persian documents. On the military side, Antonio Benzoin, *La guerra russo-turca del 1736-1739* (Archivio Veneta, series V, Vol. XIII, 186-202, 1933), also draws upon Venetian diplomatic materials.

Paul Masson, *Histoire du commerce français dans le Levant au XVIIIe siècle* (Paris, 1911), is an excellent study not only of trade in the Near East, but of diplomatic relations and general conditions. A wealth of material may be found also in Klaas Heeringa, *Bronnen tot de Geschiedenis van den levantschen Handel*, Part II (The Hague, 1917). The British side is well covered in Alfred C. Wood, *History of the Levant Company* (London, 1935).

A History of Ottoman Poetry, by Elias J. W. Gibb, ed. by Edward G. Browne, 5 vols. (London, 1905), is much more than its title implies. It is really a history of Turkish culture, and is unique in the western languages.

Special studies of internal aspects of Ottoman history are almost nonexistent excepting as they touch European countries. Thus, on the Phanariots and their role in Rumanian history see the controversial book by M. P. Zallony, *Essai sur les Fanariotes* (Marseilles, 1824), and the well-balanced recent account in R. W. Seton-Watson, *A History of the Roumanians* (Cambridge, 1934).

The following additional work, mostly recent, is suggested:

A handy general bibliography is J. K. Birge, *A Guide to Turkish Area Study* (Washington, 1949).

In the field of diplomatic history the first volume of J. C. Hurewitz, *Diplomacy in the Near and Middle East* (New York, 1956), provides many essential documents, with excellent introductory and bibliographical notes. B. H. Sumner, *Peter the Great and the Ottoman Empire* (Oxford, 1949), is a masterly essay based chiefly on Russian sources. A highly competent study, based on Turkish as well as Slavic sources, is B. Spuler: "Die europäische Diplomatie in Konstantinopel, 1699-1739," in *Jahrbuch für Kultur und Geschichte der Slaven*, XI, 1935, 53-115, 171-222.

For Ottoman institutions and conditions in the eighteenth century the magisterial study of H. A. R. Gibb and Harold Bowen, *Islamic Society and the*

West, Vol. I, parts 1 and 2 (Oxford, 1950, 1957), is in a class by itself, making full use of Oriental as well as European sources for a detailed analysis of political, economic, and religious questions. A. D. Alderson, *The Structure of the Ottoman Dynasty* (Oxford, 1956), examines in great detail various aspects of dynastic and court arrangements, S. Gorceix, *Bonneval Pacha* (Paris, 1953), provides a lively biography of a French officer engaged by the Sultan to modernize his military forces.

By far the best study of the Balkans under Turkish rule is L. S. Stavrianos, *The Balkans Since 1453* (New York, 1958), with extensive bibliographies. And on the origins of the Phanariots and their activities there is now a careful study by J. Gottwald, "Phanaristiche Studien," in *Leipziger Vierteljahrschrift für Südosteuropa,* V, 1941, 1-53.

Supplement, October, 1962

G. F. Howe and others, eds., *The American Historical Association's Guide to Historical Literature* (New York, 1961). See before, p. 264.

Hans Beyer and others, *Aufklärung und Revolution* (Bern, 1960), conventional Europe-centered collaborative scholarly work on the eighteenth century with classified bibliographies useful especially for smaller countries.

Georgio Spini, *Storia dell'età moderna dall'impero di Carlo V all'Illuminismo* (Rome, 1960), first-rate detailed survey of the sixteenth, seventeenth and eighteenth centuries.

M. S. Anderson, *Europe in the Eighteenth Century* (London, 1961), first volume of a new collaborative work, strong on Eastern Europe and diplomatic history.

J. H. Plumb, *Sir Robert Walpole: The King's Minister* (Boston, 1961), the second volume of an admirable work; see before, p. 273.

N. C. Hunt, *Two Early Political Associations, the Quakers and the Dissenting Deputies in the Age of Sir Robert Walpole* (Oxford, 1961).

Conrad Gill, *Merchants and Mariners of the 18th Century* (New York, 1961), from papers of the English merchant Thomas Hall, died 1748.

Robert Robson, *The Attorney in Eighteenth-Century England* (New York, 1959), social rather than legal history.

D. B. Horn, *The British Diplomatic Service, 1689-1789* (New York, 1961), social rather than diplomatic history.

John Carswell, *The South Sea Bubble* (Stanford, 1960), an excellent monograph.

Dora M. Clark, *The Rise of the British Treasury: Colonial Administration in the Eighteenth Century* (New Haven, 1960).

H. Lüthy, *La banque protestante en France de la révocation de l'édit de Nantes à la révolution,* Vol. I, *Dispersion et regroupment, 1685-1730* (Paris,

1959), much wider in scope than its title indicates—almost a history of France for these years.

Robert Forster, *The Nobility of Toulouse in the Eighteenth Century: A Social and Economic Study* (Baltimore, 1960), from the sources, transcending social history in importance.

John Lough, *An Introduction to Eighteenth-Century France* (New York, 1960), an excellent survey.

C. B. O'Keefe, S.J., "Conservative Opinion on the Spread of Deism in France, 1730-1750," *Journal of Modern History,* XXXIII (1961), 398-406, interesting study of a phase of public opinion.

Hans Rogger, *National Consciousness in Eighteeenth-Century Russia* (Cambridge, Mass, 1960).

G. Candeloro, *Storia dell'Italia moderna: Le origini del Risorgimento, 1700-1815* (Milan, 1956), latest on a much debated subject.

J. Vicens Vives, ed., *Historia social y económica de España y América,* Vol. III, *Imperio; aristocracia; absolutismo* by Juan Reglá and G. C. de Castillo (Barcelona, 1957), excellent general study.

R. A. Kann, *A Study in Austrian Intellectual History from Late Baroque to Romanticism* (London, 1960), a monograph on a subject little treated in English.

Geoffroy Atkinson, *Le sentiment de la nature et le retour à la vie simple, 1690-1740* (Paris, 1960).

F. L. Baumer, *Religion and the Rise of Scepticism* (New York, 1960), a very useful contemporary treatment, pertinent to the last three centuries.

INDEX

hARpER ⚜ ɔORChBOOKS

HUMANITIES AND SOCIAL SCIENCES

American Studies: General

LOUIS D. BRANDEIS: Other People's Money, *and How the Bankers Use It* ‡ TB/3081

HENRY STEELE COMMAGER, Ed.: The Struggle for Racial Equality TB/1300

CARL N. DEGLER, Ed.: Pivotal Interpretations of American History Vol. I TB/1240; Vol. II TB/1241

A. S. EISENSTADT, Ed.: The Craft of American History: *Recent Essays in American Historical Writing* Vol. I TB/1255; Vol. II TB/1256

CHARLOTTE P. GILMAN: Women and Economics. ‡ *Ed. by Carl N. Degler with an Introduction* TB/3073

MARCUS LEE HANSEN: The Atlantic Migration: 1607-1860. TB/1052

JOHN HIGHAM, Ed.: The Reconstruction of American History△ TB/1068

ROBERT H. JACKSON: The Supreme Court in the American System of Government TB/1106

LEONARD W. LEVY, Ed.: American Constitutional Law TB/1285

LEONARD W. LEVY, Ed.: Judicial Review and the Supreme Court TB/1296

LEONARD W. LEVY: The Law of the Commonwealth and Chief Justice Shaw TB/1309

HENRY F. MAY: Protestant Churches and Industrial America TB/1334

RICHARD B. MORRIS: Fair Trial: *Fourteen Who Stood Accused, from Anne Hutchinson to Alger Hiss. New Preface by the Author* TB/1335

RALPH BARTON PERRY: Puritanism and Democracy TB/1138

American Studies: Colonial

BERNARD BAILYN: The New England Merchants in the Seventeenth Century TB/1149

JOSEPH CHARLES: The Origins of the American Party System TB/1049

HENRY STEELE COMMAGER & ELMO GIORDANETTI, Eds.: Was America a Mistake? *An Eighteenth Century Controversy* TB/1329

CHARLES GIBSON: Spain in America † TB/3077

LAWRENCE HENRY GIPSON: The Coming of the Revolution: 1763-1775. † *Illus.* TB/3007

PERRY MILLER & T. H. JOHNSON, Eds.: The Puritans: *A Sourcebook* Vol. I TB/1093; Vol. II TB/1094

EDMUND S. MORGAN, Ed.: The Diary of Michael Wigglesworth, 1653-1657 TB/1228

EDMUND S. MORGAN: The Puritan Family TB/1227

RICHARD B. MORRIS: Government and Labor in Early America TB/1244

WALLACE NOTESTEIN: The English People on the Eve of Colonization: 1603-1630. † *Illus.* TB/3006

JOHN P. ROCHE: Origins of American Political Thought: *Selected Readings* TB/1301

JOHN SMITH: Captain John Smith's America: *Selections from His Writings* TB/3078

American Studies: From the Revolution to 1860

MAX BELOFF: The Debate on the American Revolution: 1761-1783 TB/1225

RAY A. BILLINGTON: The Far Western Frontier: 1830-1860. † *Illus.* TB/3012

GEORGE DANGERFIELD: The Awakening of American Nationalism: 1815-1828. † *Illus.* TB/3061

WILLIAM .W. FREEHLING, Ed.: The Nullification Era: *A Documentary Record* ‡ TB/3079

JOHN C. MILLER: Alexander Hamilton and the Growth of the New Nation TB/3057

RICHARD B. MORRIS, Ed.: The Era of the American Revolution TB/1180

R. B. NYE: The Cultural Life of the New Nation: 1776-1801. † *Illus.* TB/3026

A. F. TYLER: Freedom's Ferment TB/1074

LOUIS B. WRIGHT: Culture on the Moving Frontier TB/1053

American Studies: Since the Civil War

MAX BELOFF, Ed.: The Debate on the American Revolution, 1761-1783: *A Sourcebook* TB/1225

W. R. BROCK: An American Crisis: *Congress and Reconstruction, 1865-67* ° △ TB/1283

A. RUSSELL BUCHANAN: The United States and World War II. † *Illus.* Vol. I TB/3044; Vol. II TB/3045

EDMUND BURKE: On the American Revolution. † *Edited by Elliot Robert Barkan* TB/3068

THOMAS C. COCHRAN & WILLIAM MILLER: The Age of Enterprise: *A Social History of Industrial America* TB/1054

WHITNEY R. CROSS: The Burned-Over District: *The Social and Intellectual History of Enthusiastic Religion in Western New York, 1800-1850* TB/1242

FOSTER RHEA DULLES: America's Rise to World Power: 1898-1954. † *Illus.* TB/3021

W. A. DUNNING: Reconstruction, Political and Economic: 1865-1877 TB/1073

HAROLD U. FAULKNER: Politics, Reform and Expansion: 1890-1900. † *Illus.* TB/3020

FRANCIS GRIERSON: The Valley of Shadows TB/1246

SIDNEY HOOK: Reason, Social Myths, and Democracy TB/1237

WILLIAM E. LEUCHTENBURG: Franklin D. Roosevelt and the New Deal: 1932-1940. † *Illus.* TB/3025

JAMES MADISON: The Forging of American Federalism. *Edited by Saul K. Padover* TB/1226

ARTHUR MANN: Yankee Reformers in the Urban Age TB/1247

GEORGE E. MOWRY: The Era of Theodore Roosevelt and the Birth of Modern America: 1900-1912 † TB/3022

R. B. NYE: Midwestern Progressive Politics TB/1202

JAMES PARTON: The Presidency of Andrew Jackson, *From Vol. III of the* Life of Andrew Jackson ‡ TB/3080

---

† The New American Nation Series, edited by Henry Steele Commager and Richard B. Morris.

‡ American Perspectives series, edited by Bernard Wishy and William E. Leuchtenburg.

* The Rise of Modern Europe series, edited by William L. Langer.

** History of Europe series, edited by J. H. Plumb.

¶ Researches in the Social, Cultural and Behavioral Sciences, edited by Benjamin Nelson.

§ The Library of Religion and Culture, edited by Benjamin Nelson.

Σ Harper Modern Science Series, edited by James R. Newman.

° Not for sale in Canada.

△ Not for sale in the U. K.

1

History: Modern European

Intellectual History & History of Ideas

w. WARREN WAGAR, Ed.: European Intellectual History since Darwin and Marx   TB/1297
PHILIP P. WIENER: Evolution and the Founders of Pragmatism. △ Foreword by John Dewey   TB/1212

Literature, Poetry, The Novel & Criticism

JACQUES BARZUN: The House of Intellect △   TB/1051
JAMES BOSWELL: The Life of Dr. Johnson & The Journal of a Tour to the Hebrides with Samuel Johnson LL.D. ○ △   TB/1254
ERNST R. CURTIUS: European Literature and the Latin Middle Ages △   TB/2015
A. R. HUMPHREYS: The Augustan World: Society in 18th Century England ○△   TB/1105
RICHMOND LATTIMORE: The Poetry of Greek Tragedy △   TB/1257
J. B. LEISHMAN: The Monarch of Wit: An Analytical and Comparative Study of the Poetry of John Donne ○ △   TB/1258
J. B. LEISHMAN: Themes and Variations in Shakespeare's Sonnets ○△   TB/1259
SAMUEL PEPYS: The Diary of Samuel Pepys. ○ Edited by O. F. Morshead. Illus. by Ernest Shepard   TB/1007
V. DE S. PINTO: Crisis in English Poetry, 1880-1940 ○△   TB/1260
ROBERT PREYER, Ed.: Victorian Literature   TB/1302
C. K. STEAD: The New Poetic: Yeats to Eliot ○ △ TB/1263
PAGET TOYNBEE: Dante Alighieri: His Life and Works. Edited with Intro. by Charles S. Singleton   TB/1206
DOROTHY VAN GHENT: The English Novel   TB/1050
BASIL WILLEY: Nineteenth Century Studies: Coleridge to Matthew Arnold ○△   TB/1261
BASIL WILLEY: More Nineteenth Century Studies: A Group of Honest Doubters ○ △   TB/1262
RAYMOND WILLIAMS: Culture and Society, 1780-1950 ○ △   TB/1252
RAYMOND WILLIAMS: The Long Revolution ○△   TB/1253

Myth, Symbol & Folklore

MIRCEA ELIADE: Cosmos and History § △   TB/2050
MIRCEA ELIADE: Rites and Symbols of Initiation: The Mysteries of Birth and Rebirth § △   TB/1236
THEODOR H. GASTER: Thespis: Ritual, Myth & Drama in the Ancient Near East ○ △   TB/1281
DORA & ERWIN PANOFSKY: Pandora's Box △   TB/2021

Philosophy

G. E. M. ANSCOMBE: An Introduction to Wittgenstein's Tractatus. ○ △ Second edition, Revised   TB/1210
HENRI BERGSON: Time and Free Will ○△   TB/1021
H. J. BLACKHAM: Six Existentialist Thinkers ○ △ TB/1002
CRANE BRINTON: Nietzsche   TB/1197
ERNST CASSIRER: The Individual and the Cosmos in Renaissance Philosophy △   TB/1097
FREDERICK COPLESTON: Medieval Philosophy ○ △ TB/376
F. M. CORNFORD: Principium Sapientiae: A Study of the Origins of Greek Philosophical Thought   TB/1213
F. M. CORNFORD: From Religion to Philosophy § TB/20
A. P. D'ENTRÈVES: Natural Law △   TB/1223
MARVIN FARBER: The Aims of Phenomenology   TB/1291
PAUL FRIEDLÄNDER: Plato: An Introduction △   TB/2017
J. GLENN GRAY: The Warriors: Reflections on Men in Battle. Intro. by Hannah Arendt   TB/1294
W. K. C. GUTHRIE: The Greek Philosophers: From Thales to Aristotle ○ △   TB/1008
G. W. F. HEGEL: The Phenomenology of Mind ○ △ TB/1303
F. H. HEINEMANN: Existentialism and the Modern Predicament △   TB/28
EDMUND HUSSERL: Phenomenology and the Crisis of Philosophy   TB/1170
IMMANUEL KANT: The Doctrine of Virtue, being Part II of the Metaphysic of Morals   TB/110
IMMANUEL KANT: Groundwork of the Metaphysic of Morals. Trans. & analyzed by H. J. Paton   TB/1159
IMMANUEL KANT: Lectures on Ethics §△   TB/105

IMMANUEL KANT: Religion Within the Limits of Reason Alone. § Intro. by T. M. Greene & J. Silber   TB/67
QUENTIN LAUER: Phenomenology   TB/1169
MAURICE MANDELBAUM: The Problem of Historical Knowledge: An Answer to Relativism   TB/1338
GABRIEL MARCEL: Being and Having △   TB/310
GEORGE A. MORGAN: What Nietzsche Means   TB/1198
H. J. PATON: The Categorical Imperative: A Study in Kant's Moral Philosophy △   TB/1325
MICHAEL POLANYI: Personal Knowledge △   TB/1158
WILLARD VAN ORMAN QUINE: Elementary Logic. Revised Edition   TB/577
WILLARD VAN ORMAN QUINE: from a Logical Point of View: Logico-Philosophical Essays   TB/566
BERTRAND RUSSELL et al.: The Philosophy of Bertrand Russell   Vol. I TB/1095; Vol. II TB/1096
L. S. STEBBING: A Modern Introduction to Logic △ TB/538
ALFRED NORTH WHITEHEAD: Process and Reality: An Essay in Cosmology △   TB/1033
PHILIP P. WIENER: Evolution and the Founders of Pragmatism. Foreword by John Dewey   TB/1212
LUDWIG WITTGENSTEIN: The Blue and Brown Books ○ TB/1211

Political Science & Government

JEREMY BENTHAM: The Handbook of Political Fallacies. Introduction by Crane Brinton   TB/1069
C. E. BLACK: The Dynamics of Modernization: A Study in Comparative History   TB/1321
KENNETH E. BOULDING: Conflict and Defense   TB/3024
CRANE BRINTON: English Political Thought in the Nineteenth Century   TB/1071
ROBERT CONQUEST: Power and Policy in the USSR: The Study of Soviet Dynastics △   TB/1307
ROBERT DAHL & CHARLES E. LINDBLOM: Politics, Economics, and Welfare   TB/3037
F. L. GANSHOF: Feudalism △   TB/1058
G. P. GOOCH: English Democratic Ideas in Seventeenth Century   TB/1006
SIDNEY HOOK: Reason, Social Myths. and Democracy △   TB/1237
DAN N. JACOBS, Ed.: The New Communist Manifesto & Related Documents. Third edition, Revised   TB/1078
HANS KOHN: Political Ideologies of the 20th Century TB/1277
ROY C. MACRIDIS, Ed.: Political Parties: Contemporary Trends and Ideas   TB/1322
KINGSLEY MARTIN: French Liberal Thought in the Eighteenth Century △   TB/1114
BARRINGTON MOORE, Jr.: Political Power and Social Theory: Seven Studies ¶   TB/1221
BARRINGTON MOORE, JR.: Soviet Politics—The Dilemma of Power ¶   TB/1222
JOHN B. MORRALL: Political Thought in Medieval Times TB/1076
KARL R. POPPER: The Open Society and Its Enemies △   Vol. I TB/1101; Vol. II TB/1102
JOHN P. ROCHE, Ed.: American Political Thought: From Jefferson to Progressivism   TB/1332
CHARLES I. SCHOTTLAND, Ed.: The Welfare State   TB/1323
BENJAMIN I. SCHWARTZ: Chinese Communism and the Rise of Mao   TB/1308
PETER WOLL, Ed.: Public Administration and Policy TB/1284

Psychology

ALFRED ADLER: The Individual Psychology of Alfred Adler △   TB/1154
ARTHUR BURTON & ROBERT E. HARRIS, Editors: Clinical Studies of Personality
                               Vol. I TB/3075; Vol. II TB/3076
HADLEY CANTRIL: The Invasion from Mars: A Study in the Psychology of Panic   TB/1282
HERBERT FINGARETTE: The Self in Transformation ¶ TB/1177
SIGMUND FREUD: On Creativity and the Unconscious § △ TB/45

4